Elliott

THE PRICE OF PEACE

Incentives and International Conflict Prevention

THE PRICE OF PEACE

Incentives and International Conflict Prevention

Edited by David Cortright

Foreword by David A. Hamburg and Cyrus R. Vance

CARNEGIE COMMISSION ON PREVENTING DEADLY CONFLICT

CARNEGIE CORPORATION OF NEW YORK

ROWMAN & LITTLEFIELD PUBLISHERS, INC.
Lanham • Boulder • New York • Oxford

ROWMAN & LITTLEFIELD PUBLISHERS, INC.

Published in the United States of America
by Rowman & Littlefield Publishers, Inc.
4720 Boston Way, Lanham, Maryland 20706

12 Hid's Copse Road
Cummor Hill, Oxford OX2 9JJ, England

Copyright © 1997 by Carnegie Corporation of New York

All rights reserved. No part of this publication may be reproduced,
stored in a retrieval system, or transmitted in any form or by any
means, electronic, mechanical, photocopying, recording, or otherwise,
without the prior permission of the publisher.

British Library Cataloguing in Publication Information Available

Library of Congress Cataloging-in-Publication Data

The price of peace : incentives and international conflict prevention
  / edited by David Cortright.
      p.   cm.
    Includes bibliographical references and index.
    ISBN 0-8476-8556-X (cloth : alk. paper). — ISBN 0-8476-8557-8
(pbk. : alk. paper)
      1. Peace.   2. International relations.   3. Conflict management.
  I. Cortright, David, 1946–   .
  JZ5560.P75   1997   97-22989
                                                     CIP

ISBN 0-8476-8556-X (cloth : alk. paper)
ISBN 0-8476-8557-8 (pbk. : alk. paper)

Printed in the United States of America

 ∞ ™ The paper used in this publication meets the minimum requirements of
American National Standard for Information Sciences—Permanence of Paper for
Printed Library Materials, ANSI Z39.48—1984.

ABOUT THE
Carnegie Commission on Preventing Deadly Conflict Series

Carnegie Corporation of New York established the Carnegie Commission on Preventing Deadly Conflict in May 1994 to address the threats to world peace of intergroup violence and to advance new ideas for the prevention and resolution of deadly conflict. The Commission is examining the principal causes of deadly ethnic, nationalist, and religious conflicts within and between states and the circumstances that foster or deter their outbreak. Taking a long-term, worldwide view of violent conflicts that are likely to emerge, it seeks to determine the functional requirements of an effective system for preventing mass violence and to identify the ways in which such a system could be implemented. The Commission is also looking at the strengths and weaknesses of various international entities in conflict prevention and considering ways in which international organizations might contribute toward developing an effective international system of nonviolent problem solving. The series grew out of the research that the Commission has sponsored to answer the three fundamental questions that have guided its work: What are the problems posed by deadly conflict and why is outside help often necessary to deal with these problems? What approaches, tasks, and strategies appear most promising for preventing deadly conflict? What are the responsibilities and capacities of states, international organizations, and private and nongovernmental organizations for undertaking preventive action?

The books are published as a service to scholars, students, practitioners, and the interested public. While they have undergone peer review and have been approved for publication, the views that they express are those of the author or authors, and Commission publication does not imply that those views are shared by the Commission as a whole or by individual commissioners.

Published in the series:

BRIDGING THE GAP:
A FUTURE SECURITY ARCHITECTURE FOR THE MIDDLE EAST
by Shai Feldman and Abdullah Toukan

THE PRICE OF PEACE: INCENTIVES AND INTERNATIONAL
CONFLICT PREVENTION
Edited by David Cortright

Forthcoming:

The Ambivalence of the Sacred: Religion, Violence, and Reconciliation
By R. Scott Appleby
Turkey's Kurdish Question
By Henri J. Barkey and Graham E. Fuller
Opportunities Missed, Opportunities Seized: Preventive Diplomacy in the Post-Cold War World
Edited by Bruce Jentleson
Sustainable Peace: The Role of the UN and Regional Organizations
By Connie Peck

Reports available from the Commission:

David Hamburg, *Preventing Contemporary Intergroup Violence.* Founding Essay of the Commission, April 1994.

David Hamburg, *Education for Conflict Resolution,* April 1995.

Comprehensive Disclosure of Fissionable Materials: A Suggested Initiative, June 1995.

Larry Diamond, *Promoting Democracy in the 1990s: Actors and Instruments, Issues and Imperatives,* December 1995.

Andrew J. Goodpaster, *When Diplomacy Is Not Enough: Managing Multinational Military Interventions,* July 1996.

Jane E. Holl, *Carnegie Commission on Preventing Deadly Conflict: Second Progress Report,* July 1996.

John Stremlau, *Sharpening International Sanctions: Toward a Stronger Role for the United Nations,* November 1996.

Alexander L. George and Jane E. Holl, *The Warning-Response Problem and Missed Opportunities in Preventive Diplomacy,* May 1997.

A House No Longer Divided: Progress and Prospects for Democratic Peace in South Africa, July 1997.

Nik Gowing, *Media Coverage: Help or Hindrance in Conflict Prevention,* September 1997.

Cyrus R. Vance and David A. Hamburg, *Pathfinders for Peace: A Report to the UN Secretary-General on the Role of Special Representatives and Personal Envoys,* September 1997.

To order *Power Sharing and International Mediation in Ethnic Conflicts* by Timothy Sisk, copublished by the Commission and the United States Institute of Peace, please contact USIP Press, P.O. Box 605, Herndon, VA 22070, USA; (phone) 1-800-868-8064 or 1-703-661-1590.

Full text or summaries of these reports are available on Carnegie Corporation's Web Site: http://www.carnegie.org

To order a report or to be added to the Commission's mailing list, contact:
Carnegie Commission on Preventing Deadly Conflict
1779 Massachusetts Avenue, NW
Suite 715
Washington, DC 20036-2103
Phone: (202) 332-7900 Fax: (202) 332-1919
E-mail: pdc@carnegie.org

Members of the Carnegie Commission on Preventing Deadly Conflict

David A. Hamburg, *Cochair*
President Emeritus
Carnegie Corporation of New York

Cyrus R. Vance, *Cochair*
Partner
Simpson Thacher & Bartlett

Gro Harlem Brundtland
Former Prime Minister of Norway

Virendra Dayal
Former Under-Secretary-General and
Chef de Cabinet to the Secretary-
General
United Nations

Gareth Evans
Deputy Leader of the Opposition and
Shadow Treasurer
Australia

Alexander L. George
Graham H. Stuart Professor Emeritus
of International Relations
Stanford University

Flora MacDonald
Former Foreign Minister of Canada

Donald F. McHenry
University Research Professor of
Diplomacy and International Affairs
Georgetown University

Olara A. Otunnu
President
International Peace Academy

David Owen
Chairman
Humanitas

Shridath Ramphal
Cochairman
Commission on Global Governance

Roald Z. Sagdeev
Distinguished Professor
Department of Physics
University of Maryland

John D. Steinbruner
Senior Fellow
Foreign Policy Studies Program
The Brookings Institution

Brian Urquhart
Former Under-Secretary-General for
Special Political Affairs
United Nations

John C. Whitehead
Chairman
AEA Investors, Inc.

Sahabzada Yaqub-Khan
Former Foreign Minister of Pakistan
Chairman, Board of Trustees
Aga Khan International
University–Karachi

Special Advisor to the Commission
Herbert S. Okun
Visiting Lecturer on International Law,
Yale Law School
Former U.S. Ambassador to the
German Democratic Republic and to
the United Nations

Jane E. Holl, *Executive Director*

Contents

Part Four: Multilateral Application

Part Five: Conclusions and Lessons Learned

Foreword

The fiftieth anniversary of the Marshall Plan is an apt time to reflect on the observation that prevention is more than simply the avoidance of situations that can lead to war; it is also the creation of conditions that foster peaceful relations between states. The latter approach was one of the basic strategies of the Marshall Plan and other economic and political initiatives in Europe after the Second World War: to build capable and self-reliant partners within Europe, to strengthen relations between Europe and North America, and to reduce tensions between former adversaries and integrate them into a more cohesive political and economic community.

There have been few studies of the role of incentive strategies—of which the Marshall Plan is but one example—in encouraging responsible behavior by states, especially those that are already in difficulty and could pose a threat to international order. In contrast, vast bodies of literature exist on how to pressure states with economic sanctions and threats of force. This study proceeds from the belief that incentives—that is, positive inducements—could have great potential for conflict prevention if they were better understood.

The Carnegie Commission on Preventing Deadly Conflict distinguishes two types of preventive action, structural prevention and operational prevention, and incentives can play a role in both. Structural prevention addresses the root causes of violence. The foundation of structural prevention is the promotion of good governance that meets three core needs of society: security, well-being, and a system of justice. Governments that fulfill these needs clear a path for their citizens to live peaceful, productive lives, and they weaken the tendency of groups to redress grievances by resorting to mass violence. The most effective incentive strategies generally fall under structural prevention because they lay this groundwork for peace and cooperation.

Operational prevention addresses situations in which deadly conflict appears imminent. In such cases incentives must be used with caution because they may seem like appeasement in the face of threats of military aggression. But in other situations, many of which are described in this book, incentives can have significant advantages over punitive approaches. Conciliatory gestures frequently lead to cooperative responses, while threats often initiate spirals of hostility and defiance. If we apply such lessons to preventive action and think of ways to use "carrots" judiciously, often with implicit or explicit "sticks," we may improve chances of averting a violent outbreak.

One particularly potent inducement for effective preventive action may be "conditionality," or the forging of links between responsible, nonviolent behavior and the promise of greater reward through carefully targeted economic assistance and opportunities to gain integration into the community of market democracies. During the cold war, conditionality often focused primarily on influencing a country's international ideological leanings. Today conditionality can be directed more toward addressing a country's internal political and social ills. Associating assistance with responsible governance in this way—provided that the condition is applied consistently—may give the international community a powerful source of leverage with those who persistently use violent means to pursue their aims.

States that attach conditions to their aid are not themselves above scrutiny, however. The potential leverage of conditionality is diminished when donor states demand higher standards of behavior than they themselves are prepared to observe. No longer can established, wealthy states simply dictate behavior to the less powerful. Consistent standards must be devised that apply to all states equitably. There are small signs that this may be happening. Perhaps nowhere is this kind of reciprocal accountability in greater evidence than on questions related to the proliferation of nuclear weapons and their eventual elimination. So-called threshold states are unwilling to sign up to rules and regimes for managing the problem of nuclear proliferation until they are satisfied that future arrangements will apply with equal force and effect to the existing nuclear states.

In the international system to prevent deadly conflict envisioned by the Commission, the international community must be able to react swiftly to warning signs of mass violence anywhere in the world. Policymakers will need to choose from a full array of possible responses. The Commission hopes that this study of the role of positive inducements will encourage further investigation. We are grateful to David Cortright and the 12 case study authors for their work on this volume, and to the publisher, Rowman & Littlefield, for appreciating the value of the study and disseminating it to policymakers and scholars throughout the world.

David A. Hamburg
Cyrus R. Vance
Cochairs

Preface

This book originates from the search by the Carnegie Commission on Preventing Deadly Conflict for positive tools to address crises of international violence. The project was under the overall supervision of Jane Holl, the Commission's talented and articulate executive director. Tom Leney, senior associate at the Commission, invited me to edit the volume and gave solid direction and assistance throughout the project. Members of the Commission provided invaluable input into the study at an October 1995 meeting in New York City. The most important contribution came from Alexander George, who as a member of the Commission encouraged this project and provided constant review and intellectual input. Professor George gave generously of his time and wisdom, offering incisive commentary at project task force meetings, during scholarly conferences, and by mail, often in his small handwriting that conveys big ideas. Professor George provided essential guidance and inspiration for this book.

Additional substantive input came from Nicole Ball, Lloyd J. Dumas, Bruce Jentleson, William Long, George Lopez, Janice Gross Stein, and Raimo Väyrynen. Comments from Karl Kaiser at the October 1995 Commission meeting were also very helpful. A special word of thanks is due to Karl Kaiser and also to all the case study authors for their skilled research and writing and their diligent responses to editing queries and deadlines. I express my gratitude as well to the three anonymous external reviewers who provided sometimes critical but always constructive and helpful comments on each of the chapters and the manuscript as a whole.

This book benefited greatly from the contributions of staff members at the Carnegie Commission on Preventing Deadly Conflict, the Fourth Freedom Forum, and the University of Notre Dame. Tom Leney and Esther Brimmer of the Commission managed the project, Bob Lande served as managing editor, and Nancy Ward gave cheerful and efficient administrative support. At the Fourth Freedom Forum, indispensable help came from Jennifer Glick, who edited the text and notes of every chapter, prepared the bibliography, produced and formatted computer documents, and even found time to assist with research. Julia Wagler of the Forum also assisted with chapter editing and research. Ann Pedler and Miriam Redsecker provided essential administrative support. Carolyn Domingo of the Kellog Institute at the University of Notre Dame assisted with editing services.

The publication of this volume in the Commission series owes a great deal to Jennifer Knerr, vice president and executive editor at Rowman & Littlefield. She recognized the value of the series and skillfully and efficiently shepherded this book through the editing and production process. Knerr was the editor of two of my previous books, and it was a special pleasure to work with her again on this volume.

I owe a special debt of gratitude to Howard Brembeck, founder and chairman of the Fourth Freedom Forum, who provided continuous encouragement and financial support for the project. This volume helps to fulfill the forum's mission of examining the economic tools of statecraft, positive as well as negative. The book complements the Forum's work on economic sanctions and confirms that carrots as well as sticks have a valuable role to play in preventing deadly conflict.

The greatest credit for this volume belongs to David Hamburg, president emeritus of Carnegie Corporation of New York, and Cyrus Vance, former U.S. secretary of state, who serve as cochairs of the Commission. Through their leadership of the Commission and their emphasis on the need for new ways of thinking about security in the post–Cold War era, Hamburg and Vance have made an invaluable contribution. They have focused the attention of policymakers and scholars on the challenge of prevention and the need for new ideas and tools. The emphasis on positive measures in this volume is an essential part of their agenda for advancing new approaches for the prevention of deadly conflict.

While many have contributed to the development of this study, the responsibility for errors or omissions is mine. I hope that, despite any shortcomings, this collection of writing and scholarship can elucidate an often neglected approach to international conflict and contribute to building a solid foundation for international peace and cooperation.

David Cortright
April 1997

Part One

Overview

1

Incentives and Cooperation in International Affairs

David Cortright

WHEN THE GOVERNMENT of North Korea announced to the world its intention to withdraw from the nuclear Non-Proliferation Treaty in March 1993, political leaders in Washington faced a grim prospect. A nuclear-armed North Korea, which the truculence of Pyongyang seemed to suggest, would pose a grave threat to international security. If North Korea were to acquire the bomb, South Korea and Japan could not long resist the pressure to follow suit, and a Pandora's box would be opened allowing the spread of nuclear weapons throughout Asia and beyond. Something had to be done to contain the nuclear threat, but what?

The policy options available in the North Korean crisis were limited. Negotiations were attempted with the reclusive regime in Pyongyang, but initial discussions proved fruitless and frustrating as demands from Washington seemed only to harden North Korean intransigence. Some Americans urged the use of armed force, arguing for air strikes to destroy North Korea's nuclear industry, but others cautioned that military strikes could plunge the peninsula into a paroxysm of war and destruction even more deadly than that of forty years before. The UN Security Council debated whether to impose economic sanctions, but this option proved problematic as well, in large part because China and Japan, North Korea's largest trading partners, were reluctant to support such measures. Skeptics also asked what good it would do to sanction a country that was already one of the most isolated on earth.

With the tools of diplomacy, military force, and economic coercion largely unavailable, Washington turned to the use of incentives. In cooperation with Japan and South Korea, the United States crafted a set of economic and diplomatic incentives that eventually persuaded North Korea to abandon its apparent nuclear ambitions. In the Agreed Framework of October 1994, the United States and its partners offered to provide North Korea with fuel oil, new less-proliferation-prone nuclear reactors, and the beginnings of diplomatic recognition. In exchange, Pyongyang agreed to accept international inspections and controls on its nuclear program. As Scott Snyder recounts in chapter 3 of this volume, the use of incentives proved successful in helping to defuse a dangerous international crisis.

Incentives strategies have been used in other recent international disputes as well. In the Dayton peace accords, European nations and the United States pledged substantial economic assistance to encourage the warring parties to live up to the terms of the agreement and begin the long process of reconstruction and reconciliation. Ukraine was persuaded to give up the nuclear weapons on its soil in exchange for economic assistance, improved diplomatic relations, and security assurances from Russia and the West. In the Baltic republics and Germany, economic aid in the form of housing construction for Russian army officers helped speed the withdrawal of the Red Army and cleared away some of the last vestiges of the cold war in Eastern Europe. In El Salvador, the United States offered economic incentives both to the Salvadoran government and the guerilla forces of the Farabundo Marti National Liberation Front (FMLN) to facilitate peace negotiations and assure implementation of the resulting agreement.

These and other examples demonstrate the relevance and increasing importance of incentives strategies in the prevention of international conflict. Most of the examples reviewed here are successes, but there have also been cases where incentives proved to be ineffective. Some are examined in these chapters, notably the failure of the constructive engagement policy toward South Africa and the so-far limited impact of international economic assistance in Bosnia. In the case of China, inducements that initially were effective have gradually lost their ability to modify the recipient's behavior. Examining the cases of failure as well as of success is important for understanding when incentives are appropriate and when they are not.

The case studies illustrate other complexities in the use of incentives. In the North Korea case, critics charged that the Agreed Framework contained no assurances against future violations. They criticized aid for North Korea as a reward for wrongdoing that would encourage other states to engage in similar transgressions in the hope of obtaining like rewards. The costs of incentives policies have also stirred debate. In an era of budget constraint, why should the United States or other countries spend hundreds of millions of dollars for financial assistance in Bosnia, the former Soviet Union, or other world trouble spots when there are no assurances of success?

Perhaps the greatest concern about incentives strategies is that they may inadvertently become a form of appeasement. This is the issue of "moral hazard" about which we will have more to say in chapter 11. Making offers to aggressors can be interpreted as a sign of weakness or vacillation and may embolden an outlaw regime to further acts of belligerence. Critics warn that conciliatory gestures can be a form of perverse incentive that encourages future wrongdoing. Since Munich, the term appeasement has acquired an extremely negative connotation,[1] and partly as a result, scholars and policymakers have tended to de-emphasize the use of incentive strategies. The concern for avoiding appeasement is legitimate and necessary, but it should not blind us to the many ways in which incentives can contribute constructively to conflict prevention.

This volume examines these and other aspects of the use of incentives in international conflict resolution. The studies contained here emerge from the work of the Carnegie Commission on Preventing Deadly Conflict and its evaluation of incentives and other tools of international policy. When decision makers are faced with crises of war and deadly conflict, how do they determine the proper military, economic, or diplomatic policy responses? When coercive measures are either unavailable or too risky, as in the North Korea case, what are the alternatives? When are incentives strategies appropriate and how should they be implemented?

Defining Incentives

Much has been written about the use of economic sanctions in international relations, but surprisingly little attention has been devoted to the role of positive incentives in shaping the political relations among nations.[2] The uses of incentives are so commonplace in the conduct of international affairs that they scarcely seem to deserve separate analysis. Incentives seem inseparable from the art of diplomacy. Enter the word incentives in a library computer, and hundreds of entries appear covering a wide range of topics, from health policy to taxes—almost every subject except foreign affairs. Analysts refer frequently to "carrots and sticks" as tools of international policy, but most of their attention is devoted to the latter. The use of military, economic, and diplomatic coercion is widely studied. The role of carrots—political and economic inducements for cooperation—is often a neglected stepchild.[3] This study attempts to redress this relative neglect and focuses on the unique and often beneficial characteristics of incentives strategies in the prevention of international conflict.

The definition of what constitutes an incentive is subject to varying interpretations. The authors in this volume generally agree that the inducement process involves the offer of a reward by a sender in exchange for a particular action or response by a recipient. An incentive is defined as the granting of a political or economic benefit in exchange for a specified policy adjustment by the recipient nation. Often the incentive offered is directly related to the desired policy outcome, as when the World Bank assisted demilitarization in Uganda and Mozambique by providing financial support for demobilized combatants. It is also possible and sometimes necessary to conceive of incentives in a more unconditional manner, without the requirement for strict reciprocity. This is what Alexander George has called the "pure" form of incentives where there is little or no explicit conditionality.[4] A sender may offer benefits in the hope of developing or strengthening long-term cooperation, without insisting upon an immediate policy response. In some circumstances, such as the Council of Europe's negotiations with Estonia, the principal incentive may be the simple fact of membership itself, and the accompanying hope that a seat at the table may lead to other more concrete benefits in the future. At a minimum, incentives policies seek to make cooperation and conciliation more attractive than aggression and hostility. The goal is to achieve a degree of policy coordination in which, according to Robert Keohane, nations "adjust their behavior to the actual or anticipated preferences of others."[5]

Inducement and *incentive* are sometimes used interchangeably, but there are subtle differences between the two terms. Inducement has a more holistic and inclusive connotation and can encompass not only economic measures but also security assurances and offers of political association. Inducement is also a more directive term. It can be made into a verb and implies leading or moving one to action by persuasion or influence. The connotation suggests overcoming indifference or opposition by offering persuasive advantages that bring about a desired decision. Incentive, defined as a stimulus or encouragement to action, has many of these same connotations. In practical terms the differences between the two words are minor, and it is not necessary to distinguish rigidly between them. Incentive is the more common term and is used most frequently in this volume.

In his classic study, *Economic Statecraft*, David Baldwin offered the following examples of what he termed "positive sanctions":

- granting most-favored-nation status
- tariff reductions
- direct purchases
- subsidies to exports or imports

- providing export or import licenses
- foreign aid
- guaranteeing investments
- encouraging capital imports or exports
- favorable taxation
- promises of the above.[6]

Other examples that could be added to Baldwin's list include:

- granting access to advanced technology
- offering diplomatic and political support
- military cooperation
- environmental and social cooperation
- cultural exchanges
- support for citizen diplomacy
- debt relief
- security assurances
- granting membership in international organizations or security alliances
- lifting negative sanctions.

Many studies, such as William Long's *Economic Incentives and Bilateral Cooperation,* focus on economic instruments such as trade policy or financial assistance.[7] Much of the discussion of incentives policy and many of the cases examined here emphasize the primacy of economic incentives. Policymakers often juggle a range of policy tools, however, and it is important to consider all of the options—political and military as well as economic—that may be a part of an incentives strategy. Our approach in this volume will be to adopt a more holistic definition and examine a range of cases in which many different incentives methods are applied.

Comparing Sanctions and Incentives

Carrots and sticks are spoken of separately, but in fact they are closely related. Ending a negative sanction may be considered a positive incentive, while removing an incentive can be a sanction. In many cases the primary form of incentive is the removal of a sanction. In economic theory, incentives and sanctions are often interchangeable. An incentive is a positive sanction, a sanction, a negative incentive. Each is designed to influence the recipient and bring about a desired change of behavior.

Carrots and sticks are often combined, as the case studies in this volume amply illustrate. Incentives can be offered to increase the attractiveness of the preferred course of action, while sanctions may be threatened if the objectionable behavior is not halted. Coercive diplomacy often requires offers, in addition to threats, to achieve success.[8] According to Baldwin, the use of negative sanctions can lay the groundwork for the subsequent application of positive incentives.[9] A mix of carrots and sticks is present in almost every attempt to influence the affairs of other nations.

While sanctions and incentives have much in common, there are also significant differences between the two. For the sender state, the perceived financial impact of sanctions and incentives may vary considerably. In narrow accounting terms, a sanction is not a cost. When countries impose an embargo on an offending state, this does not show up as a line item in the national budget. As a result, some policymakers naively consider economic sanctions to be a kind of "foreign policy on the cheap."[10] In reality, sanctions can impose significant costs on private companies, local communities, and even national governments. Since these losses seldom appear as state expenditures, however, they are easy to overlook or ignore. By contrast, foreign assistance, loan guarantees, and other forms of economic incentives are usually listed as specific budgetary allocations, which can make them easy targets of budget cutters. In the current era of fiscal austerity, many nations have reduced their commitment to foreign assistance. We will comment on this trend and assess its implications for incentives strategies in the final chapter.

Trade and technology incentives impose fewer costs on governments. Partly as a result they are becoming a preferred tool of economic statecraft. While incentives do not require budget allocations, they have financial implications. U.S. budget legislation mandates that reductions in revenue from any source, including the lowering of tariffs, must be offset by tax increases or compensating budget reductions.[11] Trade incentives increase the overall level of commerce, however, and usually result in increased government revenues. Commercial incentives also open up new opportunities for commerce that can benefit domestic constituencies.[12] Where sanctions impose costs on particular industries and communities, trade incentives can bring benefits to these groups. As a result, domestic constituencies in the sender state may gain a stake in maintaining trade preferences and provide political support for sustaining the incentives policy. Incentives also create economic benefits in the recipient nation and can generate similar supportive pressures there as well. William Long has developed this theme extensively in his chapter in this volume and elsewhere.[13] In contrast to sanctions, which cause hardships for the sender and the recipient, trade incentives bring benefits to both. They are a classic win-win proposition.

Trade incentives are not without their limitations, however. With the lowering of tariffs and trade barriers through the North American Free Trade Agreement and similar arrangements, the impact of incremental trade preferences has diminished in recent years. Government policymakers have fewer commercial preference options in an era of growing free trade. There is also the problem of the apparent decline in the effectiveness of trade incentives over time. As the case of China illustrates (explained by Long in chapter 4), the development of powerful vested interests in the sender state can make it extremely difficult to withdraw benefits, even when the behavior of the recipient state no longer justifies incentives. A related problem is the tendency for a recipient's expectations to rise over time, thereby diminishing the value of previous incentives. As concessions from an earlier period are taken for granted, they tend to lose their effectiveness. A similar problem exists with sanctions, which lose their impact over time as target nations adjust to external pressures.

Incentives strategies differ significantly from sanctions in their relation to market forces. With the use of incentives there is no natural tendency, as when sanctions are imposed, for new suppliers or third-party actors to step in and circumvent trade restrictions. As political scientist Eileen Crumm has observed, "Where market forces work against negative sanctions, they can reinforce positive ones."[14] Long has emphasized the same point.[15] Many scholars have noted that economic sanctions generate countervailing market pressures that can undermine the effectiveness of such measures. A successful embargo will raise the price of imports in the target country, and in the process create powerful incentives for black marketers.[16] By contrast, an offer of incentives such as foreign aid or concessional loans will not create market pressures for another party to do likewise. Competing offers of assistance may result from political motivations, but they are not generated by market forces. During the cold war, the United States and the Soviet Union competed to provide incentives offers, but such competition is less likely now. Positive sanctions work in harmony with the natural forces of the market and thus have a significant economic advantage over negative measures.

Sanctions and incentives also have differing impacts on international trade and the prospects for economic cooperation. One of the most significant, many would say most hopeful, characteristics of the post–cold war world has been the widespread expansion of free markets and substantial increase in international commerce. Richard Rosecrance has spoken of "the trading state" phenomenon as a powerful antidote to war and armed conflict.[17] Expanding trade and economic interdependence can establish a long-term foundation for peace and enhanced international cooperation, as discussed in several of our case studies. The use of economic sanctions runs counter to this trend. Economist Peter van Bergeijk has argued that the greater use of negative sanctions may threaten the expansion of trade, thereby weakening the incentive for political cooperation that comes with increasing economic interdependence.[18] By contrast, positive measures encourage trade and international cooperation and thereby contribute to the long-term prospects for peace. Long has also emphasized the beneficial impact of trade incentives for cooperative relations among nations. Incentives provide a basis for long-term cooperation and understanding and create the foundations for international stability.[19]

Another distinction between carrots and sticks is that sanctions work better when they are multilateral, while incentives can be effective unilaterally. Sanctions scholars generally agree that in an era of expanding trade globalization, where the U.S. share of world production has slipped below 20 percent, unilateral sanctions have less ability to squeeze a target's economy. The report on economic sanctions of the Carnegie Commission on Preventing Deadly Conflict concludes that "the broader the international support, the more likely that the [sanctions] regime will be effective."[20] By contrast, unilateral incentives can be quite effective, as illustrated in the use of U.S. aid to facilitate the peace process in El Salvador or German financial support to speed Soviet troop withdrawals. Multilateral incentives are also effective at times, but sustaining common goals and levels of commitment among multiple actors can be problematic.

Perhaps the greatest difference between sanctions and incentives lies in their impact on human behavior. Drawing on the insights of behavioral psychology, Baldwin has identified key distinctions between the two approaches. Incentives foster cooperation and goodwill, while sanctions create hostility and separation. Threats tend to generate reactions of fear, anxiety, and resistance, while the normal responses to a promise or reward are hope, reassurance, and attraction.[21] Threats send a message of "indifference or active hostility," according to Baldwin, while promises "convey an impression of sympathy and concern."[22] Incentives tend to enhance the recipient's willingness to cooperate with the sender, while negative measures tend to impede such cooperation. Roger Fisher has argued that "imposing pain may not be a good way to produce a desired decision" or influence another's actions.[23] Where threats and punishment generate resistance, promises and rewards tend to foster cooperation.[24]

Although less onerous than sanctions, incentives may nonetheless arouse resentment and hostility within a recipient nation. Political officials may object to incentives as "bribes" and refuse to consider the sender's proposals. Examples abound of leaders in recipient countries declaring that national interests are "not for sale." This response is somewhat similar to the classic "rally around the flag" effect that may accompany the imposition of sanctions. As Margaret Doxey and other scholars have noted, sanctions sometimes spark a nationalist reaction that can strengthen a regime and enable it to withstand economic hardship.[25] This type of response is much less likely with the use of incentives. Moreover, the likelihood of nationalist resentment can be reduced further by de-emphasizing the requirement for strict conditionality and displaying greater sensitivity to the culture and political traditions of the recipient nation.

The differences between incentives and sanctions have important implications for the conduct of political communications between sender and recipient. Because incentives create less resentment and obstinacy in the recipient, communication is clearer and more precise, and negotiations are more likely to succeed. Punitive measures may be effective in expressing disapproval of a particular policy, but they are not conducive to constructive dialogue. Where sanctions generate communications gridlock, incentives open the door to greater interaction and understanding.[26]

Methodology

While incentives strategies have certain benefits, they also have limitations. Because of the relative lack of scholarship on the subject, many questions about how incentives function remain unanswered. The techniques for applying them are poorly understood. Scholars and policymakers lack a framework for assessing when and how incentives strategies work best. Some of the unresolved issues include the following:

- *Avoiding the appearance of rewarding evil.* When do cooperative gestures cease being inducements and become a form of appeasement? Can incentives agreements be structured to minimize moral hazards and avoid the encouragement of wrongdoing?
- *Determining the proper mix of carrots and sticks.* How are various incentives deployed in combination with coercive measures such as sanctions and the threat or use of military force?
- *Assessing the type of issues and nature of regimes that are most appropriate for the use of incentives.* Are certain problems more easily resolved through incentives than coercive measures? How do subjective perceptions, in the sender and recipient, affect the likely success of incentives? Are totalitarian or democratic governments more susceptible to incentives?
- *Improving the methods of delivery and control.* How important is the value or scale of an incentive? Are the speed of delivery and duration of incentives vital to their success?
- *Evaluating the effectiveness of incentives.* How is success measured? Can specific impacts be identified? How do the success rates of incentives compare with those of other tools of policy such as sanctions and the use of force?

Our search for answers to these and other questions uses case studies and the method of structured, focused comparison.[27] We are guided in this process by the insights and method of Alexander George, distinguished professor emeritus of international relations at Stanford University and a member of the Carnegie Commission on Preventing Deadly Conflict. George's concept of bridging the gap between theory and practice through a structured comparison of specific cases is the inspiration for this study.[28]

Through an examination of nine cases, several of which involve multiple examples, we present a rich mosaic of recent historical experience on the use of incentives for conflict prevention. Each case offers valuable lessons and conclusions on the objectives, methods, and effectiveness of incentives policies. The different cases are then compared in light of the issues and questions identified above.

The goal of this study is to provide a set of findings that can help scholars and policymakers diagnose problems of international conflict in the future. We present conditional generalizations to guide assessment and diagnosis, not a fixed set of policy prescriptions.[29] Because the context and particular conditions of each case vary, it is impossible to develop rules that apply in all circumstances. There is no "one size fits all" approach to inducement strategies. Every case is ultimately determined by conditions that are peculiar to that situation. The history and culture of the countries involved significantly influence the outcome of particular episodes. Nonetheless, common patterns are evident even across the varied examples contained in this book, and general conclusions can be drawn on when and how to implement incentives strategies. In the concluding chapter we attempt to synthesize the lessons from the different case studies into a coherent analytic framework for understanding when and how incentives can be used as effective instruments of international conflict prevention.

The Chapters in This Volume

The many examples of incentives use in recent history offer a rich and diverse range of experience from which to draw. Each episode raises anew the myriad problems and possibilities associated with incentives strategies. The selection of cases for this volume has been guided by a desire to examine the use of incentives across a wide range of issues and in many geopolitical settings. The selection is also designed to illustrate the many different forms of incentives policies. Only by reviewing the diverse uses of this instrument in a broad political and geographic context is it possible to develop tentative hypotheses on its applicability to other situations.

The issues addressed in the chapters include nuclear nonproliferation, the settlement of armed conflict, regional dispute resolution, and human and civil rights. The geographic reach covers nearly every part of the world, with cases from Asia, Europe, Africa, and Latin America. The incentive tools range from traditional forms of foreign assistance to the use of diplomatic inducements and the strategy of commercial engagement. The cases include unqualified successes such as the agreement to remove nuclear weapons from Ukraine, controversial and failed efforts such as the Reagan administration's constructive engagement policy with the apartheid regime in South Africa, and ongoing but uncertain efforts such as the civil reconstruction program in Bosnia. Each chapter yields important insights to improve our understanding of incentives policies.

The next three chapters examine the use of incentives in support of nonproliferation policy. Virginia Foran and Leonard Spector of the Carnegie Endowment for International Peace offer a comprehensive overview of the role of incentives in preventing the spread of nuclear weapons. Among the variables they identify as key to the success or failure of nonproliferation incentives are (1) the nature of the relationship between sender and recipient, (2) the intensity of the potential proliferator's desire for nuclear weapons, and (3) the sunk costs already committed to the nuclear program. Foran and Spector review the history of U.S. efforts to influence the security policy decisions of potential proliferators through such incentives as the "Atoms for Peace" program, diplomatic recognition and support, financial assistance, closer political and military ties, and security assurances. In many of the specific examples examined, Foran and Spector find that U.S. policymakers employed a package approach that included a mix of incentives and sanctions. Among the success stories they recount are Washington's efforts to dissuade Taiwan and South Korea from their brief nuclear flirtations during the 1970s, and the more recent initiative by the United States and Russia to assure the removal of nuclear weapons from Ukraine.

In chapter 3, Scott Snyder of the United States Institute of Peace provides an in-depth analysis of the North Korean nuclear crisis. Beginning with the initial response of the Bush administration and continuing through the sometimes erratic but ultimately successful efforts of the Clinton administration, Snyder traces the diplomatic history of the crisis and highlights the role of incentives in the bargaining process with Pyongyang. As noted earlier, coercive measures were threatened but never employed, and Washington had to rely almost entirely on incentives to persuade North Korea to accept limitations and external controls on its nuclear program. The Agreed Framework plan authorized international inspections of North Korea's nuclear installations, in exchange for specified economic and diplomatic commitments from the United States, Japan, and South Korea. As Snyder notes, the Agreed Framework was structured in a strictly conditional manner, with the delivery of each incentive tied to specific policy concessions from Pyongyang.

William Long of the Georgia Institute of Technology offers a systematic analysis of trade and technology incentives drawing heavily from international relations theory. He applies the findings of theoretical analysis to the examination of commercial inducements in support of nonproliferation objectives in three historical cases: Sweden, China, and democratic Czechoslovakia. The "atoms for peace" program launched by the Eisenhower administration in 1953 was effective in helping to convince Swedish authorities to abandon efforts to develop a nuclear weapons capability. Most intriguing is Long's analysis of the U.S. diplomatic and commercial opening to China. During the 1980s, Washington attempted to use its new relationship with Beijing to encourage restraint in arms transfers and greater cooperation in security matters. In recent years, however, differences between the two nations have widened, even as commercial relations have continued to grow.

In chapters 5 through 8, we review the use of incentives in the settlement of regional and civil conflicts. In chapter 5, Amitabh Mattoo of Jawaharlal Nehru University in New Delhi joins me in examining incentives strategies for addressing the security problems of South Asia. Sanctions have seldom worked in the region, while incentives have often been successful, although they were used in the past to advance cold war interests. We propose new incentive strategies that could enhance cooperation and conflict resolution within the region. Among the approaches we suggest are a partial lifting of technology restrictions and export controls on India and Pakistan, linking a possible Security Council seat for India to renunciation of the nuclear weapons option, and a limited program of debt relief. We conclude our chapter by outlining a plan for resolving the Kashmir crisis through the application of the various incentives identified above.

In chapter 6 Raimo Väyrynen, director of the Joan B. Kroc Institute for International Peace Studies at the University of Notre Dame, analyzes the Dayton peace accords and the role of economic assistance and other incentives in assuring implementation of the agreement. Väyrynen examines the range of measures, including diplomacy and military and economic coercion, that were employed in the tortured history of attempts to bring an end to the armed conflict and civil atrocities in the former Yugoslavia. He reviews the provisions of the Dayton agreements, highlighting the important role given to external economic assistance and reconstruction aid in assuring implementation. As Väyrynen notes, while the military commitments of the agreement have been implemented, the civilian dimensions of the program remain underdeveloped. He concludes his paper with a sober account of the failures and limitations of civil reconstruction efforts in Banja Luka, Mostar, and Sarajevo.

Geoffrey Thale of the Washington Office on Latin America analyzes the role of incentives in bringing an end to the long civil war in El Salvador. Noting the dominant role of the United States in funding the Salvadoran government and sustaining its ability to wage war against the guerilla forces of the Farabundo Marti National Liberation Front, Thale explains how Washington used its leverage to persuade the government to achieve a peace settlement. Diplomatic and economic incentives were also offered to the FMLN to assure its participation in the peace process. Thale describes a delicate balancing act in which Washington's offer of an incentive to one side could be used as a sanction against the other, and vice versa. While the Salvadoran case was largely a success, Thale notes several limitations in the process, including a failure to complete the reform of military and police forces. Thale concludes by observing that the recent decline in U.S. foreign assistance funding has reduced Washington's ability to influence events in El Salvador.

In chapter 8, Jeffrey Herbst of the Woodrow Wilson School at Princeton University reviews the history of the Reagan administration's constructive engagement policy toward South Africa. Herbst argues that the Reagan administration's attempts to encourage reform by the Nationalist Party government in Pretoria were constrained by domestic political factors, as activist groups argued for a more punitive approach. Deep public revulsion against the apartheid regime made the use of incentives politically untenable. The limited incentives tools available, contrasted with the vast changes required in the South African political system, also constrained administration policy. The case of South Africa partially illustrates the moral hazards of appearing to reward wrongdoers.

In chapters 9 and 10, we examine multilateral approaches to incentives policy. Heather Hurlburt, formerly of the Carnegie Endowment for International Peace, examines the efforts of the Council of Europe and Organization for Security and Cooperation in Europe (OSCE) to reduce political tensions between the newly independent Baltic states and Russia. Hurlburt recounts the sharp differences between Moscow and the Baltic states over the civil rights of Russian minorities and the pace of Red Army troop withdrawals. The Council of Europe used the process of admitting the Baltic states to encourage compromise on the civil rights and troop withdrawal issues. Targeted financial assistance and security cooperation with Moscow also played a role in assuring the completion of Russian troop withdrawals. The Baltic case illustrates the importance of political legitimation and international participation as an inducement for cooperation, although this case also shows the value of combining such inducements with concrete economic and security benefits.

In chapter 10, Nicole Ball of the Overseas Development Council is joined by Jordana Friedman of the Council on Economic Priorities and Caleb Rossiter of Demilitarization for Democracy in a case study on the use of multilateral financial assistance as an inducement for conflict prevention and resolution. Ball and her colleagues review the use of persuasion, support, and pressure by bilateral donors and multilateral agencies such as the World Bank to encourage reduced military spending, greater transparency of military budgets, postconflict reconstruction, and the demobilization of former combatants. Noting the growing consensus among international lenders that excessive military spending impedes economic development, they argue for a more concerted use of financial assistance as a peacemaking tool. Among the cases reviewed are the successful efforts of Britain and other bilateral donors to pressure Malawi into accepting democratic elections, the ambitious World Bank program to facilitate the Israeli–Palestinian peace process through economic development in Gaza and the West Bank, and World Bank funding for the demobilization of military forces in Uganda.

The final chapter attempts to synthesize the lessons learned from the various cases. Each of the variables associated with the use of incentives is analyzed in light of the case study experiences. Conclusions are drawn and a set of hypotheses presented on the most effective use of incentives for international conflict prevention. The chapter also argues for a greater commitment by the United States and other major powers to the use of foreign assistance, especially development aid, as an important tool of international policy.

The concluding comments emphasize the superiority of incentives strategies over coercive policies in the conduct of international relations. As Roger Fisher has concluded, "the process of exerting influence through offers is far more conducive to international peace than the process of exerting influence through threats."[30] While incentives are not appropriate in every setting, and may be counterproductive if employed in the face of armed conflict and overt military aggression, they have many advantages over punitive approaches. History is replete with examples of the power of positive reciprocation. Conciliatory gestures often lead to cooperative responses, while threats usually generate hostility and defiance. Applying these lessons to diplomacy, using carrots more often than sticks, offers hope for transforming the international system and creating a more cooperative and peaceful world order.

Notes

1. As Alexander George has observed, appeasement was an accepted practice of European diplomacy prior to 1938. Appeasement can be part of a strategy of conditional reciprocity to secure concessions or assurances from an adversary. Such an approach should not be employed when dealing with outlaw states. It is also much riskier for small, vulnerable nations like Israel than for powerful, relatively secure countries like the United States. See Alexander George, *Bridging the Gap: Theory and Practice in Foreign Policy* (Washington, D.C.: United States Institute of Peace, 1993), 62–66.

2. A collection of recent scholarship in this field is *Economic Sanctions: Panacea or Peacebuilding in a Post–Cold War World?* edited by David Cortright and George Lopez (Boulder, Colo.: Westview Press, 1995). The major work on the subject is Gary C. Hufbauer, Jeffrey J. Schott, and Kimberly Ann Elliott, *Economic Sanctions Reconsidered: History and Current Policy*, 2d ed. (Washington, D.C.: Institute for International Economics, 1990). See also Margaret Doxey, *Economic Sanctions in Contemporary Perspective*, 2d ed. (New York: St. Martin's Press, 1996).

Part of the explanation for this lack of attention is the overemphasis among conventional analysts on coercive strategies. See the critique of theories of deterrence and coercive diplomacy in Alexander L. George and Richard Smoke, *Deterrence in American Foreign Policy: Theory and Practice* (New York: Columbia University, 1974) and Alexander L. George, David K. Hall, and William R. Simons, *The Limits of Coercive Diplomacy: Laos-Cuba-Vietnam* (Boston: Little Brown and Company, 1971).

3. Martin Patchen, *Resolving Disputes between Nations: Coercion or Conciliation?* (Durham, N.C.: Duke University Press, 1988), 261; Peter A. van Bergeijk, *Economic Diplomacy, Trade, and Commercial Policy: Positive and Negative Sanctions in a New World Order* (Aldershot, England: Edward Elgar, 1994), 20.

4. George and Smoke, *Deterrence*, 608–9.

5. Robert Keohane, *After Hegemony: Cooperation and Discord in the World Political Economy*, (Princeton, N.J.: Princeton University Press, 1984).

6. David A. Baldwin, *Economic Statecraft* (Princeton, N.J.: Princeton University Press, 1985), 42.

7. William J. Long, *Economic Incentives and Bilateral Cooperation* (Ann Arbor, Mich.: University of Michigan Press, 1996).

8. George et al., *Limits of Coercive Diplomacy*, 25.

9. David Baldwin, "The Power of Positive Sanctions," *World Politics* 24, no. 1 (October 1971): 25.

10. Statement of Kimberly Ann Elliott, Conference on Economic Sanctions and International Relations, University of Notre Dame, Notre Dame, Indiana, April 1993.

11. Interview, David Cortright with Kimberly Ann Elliott, 26 February 1997.

12. See Long, *Economic Incentives*, especially chapter 2.

13. Ibid; see also William J. Long, "Trade and Technology Incentives and Bilateral Cooperation," *International Studies Quarterly* 40, no. 1 (March 1996): 80–82.

14. Eileen Crumm, "The Value of Economic Incentives in International Politics," *Journal of Peace Research* 32, no. 3 (1995): 326.

15. Long, "Trade and Technology Incentives," 81–82; see also chapter 4 of this volume.

16. See William H. Kaempfer and Anton D. Lowenberg, "The Problems and the Promise of Sanctions," in *Economic Sanctions*, eds. Cortright and Lopez, 61–72.

17. See Richard Rosecrance, *The Rise of the Trading State* (New York: Basic Books, 1987).

18. van Bergeijk, *Economic Diplomacy*, 12.

19. Long, *Economic Incentives*.

20. John Stremlau, *Sharpening International Sanctions: Toward a Stronger Role*

for the United Nations (Washington, D.C.: Carnegie Commission on Preventing Deadly Conflict, November 1996), 17–18.

21. Baldwin, "Power of Positive Sanctions," 32.

22. Ibid.

23. Roger Fisher, *International Conflict for Beginners* (New York: Harper and Row, 1969), 28.

24. Ibid., 35.

25. Doxey, *Economic Sanctions in Contemporary Perspective,* 98–100; Ivan Eland, "Economic Sanctions as Tools," in *Economic Sanctions,* eds. Cortright and Lopez, 32–33.

26. Long, *Economic Incentives*, chap. 2.

27. Alexander L. George, "Case Studies and Theory Development: The Method of Structured, Focused Comparison," in *Diplomacy: New Approaches in History, Theory, and Policy,* ed. Paul Gordon Lauren (New York: Free Press, 1979), 43–68.

28. George, *Bridging the Gap*.

29. The phrase "conditional generalizations" is drawn from Alexander L. George, as is the framework of our analysis.

30. Fisher, *International Conflict*, 106.

Part Two

Preventing Weapons Proliferation

2

The Application of Incentives to Nuclear Proliferation

Virginia I. Foran and Leonard S. Spector

N UCLEAR PROLIFERATION frequently has been analyzed in terms of the motivations and constraints states face in developing nuclear weapons. Less frequently discussed are the tools that have developed over the years to persuade states not to proliferate. In today's international environment, when nuclear nonproliferation has become a top foreign policy priority of the United States and many other nations, it is important to evaluate the past successes and failures of these persuasive tools to maximize their effectiveness in the future.

Since the advent of the nuclear age, states have sought to prevent the further spread of nuclear arms through a variety of unilateral and multilateral diplomatic initiatives. Mechanisms that sought to deny would-be nuclear powers the ability to develop nuclear weapons have tended to be the most visible, beginning with the 1946 McMahon Act in the United States. The use of incentives to persuade states not to proliferate has also been a long-standing part of the international effort to curb the spread of nuclear armaments, however. Like other nonproliferation tools, this approach developed over time, sometimes subsidiary to other foreign policy goals and sometimes as a distinct part of nonproliferation policy.

We wish to thank Todd Perry and Drs. Michael Cain, Harald Müller, William Long, and William Potter for their comments and editorial suggestions, and Drs. Dagobert Brito, Michael Intrilligator, and David Lalman for the original theoretical inspiration and guidance.

The best known of the incentive initiatives was the U.S. Atoms for Peace program launched in 1953.[1] In the hopes that it could discourage states around the globe from undertaking completely autonomous nuclear programs that would not be subject to any nonproliferation controls, the United States offered to share nuclear equipment, materials, and technology under Atoms for Peace with states that agreed to use such imports exclusively for peaceful purposes and to subject them to external monitoring, first by the United States and later by the International Atomic Energy Agency (IAEA). The nuclear Non-Proliferation Treaty (NPT), which was opened for signature in 1968 and entered into force in 1970, also incorporated an incentives strategy: if nonnuclear weapons states agreed to accept IAEA inspection of all of their nuclear activities, as required by Article III of the pact, such parties were to enjoy broad access to peaceful nuclear technology, as guaranteed by Article IV of the accord.

From the mid-1950s through the mid-1970s, access to the peaceful uses of nuclear energy was highly valued, and this incentive was a relatively potent one that contributed to the decisions of many states to refrain from acquiring nuclear arms. Thereafter, however, the benefits of nuclear energy became more uncertain, and nuclear commerce declined around the world. One impact of this change was to give relatively greater prominence to the "denial"-oriented inspection and export control requirements of the NPT. Also in the mid- to late 1970s, two nuclear supplier state organizations were established, the NPT Nuclear Exporters Committee and the Nuclear Suppliers Group, which sought to withhold a wide range of nuclear commodities from states thought to be seeking nuclear arms, while restricting all exports of certain classes of nuclear equipment newly recognized as sensitive. The termination of U.S. economic and military aid to Pakistan in the late 1970s, as well as the 1980 cutoff of U.S. nuclear fuel shipments to Brazil and South Africa, and the simultaneously threatened cutoff of such shipments to India, increased the salience of such denial strategies, while appearing to eclipse the use of positive inducements to achieve nonproliferation goals. This general trend continued throughout the 1980s.

While these nonproliferation incentives were developing and then waning, global nonproliferation goals also benefited from incentives in the form of security guarantees offered to certain states as the result of overarching U.S. and Soviet foreign policies. Driven by cold war politics, the alliance commitments of NATO, along with U.S. security commitments to Japan, Australia, and New Zealand, largely preempted the consideration of autonomous nuclear weapons programs in all of these alliance partners, apart from Great Britain and France, resulting in what might be termed "a priori" nonproliferation.[2] Currently, with the broadening of the definition of state security, the distinction between incentives in the form of security guarantees and other political or economic incentives is becoming increasingly blurred and somewhat artificial.[3]

The past several years have seen a dramatic resurgence of interest in the incentives approach. Several states, such as Ukraine and North Korea, have sought specific security assurances and other incentives from the United States, among others, in return for good nonproliferation behavior. Interest in this nonproliferation strategy has also been stimulated because of concerns that proliferation, and in particular nuclear proliferation, would spiral out of control as the underlying rationale for the cold war security alliances and related security ties faded away, eroding the value of the security assurance incentives they provided. This appears to have created new opportunities and perhaps new demand for developing and applying incentives strategies.

This chapter represents a first systematic effort to understand how incentives can be applied to cases of potential nuclear proliferation. We begin by proposing a rudimentary model of the basic components of how incentives have been requested and provided in the past. Then, by way of illustration, this model is applied to a selection of historical and ongoing cases: Taiwan, South Korea, Ukraine, North Korea, and Pakistan. The final section of the chapter makes an effort to draw lessons from the cases for the future design and application of this approach to nuclear proliferation.

Evaluating Incentives: Defining the Terms and Identifying the Cases

Definitions

At this early stage of analysis, questions flourish. Which states were offered incentives not to develop nuclear weapons? Did these states then choose not to proliferate? Why were not all states offered incentives? Is it easier to offer some states incentives than others? What kinds of incentives are most successful? None of these questions can be addressed without first defining some essential terms and selecting criteria for identifying appropriate case studies.

First of all, not all states need to be included. Only those states that have actually considered developing or acquiring nuclear weapons are candidates for any nonproliferation strategy. Hence, only "potential proliferators" matter for this analysis. A state will be regarded as a "potential proliferator" when it has indicated by word or deed that it has interest in developing or acquiring nuclear weapons. For the purposes of this analysis, this will include all states that: have declared their possession of nuclear weapons; had nuclear weapons on their territory at the time of the dissolution of the Soviet Union; have conducted a test of a nuclear device; have taken steps, in the absence of a credible economic justification, toward the production of weapons-usable nuclear materials (plutonium or weapons-grade uranium); or are nonnuclear weapons states that possess nuclear facilities not subject to IAEA inspection. At present, there are twenty-five states (including the United States) that are now or at one time were considered potential proliferators.[4]

Second, all potential proliferators can be further broken down into four groups divided along two dimensions: (1) whether the state was offered incentives, and (2) whether the state ultimately proliferated or not. To further classify these states, two additional definitions are needed: "nuclear proliferation" and "incentive." For the purposes of this analysis, "nuclear proliferation" will be deemed to have occurred when the state declares itself to be a nuclear weapons state, conducts a test of a nuclear device, or has acquired enough nuclear weapons components that the international community responds to it as if it had a de facto nuclear weapons capability. According to this definition, nuclear proliferation has occurred in the five declared states—the United States, Russia, Great Britain, France, and China—and the undeclared nuclear powers—India, Israel, Pakistan, North Korea, and South Africa. The Republic of South Africa, since originally crossing the nuclear weapons threshold in the late 1970s, has recently renounced its nuclear weapons capability, dismantled its weapons, and signed the Nuclear Nonproliferation Treaty as a nonnuclear weapons state.[5]

Finally, an incentive, with respect to proliferation, is defined as: *any benefit or promise of benefits offered by senders to a state thought to be considering the acquisition or development of nuclear weapons, or to a state that already has nuclear weapons, in exchange for that state's decision to halt its progress toward proliferation or for its dismantling or elimination of the weapons it already possesses.*

In practice, incentives are not offered by themselves, but as a "package" of incentives and disincentives. The package approach to nonproliferation is simply an application of the carrot and stick approach to foreign policy. The only distinction is that the particular incentives and disincentives offered are specially designed to affect the state's nuclear decision-making process. As used herein, an "incentives/disincentives package" is defined as a set of promised benefits and threatened sanctions presented by a sender state to a potential proliferator that is designed to discourage the latter from developing nuclear weapons.

At this level of analysis, it is difficult to distinguish in particular cases between the persuasive effects of the incentives and the disincentives. During the mid-1970s, for example, the United States, concerned about South Korea's clandestine nuclear weapons program, entered into discussions in which it offered to defer the proposed reduction of U.S. forces in South Korea—an incentive—while threatening the disincentive of withholding financial credits for the Republic of Korea's peaceful nuclear industry.[6] Although South Korea's abandonment of its nuclear weapons effort was a clear success for nuclear nonproliferation, one cannot be sure whether Seoul dropped its bid for nuclear arms in order to keep U.S. troops as a guarantee of its security, to avoid the financial ruin of its nuclear industry, or both.

Compounding the analytical confusion is the fact that in some cases the incentives offered a potential proliferator are ambiguous or limited to the advantage gained by remaining a member in good standing of the international community through acceptance of the nonproliferation norm. The disincentives might be similarly ambiguous and indirectly imposed by states unhappy with the potential proliferator's decision to continue developing a nuclear weapons capability. At this initial stage of analysis, it is important to select cases based on their most obvious features rather than trying to capture all the details at once. In this inquiry, we are most interested in understanding how incentives have affected a state's decision to develop or acquire nuclear weapons. Accordingly, we will focus on cases where explicit incentives were unambiguously offered by states trying to affect a potential proliferator's decision-making process.

Case Selection

Of the twenty-five states (identified in note 4) that are past or current potential proliferators, only the United States did not receive any incentives (remembering that in the context of this chapter, incentives are offered from a source external to the state). In 1946 the Soviet Union was offered what American officials considered an incentive in the nuclear disarmament provisions of the Baruch Plan, but Moscow rejected the U.S. initiative as one sided. Beginning in 1953, by which point Great Britain had become a nuclear power, each of the twenty-two remaining states that was friendly with the United States had the opportunity to benefit from the Atoms for Peace program, and many states, including India, Israel, Pakistan, South Africa, South Korea, Sweden, and Taiwan, took specific advantage of this incentive. In some cases, such as South Korea and Sweden, this appears to have played a major role in redirecting the recipient's nuclear activities away from nuclear arms. (See William Long's discussion of the Sweden case in chapter 4.) In other cases, "atoms for peace" at least led to the introduction of IAEA inspections on a portion of the recipient's nuclear program. Other countries, such as Iraq, Libya, and North Korea, enjoyed comparable incentives from the Soviet Union, which appears to have used the promise of supplying nuclear power plants—a promise never ultimately fulfilled—as an inducement to gain those countries' acceptance of the NPT. It is not clear whether the offer of access to peaceful nuclear technology contained in Article IV of the NPT by itself influenced the decision of any state to adhere to the treaty or refrain from acquiring nuclear weapons. To the extent that access to nuclear energy served as a nonproliferation incentive in particular cases, the promise of assistance from one of the major supplier states, rather than the NPT's guarantee, was probably the dominant consideration.

For the purposes of this review, the cases most interesting to analyze are the ones involving states that received incentives *above and beyond* what was widely available to the international community (i.e., incentives that went beyond Atoms for Peace, the Soviet equivalent, and NPT Article IV). These cases involve states that received specific security guarantees or other military incentives, such as special arms deals, or that received economic incentives, such as loans or special credit terms. We are also more interested in cases where the extra incentives were offered *specifically in exchange* for nonproliferation behavior, so that we can better evaluate the level of success or failure in past incentives-strategy efforts.

Given these general guidelines, the potential proliferators who received "extra incentives" include:

- *South Korea* and *Taiwan,* both of which on several occasions requested specific reaffirmation of the American security commitment as an alternative to developing nuclear weapons to defend themselves from hostile regional powers
- *Pakistan,* an ongoing potential proliferator and a currently de facto nuclear weapons state, which managed to negotiate many years of financial and military support from the United States with the implicit understanding, among other things, that it would not enrich its stockpile of uranium above 5 percent U-235 (not usable for nuclear weapons) or develop nuclear weapons, but chose to anyway
- *Ukraine,* a potential proliferator that negotiated with Russia, Great Britain, and the United States for a package of incentives, which included security guarantees, funds for dismantling nuclear weapons inherited from the former Soviet Union, raw materials, and increased political recognition from the West, in exchange for acceding to the NPT as a nonnuclear weapons state and giving up the nuclear weapons remaining on its territory
- *North Korea,* the most recent recipient of a specially designed incentives package in return for agreeing to freeze its nuclear program and fully comply with the NPT

Rudiments of a Model

Since we are selecting a few cases of potential proliferation for special scrutiny in our analysis of how incentives have been applied in the past, it is important that the same method of analysis be applied to all of our cases. What follows is a rudimentary model of what we believe are the most basic components of all applications of incentives to proliferation.[7] To discuss these components, some terms need to be created and some commonsense assumptions stated.

Actors and Motives

First and foremost, we assume that the leaders of states make decisions based on their self-interest. To remain in power, leaders must protect the state from threats to its security—whether they are military, political, or economic—originating from within the state or from outside. Second, most states have finite resources, and therefore, leaders must pick and choose how they want to use them. It follows that the leaders of a potentially proliferating state have to evaluate why they are choosing to spend finite resources on developing nuclear weapons as opposed to advancing other state objectives.

A minimum of two states is necessary: a state that is considering development or acquisition of nuclear weapons, and a state that wants to persuade the first state not to do so. For the purposes of this analysis, we refer to the first state as the "potential proliferator," and the second, as the "sender state." In some cases, there are multiple potential proliferators and several sender states, but here we will limit the model to the simplest case of one of each.

We assume the following aspects are common to each case of potential proliferation and the negotiation of an incentive.

1. Each case has actors with distinct motives; the potential proliferator has a motive to acquire nuclear weapons, and the sender state has a motive for trying to prevent proliferation; both states' motives range from weak to strong.
2. Each actor also applies certain assessment criteria in decision making; the potential proliferator assesses the costs and benefits of proliferating versus not proliferating, while the sender state assesses the costs and benefits of providing incentives versus not providing incentives.
3. Each episode entails a negotiation process between the two states where the first two components are played out.

One or the other state has to initiate an interaction for an incentive to be negotiated. If the sender state moves first, it is motivated to influence the potential proliferator's nuclear decision-making process by making proliferation too costly in comparison to the benefits of accepting the incentive. The sender state could be motivated by a nonproliferation norm, that is, a concern that the continued spread of nuclear weapons is dangerous for all states, or by something closer to home, for example, fear that the potential proliferator might eventually diminish the security or negatively affect or interfere with the foreign policy goals of the sender state or its allies.

If the potential proliferator initiates the interaction, it seeks to trade off its nuclear weapons capability for something else that it wants from the sender state. It is counting on at least one of the sender state's two motives being present. As noted above, the potential proliferator's motive in seeking nuclear weapons in the first place can vary. In the past, the security motive, that is, military threats from external sources, has been present most frequently, and the potential proliferator sought to trade its threat of proliferation for alliance-style guarantees or other outside assistance, such as arms or technology that would contribute directly to its security needs.

At times, states are motivated to acquire nuclear weapons for reasons of prestige, either to enhance the stature of the national leadership at home, or to provide advantages regionally or globally. There has even been a case in which a country believed that it could improve its economic status by raising the specter of nuclear proliferation (see the case of Ukraine, discussed below). These motives, though not related to traditional security concerns, have been interpreted since approximately the mid-1980s as contributing to the broader economic and political aspects of national security and therefore can be included in this general analysis.

The security motive continues to be a popular, publicized rationalization for nuclear-weapons programs. Potential proliferators may inflate their threat assessments to justify their programs, obscuring their true motives. This obfuscation can decrease the ability of sender states to formulate incentives that are attractive to the potential proliferator. Ultimately, however, it should be easier to strike a bargain with states that are exaggerating threats to their security than with states who face real and significant security threats that may be difficult for sender states to counter.

Some commonsense rules of thumb emerge from the above discussion. A successful negotiation of an incentive requires understanding the motives of both states involved and the relationship among those motives. Whether the sender state ultimately offers an incentive depends partially on the strength of that state's motive for doing so, a factor that may also determine the type of incentive it eventually offers. Similarly, the stronger the potential proliferator state's reason for pursuing nuclear weapons (i.e., more security, rather than prestige or economics, is the dominant motivation), the more difficult it may be to dissuade the state. This does not imply, however, that an incentives approach would not be successful, but rather that the incentive offered would have to reflect the intensity of the motive.

Further complicating this relationship is the fact that the original motive to proliferate may change or even disappear over the years, making the assessment of motivations more difficult. It is also important to recognize, when crafting an incentives strategy, that reversing a potential proliferator's nuclear weapons program is likely to become more difficult as that program advances and acquires bureaucratic and popular support.

Assessment Criteria

For the purposes of this research, we assume that all potential proliferators implicitly or explicitly assess the costs and benefits of their decision to develop or acquire nuclear weapons.[8] Assuming the leaders of the state are essentially rational and that the state does not possess infinite resources, the decision to proliferate will be made when the net benefit of doing so exceeds the net benefit of not doing so.[9] We understand that leaders do not always act in ways that others would interpret as rational, and that perceptions of costs and benefits are highly subjective and culture bound. Nonetheless, for the purposes of this chapter, we assume that leaders weigh the economic and security advantages or disadvantages of a proliferation decision before acting. Precisely when and how often the state makes this calculation depends on the motive and circumstances surrounding the decision.

Some potential proliferators embarked on a weapons program in response to severe threats to their security. They were prompted to reassess their decision when their security situation improved, when countervailing guarantees were offered, or when unanticipated costs, such as international sanctions, appeared imminent. For other states where the threat was less immediate, or in cases where the motive emerged from economic or internal political factors, a state might launch a nuclear energy program without initially deciding its end product. In such states, a program with two possible outcomes emerged: one focusing on nuclear energy and one on the materials and components for weapons. Two-track programs also emerged in states where there was internal disagreement about the end product, or where there was doubt as to whether the program would succeed. In these cases, the proliferation calculation was much more complex, requiring consideration of costs and benefits on a variety of levels and over a considerable period of time.

Prior to the emergence of an international nonproliferation norm, a state developing nuclear weapons was, first and foremost, concerned about the financial and domestic political costs of its decision and the reaction of adversary states. All nuclear programs, whether they are conceived as nuclear energy or as weapons programs, involve a serious commitment of financial and technological resources. Unless the state is governed by an absolute dictator, such a commitment requires at a minimum the acquiescence of the domestic political leadership. In some democracies, active political support from a wider segment of the population is necessary to sustain the program. Such acquiescence or active political support may be hard to come by if there are competing programs or differing views regarding the benefits of nuclear energy or nuclear weapons.[10]

Once the nonproliferation norm emerged fully in the late 1960s, states developing nuclear weapons had another cost to consider—organized international pressure. Initially, the pressure was applied in order to extract promises that the state had peaceful intentions and to ensure external monitoring of imported nuclear equipment and materials. With each test of the nonproliferation norm, by Israel, India, Pakistan, and more recently Iraq, Iran, and North Korea, the norm became more specific and so did the obligations and expectations of states belonging to the regime. Voluntary supply organizations, such as the Nuclear Suppliers Group and the NPT Exporters Committee, emerged to identify and subject to export controls specific materials and technology that could contribute to nuclear weapons programs. These organizations extended their controls to all states, even those that were not members of the NPT. The effect was to increase the cost of a potential proliferator's nuclear program by drying up all legal outside sources of nuclear equipment and material and/or driving the program underground. Getting caught trying to bypass these controls could impose political costs by souring relations with otherwise friendly states. The potential proliferator might thus be motivated to reconsider its decision to develop nuclear weapons, and, depending on its original motive (political, economic, or security), might negotiate alternative ways of gaining the expected benefits of developing nuclear weapons.

The sender's motives for intervening are also important. How much is the sender willing to pay the proliferator not to develop nuclear weapons? How crucial is it to the sender that the potential proliferator change its mind? The cost of intervention is determined in part by the assets the sender has at hand. The potential proliferator and sender state may already have a relationship in which the mere threat of damaging that relationship will be enough to change the potential proliferator's mind. On the other hand, if there is no relationship, the sender state may have to spend assets merely to establish one. In addition, if the two states are friendly, the sender state may be prepared to offer a wider variety of incentives than if the states are enemies and have no preexisting relationship. Generally speaking, the worse the relationship between the two states, the more difficult it may be to use a nonproliferation strategy that includes incentives.

Finally, understanding the motive and the assessment criteria of the potential proliferator can provide valuable information to the sender state in designing the incentive. The goal of any nonproliferation policy is to reduce the net benefit of proliferating to zero or below, if possible (assuming the state is rational). If an incentives strategy is to be successful, the magnitude of the incentive offered must be commensurate with that calculation.

When the incentive is offered also affects its relative success. An important underlying factor in all of these cases is that ten years are typically required to develop nuclear weapons, a period providing repeated opportunities for sender state intervention. A small incentive—one that generates a small reduction in the net benefit of proliferating—that is offered when a program is just beginning and when the lion's share of the costs lay in the future, might be more successful than the same incentive offered after most of the costs of proliferating had been absorbed. The general rule of thumb is that as sunk costs increase, so must the size and value of the incentive.

Essentials of Negotiation—Reaching an Agreement

The final component of the incentive approach occurs in the negotiation phase. This component is perhaps the most crucial as it involves the interaction of each state's motives and assessments, as well as the negotiation of the specific incentive or sets of incentives. At this stage, both states have decided to test out what they can obtain from the other. As in all strategic bargaining situations, both states are trying to minimize what they have to give up to maximize the benefits they hope to obtain.

Here, as in the assessment phase, the preexisting relationship between the potential proliferator and the sender state is particularly important. The degree of enmity or friendliness will determine the overall complexity of the negotiation. The more friendly the states are, the more likely they are to trust each other in word and deed. Moreover, an existing relationship can provide incentives more quickly than a situation in which a relationship needs to be created. In addition, if the two states are friendly, the sender state may be both more willing and more able to increase the value and diversity of the incentive(s) it offers than in the case of an adversary or a state with which it has no previous relationship.

The second crucial aspect to the negotiation phase is each state's understanding of its "reservation price." The reservation price is the lowest price each state will accept for what it gives up. It is commensurate in value to the benefits the potential proliferator hoped to derive from developing nuclear weapons. The reservation price is the value the sender must offer to match those benefits. The potential proliferator will hold out for the most lucrative incentives package it can obtain before agreeing not to proliferate. Its reservation price must therefore include elements essential to its motive for proliferating or to the benefits it thought it could obtain through proliferating. These essential elements need to be reflected in the incentives it receives. If the potential proliferator has been ambiguous or misleading about its motive, or its preferences change during the course of the negotiation, this can create confused and ineffective negotiations.

This is illustrated in the case of Ukraine. At first, antinuclear sentiment stemming from the Chernobyl accident dominated discussions about the disposition of the former Soviet Union's nuclear weapons based on Ukrainian territory, and it appeared that they would be removed rapidly to Russia. Gradually, concern about Russian economic and political domination of Ukraine fueled opposition to removing the nuclear arms. Some policymakers supported a Ukrainian nuclear weapons capability to deter future Russian threats to Ukrainian territorial integrity. This indecision over the fate of the nuclear weapons and concern about Russia was reflected in discussions on security guarantees that dominated the first half of the negotiation phase. Only after the disparate groups in Ukraine negotiated among themselves the costs and benefits of keeping the nuclear weapons was the government of Ukraine able to communicate the essential aspects of its concerns to sender states (Russia, the United States, and Great Britain), enabling the sender states to respond with an appropriate set of incentives. Given the lack of clarity among Ukrainians themselves, only Ukraine could signal the need to include particular dimensions in the negotiation. The sender states were not really in a position to guess. As discussed by Scott Snyder in chapter 3, a similar dynamic occurred in the lengthy negotiations the United States conducted with North Korea during 1993 and 1994.

The sender state's reservation price, on the other hand, includes the essential aspects of its nonproliferation goals. It is trying to maximize the achievement of those goals while minimizing its costs in terms of the incentives package provided. Nonetheless, a basic tenet of nonproliferation bargaining is that the incentives a sender state offers must equal or exceed the potential proliferator's reservation price. The benefits offered must match or surpass the net benefits the proliferator expects to receive from developing nuclear weapons. The sender state is not likely to offer a more valuable incentive than seems appropriate for the motive involved. In the case of inflated or ambiguous motives, it is ultimately the responsibility of the potential proliferator to signal what types of incentives are needed.

There are a number of additional elements of "getting to yes" that must be understood. First, in some cases there may be an insurmountable mismatch between the reservation price of the potential proliferator—what it must have to renounce its bid for nuclear arms—and the kind or magnitude of the incentives that the sender state is politically prepared and/or literally able to offer. Such a mismatch was seen in U.S. relations with Pakistan during the 1980s, when Pakistan required a credible military guarantee against aggression by India, which the United States, given its generally friendly relations with New Delhi, was unwilling to provide. A similar impasse would have been reached in the case of Ukraine if Kiev's reservation price had been an ironclad military alliance against Russia.

Obstacles can also arise in the negotiation phase when leaders agree to a particular trade-off, but constituencies in one or both parties exercise a veto over its implementation. The true test of the negotiation phase occurs when the deal is made public and must be sold to domestic constituencies. For example, an agreement to restore U.S. economic and military assistance to Pakistan in exchange for the dismantlement of that country's nuclear weapons program might be acceptable to some Pakistani leaders, but elements in the political opposition and in the country's armed forces undoubtedly would reject it, decrying it as a cave-in to U.S. pressure. The case of North Korea shows the other side of the coin: the possibility of a veto of the nonproliferation bargain by opposing political elements in the sender states. The price of the incentives package negotiated for North Korea was so expensive that legislators in the sender states may be unwilling to authorize all the funds necessary to implement it.

Some Hypotheses

The above discussion illustrates the difficulty of negotiating incentives even in the simplest case where only two states are involved. We recognize that our model is limited in other respects as well. Leaders of states do not always have adequate information about the costs and benefits of their actions and may lack control over the process of negotiation. Nonetheless, the abstract model may be useful in generating hypotheses that can be tested in our case studies. We offer the following three points:

1. The application of an incentives strategy is more likely to be successful when the states involved are friendly states.
2. The stronger the motive to proliferate (i.e., the more security dominant), the more lucrative the incentives package must be to gain agreement.
3. The lower the sunk costs (i.e., the earlier the stage of nuclear weapons development), the more likely the proliferator will accept an incentive.

Stated differently, these hypotheses suggest that there are three significant variables that may influence the success or failure of an incentives package: (1) degree of enmity or friendliness between the states negotiating the incentives, (2) the strength of the motive to proliferate (weak to strong), and (3) the level of investment (financial and political) in the program. These variables should be present in every case of proliferation where an incentives strategy is contemplated. The variables may interact with one another to increase or decrease the likelihood of success and failure. The success of an incentives strategy is more likely, for example, when the states involved are more friendly, the motive to proliferate is not security dominant, and the level of investment in the nuclear weapons program is low. On the other hand, an incentives strategy is less likely to succeed when the states involved are enemies or have a limited preexisting relationship, the motive to proliferate is security dominant, and the level of investment in the nuclear program is high.

In the future, objective criteria must be further developed for defining the continuum across which these variables should be measured. What precisely constitutes low, midrange, and high levels of investment? What distinguishes a security-dominant proliferator from one that is not? In the meantime, we review some of the historical cases to examine the workings of the three hypothesized variables.

Case Studies

The cases that have been identified are nonproliferation successes and failures that resulted when a special incentives strategy was applied specifically for nonproliferation purposes. These include Taiwan, South Korea, Ukraine, and North Korea as the cases of success, and Pakistan as a case of failure. Examining these cases will provide preliminary insight into why incentives may not have been offered to the other states and, perhaps, how to apply the incentives strategy to current proliferators.

Applying the proposed model to past and current cases is not as straightforward as it may first appear, in particular, because much of the record in individual instances remains classified, leaving questions as to precisely what incentives may have been offered and the response of the potential proliferator in question. Nonetheless, what *is* known about these key cases will be analyzed briefly below. A more comprehensive treatment will remain a topic for further research.

Taiwan

Actors and motives

This episode crystallized in 1975, when the United States determined that Taiwan was building a small, clandestine plutonium extraction capability, a strong indication that Taipei was launching a nuclear weapons program. From what is known about the episode, the United States—the sender state—demanded that the facility be dismantled and that Taiwan pledge not to engage in plutonium-related activities. Taiwan acquiesced, probably because of the veiled American threat to reduce U.S. security ties to the island and to terminate cooperation in peaceful nuclear electricity-generating projects, but this bitter pill appears to have been accompanied by the promise of increased cooperation in both spheres, if the plutonium issue were laid to rest.

The case highlights the tangled relationship between sanctions and in-centives. U.S. actions that gave rise to Taiwan's initial fear of reduced U.S. security ties were not stimulated by Washington's desire to sanction Tai-wan's nuclear weapons program, of which Washington was for a time un-aware, but by other foreign policy considerations. As the negotiation unfolded, however, Taiwan undoubtedly came to fear that if the nuclear issue were not resolved, U.S. security support might be reduced still fur-ther, creating the perception of a threatened sanction, which presumably affected Taiwan's calculations of the benefits of continued pursuit of nu-clear arms. It appears, however, that the U.S. intervention was framed in terms of an incentive—the reaffirmation and solidification of security links and the enhancement of nuclear trade ties.

In this case, Taiwan was clearly motivated by substantial security con-cerns. This was some four years after Nixon's opening to the People's Re-public of China dramatically unsettled the island's defense arrangements with Washington and six years after the announcement of the Nixon Doc-trine, which called upon America's Asian allies to take greater responsibil-ity for their security and reduce their reliance on the United States.[11] Washington, however, had strong incentives to arrest Taiwan's nuclear bid. Not only might a Taiwanese nuclear weapons program have derailed the growing, de facto U.S. strategic partnership with Beijing, but the epi-sode also came one year after India's nuclear test galvanized U.S. and inter-national nonproliferation efforts. In addition, because of long-standing links to a state that had been a valiant anti-Communist ally during the cold war, there was deep political support among political conservatives in the United States—elements that formed a central constituency for the Repub-lican Party of President Gerald Ford—for guaranteeing Taiwan's survival.

Unilateral assessments

The key element of the incentives package in this case was U.S. agree-ment to maintain significant security ties with Taipei, within the context of overall U.S. relations with the People's Republic of China. Facing the alternative of possible isolation and acute vulnerability for many years before it might obtain a useful nuclear deterrent, Taiwan calculated the net benefits of the alternatives confronting it and accepted what Washington offered. Importantly, the specific incentives package offered by Washington—militarily oriented security guarantees—was well suited to address the particular motivations leading Taiwan to consider developing nuclear arms. For the United States, on the other hand, the price of offering the incentive was relatively modest: maintenance of the status quo (and the promise of profitable civil nuclear cooperation). The net benefits of intervention were thus clear. The fact that there was a close, preexisting relationship between Washington and Taipei meant that there were no initial political hurdles to be overcome before the former could undertake negotiations with the latter.

Negotiations

The record concerning the communications between the parties as to Taiwan's reservation price and the availability of the U.S. incentives package remains classified, but there have been no indications of difficulties in this regard. There were obvious complications, however, for the United States in providing security guarantees to Taiwan that would not anger the People's Republic of China. Nonetheless, a formula was found that satisfied Taiwan. Finally, there were few apparent difficulties in gaining the support of interested constituencies in implementing the final bargain, and because Washington intervened when the Taiwanese nuclear weapons effort was still in its early stages, striking a bargain was not hampered by significant sunk costs on the Taiwanese side.

South Korea

Actors and motives

Many of the same calculations appear to have been at work when the United States intervened to discourage South Korea from continuing a clandestine nuclear weapons program in 1974 and 1975, a program that included the purchase of a commercial plutonium separation plant from France. Security concerns, stemming from the U.S. defeat in Vietnam and announcement of the Nixon Doctrine, motivated Seoul, while Washington feared that a nuclear-armed South Korea might destabilize the region and undermine U.S. nonproliferation efforts more broadly.

Unilateral assessments

The persuasive tools Washington employed to end Seoul's nuclear flirtation appear to have been the threat of isolation (including a halt on further peaceful nuclear cooperation)—isolation that Seoul would have had to endure for five to ten years before a nuclear deterrent was in hand—coupled with the "incentive" of reaffirmed security ties (and promises of active peaceful nuclear cooperation). These were well matched to address the anxieties that motivated Seoul. For South Korea, the net benefits of giving up its nuclear bid must have been quickly manifest. As in the case of Taiwan, a history of close ties meant that there were no preliminary political obstacles to undertaking negotiations.

Negotiations

Communications seem to have been clear between the parties, and it appears that the price that Seoul sought for renouncing its nuclear weapons effort, though not insignificant, was one Washington was able to pay politically and militarily. Gaining acceptance of the incentives package is not known to have raised serious problems in Washington, although in 1977, the incoming Carter administration would reanimate South Korean anxieties with its short-lived plan to withdraw a substantial portion of U.S. forces from Korea. In Seoul, acceptance of the nonproliferation bargain with the United States met considerable opposition from some elements in the military, but this was overcome.

One point worth underscoring here is that in both of these cases, what Washington was required to offer by way of incentives was very consistent with underlying U.S. policy in the region. In the aftermath of Vietnam, Washington clearly had no inclination to abandon two long-standing Asian allies, while conversely it had strong reason to avoid the emergence of new nuclear powers in the area. Moreover, because of its history of defending both Asian states, Washington was able to provide security guarantees (or, better, to reaffirm them) that were highly credible, so the coin it offered had recognized value. Also important was that, as indicated earlier, in both cases the secret nuclear weapons efforts were in their infancy. This meant that, on one hand, both Taipei and Seoul would have faced long periods of vulnerability had they been abandoned by Washington, and on the other, leaders in both states were not required to dismantle large-scale programs that had acquired substantial institutional/political backing.

Ukraine

Actors and motives

When the Soviet Union dissolved, Belarus, Kazakhstan, and Ukraine all retained strategic nuclear weapons on their soil. One of the foremost priorities of U.S. post-Soviet diplomacy was to ensure that none of these states took possession and exercised full control over these weapons so as to emerge as a new nuclear power.[12] Washington feared this outcome not only because the sudden emergence of new nuclear states would deal a hard blow to the nuclear nonproliferation regime, but also because the nuclear weapons in question could be targeted directly on Russia and/or the United States, a capability that could greatly complicate bilateral U.S.-Russian strategic deterrence and arms control arrangements.

Initially it appears Ukraine did not perceive the nuclear weapons on its soil to be a security asset, either in military terms or as a bargaining chip that might be spent to enhance fundamental national interests. Part of the reason was that Russia retained effective control over the weapons, both because Russian forces guarded and maintained the Ukraine-based systems on the ground and because only Russia possessed the codes and command and control systems necessary to arm and launch these weapons. In late 1991, Ukraine agreed to eliminate the nuclear arms on its territory, and in May 1992, it pledged in the Lisbon Protocol to the START I Treaty, to join the Nuclear Nonproliferation Treaty (NPT) as a nonnuclear weapons state in the "shortest possible time."

Unilateral assessments

To a far greater degree than Belarus and Kazakhstan, Ukraine was deeply embittered by its history of Russian domination. After independence in 1991, it vigorously sought to protect and enlarge its newfound autonomy. By late 1992, Kiev began to assert increasing "administrative" control over the nuclear weapons on its territory—that is, to administer custodial and maintenance arrangements for them—and to claim ownership of the weapons' components, in particular, of the valuable fissile material they contained. Although the Ukrainian executive branch and military never sought the right to control the use of the weapons (apart from a veto on their use), nationalists in the Ukrainian Parliament began to characterize the weapons as valuable military assets whose retention was essential to preserve Ukrainian independence in the face of a hegemonic Russia. At the same time, the Ukrainian Parliament refused to ratify the various denuclearization undertakings, including the Lisbon Protocol, signed by President Leonid Kravchuk of Ukraine. Meanwhile, Ukraine's economy staggered toward virtual collapse, threatening the country's very viability as an independent state.

The nuclear impasse intensified until July 1993 when, in return for Ukraine's removing the warheads from some of the missiles on its territory and shipping the warheads to Russia, Washington provided a substantial tranche of aid ($175 million) for nuclear dismantling assistance, even though Ukraine had not fulfilled a previously announced U.S. condition for such aid, namely the implementation of Ukraine's Lisbon Protocol pledge to join the Nuclear Nonproliferation Treaty as a nonnuclear weapons state. The provision of aid was intended as a gesture demonstrating Washington's interest in the survival of the beleaguered nation and in the establishment of a broad and enduring bilateral relationship.

The new opening triggered a series of negotiations among Ukraine, Russia, and the United States that intensified as 1993 ended. In November of that year, the Ukrainian Parliament (the Rada) ratified START I. However, it attached a number of conditions to be satisfied before Ukraine's adherence to the treaty could become effective. In addition, it intensified the controversy about the country's nuclear intentions by passing a resolution declaring that Ukraine was not bound by Article V of the Lisbon Protocol, the article calling for Ukraine's adherence to the NPT as a nonnuclear weapons state. Although the conditions postponed the effectiveness of the Rada's approval of the START I Treaty, they set an agenda for the ongoing incentives negotiation with the United States and Russia. The result was the 14 January 1994, Trilateral Statement, signed by presidents Leonid Kravchuk, Bill Clinton, and Boris Yeltsin, a major turning point that would lead to Ukraine's fulfillment of its denuclearization and nonproliferation pledges.

Under the Trilateral Statement, over a three-year period, Ukraine was to transfer the approximately 1,800 warheads on Ukrainian soil to Russia, where highly enriched uranium from the warheads was to be extracted and blended down to low-enriched uranium.[13] This material was then to be converted to fuel rods to be transferred to Ukraine for use in nuclear power reactors as compensation for its relinquishing the weapons-grade uranium in the strategic warheads. Ukraine was also to receive (in addition to nuclear fuel) U.S. economic aid and U.S. technical assistance for the safe, secure dismantlement of its nuclear arms. Russia and the United States also promised to provide explicit security guarantees upon Ukraine's accession to the NPT.

Over the course of 1994, Ukraine fulfilled its dismantlement and warhead return obligations on an accelerated basis. On 16 November 1994, the Rada, accepting the argument that the Trilateral Statement largely satisfied the conditions it had set for approving START, agreed to the exchange of instruments of ratification for that treaty and agreed to Ukraine's adherence to the NPT. At the 5 December 1994 summit of the members of the Conference on Security and Cooperation in Europe, Ukraine acceded to both accords, while the United States, Russia, France, and Great Britain provided Ukraine with formal security assurances, pledging not to use nuclear weapons against it and to respect the integrity of its borders.

The Ukrainian action also opened the door to significantly increased U.S. economic assistance and aid for nuclear dismantling activities.

The Ukrainian case highlights a number of elements of the assessment process that were only background issues in the previously discussed cases. First, it took Ukraine two years to determine for itself the value of the nuclear weapons on its soil. Ukraine quickly perceived the nuclear weapons to be high-value bargaining chips, and some parliamentarians apparently believed they might even have military utility in keeping Russia at bay. Gradually, however, a consensus appears to have emerged that the country's survival depended not on its military capabilities but on the establishment of cooperative relations with the West and on the receipt of Western economic assistance. In the minuet of 1993 to 1994, Ukraine traded its essentially unusable nuclear weapons for a set of relationships, especially with Washington, that would help ensure the country's future.

As in the case of Taiwan and South Korea, what the target country ultimately decided it wanted was something the sender country was only too ready to provide, and in the end the fit between Ukrainian motivations for nuclear arms and the countervailing American incentives package was a good one. Because of Ukraine's size and geopolitical position and, no doubt, because of the sizable Ukrainian community in the United States, Washington envisioned substantial bilateral ties with Kiev. Thus, aid for denuclearization and economic reform had become basic components of Washington's foreign policy in dealing with the vacuum left by the dissolution of the Soviet Union. Indeed, Washington offered—and threatened to withhold—much more, in particular, entrée into the Western economic system and the possibility of a friendly relationship that Kiev might use as a counterweight in its dealings with Moscow. Russia, it should be added, also played the role of sender state and similarly saw the trade-offs as a feasible and worthwhile arrangement.

Negotiations

Communications were difficult, with the president of Ukraine and senior parliamentarians giving, at best, mixed signals during this period regarding the country's intentions. The absence of a preexisting relationship, which might have facilitated communication and the devising of an acceptable incentives package, was another obstacle. The case also highlighted the difficulties that can arise in selling an incentives deal to interested domestic constituencies: Leonid Kravchuk, Ukrainian president during much of the negotiations with Washington, was repeatedly forced by the country's Parliament to back away from nuclear agreements he had signed.

North Korea

This case is discussed in depth in chapter 3. It is examined briefly here, however, to show how our model applies in this instance.

Actors and motives

Like many other aspects of this interaction, North Korea's motivations remain obscure. Most probably, when it launched its nuclear weapons program in the late 1970s, Pyongyang hoped that the acquisition of nuclear arms would intimidate South Korea and enhance the North's ability to reunify the Korean Peninsula on its own terms. North Korea may also have been reacting defensively to South Korea's mid-1970s bid for nuclear arms, as well as to the long-standing deployment of U.S. nuclear weapons in South Korea and to Washington's declared intention to use them in the South's defense. Whatever Pyongyang's original motives may have been, by the late 1980s it is likely that the North saw nuclear arms increasingly as a defensive military instrument intended to protect its continuing autonomy and ensure its survival at a time when its economy had been eclipsed by South Korea's and its alliances with Beijing and Moscow had withered. Thus, as its interactions with the United States began, its motivation was security dominant.

However, by the time of the October 1994 Agreed Framework understanding with the United States—the understanding that abated the North Korean nuclear threat—North Korea's motives appear to have changed, as it came to see the risk of economic collapse as the most serious threat to its survival. This made it willing to freeze its nuclear program in return for a package of incentives that included assistance for electrical power production in the form of two light-water nuclear power plants, prospects for significant economic aid, and increased integration with the world economy.[14] Pyongyang also had to weigh the costs of continuing to flout international nonproliferation norms, including its NPT and IAEA safeguards obligations, a course that had led to the threat of economic sanctions and further international isolation.

The motivations of the United States were also complex. Its fundamental objective was to prevent the emergence of North Korea as a nuclear-armed state; a secondary, but highly important set of objectives was to sustain the international nonproliferation norm and to enforce the NPT and the inspection system of the IAEA. Indeed, Washington hoped that by achieving the latter objectives, it would simultaneously thwart Pyongyang's bid for nuclear arms, forcing it to disclose and place under international inspection all of the plutonium it had produced in the past, while ensuring that any future production took place under IAEA inspection. As negotiations between the two states unfolded, Washington pursued a two-pronged strategy, offering North Korea a choice between possible UN-backed economic sanctions and increasing isolation on the one hand, and political and economic engagement through "broad and thorough" discussions that the North had long sought, on the other. The offer of the latter, intended as a clear incentive, required overcoming domestic U.S. political opposition to any opening with the North and reflected the strong security-dominant motivation of the Clinton administration to reduce the threat of proliferation in this case.

By the spring of 1994, however, Washington's incentives strategy had achieved little success, and the United States was moving toward the imposition of UN economic sanctions against the North, an uncomfortable option that few believed would ease the North Korean nuclear threat or bring about its compliance with the NPT. When, during the visit of former president Jimmy Carter to Pyongyang in June 1994, North Korean leader Kim Il Sung indicated that he was prepared for a compromise, the changed politics of the situation led the Clinton administration to adjust its focus to a strategy based predominantly on incentives.

As the bargaining between the two states ensued, Washington included elements in the incentives package of the Agreed Framework that many had thought unthinkable, especially the provision of light-water nuclear power reactors to North Korea and the agreement that the full implementation of IAEA inspections in the North and the determination of North Korea's past plutonium production would be deferred for a number of years. These developments reflected the strength of the Clinton administration's security-driven motives for containing the most dangerous elements of the North's nuclear weapons program.

Unilateral assessments

North Korea's decision making is one of the most opaque elements of this case. It is generally assumed that two camps emerged in Pyongyang, one seeking to retain the country's nuclear capabilities at all costs and the other prepared to trade them for the right package of incentives. A sudden shift in favor of the latter camp ensued when Kim Il Sung opened the door to serious negotiations. From that point, the North obviously gave considerable thought to the package it desired—to calculating its "reservation price"—and the package ultimately contained numerous elements designed to address diverse North Korean goals, including the symbolic one of having the United States validate the North's nuclear *bona fides* by agreeing to supply it with two nuclear power reactors.

As noted earlier, Washington initially weighed the likely effectiveness and risks of economic sanctions against the costs and benefits of a rudimentary incentives package. The sudden change in the political atmosphere brought about by Kim Il Sung's offer to negotiate, created a willingness to offer the highly lucrative incentives of the Agreed Framework. At the same time, however, Washington's insistence on the carefully phased implementation of the Agreed Framework, starting with North Korea's freeze of its nuclear program, reflected a very careful assessment of the quid pro quo's that would eventually make up the Agreed Framework.

The relatively advanced state of North Korea's nuclear program was also a factor in the assessment of both sides. Washington perceived these capabilities as highly threatening, which gave Pyongyang considerable bargaining leverage—and led to a very substantial incentives package.

Finally, as in many other cases, the link between the threat of sanctions and the offer of incentives was a close one. As part of its overall strategy, Washington constantly reminded the North that if it refused to accept such incentives and abandon its nuclear weapons capability, it would face sanctions and increasing isolation that would threaten economic collapse. This undoubtedly affected the North's calculations of its "reservation price."

Negotiations

The long-standing hostility between the United States and North Korea made negotiations on incentives particularly difficult. This situation was exacerbated by the fact that the North had previously obligated itself under the NPT to renounce nuclear arms and to accept comprehensive IAEA inspections. Offering incentives to the North appeared to be a reward for misconduct and a payment for actions that Pyongyang was already obligated to undertake. These obstacles were overcome only after the extraordinary exchange between Jimmy Carter and Kim Il Sung.[15]

As indicated earlier, both states ultimately determined their respective "reservation prices," but the process was a lengthy one, requiring extensive negotiations within the decision-making structures of both. In the United States, months of persuasion were needed after October 1994 to convince skeptics that a reasonable price had been obtained for U.S. concessions.

In sum, the North Korean case shows that an incentives strategy can work even in cases where key factors are unfavorable. This was an instance where the motivation to proliferate had a very strong security component; where the preexisting relationship between the potential proliferator and the sender country was hostile; and where the potential proliferator had already made a substantial commitment to its nuclear weapons effort. Unquestionably these factors contributed to the tumultuous nature of the U.S.-North Korean negotiations—and to their extended duration. Nonetheless, perhaps because the United States also had a strong security-based motivation to arrest the North Korean nuclear challenge, the incentives strategy proved workable.

Pakistan

Pakistan, along with South Africa, Israel, and India, attempted to acquire incentives in the form of security guarantees before completely committing themselves to developing nuclear weapons. Each of them, however, failed to gain the guarantees that might have persuaded it to forgo proliferating; thus, in one sense they are all failures of the incentives strategy approach. The case of Pakistan stands out from the other three because of the extraordinary effort by the United States to prevent proliferation there, although there were also inconsistencies in U.S. policy. During the late 1970s and 1980s, Pakistan and the United States negotiated several large incentives packages, each with the explicit understanding that Pakistan would refrain from various proliferation developments in return. Pakistan did not keep its end of the bargain, however.

Actors and motives

The case of Pakistan centers around the interpretation of the American military commitment to Pakistan originating with the Baghdad Pact in the mid-1950s and its successor, the 1959 Central Treaty Organization (CENTO). Since the creation of the state of Pakistan in 1947, Islamabad has fought three wars and verged on a fourth with its regional rival, India. During that time, Pakistan has sought outside assistance from the United States and China, to counter India's economic, demographic, and military advantages. The bilateral executive agreement between Washington and Islamabad drafted as part of CENTO in 1959 stated the American commitment to take appropriate action "including the use of armed forces" to protect Pakistan in the event of an attack. This agreement, however, limited American commitment to attacks from Communist sources.[16]

Hence, when Pakistan solicited U.S. assistance during its 1965 war with India, the United States was under no legal obligation to help. Instead, the United States chose to impose an arms embargo on both combatants. During the 1971 Indo-Pakistani War, triggered by the secession of East Pakistan (now Bangladesh) from Pakistan, the United States quietly "tilted" toward Pakistan against India, while proclaiming it would support neither side. At that time, President Richard Nixon saw the opportunity to reinforce the U.S.-Chinese rapprochement by deploying American warships to the Bay of Bengal in a successful effort to deter India from attacking Pakistan's west flank and contributing to an early end of the war.[17] Nonetheless, U.S. support was insufficient to prevent the loss of East Pakistan, which emerged from the war as the independent state of Bangladesh. By the end of the decade, however, the United States had reversed its policy toward Islamabad once again, twice imposing a ban on all military and economic assistance to Islamabad, when it discovered evidence of Pakistan's secret acquisition of equipment to support a nuclear weapons program.

U.S. policy was soon reversed yet again, in response to the Soviet invasion of Afghanistan in December 1979. In early 1980, U.S. Assistant Secretary of State Warren Christopher was sent to Islamabad to reaffirm the 1959 commitment to protect Pakistan from Soviet aggression. President Zia ul-Haq of Pakistan sought a new treaty with a more automatic and more explicit security commitment that would be triggered by aggression from any source. Although no new treaty commitments were made, in 1981 the Reagan administration, with the strong support of the U.S. Congress, restored U.S. economic and military assistance at higher levels than ever before, as part of Washington's effort to counter the growing threat of Soviet expansion in the region. At the time, Zia pledged to curtail Pakistan's bid for nuclear arms. Nonetheless, Pakistan continued to pursue its nuclear program aggressively, completing a crucial uranium enrichment facility in the early 1980s, engaging in nuclear smuggling in the United States in 1984, and in 1985 violating a commitment made the previous year not to enrich uranium. Because of the Afghan conflict, however, U.S. aid continued without interruption. Assuring Islamabad's cooperation in resisting the Soviet occupation of Afghanistan assumed priority over nonproliferation concerns. This pattern continued to the end of the decade.

In 1985, U.S. assistance and military sales were conditioned, in a law known as the "Pressler amendment," on a yearly certification by the U.S. president that Pakistan did "not possess a nuclear explosive device."[18] Despite increasing evidence to the contrary, certifications of this nature were provided until October 1990, when U.S. aid and military sales were cut off after Washington determined that Pakistan had assembled a number of nuclear weapons, a step Pakistan had taken earlier in 1990 in response to threatening Indian military actions. By this time, Soviet troops had withdrawn from Afghanistan.

Thus, throughout the 1980s Pakistan's nuclear program—motivated by the Pakistani's conventional military inferiority compared to India, a weak indigenous defense industry, and an American ally unwilling to support Pakistan against its foremost military rival—progressed with seemingly few setbacks, despite the incentives and disincentives strategy employed by the United States.[19]

From the U.S. perspective, during the late 1970s, the motive to intervene in Pakistan's nuclear decision making was dominated by concerns that a nuclear arms race not emerge on the subcontinent. The nonproliferation tools applied at the time were a package of disincentives in the form of reduced aid and diplomatic pressure on Pakistan, together with modest incentives in the form of offers of limited economic aid and conventional military assistance. The package thus was based on pressuring Pakistan to give up nuclear arms rather than on attempting to "buy it off."

During the 1980s, American aid to Pakistan vastly increased. Although Washington attempted to link this assistance to restraint of Pakistani nuclear activities, the dominant motive for the United States was not nonproliferation but the desire to build Pakistan into a capable strategic partner in the struggle to oust Soviet forces from Afghanistan—a hierarchy of objectives that Pakistan's leadership fully appreciated and exploited. Because of its conflicting motivations, Washington was unable to link its incentives with nonproliferation effectively.

Unilateral assessments

Throughout its history, Pakistan's efforts to acquire a stable ally have largely remained unfulfilled. While it is impossible to prove, Islamabad's efforts to develop nuclear weapons might have been averted if the United States or perhaps China had taken Pakistan under its respective wing. Without an alliance to deter India, the magnitude of the incentives and disincentives packages extended to Pakistan during the 1970s was not large enough to reduce the net benefit of proliferating to zero. In 1990, shortly after the Soviet withdrawal from Afghanistan, a crisis with India apparently led Pakistan to manufacture its first complete nuclear weapons. This triggered a cutoff of U.S. aid and military sales—but by this point, Pakistan had crossed the nuclear weapons threshold, and the sanctions were apparently able only to persuade Islamabad to accept a cap on the further production of weapons-grade uranium. The firm commitment in the U.S. Congress to a sanctions strategy, derived from the years of Pakistani disregard for U.S. nonproliferation standards, largely precluded the use of incentives at this point, which, in any event would have had to be very substantial, given the advanced stage of the Pakistani nuclear weapons effort.

Negotiations

As mentioned above, prior to the 1980s, the preexisting relationship between Pakistan and the United States was one of U.S. inconstancy. Pakistan was viewed by the United States as a willing but dependent ally. Hence, during negotiation of the incentives and disincentives, Pakistan had good cause to doubt implementation of both aspects. If the perception was that at times the United States would fulfill its alliance obligations and at other times not, then Pakistan perceived itself as having little choice but to pursue an alternative mechanism to increase its security vis-à-vis India. And if during the 1980s the United States threatened sanctions but did not impose them, then Pakistan might try to get away with more than it promised. In effect, given its regional security environment, Pakistan's reservation price was very high and the United States was never willing to meet it; simultaneously, Washington's conflicting motivations during the 1980s undermined its ability to negotiate its nonproliferation agenda effectively.

Today Washington is attempting to use more limited incentives as part of a broader policy effort to persuade Pakistan to maintain a number of existing restrictions on its nuclear capabilities, including a freeze on the production of weapons-grade nuclear materials, a freeze on nuclear exports, a voluntary ban on nuclear testing, and continued nondeployment of short-range, nuclear-capable M-11 missiles that Pakistan has apparently obtained from China. In 1995, the Clinton administration obtained a one-time exemption from the Pressler amendment's ban on aid and arms sales to permit the transfer to Pakistan of a limited quantity of military equipment for which Pakistan had previously paid. Through 1996, Pakistan was maintaining the above-noted restrictions on its nuclear program and related missile capabilities, but it was also known to be nearing completion of a new reactor for producing weapons-usable plutonium and to be working on the design of a nuclear missile warhead. It remains unclear to what extent the U.S. incentives strategy is currently influencing Pakistani decision making in these areas.

Guidelines of the Model and Case Studies

Below is a list of guidelines, derived from applying the model to the above cases, that might be used for successful application of an incentives nonproliferation strategy. Further testing and analysis is needed to evaluate whether these guidelines are useful in explaining the remaining cases of potential proliferation and to more fully specify the variables involved.

Actors and motives

  1. Proliferator perspective
     • The more security dominant the motivation for proliferation, the greater incentive required to terminate the nuclear program.
  2. Sender perspective
     • Whether the incentive provider ultimately offers an incentives

package, as well as the scale and quality of such incentives, depends on motivation of the incentive provider.

Unilateral Assessments

1. Proliferator perspective
   - Net benefit is key to decision: the value of the incentives package must be commensurate with the expected value of proliferation; sanctions and other disincentives can affect this calculation as well.
   - Status of nuclear weapons program can affect the magnitude and type of incentives demanded.
   - A decline of net benefits may initiate/signal readiness to negotiate.
2. Sender perspective
   - Intensity of motive (regional foreign policy/threat to ally; threat to sender state; sustaining nonproliferation regime)
   - Base price of intervention/negotiation (nature of preexisting relationship between proliferant and sender) will affect [1] ease of entering and conducting negotiations and [2] diversity and value of incentives package.)

Negotiation

- Essential elements of reservation price must be reflected in incentives package.
- There must be common recognition by proliferator and sender of the essential elements to permit bargaining to take place; problem of confused communication.
- Potential incentive provider must be willing and able to offer incentives that match motives.
- Bargain must obtain support of essential domestic constituencies; question of opposition veto.

Some Conclusions and Observations for Future Applications

Without additional case study work, it is premature to make a full evaluation of the usefulness of the proposed model. However, at a minimum it appears to be a reasonably good way of organizing the complex historical record and provides a consistent approach for explaining the successes and failures of the cases portrayed herein.

Since the end of the cold war, two states have made specific requests for bilateral or multilateral incentives as part of trade-off packages they claimed would enable them to renounce their nuclear weapons capability or intentions: Ukraine and North Korea. In both cases a package of incentives was negotiated. These cases are remarkable in several important respects. First, these are the first countries to request incentives in the post–cold war environment and hence it was more difficult to identify overarching foreign policy goals apart from stemming nuclear proliferation to justify granting their requests. Second, neither state had a previous security relationship with the primary guarantor of the security assurances—the United States. In the case of North Korea, this made even the opening of negotiations difficult. In addition, in each of these cases, there was considerable uncertainty on the part of the potential proliferator regarding what incentives it might accept as compensation for forsaking nuclear arms. As opposed to the cases of India, Israel, Pakistan, and South Africa, which unfolded during the cold war, the United States did not reject Ukraine's and North Korea's appeals, but negotiated a package that was closely linked to the states' renunciation of their nuclear weapons capabilities and intentions. While it is still unclear at the time of this writing whether North Korea will fulfill completely its end of the bargain, if both cases are successfully resolved it will bode well for future incentives strategies. Much can be learned from these two recent cases to streamline the incentives strategy approach and respond to its principal criticisms.

Principal criticisms of incentives strategies

A number of general objections have been raised to the use of security guarantees and other incentives for nonproliferation purposes. The approach has been challenged most frequently with the arguments that (1) it is neither credible nor feasible to extend nuclear umbrellas (i.e., the strongest incentive available) to every potential proliferator, (2) providing incentives has the effect of rewarding bad behavior by "rogue" states, and (3) providing incentives for good nonproliferation behavior creates the opportunity for states to try continually to blackmail the incentive provider.

It is true that sender states possessing nuclear arms will not be prepared to extend nuclear umbrellas in all cases. Nonetheless, such guarantees can and have been extended, and have reduced proliferation pressures in many instances. To say that they cannot be offered in every case does not diminish their utility in those where they can be. Moreover, as the discussion of Ukraine and North Korea indicates, in many cases nonproliferation objectives can be attained with less substantial incentives than ironclad security guarantees. In such instances, it is irrelevant whether the extension of a nuclear umbrella would be a viable option. Indeed, in the case of Ukraine it was the pledge not to use nuclear weapons, the negative security assurances, that proved important to reaching an agreement.

With respect to the "rewarding bad behavior" criticism, incentives, when properly applied, reward good nonproliferation behavior and should be rescinded when the good behavior ceases. Under the realist paradigm of an anarchic international system, a state seeking to develop nuclear weapons is not engaging in "bad" behavior but is pursuing its sovereign right to security. If it voluntarily forgoes a weapons system perceived as important for its security, it gives up something of considerable value, and would naturally expect to receive some type of offsetting benefit. Security assurances and other forms of incentives can provide such indemnification and are an appropriate tool for encouraging a state to decide that it is in its interest to renounce nuclear weapons. This, however, in no way guarantees that the incentives approach is foolproof, which brings us to the last, and most troublesome criticism.

How does one know whether a potential proliferator is merely attempting to blackmail a sender state to provide incentives? Clearly, there is a certain amount of gamesmanship in every negotiation, and both sides will attempt to optimize their positions. In some respects, the recipient state has the advantage, since the sender—judging from U.S. experience—is likely to make worst-case assumptions about the potential proliferator's intentions and capabilities. On the other hand, the intelligence capabilities of concerned countries, in particular those of the United States, together with IAEA inspection data, will be available to guide the sender state. At worst, it would seem, a target state's deceptive exaggeration of its nuclear potential or its repeated reopening of negotiations to demand additional incentives might lead a sender state to increase its "reservation price," by offering incentives of greater value than needed. The sender state may consider this a relatively modest cost to keep its nonproliferation diplomacy on track. On the other hand, as noted earlier, most incentives packages include the threat of sanctions (or the withholding of highly desired incentives) and this provides the sender state continuing leverage of its own to counterdemands for added benefits.

Lessons for the Future: Does Every Proliferator Have Its Price?

Several observations regarding the post–cold war cases of Ukraine and North Korea should be noted. First, in both cases, the threat of proliferation reached a crisis point before it became clear that a compromise would be possible. Second, the incentives packages that were ultimately negotiated were not limited to the traditional, military alliance-style security assurances that appear to have been so successful for nonproliferation purposes in the past. Rather they were incentives carefully tailored to the specifics of each case so as to enable the particular state to avert or reverse its decision to proliferate.

Future applications of this approach would benefit from an understanding of how to avoid the crisis point. Despite the difficulty and complexity of negotiation and the potential drawbacks to the incentives approach, perhaps the real lesson here is that every potential proliferator—even a state believed to be a determined proliferator—may have its price for refraining from the pursuit of nuclear arms.[20] Sender states may not be willing or able to meet that price at a particular time, but an incentives strategy should be considered for every potential nuclear state and should become a more prominent part of nonproliferation policy. Uncovering the motive for proliferation in each case and carefully crafting incentives to address that motive are the keys to success.

Notes

1. There was a parallel Soviet initiative as well. See William Potter, "Managing Proliferation: Problems and Prospects for U.S.-Soviet Cooperation," *Strategies for Managing Nuclear Non-Proliferation,* edited by Dagobert Brito, Michael Intrilligator, and Adele Wick (Lexington, Mass.: Lexington Books, 1983).

2. The Warsaw Pact countries would also be defined as cases of "a priori" nonproliferation. However, their nuclear decision-making process was not influenced by the presence of security guarantees, but eliminated entirely because of the political and military domination of the Soviet Union.

The cases of Britain and France are frequently cited as examples showing that security assurances are not a reliable nonproliferation tool, since both states have long been under the NATO nuclear umbrella but nonetheless developed their own nuclear arsenals. This, however, is not a correct interpretation of events. Both states had their own nuclear research and development programs underway prior to World War II and continued them to the extent possible during the war, principally in the United States and Canada. After the war, Britain and France devoted their attention to rebuilding their economies. While the North Atlantic Treaty was signed in 1949, the extension of American nuclear deterrence to Europe took many years to evolve fully. The small size of the American nuclear stockpile in the late 1940s and early 1950s did not allow adequate numbers of warheads to be deployed to Britain and Europe immediately. In addition, extending the American nuclear umbrella was hampered by secrecy concerns and the legal prohibitions against sharing nuclear technology in the U.S. Atomic Energy Act of 1946. Moreover, in the case of France, the Suez Crisis of 1956 made clear that France's security objectives did not necessarily coincide with those of the rest of the alliance. For a discussion of American nuclear strategy and diplomacy and its relationship to proliferation, see George Quester, *Nuclear Diplomacy: The First Twenty-Five Years* (Cambridge, Mass: Dunellen, University Press of Cambridge, 1970), 83–87, and Richard N. Rosecrance, ed., *The Dispersion of Nuclear Weapons* (New York: Columbia University Press, 1964), 72–86, 113–25. For detailed accounts of the British and French decisions to develop nuclear weapons, see, respectively, Timothy J. Botti, *The Long*

Wait: The Forging of the Anglo-American Alliance, 1945–1958 (New York: Greenwood Press, 1987), and Wolf Mendl, *Deterrence and Persuasion: French Nuclear Armament in the Context of National Policy, 1945–1969* (New York: Praeger Publishers, 1970).

3. See Richard Ullman, "Redefining National Security," *International Security* 8, no. 1 (1983): 120–53; Joseph Nye, "Problems of Security Studies" (paper presented at the Fourteenth World Congress of the International Political Science Association, Washington, D.C., August 1988; and Sean M. Lynn-Jones, "International Security Studies," *International Studies Notes* (Fall 1991/Winter 1992): 53–63.

4. The twenty-five potential proliferators are the five nuclear weapons states—the United States, Russia, Great Britain, France, China—and, in alphabetical order, Algeria, Argentina, Belarus, Brazil, India, Iran, Iraq, Israel, Kazahkstan, Libya, North Korea, Pakistan, Romania, Saudi Arabia, South Africa, South Korea, Sweden, Switzerland, Taiwan, and Ukraine. The classification of states as potential proliferators is based on open source information collected by the Carnegie Endowment's Nuclear Non-Proliferation Project.

5. Leonard Spector, Mark McDonough, and Evan Medeiros, *Tracking Nuclear Proliferation: A Guide in Maps and Charts* (Washington, D.C.: Carnegie Endowment for International Peace, 1995), 161–62.

6. Mitchell Reiss, *Without the Bomb: The Politics of Nuclear Nonproliferation* (New York: Columbia University Press, 1988), 92–93.

7. This model could also be further generalized to incorporate disincentives as well, but in this case we will limit the discussion to incentives only.

8. At this point in the analysis we discuss modeling the behavior of states *as if* it were the result of decisions made by a single actor. We do not assume, however, that only one actor influenced the decisions, but that decisions are the product of various actors and institutions and that each, to varying degrees, has a stake in the outcome.

9. In the academic literature, the rationality assumption has two components: (1) that the state has preferences that can be identified such that if the state prefers A to B to C, then the state will prefer A to C; and (2) that the state will prefer A to C consistently when offered the choice repeatedly. In the real world, rationality is constrained by imperfect information, making it difficult to know one's true preferences and thus act accordingly. This analytical approach to assessing behavior is frequently criticized especially when its results are oversold. We will try not to do that here. Given the vagaries of foreign policy decision making, it is difficult to assess all the factors that influence an outcome. We are simply trying to identify the most prominent, consistent factors.

10. The disincentives portion of an "incentives/disincentives" package proffered to a state would also affect these calculations of the costs of nuclearization.

11. Robert S. Litwak, *Détente and the Nixon Doctrine* (Cambridge: Cambridge University Press, 1984), 40.

12. Moscow acted swiftly to remove tactical nuclear weapons from these states and other Soviet successor states, and by April 1992 all had been transferred to Russia.

13. Although the text of the Trilateral Statement declared that the weapons would be returned to Russia within seven years, in one of several confidential side letters, Ukraine privately agreed to the three-year transfer period, and Russia promised to forgive large portions of Ukraine's debt for energy supplies as compensation for Ukraine's prior transfer of tactical nuclear weapons to Russia.

14. Under the Agreed Framework, North Korea immediately received interim supplies of heavy oil (for the production of electricity), which are to continue until the first light-water nuclear power reactor promised under the framework is completed. In addition, in the framework the United States promised to ease restrictions on trade with Pyongyang. Moreover, as diplomatic tensions with the United States and its allies abate, North Korea can expect considerable economic assistance from Japan, including billions of dollars in compensation for the decades of Japanese occupation during the first half of this century. The understanding also provides for gradual movement toward U.S. diplomatic recognition of North Korea, which Pyongyang has sought for many years.

15. Negotiations were further complicated for the United States by the need to avoid undercutting South Korea by offering the North political concessions or economic benefits beyond those that the South deemed acceptable.

16. Christopher Van Hollen, "Leaning on Pakistan," *Foreign Policy* 38 (Spring 1980): 40.

17. Francine R. Frankel, "India's Promise," *Foreign Policy* 38, (Spring 1980): 52–53.

18. Leonard S. Spector with Jacqueline R. Smith, *Nuclear Ambitions* (Boulder, Colo.: Westview Press, 1990), chap. 7. In 1984, the Reagan administration actually opposed legislation that would have cut off aid unless the president certified that specific thresholds short of Pakistan's possession of a nuclear device had not been crossed. Aides claimed that the president would not be able to make these certifications and that the assistance cutoff that this would trigger would be unacceptable. See Leonard S. Spector, *The Undeclared Bomb* (Cambridge, Mass.: Ballinger Publishing Co., 1988), 365, n17.

19. Van Hollen, "Leaning on Pakistan," p. 44.

20. This concept has its origins in a short article by Bob Brito and Michael Intrilligator, "Buy the Missiles, Feed the People," *The Los Angeles Times*, 9 September 1991.

3

North Korea's Nuclear Program: The Role of Incentives in Preventing Deadly Conflict

Scott Snyder[1]

T HE POLICY CHALLENGE posed by North Korea's nuclear program has been a particularly vexing test case for U.S. policymakers in the transition to a post–cold war security environment in Northeast Asia. The methods employed to cope with the North Korean nuclear challenge as it evolved, the responses that were employed at various stages, and the unusual solution projected by the 1994 Geneva Agreed Framework are worthy of careful consideration to identify lessons learned that might be transferable to other contexts. Initial assessments have already detailed the history of the U.S.-Democratic People's Republic of Korea (DPRK) negotiations and have drawn preliminary conclusions regarding the implications of the North Korean nuclear issue for nonproliferation and for security on the Korean peninsula.[2] This paper will analyze the effectiveness of inducement strategies in the Korean case as one policy tool among many that may be used to achieve U.S. interests without resort to deadly conflict.

This examination of the role of incentives in dealing with the North Korean nuclear challenge is divided into three primary phases: (1) the Bush administration response (January 1989 through October 1992), during which the conceptual framework of combining incentives and disincentives to induce North Korean cooperation was first identified; (2) the initial approach of the Clinton administration (March 1993 to June 1994), during which the Clinton administration's response was defined largely by North Korea's refusals to fulfill its obligations under the International Atomic Energy Agency (IAEA) and nuclear Non-Proliferation Treaty (NPT), and resulting concerns that incentives might be seen as a reward for North Korean intransigence; and (3) the "comprehensive" approach (October 1993 to June 1995), in which the focus was on achieving a package deal. As part of such a deal, the United States would provide concrete economic and political inducements in combination with clearly defined pressure in return for North Korean cooperation to freeze and roll back its nuclear program. This approach uses simultaneous actions and phased progress as a means by which to draw North Korea into a longtime cooperative process in which each series of steps is verifiable.[3]

One potential difficulty of drawing lessons from the North Korean case is the unique context in which North and South Korea continue to struggle for legitimacy on the Korean peninsula. In the case of North Korea's nuclear program, post–cold war proliferation concerns were superimposed on a preexisting conflict on the Korean peninsula. The fact of Korea's division following World War II, the legacy of the Korean War and continuing inter-Korean confrontation, and the continuation of the U.S.-Republic of Korea (ROK) security alliance as a deterrent to possible North Korean aggression are essential characteristics of the Korean confrontation that have remained unresolved, despite the end of the cold war. To a large extent, the North Korean nuclear challenge was viewed as either another stage in an ongoing inter-Korean rivalry or as a vestige of the cold war, not as a "new" problem that could be isolated and defined functionally as solely a proliferation problem. This context has had a substantial effect on the perceptions and use of incentives as a diplomatic tool in preventing deadly conflict.

The Bush Administration Effort: An Initial Attempt To Define "Carrots and Sticks" for North Korea

The Drive To Develop Nuclear Weapons

Although the history of North Korea's efforts to develop nuclear capabilities dates back to the 1950s, it was not until 1988 that U.S. satellite intelligence revealed alarming evidence that the North Korean drive to build a nuclear weapons program included a plutonium reprocessing capability.[4] In addition to the 5-megawatt experimental reactor and the reprocessing plant located at Yongbyon—which subsequently became the focal point of public attention with regard to North Korea's nuclear program—Bush administration officials were disturbed by evidence of construction of two larger plants (50 and 200 megawatts, respectively) that, when finished, might produce enough plutonium to allow the manufacture of thirty to forty nuclear bombs per year.[5] These developments pushed North Korea's nuclear program onto the policy radar screen, and the United States and South Korea began to discuss counterstrategies in the spring of 1989.

An interagency working group was formed in Washington to sketch out specific elements of a "carrot and stick" strategy that might bring the North Korean program under international inspection. This group issued an internal report that supported the withdrawal of tactical nuclear weapons based in South Korea. The group also recommended providing North Korea with limited security assurances as incentives to accept international inspections of its nuclear program in combination with diplomatic pressure from a coalition including South Korea, Japan, Russia, and China. Beyond this initial offer, the report recommended that the United States avoid protracted negotiation with or additional concessions to the North.[6]

The opportunity to implement this strategy came about as a result of President Bush's 27 September 1991 announcement that the United States would unilaterally withdraw land- and sea-based tactical nuclear weapons in response to changes in the global strategic environment.[7] That announcement created an opening to press North Korea to accept nuclear inspections and coincided with historic progress in North-South relations, culminating in the announcement in December 1991 of two agreements: the North-South Agreement on Reconciliation, Nonaggression, Exchanges, and Cooperation—hereafter referred to as the Basic Agreement—and the Joint Declaration on the Denuclearization of the Korean Peninsula.[8]

These two agreements identified areas of mutual exchange and contained pledges of nonaggression by both sides as well as mutual commitments neither to pursue the development of nuclear weapons nor to reprocess plutonium. In addition, a joint, mutual inspections regime (yet to be implemented) was mandated to verify compliance with the provisions of the Joint Declaration. To enhance the likelihood that the denuclearization agreement would be implemented, the United States indicated its willingness to allow North Korean inspections of U.S. military bases in South Korea as part of the proposed mutual inspections. However, procedural issues on implementation remained unresolved in subsequent working-level discussions during 1992. North Korea decided to go ahead with IAEA inspections, but would not accept an extensive range of highly intrusive demands accompanying the proposed inter-Korean inspections regime.

To build on momentum provided by the two inter-Korean accords of December 1991, some carrots and sticks intended to induce North Korean cooperation and participation in IAEA inspections were unveiled during President Bush's summit meeting with President Roh Tae Woo of South Korea in January 1992. Presidents Bush and Roh announced on 6 January that the 1992 Team Spirit exercise would be canceled if North Korea agreed to join the IAEA and allow international inspections of its nuclear facilities. To balance this incentive, Secretary of Defense Richard Cheney had announced during his November 1991 visit to Seoul that the projected reduction in U.S. troop presence below thirty-seven thousand under the East Asian Strategy Initiative would be suspended until after the North Korean nuclear problem had been resolved.

In addition, the United States agreed that Undersecretary of State for Political Affairs Arnold Kanter would have a single meeting with the (North) Korean Worker's Party secretary for international affairs, Kim Yong Sun, to underscore U.S. concerns about North Korea's nuclear program. The purposes of this meeting were to reiterate U.S. expectations regarding North Korea's nuclear program and to directly communicate other obstacles to improved U.S.-DPRK relations. This high-level meeting was seen by some hard-liners as a concession that attributed undeserved legitimacy to North Korea. As a result of these concerns, the meeting was the "carrot," and the message was the "stick."

The U.S. message emphasized the need for North Korea to comply with international inspections of its nuclear program, while prospects for eventual normalization of relations or even the possibility of a follow-up meeting at the political level remained vague. For his part, Kim Yong Sun tested U.S. willingness to develop closer relations—seeking a joint communiqué and additional meetings at the political level—but he achieved neither objective. The North Korean delegation also suggested that U.S. troop withdrawals from South Korea were not a prerequisite for improved relations and proposed U.S.-DPRK cooperation to contain the possibility of a remilitarized Japan, an idea the U.S. delegation rejected vigorously.[9]

Although the Kanter-Kim meeting may have been useful in reinforcing U.S. concerns and encouraging North Korea to allow IAEA inspections, the apparent gains of December 1991 and January 1992 unraveled as 1992 progressed. North and South Korea could not agree in working-level meetings on the guidelines for mutual challenge inspections, and there were discrepancies between North Korean reports to the IAEA regarding its past nuclear activities and the findings of the IAEA inspections through the summer of 1992. Reacting to the failings of the IAEA inspections regime in Iraq revealed following the Persian Gulf War, IAEA director Hans Blix pushed to implement previously unprecedented "special inspections" of undisclosed North Korean nuclear sites in the fall of 1992, provoking North Korean charges that the IAEA demands were unfair and leading to a breakdown in DPRK-IAEA negotiations.

Working-level meetings to implement the Basic Agreement were suspended in the fall of 1992, as moderates and hard-liners in the ROK struggled with each other for control over policy toward the North. The primary difficulties in these channels included not only the nuclear question, but also a broader range of issues regarding the pace, scope, and order of the implementation of the Basic Agreement. Discoveries of a North Korean spy ring in South Korea, the heated rhetoric of the campaigns for president in both South Korea and the United States, and an announcement that planning for the Team Spirit exercises suspended in 1992 would be resumed in 1993 combined to wipe out earlier gains, exacerbating North Korean anxieties and feeding paranoia concerning Western intentions.

Lessons Learned from the Bush Administration Approach

What observations can be drawn—with the benefit of hindsight—from the first phase of American efforts to neutralize North Korea's nuclear program, and why did a strategy that initially seemed promising fall apart so quickly? The following successes and problems characterized the Bush administration strategy toward North Korea:

1. *Taking the initiative with North Korea.* A major advantage of the U.S. initiative toward North Korea—and President Bush's decision to withdraw tactical land- and sea-based nuclear weapons worldwide—is that it allowed the United States to make the first move, rather than finding itself on the defensive. Second, the decision to engage in direct talks with North Korea at the political level was indeed an incentive for North Korea to engage in limited cooperation with the United States, although the one-time nature of the Kanter-Kim meeting may have also served to ensure that North Korean cooperation was limited, rather than ongoing.

2. *Failure to lay the groundwork to ensure full success.* By the same token, North Korea may not have initially been prepared to respond to the unilateral concessions made by the United States in the form of negative security assurances and the elimination of tactical nuclear weapons from the Korean peninsula. Perhaps if the United States had moved earlier to a higher-level political dialogue with the DPRK in parallel with high-level talks between Seoul and Pyongyang, it might have been possible for the United States to prepare North Korea to make a more generous response to the United States' historic announcement.[10] North Korea had previously taken a host of symbolic

gestures to show its desire to improve relations with the United States during the period from 1988 to 1991.[11] No official U.S. response to these symbolic gestures was forthcoming prior to the Kim-Kanter meeting.

The calculation that North Korea's straitened economic circumstances would be a significant factor in bringing about cooperation—a significant part of the rationale for moving ahead with a direct meeting between the United States and the DPRK—was not fully tested in any concrete way as part of the Kanter-Kim meeting. Many analysts may have misperceived that for a North Korean system in which political imperatives dominated other considerations, the opportunity not to be isolated *economically* had relatively little significant value as an inducement for cooperation. Rational self-interest in the North Korean context was measured overwhelmingly by political and ideological considerations; from the outside, North Korean choices appeared irrational and self-defeating, further inhibiting the ability of U.S. policymakers to determine an appropriate incentives structure for North Korea.[12]

3. *The legacy of the Korean War as an obstacle to dealing with North Korea.* There appears to have been a generational gap in attitudes toward North Korea among high-level officials in the Bush administration, with those individuals from the generation occupying the most senior levels of government the most strongly opposed to adjusting policy toward North Korea.[13] In this respect, North Korea may have continued to suffer from the legacy of the cold war even as it tried to react to the end of the cold war by improving relations with the United States. Without having faced a transition in leadership since 1945 and unable to provide a strategic rationale that might induce the United States to improve relations, North Korea may have found itself immobilized by its own slowness to adapt to external changes.

4. *Could the Bush administration have gotten a better deal?* Finally, the Bush administration appears to have enjoyed more latitude from South Korea than the Clinton administration—if only it had been willing to take a bolder, more direct approach in dealing with North Korea. Granted, no South Korean administration would have been entirely comfortable in the context of any contact between the United States and North Korea; however, the Bush administration might have benefited in South Korea from the "Nixon-to-China factor," in which conservatives with strong anti-Communist credentials could travel to Beijing (or talk with Pyongyang), whereas others were likely to encounter significantly more political opposition—or mistrust—in Seoul.[14]

Interestingly enough, it was the United States that urged South Korea to be cautious in moving toward a presidential summit between South Korea's Roh Tae Woo and North Korea's Kim Il Sung in early 1992, arguing that the North Korean nuclear issue should be resolved before South Korea moved ahead with North Korea on the economic front. American strategic thinking significantly influenced Seoul regarding the substance of the Joint Declaration on the Denuclearization of the Korean Peninsula, the strictness of the South Korean negotiating position, and the conceptual shape of the implementation mechanism of mutual challenge inspections. This was the case despite the fact that progress in South Korean relations with Russia, China, and North Korea (as part of President Roh's "Nordpolitik" strategy) implicitly indicated acceptance by the South Korean government of improved relations between the United States and North Korea.[15] The critical importance of managing the U.S.-ROK relationship as part of any negotiating strategy with North Korea would become a critical factor in the Clinton administration's efforts to deal with North Korea.

The Clinton Administration's Initial Response to the North Korean Nuclear Challenge

By the time the Clinton administration's foreign policy team had been put into place, the nature of the problem posed by North Korea's nuclear program had been fundamentally transformed. Evidence of North Korean cheating since 1989, uncovered through IAEA inspections during the summer of 1992, resulted in a North Korean breakdown in cooperation with the IAEA, South Korea, and the United States. Then came the stunning 12 March 1993 announcement that North Korea intended to withdraw from the NPT effective three months from the date of the announcement, in accordance with provisions of the treaty. For the next fifteen months, the Clinton administration would find itself on the defensive, scrambling to corral North Korea and bring its potentially dangerous nuclear program under control while preserving the integrity of the NPT.

Initial efforts to address North Korea's NPT withdrawal included a referral of the issue by the IAEA Board of Governors to the UN Security Council, requiring multilateral cooperation in fashioning a response by the Security Council members—including China—to pressure North Korea to reverse its decision to withdraw from the NPT and to continue IAEA inspections under the treaty.[16] Although all the major powers including China shared the objective of containing North Korea's nuclear program, Chinese officials consistently advocated that the nuclear issue be solved through dialogue, including direct negotiations between the United States and North Korea.[17] Unable to convince China to sign on to a resolution that included punishments for North Korean intransigence, administration officials were left with little choice in the UN Security Council (UNSC) but to accept a resolution—passed on 8 April 1993—condemning North Korea's decision to withdraw from the NPT and welcoming "all efforts aimed at resolving this situation," including an invitation from the UNSC to the United States to initiate a bilateral dialogue with North Korea.[18] Given the lack of satisfactory available alternatives, Seoul reluctantly supported U.S.-DPRK direct talks on the nuclear issue, despite concerns that North Korea might use such talks to attempt to drive a wedge in the U.S.-ROK security alliance.

To reinforce the message that U.S.-DPRK talks were intended solely to address nuclear issues with North Korea, Assistant Secretary for Political-Military Affairs Robert Gallucci, a holdover from the Bush administration, was appointed to lead talks in New York with Vice Foreign Minister Kang Sok Ju of North Korea, starting on 5 June 1993. There was little room for failure, and a very high level of expectation on the U.S. side regarding the definition of "success." A newly chosen, untested Clinton foreign policy team was just coming into place, and faced the almost impossible challenge of reconciling widely differing intelligence estimates across the U.S. government regarding the progress and intentions of North Korea's nuclear efforts. In addition, a reorganized Department of Defense reflected the priority placed by the Clinton administration on counterproliferation, and included officials who had defined its counterproliferation goals by the highest standard—in absolute terms that refused to tolerate actions such as a North Korean threat to the NPT.[19] Also, there had been a decision at the end of the Bush administration to include the Joint Chiefs of Staff in the interagency process to define U.S. policy—including the approval of talking points for negotiations. Reportedly uncomfortable with some members of the Clinton foreign policy team, the Joint Chiefs adamantly opposed any offer of incentives to North Korea in the initial stages of the negotiations.[20]

According to one State Department official involved in the first round of U.S.-DPRK talks, negotiating with the DPRK in this context was "like learning how to fly while rolling down the runway."[21] To make matters worse, it became apparent at the very beginning that North Korea also had strict instructions that eliminated almost any chance for compromise. During the first two days, both sides were talking past each other. Another State Department official involved in the talks characterized the U.S. strategy as one of "showing the sticks first, and holding the carrots in reserve," only to be used as a reward for good North Korean behavior. Gallucci had been authorized to take to New York "a fistful of carrots. The carrots were in a basket, and the basket was kept squarely on the floor behind him." When any "carrot" was presented, it came with a precondition for North

Korean action, and as a result was unacceptable to the North Koreans, who showed themselves to be extremely sensitive to signals of superiority or absence of reciprocity or equality in American words or actions.

Moreover, some of the "carrots" Gallucci had on offer were "recycled carrots," such as negative security assurances, pledges the United States had made in the Kanter-Kim negotiations the previous year. Despite the fact that Gallucci had publicly floated the offer of negative security assurances to North Korea in exchange for a return to the NPT weeks before the negotiations, that carrot was held in reserve as a fallback position and was not even included in the talking points for Gallucci's initial presentation.[22] Given the fact that North Korea had stumbled on a highly effective means by which to "manufacture" leverage by challenging the top U.S. strategic priority of containing proliferation, it should not be surprising that, ironically, North Korea achieved both of the objectives it had failed to achieve in the January 1992 meetings: a joint statement and the explicit promise of a further meeting in return for a "suspension" of North Korea's withdrawal from the NPT. The United States had failed to convince North Korea to return fully to the NPT, but had given up nothing more than a recycled assurance that it would not attack North Korea with nuclear weapons.[23]

At the second round of U.S.-DPRK negotiations in Geneva in July of 1993, the idea of a package deal came up for the first time, although the elements of such a deal remained undefined. During the second round of negotiations in Geneva, the United States supported in principle a North Korean proposition that North Korea be supplied with proliferation-resistant light-water reactor (LWR) technology to replace its graphite-moderated reactors, which are capable of producing weapons-grade plutonium. Prior to the resumption of talks—scheduled for September 1993—the United States insisted on two preconditions that served to effectively stall further negotiations for over a year. The United States demanded that North Korea cooperate with the IAEA to allow inspections that would preserve the continuity of safeguards of North Korea's nuclear program and—at the insistence of the ROK—that direct working-level dialogue with South Korea be resumed.[24]

The Emerging Debate over Incentives for North Korea

Throughout the spring and summer of 1993, the basic parameters of a relatively active debate on strategy and tactics toward North Korea had begun to emerge both inside and outside the government. It became apparent that a UN-supported economic sanctions regime would not gain sufficient support from China unless the United States was perceived as having made its best efforts through direct negotiations to induce North

Korea to return to the NPT. On the other hand, there was staunch opposition within the Joint Chiefs of Staff and the counterproliferation community to offering any deal that might be seen as a reward for North Korea's having "been caught red-handed taking the last cookie from the cookie jar."[25] During the fall of 1993, as the basis for continuing high-level U.S.-DPRK talks began to break down, the continuity of safeguards under IAEA inspections eroded, and no progress was made in North-South dialogue, the debate intensified as the stakes appeared to increase.

The Rockefeller Foundation commissioned a survey of specialists on Korea and on nuclear issues in October 1993 to define more concretely the range of incentives that might be considered as part of a package to encourage North Korea to give up its nuclear program.[26] The schools of thought among respondents roughly reflected the ambivalence of the ongoing public policy debate on North Korea, among both U.S. and South Korean experts. There was widespread agreement among those surveyed that fundamental U.S. policy objectives were to maintain close cooperation with South Korea and Japan and to preserve the integrity of the NPT. A sizable minority of respondents felt that no incentive—only negative pressure such as sanctions or possibly military action—would be sufficient to induce North Korea to give up its nuclear program.[27] The majority of respondents supported exploration of incentives, but felt that "disincentives must be used in a flexible, continuous process in order to ensure progress in the right direction."[28] A third group felt that the DPRK nuclear threat was exaggerated and that time was on the side of the United States—artificial negotiating deadlines served to give North Korea leverage that would otherwise have been unavailable.[29] Finally, a small group felt that no negotiation with North Korea was likely to succeed unless the top level of the North Korean leadership was engaged directly in the process—perhaps through a high-level envoy of President Clinton who would travel to Pyongyang to present U.S. concerns directly to Kim Il Sung.[30]

Another element of the debate over incentives was put forth by Paul Bracken in an article in the autumn 1993 issue of *Survival*. This article suggested that the institutional weakness of the North Korean state structure doomed it to collapse, and that most of the possible incentives on offer to North Korea were likely to have the practical effect of accelerating North Korea's demise. These "poisoned carrots," or policy openings to North Korea that might ultimately have the effect of destabilizing the North Korean regime, included initiatives that involve foreign economic aid or direct engagement with North Korea. These types of incentives might in fact not be carrots at all, but instead might "constitute a greater threat to its [North Korea's] security than would the threats."[31]

A further addition to the debate over North Korea was a February 1994 report by a working group on North Korea convened by Richard Solomon, president of the United States Institute of Peace. The report, titled "North Korea's Nuclear Program: Challenge and Opportunity for American Policy," suggested that North Korea's nuclear program need not precipitate an immediate military crisis, and urged the Clinton administration to pursue a negotiating strategy on the basis of a package proposal that "clearly spelled out for Pyongyang a strategic choice of two paths to its future."[32] In addition, noting that interagency dissonance was affecting the ability of U.S. negotiators to put forward a unified position, the working group recommended that the Clinton administration appoint a senior coordinator within the administration to deal with North Korean nuclear issues.[33]

Although U.S.-DPRK negotiations in New York opened the way for partial IAEA inspections of North Korean nuclear sites in February 1994, it became clear that North-South dialogue was a particularly serious stumbling block that might be used by either side to impede progress. The phenomenon whereby South Korean policy would "flip" based on perceptions of whether the United States was taking too hard or too soft a position toward North Korea proved to be particularly frustrating to many observers in both the United States and South Korea. Finally, the ROK government's decision to drop the condition of North-South dialogue in late April 1994 appeared to open the way for renewed high-level dialogue in combination with the satisfactory completion of IAEA inspections to ensure the continuity of safeguards.

However, North Korea simultaneously removed fuel rods from the five-megawatt experimental reactor at Yongbyon in the absence of IAEA inspectors. These fuel rods could be reprocessed to produce more plutonium for North Korea, enough to make several nuclear bombs. This North Korean challenge appeared to cross one of three "red lines" established by the United States in the first round of U.S.–DPRK negotiations in June 1993.[34] In the context of this provocation, the anticipated resumption of high-level U.S.–DPRK negotiations was impossible, and the United States initiated a drive for a two-phased sanctions regime to be imposed against North Korea through the United Nations. In response to the IAEA's cutoff on 10 June of economic assistance to North Korea—provided as part of the IAEA's ongoing technical cooperation with North Korea's nuclear program—Pyongyang announced that it would withdraw from the IAEA.

The deterioration of the situation was the height of the crisis, and generated a number of editorial comments, including opinions from former officials including Brent Scowcroft, Arnold Kanter, and Henry Kissinger.[35] These columns stressed the seriousness of North Korean provocations, advocated economic sanctions, and hinted at the possibility that military action might become necessary to remove North Korea's reprocessing capability.

Lessons Learned from the First Phase of Clinton Policy

1. *The dangers of a purely reactive policy.* The first phase of the Clinton administration's policy was driven almost entirely by North Korean actions. By June 1994, there was a major need to reestablish control of both the parameters of the interaction and the negotiating agenda, which had been driven by North Korean challenges and failed responses by the Clinton administration. It appeared that the governments in Washington, Seoul, and Pyongyang had put themselves into a policy "box canyon," in which the only acceptable way out was either military confrontation or mutual retreat.

2. *Unrealistic statements of policy objectives undermine prospects for negotiations.* The Clinton administration's absolutist statements of its policy goals regarding North Korea's nuclear efforts were untenable and helped to undermine the possibility of a negotiated solution.[36] This was particularly so given the constraints imposed by the need to maintain solidarity with Asian allies, who rejected military confrontation as an acceptable outcome while at the same time relying on the United States to lead. A corollary of this lesson was that for the United States to be perceived as having preserved the NPT, it would be necessary to have gained North Korean concessions beyond the minimum of what the NPT required before the negotiation effort could be seen as politically justifiable.

3. *Preconditions heighten the likelihood of confrontation and remove possibilities for dialogue.* Finally, it had become apparent through experience gained in contacts since the first round of U.S.-DPRK negotiations in New York in June 1993 that preconditions in dealing with North Korea breed intransigence rather than force cooperation. To claim that North Korean principles of sovereignty and self-reliance had been preserved, it had become inevitable that Pyongyang, when faced with a demand from the United States, would choose to take exactly the opposite action—even if that action appeared to damage North Korean national interests—rather than be seen as capitulating on its core principles.[37] One key to turning the situation around was to find a way out of the escalating war of threats before military conflict became inevitable.

The Clinton Administration's Second Chance: A Package Solution for North Korea

Former president Jimmy Carter's June 1994 decision to travel to Pyongyang for a face-to-face meeting with Kim Il Sung was a dramatic turning point in the direction of U.S. policy toward the DPRK, creating an open-ing for a renewal of high-level discussions to negotiate a package deal with the North. Clinton administration officials had been preparing for the op-portunity to finally lay on the table a "comprehensive" solution for dealing with North Korea's nuclear program since the late fall of 1993, when a number of signs indicated that North Korea was also ready to negotiate a solution to the nuclear issue. First, Congressman Gary Ackerman brought back the general outlines of what North Korea sought as part of a "package solution" to the nuclear issue.[38] Second, Vice Foreign Minister Kang Sok Ju publicly reaffirmed many of the elements of such a "package solution" in public comments on 11 November 1993.[39]

By this time a debate had developed at the State Department regarding the elements of a possible package deal with North Korea—both in terms of what specific incentives the United States might be willing to offer and what would constitute a satisfactory North Korean response. During the Asia-Pacific Economic Cooperation (APEC) meeting in Seattle a few days prior to the Clinton-Kim summit in Washington, D.C., members of the South Korean delegation learned of preliminary internal State Department discussions regarding the deal, which had not yet been briefed to counter-parts at the Korean Embassy. Kim Young Sam, suspicious of a comprehen-sive approach developed within the U.S. government in the absence of full South Korean consultation, was not ready to fully back such an initiative in his meeting with President Clinton. The result was an awkward, drawn-out White House meeting from which Presidents Clinton and Kim emerged to announce the concept of a "broad and thorough" approach, the details of which had not yet been fully resolved. This approach in-cluded a renewed emphasis on North-South dialogue, a politically neces-sary addition President Kim needed to take back to Seoul to demonstrate that South Korean interests were being protected as part of U.S.-DPRK negotiations.[40]

Under the newly announced "broad and thorough" approach, Tom Hubbard, deputy assistant secretary of state for East Asia, and Gary Sa-more, deputy assistant secretary of state for political-military affairs, shut-tled to New York for discussions with members of the DPRK Mission to the UN. These discussions continued for over three months under arduous circumstances; ever more dire Central Intelligence Agency (CIA) and De-fense Intelligence Agency (DIA) assessments appeared in the press, as did misleading Korean press stories suggesting secret U.S.-North Korean deals were in the works that might disadvantage South Korea. Meanwhile, the Damoclean sword of continuously eroding IAEA safeguards hung over the talks, as Director General Hans Blix of the IAEA came closer to admitting that the IAEA inspections regime had for all practical purposes broken down. Finally, on 25 February 1994, the United States and North Korea announced the Agreed Conclusion,[41] in which Team Spirit would be suspended, IAEA inspections would be reinitiated, North-South work-ing-level contacts would be resumed, and a third round of U.S.-DPRK high-level talks would be resumed in Geneva on 21 March 1994.

The key factors allowing the successful negotiation of the modest Agreed Conclusions were that they avoided preconditions and emphasized simultaneity of action among the IAEA, North Korea, South Korea, and the United States and that they required concessions from both sides. However, the timing of implementation was thrown off by a seventy-two-hour delay in the resumption of working-level dialogue at Panmunjom brought about by a policy debate in Seoul over whether the DPRK should be required to send a special envoy to Seoul as a precondition for resuming inter-Korean dialogue. As a result, Pyongyang blocked the last of seven required IAEA inspections necessary to maintain continuity of safeguards, postponing the resumption of the U.S.-DPRK talks that had been set to resume in Geneva. Meanwhile, the working-level talks between North and South Korea were attempting to set the stage for higher-level dialogue and possibly a North-South presidential summit, but when Seoul threatened to push for international economic sanctions if the North failed to meet its preconditions for the holding of such a summit—even though the North had earlier dropped its conditions—the North Korean delegate is-sued his infamous statement that Seoul would be turned into a "sea of fire."[42]

It was in this steadily deteriorating environment that a number of at-tempts were made to establish communication directly with Kim Il Sung. First, Billy Graham delivered a message from President Clinton to Kim Il Sung during a January 1994 visit to Pyongyang.[43] Second, Secretary of Defense William Perry called on Senators Sam Nunn and Richard Lugar to be prepared to travel to Pyongyang and meet with Kim Il Sung in late May as part of a last-ditch effort to turn around the rapidly deteriorating environment between the United States and North Korea. North Korea mysteriously failed to respond to this offer for urgent talks between Kim Il Sung and a bipartisan team of respected senators.[44] Third, Selig Har-rison, a researcher at the Carnegie Endowment for International Peace, returned from meetings with Kim Il Sung in Pyongyang, again reporting the outlines of a package deal that North Korea would reportedly find acceptable.[45]

But it was the Carter visit in June 1994 that provided the basis for head-ing off an impending escalation of tensions as a result of North Korea's decision to remove spent fuel rods from its five-megawatt experimental reactor. As Secretary Perry was about to recommend to President Clinton a ten-thousand-man "augmentation" of U.S. forces in South Korea, Carter called the White House from Pyongyang to report that Kim Il Sung had agreed to allow IAEA inspectors to remain at Yongbyon to ensure continuity of safeguards. In addition, the North Koreans would maintain a freeze on all their nuclear activities and defer reprocessing of spent fuel rods as the basis for resuming high-level negotiations. Following independent confirmation by the Clinton administration of the pledges brought back by former president Carter, the third round of U.S.-DPRK talks was scheduled to resume in Geneva on 8 July 1994, but was interrupted following the morning session by the announcement that Kim Il Sung had died. In the context of Kim's death and the uncertainty of whether the U.S.-DPRK negotiations would be continued, President Clinton renewed an outstretched hand to the North by offering his condolences.[46]

Upon the resumption of U.S.-DPRK negotiations, the outlines of a possible package deal quickly began to take shape, although major details emerged as potential stumbling blocks between the United States and North Korea, which threatened to upend the negotiations. The three most significant issues were the need for North Korea to agree to special inspections of its nuclear facilities as part of its return to the NPT, the question of whether North Korea could accept a South Korean-style light-water reactor, and the issue of South Korea's central role as a participant in any multinational effort to replace North Korea's graphite-moderated reactors with light-water reactors. Compromise on the issue of special inspections made possible the announcement of the Geneva Agreed Framework, signed on 21 October 1994.

The major elements of the package deal presented in the Agreed Framework were that Pyongyang would continue to freeze all elements of its nuclear program, that North Korea would return to the NPT and accept full-scope safeguards on its nuclear program, and that its current graphite-moderated reactors would eventually be dismantled. In return, the United States agreed to organize an international consortium to finance and supply two one-thousand-megawatt LWRs to North Korea and to supply North Korea with approximately five hundred thousand tons of heavy oil per year as compensation for energy that might otherwise have been gained through the construction and completion of the fifty and two-hundred-megawatt reactors.

Before any essential nuclear components for the construction of the LWRs are provided (essential nuclear components are usually supplied about five years into the construction of an LWR), North Korea is required to implement its safeguards agreement under the NPT, allowing any inspections necessary—including special inspections—to ensure that North Korea is in compliance with the treaty. In addition, the Agreed Framework stipulates that North Korea must allow spent fuel rods from the five-megawatt experimental reactor at Yongbyon to be shipped out of the country before the completion of the first light-water reactor, and that graphite-moderated reactors and related facilities would be dismantled upon the completion of the second light-water reactor. As the light-water project proceeds, the United States and North Korea will gradually improve their bilateral relationship, initially through the exchange of liaison offices and later through negotiations over other outstanding issues in U.S.-DPRK relations including missile exports, levels of conventional military deployments on the Korean Peninsula, and human rights. Also included is a stipulation that North and South Korea resume a direct dialogue to discuss outstanding issues on the Korean peninsula.

Difficulties regarding South Korea's role were skirted in the Agreed Framework, although U.S. negotiators claimed to have made the U.S. position clear on these issues during discussions in Geneva. Nonetheless, it took eight months of subsequent negotiations at various levels in Berlin and Kuala Lumpur before North Korea accepted a complex, face-saving compromise. The Korean Peninsula Energy Development Organization (KEDO)—an international organization with an American executive director created to implement the provisions of the Geneva Agreed Framework—was designated to negotiate with North Korea and oversee the implementation of the light-water reactor project. At the same time, KEDO made clear at a board of directors meeting in Seoul that the primary contractor for the project would be a South Korean company, the Korean Electric Power Company (KEPCO), and that the light-water reactor to be built would be based on the Ulchin-3 and Ulchin-4 plants, the most advanced LWRs to have been built in South Korea. KEDO subsequently negotiated with the DPRK a contract to provide a light-water reactor. KEDO and U.S. government representatives noted North Korea's compliance with the Agreed Framework in its two-plus years of implementation.

Debating the Merits of the Geneva Agreed Framework

In the months following the signing of the Agreed Framework in Geneva, extensive debate occurred over the merits and deficiencies of the agreement and its implications both for U.S. counterproliferation efforts worldwide and for the situation on the Korean peninsula. The most significant concerns raised in congressional hearings focused on whether the "package solution" approach of the administration had fallen into the moral hazard trap by rewarding North Korea for noncompliance with the NPT. By rewarding instead of punishing the DPRK, the Clinton administration was vulnerable to charges from critics who argued that the United States had helped to undermine the ability of the NPT to deter nations from pursuing nuclear proliferation. The precedent set by a special deal with North Korea might encourage states such as Iran or Libya to develop nuclear weapons and challenge the nonproliferation regime as a means by which to blackmail the international community into providing a "ransom" and, as a result, to reap the potential benefits of their own package deal.

To a certain extent, these concerns were buttressed by Russian criticisms of the agreement with North Korea that U.S. and South Korean commercial interests were supported at the expense of Russia, since the former Soviet Union had discussed the possibility of building a light-water reactor in the DPRK in the 1980s. At the same time, the Russians were actively pursuing an LWR contract with Iran, a step that the United States vigorously opposed on the grounds that providing LWR technology to Iran might bolster a nuclear weapons production effort.

Administration officials justified dealing with the DPRK as unavoidable since the North Koreans were already so far down the road to building a bomb. Therefore, it was necessary to provide inducements sufficient to forestall the further development of the program. In addition, government officials added, the North Korean deal arose from a unique situation in which South Korea was willing to take on the lion's share of the burdens associated with the construction and financing of a light-water reactor in North Korea, whereas South Korea—the only viable source for financing an LWR project in North Korea—would not be interested in financing the construction of another country's reactor in the North.

Another major criticism of the North Korean nuclear deal was that the provision of heavy oil and other financial benefits to North Korea served to prop up a regime that otherwise would have been headed the way of other communist dictatorships. Despite the fact that heavy oil—or sludge—is relatively useless for military activities, the issue of diversion for uses other than humanitarian ones—including economic uses—proved to be a particularly sensitive political issue.[47] Although analysts disagree regarding the staying power and adaptability of the North Korean regime and its leadership, a consensus developed among all of North Korea's neighbors that a "soft landing" for North Korea is preferable to a violent collapse or prolonged instability. The uncertainties surrounding the future of North Korea following the death of Kim Il Sung made less abstract the debate over North Korea's future and its implications for South Korea.

A third major concern regarding the Geneva Agreed Framework was whether it sufficiently supported North-South dialogue as a direct vehicle for easing the core tensions on the Korean Peninsula. This concern is reflective of sensitivities alluded to above regarding whether South Korean interests in the nuclear issue—an issue that directly threatened South Korean security interests—had been sufficiently represented by the solution posed in the Agreed Framework. Although the U.S.-ROK governmental consultation was intensive, sensitivities remained on key issues, particularly with regard to the South Korean role. These concerns, while not fatal to the Agreed Framework, were expressed through the passage of a nonbinding congressional resolution urging the United States to pressure North Korea to implement the provisions of the Basic Agreement, if necessary by withholding key political and economic incentives that are part of the Agreed Framework.

The sharpest criticisms of the Geneva Agreed Framework came from Senator John McCain in his remarks at a Heritage Foundation forum to assess the results of the Kuala Lumpur negotiations between the United States and North Korea in May and June of 1995. While indicating that he did not object to the results of the Kuala Lumpur negotiations (clarifying KEDO's role with regard to the provision of South Korean reactors to North Korea), McCain took issue with the fundamental approach of the administration with regard to the North Korean nuclear issue. McCain asserted that "the administration could have given less and received more. However, the less which I had in mind is nothing, and the more would be nothing short of North Korea's full compliance with the nuclear nonproliferation treaty." Arguing that the North Korean "regime is constitutionally disposed to treachery," McCain predicted that North Korea would not live up to its obligations under the framework agreement, and expressed concern that North Korea had been given five years to continue to develop any covert nuclear weapons program that might exist in North Korea before special inspections consistent with IAEA or NPT obligations would be required. He also elaborated on the theme sounded in earlier congressional testimony by former secretary of state James Baker and others that the Clinton administration had pursued a "carrots-and-carrots" policy. McCain argued that:

> To get a mule to move, you have to show it the carrot and hit it with a stick at the same time. Despite the many reverses that have plagued the Clinton Administration's North Korea policy, one quality of their diplomacy has remained constant. Their approach to the crisis has always reflected the mirror opposite of North Korea's. Our diplomacy employs only carrots; theirs only sticks. Whenever our carrots have failed to prevent North Korean transgressions, the administration has limited its choice of sticks to the withdrawal of the carrot. The North Koreans repeatedly raise, then withdraw, a threat, masking their forbearance as a carrot. Using sticks such as their latest threat to reprocess their fuel rods, the North Koreans have consistently sought and received a better deal.[48]

Ambassador Gallucci's response to Senator McCain's criticisms argued that a negotiated approach had succeeded in achieving the administration's objective of freezing North Korea's nuclear program, halting a proliferation threat without capitulating wholesale to North Korean demands. Gallucci recognized the difficulties inherent in the moral hazard of dealing with North Korea ("We did not trust these guys. We knew they were not Canadians"), but he underscored and dramatized the risk inherent in the "stick" that had remained available to the administration throughout the negotiations:

> When I come home and I actually find my kids asking me why such bad people as the North Koreans are getting such good things, like a $4 billion power reactor, I have to sit down and explain that. That is not immediately obvious. It's not obvious to a 14-year-old, and it's not obvious to people who are a lot older and wiser. . . . I think sanctions are very important. But they don't stop reprocessing. Something else stops reprocessing that the senator is much more familiar with than I am, but I'm not unfamiliar with it. I know what's involved. So does the administration. That's an option that's always been there, it always will be there. It sits like a specter over our negotiations. It's good that it does. But it's not a happy option.[49]

Regardless of the potential rewards that might accompany conflict avoidance, a major political risk of incentives in the Korean case was the need by the Clinton administration to show its resolve sufficiently that critics' charges of appeasement might be neutralized—without losing the opportunity for a negotiated settlement.

Lessons from the Second Phase of Clinton Administration Policy

The Clinton administration showed a quick learning curve once an opportunity was created to get back to the negotiating table with North Korea following the Carter visit to Pyongyang. The need for multilateral cooperation forced the Clinton administration to accept the "lowest common denominator" option of fully testing the opportunities for dialogue before it was possible to execute a more pressure-oriented, confrontational approach. However, the experience gained from initial encounters with North Korea proved to be extremely useful as preparation for the resumption of high-level dialogue in Geneva in August 1994. Four preliminary lessons learned are explored below:

1. *Negotiation and the demythologizing of North Korea.* A major benefit of pursuing a negotiated settlement with North Korea was the experience gained in observing the capacity of the DPRK to react to fundamental foreign policy challenges. The use of incentives as a means by which to signal prospects for cooperation provided an opportunity to observe the reactions of North Korean negotiators at various levels and to understand in a more detailed way the workings and positions of concerned North Korean bureaucratic interests.

   In addition, it provided U.S. negotiators with a more comprehensive view of the kinds of inducements—political, economic, or otherwise—that might be most effective in encouraging North Korean cooperation. As has been noted earlier in this paper, the experience of direct contact through negotiations with North Korea proved vital to achieving a solution without resort to deadly force. In this respect, the perception that direct talks were a carrot (or a reward) to North Korea for good behavior was misguided, and may have served to heighten tensions and increase the potential for misunderstanding and confrontation. In addition, given the importance of perceptions of "equality" and reciprocity to North Korean political needs, the perception of parallel action and simultaneity rather than the imposition of preconditions—was particularly important in achieving progress.

2. *Be prepared to use real, not recycled carrots.* Although it may seem intuitive, incentives can only work if they indeed provide an inducement for the receiving party to act in the desired fashion. Negative incentives (disincentives) are an essential part of a carrots and sticks strategy, but it is unlikely that satisfactory cooperation with North Korea could have been achieved without constructing a plan of action that was perceived to be in the mutual interests of both parties.

One of the strengths of the Geneva Agreed Framework was precisely that, as Ambassador Gallucci said repeatedly in defending the agreement, "it is not based on trust." The structure of the agreement, in which a series of parallel movements are made on the basis of clearly delineated, concrete steps, provides verifiability and helps to ensure that neither side may pocket a concession by taking unfair advantage. For this reason, disincentives for breaking an agreement are essential, but a successful agreement will not be achieved unless both parties construe it to be in their respective national interests.

Another benefit of the package solution in the case of North Korea is that the proposal—in combination with other measures including the North Korean commitment to freeze its nuclear program—provided a basis for the United States to take the initiative in a way that was not seen as immediately threatening to North Korean national interests. Even if the carrots inherent in the LWR agreement prove to be poisoned carrots (or a Trojan Horse) in the end, as long as both sides perceive the agreement to be in their national interests, implementation can be expected to proceed in a positive direction. In addition, it is gradually becoming apparent that the process of cooperation with North Korea on this project, however arduous, is creating new leverage through which the U.S. influence in Pyongyang has grown in significant ways.

3. *Incentives will always be vulnerable to attack as political capitulation.*

Arguments such as those made by Senator McCain or former secretary Baker that agreements involving incentives are "carrots and carrots" deals and are to a certain extent inevitable in a political environment. Whether those political arguments have substantive merit, however, will ultimately be determined by whether an agreement is perceived as potentially damaging to the national interest or whether a less costly, more effective alternative can be put forward.

For this reason, one must be sure that there is a rationale for concessions made and that the technicalities of agreements can be clearly and simply explained. The technical nature of the solutions embodied in the Geneva Agreed Framework were a potential stumbling block to broader support for the agreement, but the administration managed to make its case sufficiently that the agreement was able to survive. In addition, the concrete benefits were sufficiently tangible and the stakes associated with dismantling the agreement sufficiently large that it survived intact. The fact that no concrete, cost-free alternative path could be identified was a major factor in the survival of the framework as it was examined by unfriendly critics.

4. *Incentives and the psychology of national insecurity and regime survival.* It has already been stated clearly on many occasions that North Korea's primary objective in the post–cold war environment has been to assure the survival of its regime in the face of the collapse of communism elsewhere. Given the insecurities of North Korea's apparently precarious position, a reexamination of the analogy of the hand in the cookie jar—which suggests the need to punish North Korea's dysfunctional behavior and inability to accept international norms—may be necessary.[50] In cases of such deep insecurity, the "stick" of punishment may only reinforce the likelihood of more flagrant violations, while positive measures are more likely to resolve core insecurities and encourage cooperative behavior. In the case of North Korea, it appears that incentives played an important role as a means by which to induce positive national behavior precisely because of the underlying North Korean policy objective of obtaining greater recognition from the United States.

Conclusion

Thus far, the provisions of the Agreed Framework have been observed and implemented, albeit at a slightly slower pace than was originally envisioned. KEDO has successfully negotiated the terms of a light-water reactor supply contract with the DPRK and has begun preparations for construction, although potential difficulties remain at every turn in this extraordinarily challenging technical process of constructing a light-water reactor in an isolated nation such as the DPRK.

Interestingly enough, it is not the DPRK that is in danger of breaching the Geneva Agreed Framework, but the United States. While the "lawless North Koreans" have lived up to their agreements thus far, some have suggested that the DPRK could be within its rights to abandon the Agreed Framework if KEDO were to fail to deliver on promised heavy oil supplies financed by an inadequate shoestring budget. Other critics charge that the United States has also moved too slowly in removing economic barriers as promised under the agreement.

Although KEDO has provided a new means by which indirect North-South dialogue might occur, the DPRK has failed thus far to live up to the spirit of one provision of the Geneva Agreed Framework calling for a renewal of North-South dialogue on a governmental level. Despite promising signs of greater interaction during the summer of 1995 through "rice talks" between representatives of Pyongyang and Seoul that were held in Beijing, there has been no significant substantive development on a government-to-government level, although proposed Four-Party meetings between the United States, China, and the two Koreas hold open the possibility that North–South dialogue may be reinitiated.

Perhaps the most startling development since 1994 is that the DPRK is now perceived as a threat due to its own weakness rather than due to the strength that accompanied its threat to gain nuclear supremacy on the peninsula. The structural economic problems that have resulted from decades of economic mismanagement have pressed down in earnest, leading some analysts to predict that it is only a matter of time before the DPRK collapses under the weight of its own economic mistakes.

These developments have given the United States and the ROK considerable potential leverage in dealing with the DPRK, but at a cost. The nature of the threat that accompanies North Korea's economic weakness is such that it has proved to be at least as divisive as the challenging task of coordinating policy during the height of the nuclear crisis, underscoring the fact that the underlying dangers of tension on the Korean peninsula remain, and that both the existence of an aggressive, hostile DPRK and the possibility of its sudden demise are equally worrisome and potentially unpredictable challenges for U.S. policymakers.

Incentives continue to be a part of the policy debate over how to induce political and economic changes that will integrate the DPRK with the outside world. Among the bolder prescriptions designed to induce change in the DPRK have been recommendations to proceed with economic incentives such as the lifting of all governmental restrictions on South Korean trade and investment in the North, the elimination of the U.S. economic embargo on trade with North Korea, and encouraging North Korea's membership in international financial institutions such as the Asian Development Bank, World Bank, and International Monetary Fund. All of these potential inputs will require structural changes in North Korea's system as it responds to Western demands for North Korea to live up to international standards of verification and accountability. Washington is already employing some of the most powerful of economic sticks in the form of the continued isolation of the DPRK from the economic inputs that are necessary for its long-term survival. Might incentives again provide a means by which to pacify North Korean leaders and tempt them on the way to reforms, or will this kind of poisoned carrot ultimately prove to be unavailable, paving the way to future conflict?

Notes

1. Scott Snyder, program officer at the United States Institute of Peace (USIP), is the author of USIP's November 1996 report entitled "A Coming Crisis on the Korean Peninsula?" The views presented here are his own, and do not represent those of the United States Institute of Peace. Questions or comments may be directed to Scott Snyder at the U.S. Institute of Peace, 1550 M St., NW, Washington, D.C., 20005.

2. Among the initial studies that are of particular note are the following: Michael J. Mazarr, *North Korea and the Bomb: A Case Study in Nonproliferation* (New York: St. Martin's Press, 1995); Mitchell Reiss, *Bridled Ambition: Why Countries Constrain Their Nuclear Capabilities* (Washington, D.C.: Woodrow Wilson Center Press, 1995), 231–321; Chung Ok-nim (in Korean), *588 Days in North Korea's Nuclear Program: The Tactics and Strategy of the Clinton Administration* (Seoul: Seoul Press, 1995); Byung Chul Koh, "Confrontation and Cooperation on the Korean Peninsula: The Politics of Nuclear Proliferation," in *Korean Journal of Defense Analysis* 6, no. 2 (Winter 1994): 53–85; Young Hwan Kihl, "Confrontation or Compromise on the Korean Peninsula: The North Korean Nuclear Issue," in *Korean Journal of Defense Analysis* 6, no. 2 (Winter 1994): 101–31; and Susan Rosegrant, "Carrots, Sticks, and Question Marks: Negotiating the North Korean Nuclear Crisis" (Kennedy School of Government Case Studies in Public Policy, Harvard University, 1995).

3. We are now moving into a fourth phase not covered in this paper, in which the Korean Peninsula Energy Development Organization (KEDO), a multinational organization created to provide North Korea with light-water reactors (LWRs) under the Geneva Agreed Framework, negotiates directly with North Korea to oversee the details of implementation.

4. Dr. Stephen Linton, a longtime observer of North Korea, has noted that Kim Il Sung—as a guerilla fighter against Japanese colonial rule—must have been particularly impressed with the effects of the atomic bomb in bringing the Japanese empire to its knees and ending World War II. As a result, Kim probably maintained a direct personal interest in developing the bomb as an insurance policy against

larger and more powerful neighbors. (Dr. Stephen Linton, Korea Society Tuesday Lunch Group Presentation, Washington, D.C., February 1995.)

5. The Bush administration had inherited from the Reagan administration a "modest initiative" to improve political relations with the DPRK initiated by Gaston Sigur in 1988. U.S. diplomats were allowed to have informal contact with North Korean counterparts at unofficial meetings, and a low-level U.S.-DPRK dialogue was initiated in Beijing, but that channel was relatively ineffectual in dealing with political issues, including questions about the North Korean nuclear program.

6. Mazarr, *North Korea and the Bomb*, 55–79.

7. This announcement was originally scheduled to be made by President Bush in a 2 August 1990 speech to the Aspen Institute, but announcement of the initiative was delayed as a result of worries that it would send the wrong signals following Iraq's invasion of Kuwait (Mazarr, 60–61).

8. The failed Soviet coup of August 1991, and the impending dissolution of the Soviet Union, which occurred shortly after the signing of the Basic Agreement were also probably key factors in North Korea's decision to conclude the landmark agreement with Seoul. In addition, U.S. policymakers identified North Korea's economic weakness as a factor that encouraged "some hope that the North was finally emerging from its isolation and was prepared to become a more normal member of international society." (See Rosegrant, 10–11.)

9. Rosegrant, 7–17, and interviews with former Bush administration officials.

10. The United States and North Korea had initiated a low-level dialogue in Beijing in 1988, but these meetings have been described as pro forma, heavily scripted contacts in which the possibilities for progress were limited.

11. North Korean gestures included the return of the bodies of some MIAs from the Korean War, aggressive pursuit by North Korean diplomats at the United Nations of opportunities to speak with State Department officials at unofficial functions, increased invitations to American scholarly delegations to visit Pyongyang to discuss policy issues, North Korean proposals on arms control and confidence-building measures, and the initiation of high-level talks at the prime minister level between Seoul and Pyongyang.

12. Denny Roy, "The Myth of North Korean 'Irrationality,' " *The Korean Journal of International Studies* 25, 2 (Summer 1994).

13. Public reactions of former Bush administration officials such as Brent Scowcroft, James Baker, and Lawrance Eagleburger to U.S.-DPRK developments have been instructive regarding the constraints of U.S. policy toward North Korea during the Bush administration. See Brent Scowcroft and Arnold Kanter, "Korea: A Time for Action," *Washington Post,* 15 June 1994; "Brent Scowcroft Discusses North Korean Sanctions," NPR Interview, Morning Edition, 16 June 1994 (Nexis); Federal News Service, "Testimony of James Baker to the House Committee on International Relations," 12 January 1995 (Nexis); Maureen Dowd, "Baker Basks in House, Warns on Meddling," *New York Times,* 13 January 1995, A8; MacNeil-Lehrer News Hour, 2 June 1994 (Nexis); "Observers Mixed about Carter's Diplomatic Missions," CNN, 16 December 1994 (Nexis).

14. Another factor that might have reinforced such attitudes in South Korea

was the abortive Carter effort to remove U.S. troops from South Korea in the late 1970s.

15. Roh Tae Woo Declaration on North-South Relations, 7 July 1988.

16. International pressure had been a lever by which North Korea had been induced to take positive action on nuclear issues since the United States had requested the Soviet Union to pressure North Korea to join the NPT in 1985.

17. Chinese representatives were consistently skeptical of U.S. and South Korean estimates regarding the level of North Korea's technical ability to pursue a nuclear weapons program.

18. UN Security Council Statement (S/25562), 8 April 1993.

19. Mazaar, 109–18, 190–92.

20. Interviews with State Department officials, August 1995.

21. Interviews with State Department officials, April 1995.

22. Interviews with State Department officials, August 1995.

23. U.S.-DPRK Joint Statement, Department of State, 11 June 1993.

24. U.S.-DPRK Press Statement, Department of State, 19 July 1993.

25. Interviews with State Department officials, August 1995.

26. Scott Snyder (unpublished manuscript), "Possible Areas of Cooperation with the Democratic People's Republic of Korea," An Asia Society Research Project for the Rockefeller Foundation, 24 November 1993.

27. See James Lilley, "Get Tough with North Korea," *Wall Street Journal,* 29 March 1994, A16; Karen Elliott House, "Korea: Raise Another Desert Shield," *Wall Street Journal,* 15 June 1994, A18; Karen Elliott House, "Korea: Clinton's Cuban Missile Crisis," *Wall Street Journal,* 5 January 1994, A14; William Taylor, "Heading Off a Korean Showdown," *Washington Post,* 19 November 1993, A29; Nicholas Eberstadt, "North Korea: Reform, Muddling Through, or Collapse?" *The National Bureau of Asian Research Analysis* 4, no. 3 (September 1993).

28. Snyder, "Possible Areas of Cooperation," 5.

29. Robert Sutter, Rinn-sup Shinn, and Lawrence Krause were among those who held this view (Ibid., 5).

30. Steve Linton, Robert Manning, and Antonio Betancourt advocated this approach (Ibid., 6).

31. Paul Bracken, "State Survival and Nuclear Weapons in North Korea," *Survival* (Autumn 1993): 137–53, and "The Prudent Course in North Korea," *Orbis* 39, no. 1 (Winter 1995): 55–64.

32. U.S. Institute of Peace North Korea Working Group, "North Korea's Nuclear Program: Challenge and Opportunity for American Policy," United States Institute of Peace, February 1994, 2.

33. Subsequently, Robert Gallucci was promoted to the rank of ambassador at large and given greater responsibility for coordinating the Clinton administration's positions on the North Korean nuclear issue.

34. The three conditions under which the United States had threatened to break off talks with North Korea were (1) a break in the continuity of safeguards, (2) a defueling and reloading of the core of the DPRK's reactor outside of the IAEA's inspections process, and (3) the resumption of reprocessing.

35. Henry Kissinger, "No Compromise, But a Rollback," *Washington Post,* 6

July 1994; Brent Scowcroft and Arnold Kanter, "Korea: A Time for Action," *Washington Post*, 15 June 1994.

36. Mike Mazaar makes this point very effectively in *North Korea and the Bomb*. See chaps. 1 and 9.

37. Steve Linton, Presentation at Columbia University Center for Korean Research, November 1993.

38. Interviews with U.S. State Department officials, August 1995.

39. R. Jeffrey Smith, "North Korea Deal Urged by State Department: Canceling Exercise Linked to Inspections," 15 November 1994, A15.

40. Thomas Friedman, "U.S. and Seoul Differ on Approach to North Korea on Nuclear Sites," *New York Times*, 24 November 1995, 16.

41. Agreed Conclusion, U.S. Department of State, 25 February 1994.

42. Michael Gordon, "U.S. Will Urge UN to Plan Sanctions for North Korea," *New York Times*, 20 March 1994.

43. Graham's advisors anticipated that the Clinton message might be too blunt—given considerations of "face" and North Korean sensitivities—to be an effective attempt to set the stage for a positive exchange. Even the slightly warmer revised message produced for Clinton by National Security Council staff drew a vigorously emotional response from Kim Il Sung, despite Graham's efforts to soften the tone of the message, according to Steve Linton, Graham's interpreter during the visit. Graham tried to explain the difficult situation in which President Clinton found himself, including the pressures of public opinion and from Congress, to calm down Kim Il Sung, and to vouch for President Clinton's sincerity in seeking a fair resolution of the issue. (Mazaar, 123–25, "Kim Il Sung, Up Close and Personal," *The New Yorker* 70, no. 4 [14 March 1994]; and conversations with Steve Linton, March 1994.)

44. Steve Coll and David B. Ottoway, "New Threats Create Doubt in US Policy," *Washington Post*, 13 April 1995, 1.

45. McNeil-Lehrer News-Hour, 2 June 1994; Selig Harrison, "What North Korea Really Wants from the US," *USA Today*, 7 July 1994.

46. The Kim Young Sam-Kim Il Sung summit meeting brokered by Jimmy Carter had been scheduled for 23 July but was canceled following Kim Il Sung's death. The summit was more politically difficult than the resumption of U.S.-DPRK negotiations, but ROK president Kim Young Sam's inability to offer condolences for domestic political reasons gave the DPRK a ready-made excuse to delay the presidential summit indefinitely.

47. The North Koreans had diverted some of the heavy oil from the first shipment to power a steel plant, a diversion that might have some indirect military significance. Congressional hearings revealed the potential sensitivity of the issue, since the question reflects whether North Korea is living up to its obligations under the Geneva Agreed Framework. Subsequently, it was agreed that monitoring equipment would be installed to provide verification that no future diversion of U.S.-provided heavy oil could take place.

48. John McCain, remarks at "The U.S.-North Korea Nuclear Agreement: Current Status and Prospects for the Future," The Heritage Foundation, 15 June 1995.

49. Robert Gallucci, remarks at "The U.S.-North Korea Nuclear Agreement: Current Status and Prospects for the Future," The Heritage Foundation, 15 June 1995.

50. A less-benign analogy among those who are skeptical about the capacity for systemic adaptation to external changes in North Korea is that of a cancer that must be removed from the body before health can be restored.

4

Trade and Technology Incentives and Bilateral Cooperation

William J. Long

AN TRADE AND TECHNOLOGY incentives shape national preferences and create a measure of bilateral cooperation? The case studies synopsized below suggest the answer may be a qualified yes. Although this finding may be surprising or suspect to those who doubt the effectiveness of economic measures in fostering interstate cooperation, the point of this chapter is not to debate *whether* incentives work as policy instruments. Rather, it provides a brief theoretical explanation of *how* incentives might work to affect the prospects for bilateral cooperation. It explains the way incentives can foster bilateral cooperation by both changing the external environment facing states and by altering the domestic political and economic determinants of a state's policy preferences. The chapter then considers three historical cases: (1) the transfer of American civilian nuclear technology and materials to Sweden during the 1950s and 1960s to discourage Sweden's development of nuclear weapons manufacturing capabilities; (2) the exchange of U.S. trade, technology, and other economic benefits to the People's Republic of China (PRC) during the 1970s and 1980s in return for improved Sino-American political-strategic cooperation; and (3) the extension of most-favored-nation (MFN) trading status,

This is a shortened version of an article that appeared in *International Studies Quarterly* (Spring 1996). It is reprinted here with the permission of Blackwell Publishers, Inc.

preferential financing, and access to advanced technology to Czechoslovakia during the early 1990s in exchange for cooperation in controlling the proliferation of weapons of mass destruction. The purpose of the cases is to inform and illustrate the theory of incentives through systematic empirical research. This chapter also claims a degree of practical relevance to policymakers. Having explained the general logic behind the operation of economic incentives and considered their operation in several situations, it offers some policy advice as to *when* incentives might work in contrast to economic sanctions. The chapter concludes with suggestions for further research.

The Independent and Dependent Variables

The independent variable is trade and technology incentives—an important form of economic incentives. Trade and technology incentives are a mode of power exercised through the promise or giving of an economic benefit to induce a state to change its political behavior. They contrast with economic sanctions and coercion that aim to force an alteration in the target's behavior by impeding its welfare. The policies at issue are medium to long term and, although not overtly "coercive," clearly aim to influence the recipient state's behavior in a preferred direction in specific areas.[1]

As a matter of practical policy, states often employ trade or technology transfer measures to strengthen an ally or decrease the dependency or vulnerability of a potential ally or friend to a common adversary. States offer trade and technology incentives in varying forms to foster a preferred form of economic development, to instigate or promote particular values or interests in the recipient, or to create conditions for the provision of a collective good. Indeed, the use of trade denial strategies—a popular cold war instrument—created opportunities to relax or remove such restrictions as a means of influence. In David Baldwin's words, "Today's reward may lay the groundwork for tomorrow's threat, and tomorrow's threat may lay the groundwork for a promise the day after tomorrow."[2]

Programmatic incentives are important policy instruments, but, with the exception of foreign aid, they have not been extensively examined. Likewise, although scholars have given considerable attention to the coercive uses of trade and technology in the form of sanctions or boycotts, they have largely ignored incentives. International relations theorists typically discount the use and potential of trade and technology incentives as a tool of foreign policy. Many reject incentives on theoretical grounds as power relations between states.[3] Other analysts, while acknowledging that they should theoretically include trade and technology inducements as a means by which states pursue their goals and affect the behavior of other actors or their environment, argue on practical grounds that these forms of economic incentives are of limited significance. They dismiss the availability of economic rewards for capitalist states, noting, for example, the difficulty of directing trade for political purposes in such societies and the general prohibitions against the use of selective preferences in trade for market societies.[4] As Baldwin notes, this depoliticization of trade fails to recognize that, while private actors carry out trade, "Attempts by statesmen to influence the pattern of international trade through manipulating this legal and political framework can be regarded as acts of economic statecraft."[5] Policies that create the possibility for international exchange, alter the terms of exchange, or enhance the technological capabilities of others are pervasive and powerful features of international relations worthy of investigation.

Incentives influence both international behavior and domestic politics. Therefore, there are both structural and agent-level dependent variables in the study—bilateral cooperation and domestic policy preferences—and these dependent variables are themselves interdependent. At the level of international relations, we are concerned with how incentives affect the environment for bilateral "cooperation," that is, policy coordination where "actors adjust their behavior to the actual or anticipated preferences of others."[6] Embedded in this definition of cooperation is the formation of national policy preferences. Understanding how incentives shape interstate strategic interaction *and* how they alter national preference formation is necessary to explain how they affect behavior.[7]

Toward a Theory of Incentives

At the level of the international system, incentives can shape state behavior much like sanctions. Incentives alter a state's payoff environment by offering an exchange of economic gains from trade and technology transfer for political concessions.[8] A sender offers to open mutually beneficial trade or to grant the recipient state better terms of trade (relaxing a tariff, for example) in exchange for a desired policy adjustment (political cooperation). In a sanctions case, the sender is trying to collect a political concession for bargaining gains it has forgone earlier. With incentives, the sender is offering new or additional gains from trade and technology transfer for the concession.

R. Harrison Wagner suggests incentives should be less powerful than sanctions because the recipient state necessarily values more highly the marginal unit of a good taken away (via sanctions) than an additional economic benefit of the same amount (via incentives).[9] He also claims the reallocation costs associated with the loss of existing trade are likely to exceed those associated with new trade and, thus, sanctions should be a more influential policy instrument.

Wagner's analysis allows us to see some important points about incentives operating at the level of international exchange, and it illustrates how private exchange does not preclude the state from using trade for political influence. Unfortunately, Wagner's conclusion that incentives are merely weak sanctions ignores many important differences between the two instruments, particularly the sources of incentives' strength and their potential for cooperative influence.

Under certain conditions, incentives may be compelling in altering the international environment facing states. First, although a recipient necessarily has a declining marginal utility for an incentive, what may be more important is the recipient's total utility for the goods or gains from trade and technology. If total utility remains substantially positive during the influence attempt, the incentive could represent a powerful inducement. Enduring positive utility is more likely when advanced technology is part of the package, as technology is integral to a state's overall productive capability.[10] The importance of technology as an incentive is best illustrated in the U.S.-PRC case. A new policy line emerged in China in the 1970s that increasingly relied on foreign goods and technology to speed China's development and modernization, making Western incentives a particularly powerful inducement.

Second, with regard to costs, incentives, unlike sanctions, to the extent they open new opportunities for trade and exchange (relaxing an embargo, for example), create opportunities for both the sender and the recipient to garner new benefits—an improvement in economic utility for both. This important difference between incentives and sanctions means the sender will have greater interest in maintaining the policy and implies that incentives are less likely to collapse under their own weight. Many forms of trade and technology incentives are "off-budget" policy instruments and differ from foreign aid, which is costly to the sender. Simply put, incentives can be a win-win instrument, whereas sanctions are a lose-lose instrument, whose effectiveness depends on which party is better able to withstand the attendant costs. This difference carries important implications for the domestic political effects of incentives discussed below.

Finally, in those instances where the sender possesses market power in the incentive, the impact of an incentive is enhanced because market power creates a larger potential benefit to exchange for the desired political concession. Unlike economic sanctions, however, market power is not a strict necessity. In the cases that follow, the sender had substantial market power in the incentive goods.

The international exchange model, like much economic and international relations theory, assumes a set of fixed preferences and is an incomplete conceptualization.[11] Much of the explanation for how incentives work is found in the domestic politics of the sender and recipient and the formation of their policy preferences.[12] An internal choice or exchange as well as an external exchange occurs for both the sender and the recipient state. Before an international exchange of economic benefits for political concessions can occur, a sender state must change its preferences for political concession versus relative economic gain to alter the terms of trade, and a recipient state must adopt an internal exchange function favoring gains from trade (and political concessions), rather than political autonomy. At this level, the argument draws on several approaches suggested by the case studies—statism, institutionalism, interest group explanations, and decision-maker cognition—to understand state preference formation and change. This chapter suggests four ways in which the power of economic incentives is enhanced or less likely to be diminished by its domestic operation, in contrast to sanctions.

First, in the sender state, sanctions invariably cost societal actors and create conflict between the state and society. For example, the study of economic sanctions by Gary Hufbauer et al. concludes that with regard to societal groups in the sender state, "Business firms at home may experience severe losses when sanctions interrupt trade and financial contacts. . . . After the first flush of patriotic enthusiasm, such complaints can undermine a sanction initiative."[13] As for the larger public, they assert, "Even though popular opinion in the sender country may welcome the introduction of sanctions, public support often dissipates over time."[14]

In contrast, incentives are more likely to maintain or increase their base of support in the sender state over time or, at least, create less state/society antagonism. Unlike sanctions, support for trade and technology incentives spreads as exporters and investors take a growing interest in the gains from trade and technology transfer associated with new or expanded commercial relations. Incentives do not necessarily create a state/society antagonism in the sender nation, and, in many cases, the interest of the sender state and its societal groups strongly affected by the policy are reinforcing. In the case of civilian nuclear technology incentives offered to Sweden, the chief societal beneficiary in the sender state was the emerging nuclear reactor industry headed by industrial giants like General Electric and Westinghouse. In the other two cases, a wide group of medium- and high-technology American exporters stood to gain by an incentive policy that would open an important new market and investment opportunity.

It is true that import-competing producers in the sender state might oppose an incentives policy because of the economic adjustment costs it imposes on them—a case in point would be American textile industries adversely impacted by expanded trade with the PRC. Although adjustment costs pose a domestic obstacle to some trade incentive policies it is not an insurmountable problem. States regularly incur the costs of domestic adjustment for overall welfare gains from expanded trade. Indeed, the history of international trade liberalization of the past fifty years attests to the willingness of states to make this trade-off. In the case of trade incentive policies, the sender state anticipates gaining both politically and economically from expanded trade with the recipient state. The potential political and economic gains for the sender state should make it more willing to shoulder any domestic adjustment costs attending its policy.

As to orchestrating broader domestic support, incentives may be an easier policy instrument to rally a winning domestic coalition behind than other economic instruments. Because incentives have an overtly political purpose (unlike, say, a GATT-mandated tariff reduction), policymakers can more credibly invoke ideals such as global peace or national security (in addition to economic benefit for the domestic sectors) to garner support for the incentive strategy. Incentives, unlike more bellicose measures like sanctions, raise few fears or concerns in the sender state's populace and, indeed, are generally good for domestic propaganda purposes. President Eisenhower's "atoms for peace" initiative directed to Sweden, among others, was particularly ingenious in this respect. That incentive strategy allowed the president to transcend his advisors' recommendation for greater candor with the American people about the potential (good and evil) of the atom and give concrete meaning to a positive vision of using new knowledge and technology to build greater world peace and prosperity. Similarly, the reopening to China was a propaganda plus for American policymakers, resonating with the public's desire to see a relaxation in cold war tensions and widespread (but naive) belief that America had reestablished its special relationship with China dating back to the Open Door era.[15]

Incentives also operate differently than sanctions in the domestic politics of the recipient state. The sanctions literature repeatedly asserts that domestic antidotes generated in the recipient state limit the power of economic sanctions. The two antidotes most often cited are the tendency of economic sanctions to (1) unify the target country to an external threat and (2) compel the target country to search for commercial alternatives.[16] Both reactions move the target country away from a preference for the sender's desired political concession.

The first antidote, the "rally-around-the-flag" effect, has two dimensions. Politically, because sanctions are a threat to harm the target state, its leaders can marshall popular support and suppress societal dissent by an appeal to national pride and survival. Fidel Castro and Saddam Hussein provide two recent examples.[17] Economically, a sanction, by raising the domestic price of the sanctioned import, will cause the target government to intervene extensively in the market to organize trade in that sector as a monopsonist and capture some of the economic rents generated by the sanctions.[18] The target government then can use the difference between domestic and world prices to ration the goods as a political resource to consolidate its ruling coalition by offering access to the sanctioned good to preferred domestic groups in return for political resistance to the sanctions. Furthermore, sanctions create groups in the target state with a vested interest in seeing the sanctions continue. Sanctions create a transfer of surplus from domestic consumers of the imported good to import-competing producers, who capture a windfall as long as the sanctions persist. This group, which typically is better organized than consumers, has a strong economic interest in encouraging the target government to reject the demands of the sanctioning state.[19] For political and economic reasons, therefore, sanctions encourage the target state to form or maintain preferences rejecting the sender's demands.

Incentives are less likely to produce this antidote. Because incentives are noncoercive instruments providing a tangible material benefit that some recipient actors can appropriate (as well as nontangible benefits such as recognition or legitimacy), they do not threaten the target state so as to instinctively provoke rally-around-the-flag reactions, and they find natural allies in the recipient state who reinforce the sender's message and influence. Arguably, incentives, if overreaching or overbearing, could antagonize the recipient rather than encourage cooperation. However, unlike sanctions, they do not necessarily challenge the sovereignty of the recipient state or reduce its net welfare.

Within the political economy of the recipient state, incentives encourage those state or societal actors who have the most to gain economically to be more sympathetic or less resistant to the political concessions the sender seeks. Regarding technology transfer to Sweden, for example, the internal ally was Sweden's emerging civilian nuclear power industry (ASEA), which was eager for American nuclear technology and material and unconcerned about the nonproliferation commitments that accepting the technology entailed. In China, the economic and modernization benefits derived from expanded commercial relations strengthened the hand of Deng Xiaoping and the reformers at a critical juncture in China's foreign policy. In the Czech case, the economic benefits not only offered new technology and material rewards to emerging private sector actors, but strengthened the legitimacy of new leaders, like Vaclav Havel, who had committed themselves to reintegration with the West. Each of these allies assisted the sender in moving the recipient toward cooperative adjustment.

One qualification to this point should be noted, however. Analogous to the possibility of import-competing producer opposition to incentives in the sender state, incentives also can create opposition among adversely affected economic actors in the recipient state. The case of U.S. and Western economic incentives to Czechoslovakia in exchange for arms transfer restraint illustrates the point. In that instance, recipient cooperation was complicated because the costs of arms export restraint fell heavily on munitions manufacturers in Slovak regions. Nonetheless, although societal recipient groups actually or potentially hurt by an incentives policy may raise objections, such incentives also create potential partners in the recipient state who benefit economically and are motivated to see incentives work. While the outcome of contending domestic interest is never certain, incentives create a clear possibility that a recipient interest group with a potential stake in the gains from trade will join the sender in urging cooperative adjustment.

The second cited antidote to sanctions is the tendency to drive the target in search of alternative suppliers who are encouraged to supply the target state because the politically created scarcity of economic sanctions offers them unique economic opportunities. The power of sanctions can be "broken" if the target can locate an alternative source of supply for the embargoed good(s).[20]

In contrast, the offer of an economic incentive providing new gains from trade and technology transfer does not create in the recipient a strong desire to undermine the influence attempt by seeking an alternative supplier. Furthermore, incentives do not create economic conditions that encourage new entrants or third-party suppliers to offset the sender's efforts. When an incentive is offered, the potential recipient can choose to reject it and maintain its political autonomy, leaving it no worse off than before. Third-party suppliers are important in incentives cases only to the extent a potential recipient could "shop" the offered incentive among potential senders. The ability of small states to entice the United States and the former Soviet Union into a bidding war for political influence would be a case in point, albeit an exceptional one. Moreover, it is unlikely a potential recipient would even try to "break" an incentive. Many theorists suggest that states concern themselves with the potential of loss far more than the possibility of additional gain.[21] Thus, unlike sanctions, whose threatened economic and reputational losses motivate and mobilize the recipient to search for third-party suppliers, incentives do not compel a potential recipient to pursue a better offer. As to third-party suppliers, politically created scarcity precipitated by sanctions induces the entry of new suppliers. A sender's offer of goods and technology on more favorable terms has the opposite effect. The first case study illustrates these points as America's incentives strategy shaped Sweden's decision-making environment for over a decade without inviting third-party interference.

Incentives may operate differently than sanctions at the level of national decision making as well. Scholars who have examined decision-maker cognition and choice as a source of national preferences tell us that decision makers often used established images to filter information and to resist negative feedback once committed to a course of action.[22] Some suggest that warnings, threats, and the possibility of loss often lead decision makers to be insensitive to information critical of their policies—a pattern of defensive avoidance.[23]

These insights imply that sanctions are more likely to engender or aggravate misperception or produce these cognitive pathologies than incentives and, therefore, may impede cooperation where incentives encourage it.[24] Incentives, a noncoercive influence attempt, do not threaten a decision maker in the recipient country with loss (both tangible loss of an existing gain from trade and loss of reputation at home). Unlike sanctions' punishment or opprobrium, incentives should be less likely to produce defensive, rigid, or obstinate reactions that impede clear communication and policy adjustment between countries over the long term. Instead, incentives show, through a beneficial act, that the sender expects the recipient to cooperate, thereby changing the intersubjective identities of the parties.[25]

Incentives can open new channels of communication, encourage further negotiation, reduce the fear and hostility that may have characterized the bilateral relationship, and permit the recipient greater freedom to react cooperatively without fear of economic or reputational loss. Ironically, the ability of the recipient to characterize its policy adjustment in response to an incentive as self-motivated (rather than coerced) may be an important strength of incentives as a policy instrument, and yet one of the reasons it is easy to overlook or underestimate their effects. The China case illustrates this point best as incentives in the economic and technological sphere help dissolve decades of mistrust and mutual hostility.

Further, incentives, by highlighting the desired policy adaptation sought in the recipient, rather than singling out the undesired direction in another state's policies, may convey more precise and constructive information than sanctions. Incentives show the sender's desired or preferred course of adjustment rather than sanctioning an existing or anticipated policy. In this respect, incentives may perform the information-providing function of regimes in developing cooperation. Punishment does not, in itself, communicate the sender's desired response. It merely points out one of the many undesired responses. Punishments have value in indicating the sender's displeasure, blocking the actions of the target, or satisfying the sender's desire for justice or revenge, but they are less than ideal for communicating the desire or direction for long-term cooperation. In fact they can quickly lead to communication gridlock.[26] Simply put, if long-run cooperation is the goal, incentives communicate better than sanctions. In many cases, but not all, clearer communication can facilitate cooperation.[27] In moving away from trade and technology denial and toward expanded commercial contact with reform-minded countries of Central Europe like Czechoslovakia, the United States communicated clearly and specifically its desired quid pro quo—the establishment of internal nonproliferation technology control institutions—and worked closely with these countries in realizing this objective. In contrast, the cold war policy of trade and technology denial, while serving the goal of containment by imposing costs on a military and political rival, did little to communicate a preference or path for cooperation.

To sum up, incentives alter international structures (the terms of trade and the potential technological frontier), and they affect the domestic political economy of agents (states). The dual effects are interdependent, and an appreciation of both is necessary to understand how incentives might foster bilateral cooperation.[28] Incentives are not simply weak versions of economic sanctions; the two instruments operate in substantially different ways.

Incentives alter the payoff environment of states by offering an exchange of economic gains from trade and technology transfer for political concessions. Incentives may be compelling in altering state behavior when (1) the recipient's marginal utility for the goods or gains from trade remained substantially positive, that is, total utility is increasing (likely in instances where advance technology is part of the package), (2) both the sender and the recipient stand to gain in economic terms through the creation of new trade, and (3) the sender possesses market power in the incentive goods. Incentives also affect the domestic political economy of states by shaping preferences in the sender and recipient in a manner that enhances or is less likely to impede cooperation. First, societal actors in the sender state who stand to gain economically from expanded trade lend support over time for an incentive, thereby improving the policy's legitimacy and endurance. Public opinion in the sender state is unlikely to oppose an incentive. Second, certain actors in the recipient state who can appropriate the economic benefits tend to ally with the sender state and reinforce its efforts to move the recipient's policy preference in the direction of the sender's intent. Third, incentives are unlikely to create an impetus to elude or undermine the sender's influence through the search for third-party suppliers or create the economic conditions that invite new entrants. Finally, incentives convey more precise information to decision makers in the recipient state in a manner that is unlikely to be filtered, avoided, or resisted by them.

To illustrate some of these hypotheses and provide an empirical foundation for discerning general insights about the operation and effect of incentives for policymakers, the next section synopsizes three historical incentives programs. Each case was a long-term, diffuse attempt to influence and regularize behavior and cooperation, and each was an important policy initiative. To isolate somewhat the impact of incentives, the cases selected involve cooperative interaction attempts occurring outside the context of shared regimes, that is, sets of rules, principles, norms, or decision-making procedures around which actors' expectations converge. Cooperative efforts in these cases did not occur within formal institutions to help regularize behavior and cooperation, to inhibit cheating, to sanction noncompliance, or to facilitate side payments between sender and recipient. Further, the states interacting in the U.S.-PRC case possessed different political and economic systems or, in the Czech case, lacked long-standing patterns of trust and cooperation. Sweden, too, remained outside the East-West alliance structures of the period and had a strong tradition of looking after its own defense outside formal institutions. Thus, while numerous variables affected the outcome of the cases, the studies do control, to the degree permitted in international relations, some of the variables—regimes, institutions, and norms—that have been the foci of many studies of international cooperation and allow us to trace the process of incentives and cooperative influence.[29]

These cases are also important because they present situations where the sender offers an economic and civilian technology package in exchange for recipient adjustments in the area of "high politics" (political military-security relations), as opposed to adjustments in the "low politics" arena (economic or technological cooperation) alone. These cases are programmatic incentives offered by the sender to foster policy adjustment in areas directly related to the recipient's vital security interests. The cooperation sought is not a trivial, inconsequential, or secondary matter to either the sender or recipient.

Methodologically, exploring the question of the relationship between an incentive program and cooperation requires a thorough understanding of actions, and interactions, and an estimation of the motives of two or more states—the sender(s) and the recipient(s). To locate patterns of cooperation or their absence, one must first identify the sender state's goals and the incentives it devises to achieve cooperative adjustment from the target state. Next, the target state's actions in the sender's areas of interest before and after the receipt of the incentive (or promise thereof) must be analyzed to determine if the recipient's policies are adjusting along the lines desired by the sender state. If so, then the study must judge if the apparent adjustment is in some measure other-regarding or merely reflects the recipient's pursuit of self-interest, that is, when the policies of the sender and the recipient coalesce, is it a case of harmony or is it cooperation?[30] To answer this question one must consider a state's motivation. Judging a recipient's motives contains a measure of subjectivity and is influenced by the observer's preexisting beliefs. This study identifies cooperation or noncooperation based on an informed assessment of the recipient's actions gained by an empirical examination of the bilateral relationship during the incentives program and a synthesis of the expert interpretations of specialists and policymakers involved in the bilateral relationship. This historiographic method is appropriate when the goals are hypothesis generation and policy insight.[31]

Civilian Nuclear Technology Incentives and U.S. Nonproliferation Policy: The Case of Sweden

Changing the External Environment to Induce Cooperation

In 1954, following President Eisenhower's "atoms for peace" address to the United Nations, the United States abandoned a policy of strict secrecy surrounding civilian nuclear technology transfer with passage of the Atomic Energy Act. If the Soviet Union possessed nuclear capabilities, it made little sense for America to deny nuclear information, technology, and material to its allies. Failure to share atomic technology could cost the United States greatly in prestige and influence during a period of intense cold war rivalry.

Beginning in 1955, the United States adopted a policy of technology exchange through a series of bilateral agreements for cooperation with several nations that transferred nuclear research and power reactors, enriched uranium, and training in exchange for the recipient's assurances that it would not divert the technology and materials to military purposes, that is, building atomic bombs, and guarantees that the United States could exercise certain forms of safeguards to verify the material's disposition. Recognizing both the inevitable spread of nuclear technology and the incentive power of the virtual American monopoly over certain nuclear technologies and enriched uranium, the United States hoped to shape the desires and direction of countries like Sweden away from developing a weapons capability based on natural uranium and technology outside American control and safeguards.[32] On 18 January 1956, an "agreement for cooperation" with Sweden took effect.[33]

Appreciating the nonproliferation effect of America's incentives strategy requires a basic understanding of reactor technologies. Essentially two types of civilian nuclear technologies were available during the 1950s and 1960s. Both produced plutonium (a weapons material) as a byproduct, but from the standpoint of proliferation, they presented very different implications. One method, the approach originally favored by Sweden, relied on natural uranium and heavy-water reactors (HWRs). Reactors can use natural uranium as fuel with heavy water (D_2O) to generate energy. An HWR "burns," or fissions a portion of its radioactive uranium (U-235) and converts another portion of its inert uranium (U-238) into the element plutonium. Technicians can reprocess plutonium from the spent fuel to make a nuclear weapon core. Because natural uranium was available from several sources outside U.S. control, the HWR approach presented proliferation problems from an American perspective. A country with a viable HWR program would have an independent supply of plutonium for the manufacture of nuclear bombs.

In contrast, the American approach used enriched uranium fuel (that is, with a higher concentration of U-235) and light-water reactors (LWRs) with H_2O as a moderator in creating nuclear energy. During the 1950s and 1960s, the United States had a free world monopoly on enriched uranium and enrichment capabilities, that is, market power in the incentive goods. Enriched uranium, once created, could release vastly greater quantities of energy than natural uranium.

By encouraging countries to rely on enriched uranium and LWR for their energy needs, the United States could inhibit weapons proliferation. Under the agreements for cooperation, the United States made generous offers to sell or lease enriched uranium to friendly nations for exclusively peaceful purposes. The United States also offered technology along with the safeguarded fuel: first research reactors and, later, commercially viable electricity reactors. Furthermore, the U.S. Atomic Energy Commission (AEC) priced the enriched uranium fuel so low compared to the cost of developing independent enrichment capabilities that the American offer created a powerful economic rationale for Western European nations to forgo development of uranium enrichment plants.

Equally important to the bilateral agreements in serving the nonproliferation strategy, the passage of the Atomic Energy Act of 1954 opened the door for the creation of a civilian nuclear energy industry that would become an important societal ally of the incentives strategy. Domestically, the new legislation reduced the government's control over nuclear energy technology and strengthened private initiatives for developing nuclear power. Within three years of the new act, the first U.S.-powered LWR demonstrated the technological feasibility of civilian nuclear energy. Privately owned, commercial-sized plants followed in the early 1960s.[34]

The domestic and international programs launched in 1954 were interdependent. The ability to achieve the foreign policy goals of the peaceful atom was linked to the creation of technologically viable and eventually, economically competitive, civilian LWRs. The United States could not undertake a policy of international nuclear cooperation in the peaceful uses of the atom without a competitive domestic technological base in nuclear energy technology and materials. Private sector interest in the new technology would not last without commercial applications on the horizon. The continuing attractiveness of American technology and material from the first bilateral agreements for cooperation to the commercialization of

LWRs and the domination of the civilian nuclear power plant market leveraged U.S. nonproliferation policy.[35]

The pattern of U.S.-Swedish relations in civilian nuclear technology corresponds with American use of technology as part of a nonproliferation policy strategy. In addition to a research reactor and enriched fuel, in the mid-1950s the AEC provided Sweden with a host of other forms of technical assistance.[36] In addition, as early as 1956, the United States and Sweden began discussions for more substantial cooperation governing future power-reactor technology. Negotiating a power-reactor agreement began in earnest in 1962 and was concluded in 1966.[37] Over time, these tacit incentives and a unique set of domestic factors helped dissuade Sweden from developing the technological capability to produce nuclear weapons.

Sweden's Domestic Situation: Incentives and Shifting Preferences

In the 1940s and 1950s, Sweden pursued both the military and civilian possibilities of nuclear energy. Nuclear energy held the promise of breaking its oil dependence and replacing it with a clean, efficient source that relied on Sweden's considerable technological competence.[38] Sweden also saw the clear military possibilities of nuclear power from America's use of the bomb during World War II, and, in the postwar world, assumed that nuclear weapons would soon be part of its arsenal.[39] Because the nuclear powers would not sell nuclear weapons, Sweden would need to manufacture nuclear material for a bomb itself.[40]

During this period, it did not appear that Sweden faced insuperable technical obstacles in nuclear weapons development as a byproduct of its civilian nuclear energy program. Recently declassified information revealed that in 1950 the Swedish cabinet approved a secret memorandum of agreement regulating the exchange of information and personnel between military and civilian organizations "to avoid duplication and to coordinate efforts in a joint plan."[41] These decisions reflected the government's early conclusion that Sweden could not keep the pursuit of the atom's peaceful and military applications separate. Economic costs and finite technological resources required coordination of the civil and military programs.[42]

In pursuing its civilian energy goals, Sweden's initial preference was for a program based on potentially self-supporting natural uranium and HWRs that could serve as the basis for its military needs as well. Sweden's political leadership in the early 1950s recognized that an ability to produce atomic weapons would be a potential byproduct of the civilian program through the development of nuclear expertise and the possibility of extracting and reprocessing spent civilian reactor fuel into weapons-grade plutonium outside of foreign control, inspection, or restriction.[43] Sweden's defense establishment concluded that developing sufficient plutonium for nuclear weapons cores would require a large HWR and would take between eight and thirteen years. Thus, it was important the civilian reactor program make progress toward the goal of successful reactor design and maintain the military's secret link to the civilian reactor program over that period.[44]

When the nuclear weapons issue surfaced publicly in 1954, it set off a storm of political debate in the Swedish Parliament and press. Because of lack of consensus within the ruling Social Democratic Party on the issue, the government publicly demurred on the question of nuclear weapons acquisition. Behind the scenes, the joint civilian-military nuclear program took a large step forward, however. That step was Sweden's decision to develop large heavy-water plutonium-producing reactors.[45] The decision, publicly taken for civilian purposes, was supported by a detailed defense study of the premises for developing nuclear weapons, which concluded that the best course of action remained a dual-purpose program where reactors would produce heat and electricity for civilian purposes and plutonium for military ones. Under this plan, Sweden would soon have modest HWR producing plutonium at Agesta, then a larger reactor at Marviken.

In 1957, the issue of nuclear weapons returned to test the Social Democrats. To prevent the issue from dividing the party and dissolving the government (the Social Democrats governed with a single-seat plurality in association with the Communist Party), the party organized a special committee of eighteen leaders to examine the issue in November 1958. The committee recommended postponing a definite decision on nuclear weapons acquisition until 1963–64 when Sweden would have the technical capability and nuclear material from its reactors for manufacturing nuclear weapons. The decision was viewed by nuclear weapons proponents as a green light to continue working to reduce the time between a decision to build nuclear weapons and their actual production, whereas opponents to nuclear-weapons acquisition considered it a way of gaining time to let resistance grow.[46] It also created a window of opportunity for American technological influence.

In the spring of 1961, Sweden's defense research lab reported that most theoretic problems with the construction of a nuclear charge had been solved, and a simple prototype could be assembled if the necessary weapons-grade material became available.[47] For Sweden to achieve its military aspirations, "all that was needed was for the civilian program to keep pace with the military one."[48]

The civilian side of Sweden's nuclear program was not keeping pace, however, straining the linkage between the civilian and military programs. The Agesta and Marviken HWRs under development by the state were facing delays, cost overruns, and technological problems. The completion date for Agesta was postponed from 1961 to 1963 and then to 1964, and the cost of the project nearly doubled. The delays at Agesta meant it had fallen behind the schedule set by the defense staff projections for the production of militarily useful plutonium. Marviken experienced similar delays and cost overruns. "Altogether, this finally led to doubts about the whole HWR program in comparison with the emerging light water reactor systems."[49] Marviken became unjustifiable except for its role in the fuel cycle for the production of materials useful to the military.

As James Jasper writes, "Mild disenchantment with the Swedish heavy water line was reinforced by the rising tide of enthusiasm for LWRs emanating from the United States and advancing across Europe."[50] News of the American breakthrough to commercially competitive light-water nuclear electricity spread quickly among the international nuclear energy community.[51] The technical problems at Marviken had weakened the government's role and strengthened the hand of private industry, such as power firm ASEA, which preferred the LWR approach.

Sweden's nuclear power-planning began shifting to LWRs. By the early 1960s, Sweden's power companies had concluded that delays in the domestic program would force them to purchase foreign reactor technology rather than waiting for domestic models. These imported reactors' reliance on safeguarded enriched fuel was of no concern to the utilities.[52]

The Swedish power utilities were anxious to obtain experience in constructing and operating LWRs. The government insistence on the HWR approach adopted in the 1950s made little sense considering current technologies and a U.S. offer of long-term fuel supply. By 1962, the AEC and Sweden were in serious negotiations over the transfer of reactor technology and fuel for large-scale LWR power production. Negotiations on this point culminated in a new cooperation agreement in 1966 for the United States to supply enriched uranium, under safeguards, for the first six Swedish nuclear power units up to 1996.[53]

The emerging Swedish reactor industry, in particularly the Swedish firm ASEA, lobbied AB Atomenergi hard and successfully for scuttling the heavy line of reactors in favor of light-water designs.[54] The American incentive strategy had mobilized an important recipient ally that stood to gain from the new technology and would exercise influence in reshaping the recipient state's preference. In 1964, the state withdrew from the Marviken project. ASEA, meanwhile, had adapted its technology to LWR design and sold its first LWR to a Swedish electric utility consortium in 1965. The withdrawal of support by the state and private utilities sealed the fate of Swedish HWRs.

The Swedish nuclear-weapons option died sometime during the mid-1960s. In February 1968, the Parliament dryly stated, "It is not in our country's political interest to acquire nuclear weapons." In 1970, AB Atomenergi formally canceled the Marviken reactor because of design problems. Swedish authorities would also close Agesta. Because of economic, technological, and political necessity, Sweden turned to American-safeguarded enriched uranium fuel and power stations relying on LWR technology.[55]

The United States monitored Swedish developments closely, and its technology transfers were purposeful.[56] Consistent with its political and commercial interests, the United States sold LWRs and safeguarded materials to Sweden to halt the proliferation danger posed by operating HWRs in countries with nuclear weapons potential. The United States aimed its offers at making LWRs the sole economic choice for energy production through technology transfer and concessionary long-term contracts on U.S.-controlled uranium as a barrier to nuclear weapons proliferation. "In effect the bargains offered by the U.S. AEC had quietly undone a Swedish defense plan."[57] In considering the impact of U.S. policies on Swedish decisions, Garris concludes, "Sweden's own civilian atomic energy setbacks and the policy of the United States in providing controlled nuclear materials ensured that Sweden's nuclear weapons capability was never very well developed."[58] In short, American civilian nuclear technology incentives encouraged Sweden to abandon its HWR approach, shift its preference to LWRs, and forgo the possibility of an independent military nuclear capability in the early 1960s.

Trade and Technology Transfer to the People's Republic of China, 1978-1986

From Embargo to Incentive: Changing the Strategic Environment

America's incentive program toward China followed a long period of embargo that began in 1949. As the Chinese Communists gained control, the United States imposed an export embargo with its allies in the Coordinating Committee for Multilateral Export Controls (COCOM), seized Chinese assets, denied MFN treatment to Chinese imports, and withdrew Export-Import Bank financing.[59]

The movement away from sanctions did not begin until the Nixon administration. On taking office, President Nixon signaled a relaxation in America's policies toward China by expanding commercial exchange and liberalizing restrictions on travel to China. By May 1972 Nixon had accepted Premier Zhou Enlai's invitation to seek normalization of relations.[60] In explaining the new direction in U.S. policy, administration officials pointed to a recalculation of the nature of the strategic threat posed by China.[61] Specifically, American policymakers increasingly viewed

the Sino-Soviet schism and the emerging power of Japan as creating coun-
terweights to Chinese influence that, except for the ongoing war in Vietnam, did not pose a direct threat to Southeast Asia.

China was reassessing the international environment as well. The Soviet
invasion of Czechoslovakia in 1968 and Sino-Soviet border clashes in
1969 led China's leaders to emphasize the security threat from the Soviet
Union rather than the West. Moreover, some Chinese leaders were beginning to see the United States as useful for its emerging economic strategy.

After Nixon's visit, the two countries announced the first major thaw in
U.S. embargo policy in the Shanghai Communiqué of 1972.[62] The communiqué officially marked the resumption of commercial relations between the United States and China. The United States relaxed trade
restrictions with China to those with the USSR, a policy of "evenhandedness" in economic relations. Despite some early enthusiasm, the growth in
U.S.-PRC trade was slow and uneven.[63]

Although progress was not dramatic, the outlines of greater Sino-American cooperation took shape in the 1970s. By the late 1970s, conditions
for the effective use of American economic incentives were in place. First,
China's desire for the incentive goods strengthened. Second, both the
United States and China stood to gain economically from relaxing the
embargo. Finally, the United States, in concert with its Western allies in
COCOM held substantial market power in the incentive goods.

In 1978, Deng Xiaoping and the reformers relaunched the Four Mod-
ernizations Policy designed to revitalize the Chinese economy in agriculture, industry, national defense, and science and technology by the year
2000. Crucial to the program's success was an "opening to the West," to
obtain the goods and services necessary for the modernization process.
Full implementation of the program began when Deng purged the remaining Maoists and gained full control over the CCP Central Committee
in 1979. The emergence of the reformers as the dominant political actors
led to policies premised on the belief that foreign technology and capital
were necessary to modernize China and to maintain a high level of economic growth.[64] They would become the recipient ally of an American
incentive program.

The United States, meanwhile, was reassessing China's strategic importance and economic needs and would fashion an economic incentive program to encourage closer strategic cooperation between the two countries.
For the incoming Carter administration, fuller normalization of relations
with China was a goal that would gather momentum in the late 1970s
under the auspices of National Security Advisor Zbigniew Brzezinski.[65]
Brzezinski believed economic exchange and widened opportunities for
commercial flow of technology with China would lay the groundwork for

improved Sino-American security relations and a further deterioration in the Sino-Soviet link.[66]

Shortly after submitting a normalization agreement to Congress, Carter granted annually renewable MFN treatment to China by waiving the prohibitions on China's receipt of MFN and submitting a Sino-American trade treaty to Congress. Carter intended economic measures to strengthen broader political and strategic cooperation over time.[67] The MFN agreement led to an improvement in the welfare of both states through an acceleration in U.S.-China trade—from $2.45 billion in 1979 to $6.85 billion in 1981—and broke the policy of evenhandedness in U.S. economic relations with the two communist powers.[68]

The United States also altered the policy of evenhandedness in technology transfer by promoting the export to China of dual-use and nonlethal military technology not available for export to the Soviet Union, signaling a new stage in Sino-American strategic relations.[69]

In April 1980, the Carter administration created new, less-restrictive guidelines for dual-use technology exports to the PRC. In June 1981, President Ronald Reagan followed the Carter administration's decision to relax U.S. export controls by issuing a directive allowing approval of technology and equipment exports to China at levels generally twice those approved for the USSR—the so-called two-times policy. Problems of implementation immediately followed the two-times decision, however, and continued following the policy's promulgation. Responding to the complaints of American exporters and the Chinese government, in May 1983 President Reagan announced a new policy of treating China like other Western nations for most high-technology exports. In this respect, the China case best illustrates the mobilization of sender state interest groups (American exporters) to bolster the endurance of an incentives program. Implementation of the 1983 reforms led to a rapid growth in technology transfer between the United States and China, expanding tenfold from 1980 to 1986.[70]

Although directed toward the achievement of several objectives, the overarching purpose of U.S. policy was to protect and enhance Sino-American political and strategic cooperation by giving the Chinese an economic and technological stake in preserving good relations with the United States and the West.[71] The level of cooperation between China and the United States has varied over time and across issue area, yet in several important areas China adjusted its foreign policy in a cooperative fashion influenced in part by its interest in securing and expanding its economic and technological link to the United States and the West.

In many respects, U.S. and Chinese goals were harmonious. The goals were far from identical, however. A basic complementarity (rather than identity) between U.S. and PRC interests was the underlying basis for cooperation. As noted, security motivated the United States. The United States also had a complementary economic logic to its security policy "which sought not simply an anti-Soviet China but also a China that would be, for the foreseeable future, enmeshed with and dependent upon the U.S.-managed world economy."[72] From the Chinese perspective, economic concerns took highest priority by the late 1970s and 1980s. China's leaders emphasized "economic diplomacy," that is, China should use its foreign policy to serve the nation's paramount interest—economic development. This economic emphasis encouraged Beijing to seek a stable and peaceful international environment so China would not divert its energies from the goal of economic modernization. As Deng Xiaoping succinctly said, "China needs at least 20 years of peace to concentrate on our domestic development."[73] This approach to foreign relations encouraged greater pragmatism and a willingness to find common ground with the United States and other states on an issue-by-issue basis. Thus, the shared goals in constraining Soviet influence and in expanded commercial ties should not obfuscate that both states cooperatively adjusted their policies in view of the other's primary interest.[74]

PRC Policy Adjustment

The PRC initially demonstrated cooperative adjustment in its willingness to normalize relations with the United States despite U.S. assertions that it would continue to sell weapons to Taiwan.[75] Other less-dramatic evidence of Chinese accommodation with the United States and the West included the elimination of its rhetorical support for a "New International Economic Order" and the removal of the United States from its list of hegemonic powers (leaving the Soviet Union and its allies).

By 1980 to 1981, cooperation between the two countries had expanded in the strategic and economic spheres. Notably, the United States and China began to coordinate policy on regional issues. The PRC sought to align itself with the United States over continuation of the Japanese-American security relationship, maintenance of peace on the Korean peninsula, and opposition to Vietnam's invasion of Cambodia. The two countries also began limited cooperation in security affairs—the United States relaxing restrictions on military equipment sales and China agreeing to establish a joint surveillance facility to monitor Soviet missile tests.[76]

The evolution of U.S.-PRC relations was not one of unremitting progress. This case illustrates several important limits to cooperation. Several irritants contributed to a cooling in Sino-American relations during the period 1981 to 1983.[77] Further, a divergent reappraisal by the United States and China over the nature of the Soviet threat and the importance of Sino-American strategic cooperation slowed cooperation. The Reagan administration came into office perceiving an immediate need to directly challenge Soviet military capabilities. In 1981 to 1982, China, in contrast, appears to have concluded that the Soviet threat had lessened because of Soviet difficulties in Afghanistan and Eastern Europe and economic problems at home. Thus, the PRC saw a reduced need for strategic cooperation with the West. Yet, "good relations with the United States would remain very important, especially if China were to benefit more fully in the areas of economic collaboration and technology transfer."[78]

A series of measures, including the promise and delivery of U.S. high technology, a compromise on arms sales to Taiwan, and the settlement of a textile dispute, contributed to a second wave of bilateral cooperation in 1983 and 1984.[79] Recognizing the importance of access to U.S. and Western technology, capital, and expertise, the Chinese responded directly to the May 1983 announcement to ease technology transfer restrictions by agreeing to schedule a long-delayed exchange visit of defense ministers.[80] This process of reconciliation culminated in an exchange of visits between Premier Zhao and President Reagan in early 1984.

Although portrayed by Beijing as independent steps, it was clear that China was reviving defense cooperation and high-level political contacts and moderating demands and threats of retaliation over Taiwan for the sake of improved Sino-American economic relations. The cooperative adjustments by the PRC during this period included changing its policy on purchasing arms from the United States, soft-pedaling past demands and threats, joining the Asian Development Bank despite Taiwan's membership, and others.[81]

The slow but steady expansion of U.S.-PRC military links in the mid-1980s, despite China's view that the Soviet threat to the mainland was continuing to recede, is also significant. Considering these developments, some China scholars have asked, "Why did Peking move ahead with security cooperation with the United States just as it was becoming confident that the Soviets would not attack mainland China [and] a U.S. security link. . . was certain to antagonize Moscow?"[82] Analysts have concluded that China acceded to U.S. demands for active military links to guarantee access to U.S. technology and economic benefits essential to China's modernization.[83] Others have maintained that the United States made China's military cooperation a test of China's sincerity in opposing Soviet hegemony. According to this analysis, China's refusal to cooperate could have adversely affected China's access to U.S. technology.[84]

Differences between the United States and China remained in the mid-1980s and relations would deteriorate by the late 1980s, but in this earlier period both sides recognized and worked with reasonable success in managing those differences to avoid serious interference in what they came to see as their mutually beneficial relationship: "the PRC gets a peaceful environment in which to develop . . . technology, access to the American market, and capital from international institutions and American investors. The United States gets strategic benefits."[85] As Harding observed, China's stress on economic modernization and its growing economic interaction with the United States during this period "will give Peking a lasting incentive to manage and moderate any geopolitical tensions in its relationship with Washington."[86]

In sum, the PRC took pains to ensure that its foreign policy did not jeopardize the flow of U.S. and Western technology, capital, and access to markets, and the United States delivered a measure of advanced technology and facilitated China's access to its market and to public and private capital to improve political and strategic cooperation with the PRC. Bilateral frictions and adjustments continued to be a part of Sino-American relations during this period. Overall, however, American economic incentives broadened the cooperative interactions between the two countries, contributed to the achievement of their respective objectives, and produced a measure of cooperative "spillover" in their concurrent relations.

Since the Tiananmen incident of 4 June 1989, U.S. trade and technology transfer ends and means vis-à-vis China have oscillated between reinforcing shared commercial and geostrategic interests through continued exchange to castigating China's human rights and arms proliferation practices through selective economic sanctions and threats to withdraw MFN tariff treatment. As a result, the level of bilateral cooperation has declined markedly in the 1990s. This lack of bilateral cooperation reflects both the contradictory and sometimes confused state of U.S. policy and the limits of influence (in terms of scope and duration) of trade and technology incentives generally.

Incentives and Czechoslovak Cooperation in Stopping the Proliferation of Dangerous Technology

Changing the External Environment: From Boycott to Engagement

Czechoslovakia, a staunch supporter of the Soviet Union and its Warsaw Pact ally, was among the targets of an American-led embargo designed to contain the economic and military potential of adversary nations. The United States denied Czechoslovakia loans and export credits and maintained prohibitive tariffs against Czechoslovakia in the post–World War II era.[87] With the help of other Western countries in COCOM, the United States also embargoed technology transfer. These prohibitions remained remarkably constant features of U.S. policy from the 1950s through the 1980s.

The end of the cold war forced a realignment of policy to meet new challenges. The basic Western security concern of a sudden Warsaw Pact attack on Western Europe dissolved and was replaced by concerns over centrifugal tendencies and economic decay in these nations, or the possible export of dangerous technologies from former East bloc states to unstable regimes. Sudden oversupply and overcapacity in military and military-related technology in the former Warsaw Pact was an unfortunate consequence of the cold war's end. Czechoslovakia, a small country no longer part of a larger alliance, could not sustain its arms industries through purchases for its own forces or those within its former alliance. Until the eventual conversion of defense industries to civilian projects, arms producers in Czechoslovakia and elsewhere faced considerable economic pressure to export weapons and weapons-related technology to any potential buyer to earn foreign exchange, and, ironically, to finance military conversion and economic modernization. Ensuring that Western technology was not retransferred to unstable areas and engendering responsible policies over arms manufacturing and exporting soon became important aspects of U.S. nonproliferation policy toward Czechoslovakia.

The United States encouraged Czechoslovakia to develop an indigenous technology control system and to join other multilateral export-control arrangements. In addition to COCOM, the late 1980s saw the emergence of three independent multilateral regimes—the Nuclear Suppliers Group (NSG), the Missile Technology Control Regime (MTCR), and the Australia Group (AG)—addressing the question of regulating dual-use technology for nuclear, missile, and chemical weapons technology, respectively. Strengthening nascent multilateral technology control regimes to combat the proliferation of dangerous technologies and expanding their membership to include countries like Czechoslovakia became an important American goal.

From 1990 through 1992, the United States made a strategic reassessment of the situation in Eastern Europe and offered the reform-minded countries of that region (Czechoslovakia, Hungary, and Poland) a new economic bargain—trade and high technology for responsible nonproliferation policies. The elements of the American economic incentives program for Czechoslovakia offered during the 1990 to 1992 period included (1) IMF and World Bank resources; (2) market access in the form of most-favored-nation tariff status and, in some cases, preferential access under the Generalized System of Preferences; (3) economic assistance; (4) investment guarantees and credits; and (5) transfer of American and Western high technology.[87] Bilateral trade and investment flows grew rapidly.[88]

The United States pursued several goals through its incentives policies. Some of these goals were quite specific. For example, the creation of an internal licensing and export control apparatus that could regulate the disposition and prohibit the undesired retransfer of Western technology imported by Czechoslovakia was an explicit requirement for the liberalization of U.S. and Western technology transfer restrictions. The United States and COCOM countries also wanted safeguards created to prohibit unauthorized export of indigenous Czechoslovak technology. Relatedly, the United States sought cooperation in Western efforts to strengthen emerging nonproliferation export-control regimes.

Beyond these specific expectations, the United States also hoped Czechoslovakia would exercise restraint in making conventional arms sales to countries or areas of instability. To reduce the oversupply of arms, the United States anticipated to see the conversion of much of the Czechoslovak arms industry to civilian production. Finally, the United States wanted to see the country continue on the path of democratization, free market reform, and reintegration into the world economy—of which conversion of its armaments industries was an important step.[89]

Changing Preferences in the Recipient State

In Czechoslovakia, the "velvet" revolution at the end of 1989 toppled one of the staunchest of communist regimes and replaced it with a new government. Czechoslovakia held free elections on 8 June 1990, ousting the Communist Party and giving the reformers a strong mandate to move the country toward democracy and a free market economy.[90] In November 1990, the republics, Czech and Slovak, signed a power-sharing agreement with the central government that transferred considerable power to them and renamed the country the Czech and Slovak Federal Republic (CSFR).[91]

Becoming part of Western society and gaining access to Western goods, markets, and technology became explicit goals of the new nation. The postcommunist government saw access to modern Western technology in telecommunications, computers, machine tools, and other sectors as essential to its ability to eventually compete in the global economy. It lacked the capacity to foster any substantial progress from within because of its economic problems and a legacy of technological backwardness.[92] As in the China case, the recipient's utility for the incentive was strongly positive, the sender's market power substantial, and both parties could improve their economic gains.

Obtaining access to the West's resources and markets essential for modernization and growth required incurring certain obligations, however, including cooperation with the West on nonproliferation export controls. In addition to the economic benefits, cooperation with the United States and the West in this area bore considerable symbolic significance for all parties—a concrete expression of the end of cold war technological isolation and a symbol of the CSFR's reintegration with, and acceptance by, the West.[93]

To qualify for Western technology, the CSFR created a new export-control apparatus. Despite the organizational, legal, technical, and economic challenges associated with creating this new governmental function, a broad consensus existed within the new government over the need for such controls. The CSFR quickly implemented controls on imported advanced technology by passing legislation empowering the Federal Foreign Trade Ministry to license the import and export of controlled goods and giving the customs administration authority to inspect for compliance with the law and identify violators. A separate law created criminal penalties and punishment for violations. The two provisions created the initial framework for compliance with Western demands for a technology-control system.

In addition to addressing COCOM's immediate concerns for control over the proliferation of strategic dual-use technology, the CSFR continued its support for other multilateral export-control arrangements. The CSFR signed the "declaration of the CSCE (Conference on Security and Cooperation in Europe) Council on Nonproliferation and Arms Transfers," promising to prevent the proliferation of weapons of mass destruction and delivery systems. It renewed its support for a comprehensive chemical weapons convention to be concluded in 1992.[94] The CSFR adopted the list of chemical export restrictions of the AG and, in November 1990, removed any objection it had to the ban on chemical weapons in the proposed Convention on Chemical and Biological Weapons then under negotiation in Geneva.[95] In the area of nuclear-related exports, the new federation committed itself to the strict guidelines of the NSG, an organization that Czechoslovakia had joined in an earlier incarnation in 1978 and became a proponent of a global nuclear test ban.[96] In conventional arms, the CSFR joined the United Nations embargo on Iraq and European Community restrictions applied to Yugoslavia.[97] The federation also approved a CSCE agreement on the maximum levels of conventional weapons and technology in the former Warsaw Pact countries.[98]

Despite these considerable cooperative efforts, the CSFR faced many obstacles in meeting Western expectations for limitations on arms exports and defense industry conversion. Unlike dual-use technology exports, the government of the CSFR was unable to pass legislation controlling the licensing and export of arms, leaving arms sales and licensing to a case-by-case process.[99] Despite U.S. encouragement to have CSFR arms export policies conform to COCOM munitions lists, and statements of CSFR good intentions, actual policy in this area was strongly influenced by economic necessity and particular interests.

The CSFR's process of bureaucratic implementation of arms technology licensing complicated efforts to cooperate fully with the West. The Foreign Trade Ministry generally supported the granting of export licenses along with the Ministry of Defense (which had an interest in maintaining the defense industry of the CSFR through exports). These views were often contested by the Ministry of Foreign Affairs, which advocated stricter controls over the export of arms in part because of its greater concern over external relations with the West.[100] The process of removing government control over the economy and the consequent burgeoning number of companies involved in arms trade also complicated arms sales restraint.[101] Relatedly, the development of a powerful arms lobby that included weapons producers, factory managers, and private dealers impeded the ability of the federal legislature to fashion a more coherent arms policy.[102]

A major hindrance to adopting and implementing new arms-export-control policies arose from growing interrepublic differences. Under its new government, the federal state granted substantial authority over the economic sphere to the Czech and Slovak Republics. One immediate result of this dispersion of power was the decision by the government of the Slovak Republic to adopt a different posture regarding arms exports and slow the pace of the federal government's defense conversion plans.[103] Higher levels of unemployment, concentrated defense production, rigid labor markets, uncompetitive industries, inability to absorb advanced technology, greater suspicion of the West, and reemerging nationalism all made the Slovak Republic less cooperative with Western demands for arms-sales restraint and defense-industry conversion. Growing support for Slovakian independence in 1992 and local interest in maintaining arms exports constrained the negotiating position of the CSFR in dealing with Western demands for restraints on arms sales and defense-industry conversion.

Another factor complicating Czech and Slovak cooperation with the West on arms sales and conversion was the declining importance of greater access to Western technology as a factor in shaping policy by year-end 1992. As Wagner predicts, declining marginal utility can limit influence. Having secured favorable consideration status from Western exports from COCOM, enterprises in the CSFR had access to all but the most technologically sophisticated items. Most CSFR enterprises, especially those in the Slovak Republic, had little interest in further liberalization governing cutting-edge technologies they could neither absorb nor afford. Moreover, U.S. assistance was largely limited to encouraging private-sector participation in the CSFR, rather than making large official financial transfers as many in the CSFR anticipated. Slovak leader Vladimir Meciar captured the sentiment well: "The federal government understood conversion as a gesture of cooperation toward the West. They hoped there'd be a payoff, but they're still waiting."[104]

Generally, however, CSFR policies were cooperative or harmonious with the United States and the West. It established an internal technology-control system, continued and expanded policies in support of weapons nonproliferation, restrained some of its arms sales, and continued on an uneven path of defense conversion. Western incentives were an important factor in shaping these policies because they conditioned receipt of goods and technology critical for the CSFR's economic development on cooperation with COCOM and other multilateral proliferation-control regimes. Failure to comply could mean the loss of necessary technology and capital. From an American perspective, CSFR policies were also favorably influenced by that country's desire to rejoin the West and a decline in the international arms market, whereas cooperative influence was limited by the split between the two republics, economic dislocation associated with the movement to a free market economy, and problems of CSFR bureaucratic coordination.

Trade and Technology Incentives and Foreign Policy

Alexander George has argued that scholars can aid policy judgments by providing "generic knowledge" of policy instruments that identify their uses and limitations and the conditions on which their effectiveness depends based on a study of past experience.[105] The conceptual framework and case studies in this chapter provide a basis for making some policy generalizations regarding economic incentives.

The necessary conditions for economic incentives include the existence of, or potential for, a bilateral exchange relationship. Further, the relationship must be one in which the sender country has in some way impeded the full recognition of the gains from trade available to the potential recipient (such as an embargo, tariff or nontariff barrier, capital restriction, or other impediment) or has used policies to obtain preferable terms of trade or restrict technology transfer. Political influence comes from forgoing part of one's gains from trade for a change in the recipient's political behavior. If market forces alone have set the terms, then there is nothing for the sender to offer affirmatively.

In addition to the existence of an economic market, the case studies suggest a second potentially necessary condition, the existence of a minimum degree of trust or confidence in the bilateral relationship. Just as an economic market between the parties is necessary, a "political market" for exchange is necessary, too. In relationships characterized by an atmosphere of hostility, mistrust, and misunderstanding, ambitious incentives may be a premature, if not dangerous, policy choice. In popular parlance, confidence-building measures may be necessary before a programmatic incentive is possible or warranted. The China case study helps illustrate this point as significant cooperation only became possible as the threat of China to the United States diminished, and a reasonable basis existed to conclude that each country sought improved relations.

Other factors contribute to, or detract from, the success of economic incentives. At the level of the international exchange, market power is an important condition favoring the success of an incentive. Unlike sanctions, market power is not a strict necessity (any gainful exchange relationship and any governmental policy that affects the distribution of the gains from trade in favor of itself creates a potential avenue for political influence). Nonetheless, more market power in the incentive goods creates a larger potential economic benefit that can be exchanged for the desired political concession. In the cases considered, the United States had significant market power in the incentive goods.

The incentive is more likely to be influential if the recipient state values highly the incentive and the acquisition of the incentive is linked to abiding state interests. It is true, as seen in the Czech case, that the utility a recipient attaches to an incentive declines with additional units of the good or technology. Nonetheless, to the extent the recipient continues to attach significant positive value to the incentive, that is, as long as total utility is rising, incentives may be powerful tools of influence.

The cases suggest that policymakers must also consider several domestic conditions in weighing the possible employment of an incentives strategy. First, incentives, if accepted by the recipient in the sense that the recipient indicates a likelihood of cooperating, require steady and protracted implementation on the part of the sender. This feature is in contrast to sanctions that require swift and sure implementation when the recipient indicates an intention *not* to adapt its policies in the direction desired by the sender.[106] The burden of implementation means that an effective incentives policy may require sustained bureaucratic coordination and followthrough and, while most advanced states possess this institutional capability, its effective use cannot be assumed. For example, problems of implementation characterized the U.S. decision to liberalize technology transfer to the PRC in the early and mid 1980s. Although these problems did not fundamentally undermine the initiative, the problem of bureaucratic implementation and interagency coordination remained an impediment to a more effective incentives policy. In short, an incentive strategy works best when the bureaus charged with its implementation have the capability to see that the policy is fully effected.

Second, because incentives create economic gains that can be captured by both parties, policymakers should recognize that incentives are more successful when domestic partners can be identified and mobilized in support of the strategy and societal groups actually or potentially adverse to the policy can be compensated materially or placated politically. Likewise, incentives work well at home for the sender to the extent they can be promulgated to appeal beyond narrow economic or political gain to broadly held ideals or aspirations. As discussed below, this favoring condition may be an impediment to the policy's success to the extent that keeping an incentives policy quiet permits the recipient greater freedom to accommodate the sender's wishes without creating impressions in *its* domestic society that it is capitulating to foreign influence.

Paradoxically, because incentives often create economic gains for the sender and gather support in the sender society over time, they may eventually shift some influence back to the recipient. After the initial establishment of incentives programs, the recipient society's interest in maintaining incentives may limit the sender state's flexibility in rescinding benefits, thus diminishing its influence vis-à-vis the recipient state. The American difficulty in making a credible threat to China over the possible withdrawal of its MFN status post-Tiananmen is an example of the sender state becoming captive to its own policy.

Domestic conditions favoring or disfavoring successful operation of incentives in the recipient state are also critically important considerations for policymakers. Because incentives create partners in the recipient state who favor executing the incentives policy and will, therefore, exert pressure in the recipient state for the desired political adaptation, policymakers should identify and target those groups in the recipient state that have an economic or political stake in the acceptance, continuation, or expansion of an economic incentive. These allies may be private groups—the civilian power industry in Sweden that sought the latest and cheapest technology and nuclear fuel, for example—or state actors—such as modernizers in China or political and economic liberals in the CSFR. In general, incentives work better when important allies in the recipient state help sell the desired policy adaptation to, or within, the recipient's government.

In deciding how much visibility to give to an incentives strategy, policymakers should consider the need for public support for cooperative adjustment in the recipient state. It may be necessary to balance the advantages of publicity at home against the recipient state's need for discretion. In certain situations, casting cooperative adjustment as harmony ("we are acting only in the interest of China, not in response to foreign pressure") may be beneficial for the recipient government's image. Alternatively, publicizing an incentive may carry important symbolic value that the recipient can use to bolster its domestic legitimacy. For example, the new CSFR government craved recognition and acceptance by the West and was not adverse to the image that it was paying the political dues necessary to join the club. Generally, incentives may work best when both the sender and the recipient can use the policy for public propaganda purposes or to bolster their self-images.

The theoretical argument also hypothesizes as to the superior communication potential of incentives relative to sanctions. Policymakers should make the most of this function by delivering a message of desired policy adaptation. It may be advantageous to make the desired adaptation quite specific, for example, the requirement that the CSFR develop a minimally acceptable level of internal controls on imported technology, or more diffuse, the desire for Chinese cooperation across a broad spectrum of political and strategic issues. The cases are too few to suggest when demands should be more specific or more diffuse, but because incentives can give a precise and nonthreatening signal of the desired policy adaptation, the sender should be clear and purposeful as to its message.[107] The U.S.-Iraq situation before the Gulf War, although not examined in this study, may illustrate the danger of an incentives policy in which the sender had muddled or ignored the communication function of incentives.

How do incentives compare in effectiveness with other policy instruments? Although the chief purpose of this study is to suggest how and when incentives work, rather than how well, the cases allow us to speculate in a preliminary way on the question of the efficacy of economic incentives. The cases suggest that incentives may, in some situations, work relatively well in fostering bilateral cooperation and at reasonable cost. Like most economic instruments, the cost of economic incentives is generally far lower than the cost of military statecraft. Moreover, as noted, the material costs of incentives may be lower still than the cost of other forms of economic statecraft, such as sanctions. To the extent that policymakers seek efficient policies, much commends economic incentives.

Incentives' potential as a tool of long-run cooperation is in contrast to sanctions, which serve other goals somewhat better. Sanctions are valuable instruments for indicating a sender's displeasure, blocking a target's actions or increasing its costs in the short term, satisfying a sender's desire for justice or revenge, demonstrating outrage or resolve to foreign audiences, or fulfilling a political or a psychological need to "do something" without incurring the cost associated with military intervention. However, if cooperation is the goal, then incentives may be a more appropriate—and available—policy instrument. As discussed throughout this chapter, incentives have several overlooked strengths. Further, incentives do not require the stringent conditions of sanctions—monopoly over targeted trade, asymmetrical dependence, and speed of implementation—to generate some influence in encouraging policy adjustment.

Having given a qualified endorsement of incentives as potentially influential, low-cost policy options, this study also cautions against overestimating the political concessions or degree of cooperation that can be purchased through economic incentives. Each case demonstrates some limit to cooperative influence. In the case of U.S. civilian nuclear technology incentives to Sweden, this factor was one of many at play in influencing the outcome of events. American incentives conditioned the payoff environment facing Swedish decision makers in a way that favored relinquishing its independent nuclear capabilities needed to produce a bomb. Other external factors were also important. At the agent level, the incentive combined with other forces in Swedish domestic policies to influence that country's preferences and choice, but was not uniquely or solely determinative of the outcome.

The China and CSFR cases reveal other limits to the power of incentives. While China moved closer to the United States in several areas of political and strategic importance, cooperative adjustment was uneven and often contentious, perhaps because of its novel and uninstitutionalized nature. Since Tiananmen, U.S. economic measures (both incentives and sanctions) have shown limited ability to influence China's human-rights or arms-sales policies. This apparent decline in U.S. influence suggests several possible limitations to economic incentives. Putting aside the problem of inconsistency in American policy, the recent course of bilateral relations suggests that the influence of incentives may decline over time as vested interests in the sender state vitiate the ability to make a credible threat to withdraw benefits for recipient noncooperation. Further, influence may decline as the recipient's "baseline of expectation" shifts upward over time and what was viewed as a favorable concession in an earlier period is taken for granted in a later period. Finally, it suggests that influence over certain fundamental state preferences may be especially difficult to alter. As the Tiananmen incident demonstrates, China willingly put economic incentives at risk when it suppressed and killed its own people, judging fundamental internal stability was at stake. Certain political concessions are not for sale. The CSFR case, while less dramatic, makes a similar point: that a political concession may be for sale, but the price may be too high for the sender state. The United States failed to dissuade the CSFR from making certain military sales where the political and economic advantages of concluding sales overmatched those of incentives designed to encourage the CSFR to forgo them. Interestingly, CSFR politicians often made clear that the scales would have been tipped the other way had foreign incentives been more substantial. In other words, cooperative concessions on arms sales had their price, but the sender failed to meet it.

Finally, as alluded to above, incentives are ill suited for certain purposes. They are tools for patient and programmatic policies designed to encourage cooperation over the long term. If, instead, the goal is punishment, short-run prevention, or demonstration of resolve, then sanctions are the more appropriate policy choice. Misuse of incentives as ad hoc crisis-management tools or as a substitute for sanctions in deterring unwanted actions can make incentives merely a form of appeasement.

Conclusion

The goal of this study is twofold: first to generate hypotheses on how incentives work in bilateral relations, and second, in light of theory and the cases examined, to suggest when incentives work best as a policy instrument. The theory combines the notion of international exchange of economic benefits for political goods with a set of logically consistent hypotheses on the domestic political economy of incentives. Many of the hypotheses merit further investigation and could be strengthened, refined, or rejected through a "large n" study employing statistical methods. Another avenue of future theoretical investigation could explore the relationship between incentives and other factors that influence cooperative adjustment by looking at incentives cases with more variance on the dependent variable. Unlike this study where the cases were qualified successes, by considering cases of success and of failure one might tease out relationships between incentives and other factors operating at the agent or system level that determine the level of cooperative influence. As the theory of incentives is improved, so too will the generic policy advice that flows from it.

Although this work is concerned with improving our understanding of an independent variable, it also carries implications for those interested in the dependent variable—international cooperation. The chapter suggests that incentives can be an important factor in fostering a degree of bilateral cooperation. To some this assertion is unremarkable, to others contentious. In either event, it has gone largely unnoticed and "undertheorized" in the international relations literature. As discussed, this chapter is an early attempt at such a conceptualization. In addition, by suggesting the potential efficacy of incentives in shaping state behavior, this study commends further investigation not only of incentives, but of other diffuse factors that may contribute to international cooperation. Although not strictly defended in this chapter, the effectiveness of incentives implies that noninstitutionalized cooperation may be more prevalent than previously acknowledged and that diffuse factors (like incentives) can affect interstate cooperation.

To date, much of the literature on factors shaping cooperation has focused intensely on institutionalized forms of cooperation, the role of regimes, and strategies of specific reciprocity. This study suggests that understanding patterns and processes of international cooperation could also benefit by widening the aperture of investigation beyond direct reciprocity and the role of institutions and regimes to look at other factors pertinent to the process of interstate cooperation.

Notes

1. States can also use economic inducements or rewards such as trade or technology transfer more directly as a specific, short-term benefit exchanged for an explicitly delineated response from the recipient. For a review of some of this literature, see R. J. Leng and H. G. Wheeler, "Influence Strategies, Success and War," *Journal of Conflict Resolution* 23 (1979): 655–84; J. S. Fieldstein and J. R. Freeman, *Three-way Street: Strategic Reciprocity in World Politics* (Chicago, Ill: University of Chicago Press, 1991), chap. 1. See also D. A. Baldwin, "Power and Social Exchange," *American Political Science Review* 72 (1978):1229–42; J. Garenta, *Power and Powerlessness* (Urbana, Ill.: University of Illinois Press, 1980); and S. Lukes, *Power: A Radical View* (London: Macmillan, 1974).

2. D. A. Baldwin, "The Power of Positive Sanctions," *World Politics* 24 (1971): 19–38.

3. On this conceptual bias see D. A. Baldwin, *Economic Statecraft* (Princeton, N.J.: Princeton University Press, 1985), 117–18.

4. K. Knorr, *The Power of Nations* (New York: Basic Books, 1975). This claim is raised despite the fact that international trading rules under the General Agreement on Tariffs and Trade recognized the extension of nonreciprocal trade benefits such as the Generalized System of Preferences (GSP), and states have often tied the extension or removal of GSP treatment (or MFN treatment for that matter) to political concessions.

5. Baldwin, *Economic Statecraft*, 46.

6. R. Keohane, *After Hegemony* (Princeton, N.J.: Princeton University Press, 1984), 51.

7. A. Moravcsik, "Preferences and Power in the European Community: A Liberal Intergovernmentalist Approach," *Journal of Common Market Studies* 31 (1993): 52.

8. R. H. Wagner, "Economic Interdependence, Bargaining Power, and Political Influence," *International Organization* 42 (1988): 461–83.

9. Ibid.

10. For economists a society's ability to produce a given level of output from existing factor inputs is dependent on the state of technology. For example, the simple Cobb-Douglas production function is $Q=AL^aK^b$ where output (Q) is a function of labor (L) and capital (K) adjusted for their respective output elasticities $(a$ and b respectively) *multiplied by* the level of technology (A).

11. R. Jervis, "Realism, Game Theory, and Cooperation," *World Politics* 40 (1988): 322.

12. H. Milner, "International Theories of Cooperation among Nations," *World Politics* 44 (1992): 466–97.

13. G. C. Hufbauer, J. J. Schott, and K. A. Elliott, *Economic Sanctions Reconsidered*, 2d ed. (Washington, D.C.: Institute for International Economics, 1990).

14. Ibid.

15. This assertion does not imply that domestic interests will uniformly endorse incentives. Every major policy departure has its legitimate critics and those looking for partisan advantage. Because of their noncoercive character, incentives policies are particularly vulnerable to attack as "weak" responses or as "appeasement." Recent criticism of U.S. incentives policies toward North Korea provide an example. Policymakers may need to take such warnings seriously because, as discussed in a later section of this article, inappropriately applied or executed incentives can lead to appeasement.

16. Hufbauer et al., *Sanctions Reconsidered,* 10; P. Wallenstein, "Characteristics of Economic Sanctions," *Journal of Peace Research* 5 (1968): 248–67; Margaret Doxey, "International Sanctions: A Framework for Analysis with Special Reference to the U.N. and South Africa," *International Organization* 26 (1972): 527–50; J. Green, "Strategies for Evading Economic Sanctions," in *Dilemmas of Economic Coercion: Sanctions in World Politics,* eds. M. Mincic and P. Wallenstein (New York: Praeger, 1983).

17. P. Clawson, *How Has Saddam Hussein Survived?* (Washington, D.C.: National Defense University, 1993); A. P. Schreiber, "Economic Coercion as an Instrument of Policy: U.S. Measures Against Cuba and the Dominican Republic," *World Politics* 25 (1973): 387–413.

18. D. M. Rowe, "The Domestic Political Economy of International Economic Sanctions" (paper prepared for the Annual Meeting of the American Political Science Association, Washington, D.C., 1993), 8–11.

19. Ibid.

20. L. L. Martin, *Coercive Cooperation: Explaining Multilateral Economic Sanctions* (Princeton, N.J.: Princeton University Press, 1992), 3.

21. J. S. Levy, "Prospect Theory and International Relations: Theoretical Applications and Analytical Problems," *Political Psychology* 13 (1992): 284.

22. R. Jervis, *The Logic of Images in International Relations* (Princeton, N.J.: Princeton University Press. 1970).

23. I. L. Janis and L. Mann, *Decision-Making: A Psychological Analysis of Conflict, Choice, and Commitment* (New York: Free Press, 1977).

24. Although misperception does not always lead to noncooperative outcomes, game theory suggests it does when an actor's choice is contingent on the actions of others and the misunderstood actor has a dominant strategy of noncooperation or is a "tit-for-tat" reciprocator. See A. Stein, "When Misperception Matters," *World Politics* 34 (1982): 505–26.

25. A. Wendt, "Collective Identity Formation and the International State," *American Political Science Review* 88 (1994): 390.

26. J. R. Raser, "Learning and Affect in International Politics," *Journal of Peace Research* 2 (1965): 223.

27. On the possible value of ambiguity in threats and promises see D. A. Baldwin, "Thinking about Threats," *Journal of Conflict Resolution* 15 (March 1971): 75.

28. A. Wendt, "The Agent-Structure Problem in International Relations Theory," *International Organization* 41 (1987): 338.

29. A. L. George, "Case Studies and Theory Development" (paper presented

to the Second Annual Symposium on Information Processing in Organizations, Carnegie Mellon University, 1982); A. L. George and T. J. McKeown, "Case Studies and Theories in Organizational Decision-Making," in *Advances in Information Processing in Organizations,* eds. R. Coulum and R. Smith (Greenwich, Conn.: JAI Press, 1985), 21–58.

30. On this distinction, Keohane argues that "harmony" is "a situation in which actors' policies (pursued for their own self-interest without regard for others) automatically facilitate the attainment of other's goals." Keohane, *After Hegemony,* 51–52.

31. A. Lijphart, "Comparative Politics and the Comparative Method," *American Political Science Review* 65 (1971): 658–86.

32. U.S. National Security Council, *Statement of Policy on Peaceful Uses of Atomic Energy, General Considerations,* Document 5507/2, 12 March 1955, 12.

33. U.S. Department of State, "Atomic Energy (Cooperation for Civil Uses)," 1956, TIAS no. 3477, *U.S. Treaties and Other International Agreements,* vol. 7, pt. 1.

34. D. Burn, *The Political Economy of Nuclear Energy* (London: The Institute of Economic Affairs, 1967), 11.

35. G. Quester, *The Politics of Nuclear Proliferation* (Baltimore, Md.: Johns Hopkins University Press, 1973), 19; W. Walker and M. Lonnroth, *Nuclear Power Struggles* (London: Allen & Unwin, 1983), 25.

36. U.S. Atomic Energy Commission, "International Cooperation in the Peaceful Uses of Atomic Energy through the Instrument of the Bilateral Agreement for Cooperation," *Review of the International Atomic Policies and Programs of the United States,* vol. 2, U.S. Congress, Joint Committee on Atomic Energy, 86th cong., 2d sess., 1960, 130–31, 163, 185, 271, 279, 358–59.

37. U.S. Department of State, "Atomic Energy (Cooperation for Civil Uses)," 1966, TIAS no. 6076, *U.S. Treaties and Other International Agreements,* vol. 17, pt. 1.

38. T. B. Johansson, "Sweden's Abortive Nuclear Weapons Project," *The Bulletin of the Atomic Scientists* 42, no. 3 (1986): 33; M. Reiss, *Without the Bomb: The Politics of Nuclear Nonproliferation* (New York: Columbia University Press, 1988), 39.

39. W. Agrell, "The Bomb That Never Was: The Rise and Fall of the Swedish Nuclear Weapons Programme," in *Arms Races: Technological and Political Dynamics,* eds. N. P. Gleditsch and O. Njølstud (Oslo, Norway: International Peace Research Institute, 1990).

40. L. Wallin, "Sweden," in *Security with Nuclear Weapons: Different Perspectives on National Security,* ed. R. Cowen Karp (Stockholm: Stockholm International Peace Research Institute and Oxford University Press, 1991), 361; Agrell, "The Bomb That Never Was," 157.

41. Johansson, "Sweden's Abortive Nuclear," 31–34; C. Larsson, "History of the Swedish Atomic Bomb, 1945–1972," *Ny Teknik* (April 1985).

42. J. H. Garris, "Sweden and the Spread of Nuclear Weapons: A Study in Restraint" (Ph.D. diss., University of California, Los Angeles, 1972), 43.

43. M. Fehrm, "Sweden," in *Nuclear Non-proliferation: The Why and the Wherefore,* ed. J. Goldblat (London: Taylor & Francis, 1985), 213–14.

44. Agrell, "The Bomb That Never Was," 159.

45. Ibid., 161–62.

46. Johansson, "Sweden's Abortive Nuclear," 33.

47. To generate the plutonium-239 necessary for weapons, the government relied on secret plans designated the "L-Program." The L-Program envisioned weapons-grade plutonium from the Agesta and Marviken plants. See P. A. Cole, "Neutralité du Jour" (Ph.D. diss., Johns Hopkins University, 1990), 386.

48. Agrell, "The Bomb That Never Was," 167.

49. Larsson, "History of the Bomb."

50. James Jasper, *Nuclear Politics: Energy and the State in the United States, Sweden, and France* (Princeton, N.J.: Princeton University Press, 1990), 67. Swedish power industry representatives frequently visited their American counterparts in the early 1960s to keep track of light water developments. Interview data, Stockholm, 10 September 1992.

51. I. C. Bupp and J. Derian, *Light Water* (New York: Basic Books, 1978), 64–65.

52. Garris, "Sweden and the Spread," 290.

53. O. Gimstedt, "Three Decades of Nuclear Power Development in Sweden," in *Nuclear Power Experience: Proceedings of an International Conference on Nuclear Power Experience* (Vienna: International Atomic Energy Agency, 1983), 133–34.

54. Ibid.

55. Garris, "Sweden and the Spread," 358.

56. Johansson, "Sweden's Abortive Nuclear," 32.

57. Quester, *Politics of Nuclear Proliferation,* 129.

58. Garris, "Sweden and the Spread," 388–89.

59. S. G. Seabolt, "United States Technology Exports to the People's Republic of China: Current Developments in Law and Policy," *Texas International Law Journal* 19 (1984): 599–600; P. M. Evans, "Caging the Dragon: Post-War Economic Sanctions Against the People's Republic of China," in *The Utility of International Economic Sanctions,* ed. D. Leyton-Brown (New York: St. Martin's Press, 1987), 59–86.

60. Evans, 59–60.

61. House Committee on Foreign Affairs, *United States-China Relations: A Strategy for the Future,* 91st Cong., 2d sess. 6 October 1970, 290.

62. "Shanghai Joint Communiqué," *Weekly Compiled Presidential Documents* 8 (Washington, D.C.: Office of the Federal Register, 1972), 473.

63. During the 1970s, the United States accounted for only 3 percent of China's foreign trade. After three years of rapid growth following the resumption of commercial relations, U.S. exports to China actually declined during the period between 1974 and 1977, and a two-way trade did not surpass one billion dollars until formal diplomatic recognition on 1 January 1979. See J. Tsao, *China's Development Strategies and Foreign Trade* (Lexington, Mass.: Lexington Books, 1987), 92.

64. C. Qiwei, "Why Is China Opening to the Outside?" *Beijing Review* (April 1985): 18–22.

65. Z. Brzezinski, *Power and Principle: Memoirs of the National Security Advisor*

1977–1981 (New York: Farrar, Straus, and Giroux, 1983), 403; C. Vance, *Hard Choices: Critical Years in American Foreign Policy* (New York: Simon and Schuster, 1983), 76.

66. M. Oksenberg, "A Decade of Sino-American Relations," *Foreign Affairs* 61, no. 1 (1982): 178.

67. "Chinese Trade Pact Is Sent to Congress," *New York Times,* 24 October 1979.

68. Tsao, *China's Development Strategies,* 96.

69. Oksenberg, "Decade of Sino-American," 190.

70. *Technology Transfer to China,* Office of Technology Assessment, U.S. Congress (Washington, D.C.: GPO, 1987), 206.

71. T. Qingshan, *The Making of U.S. China Policy* (Boulder, Colo.: Lynne Rienner Publishers, 1992), 13–14.

72. B. Cummings, "The Political Economy of China's Turn Outward," in *China and the World,* 2d ed., ed. S. Kim (Boulder, Colo.: Westview, 1989), 222.

73. H. Harding, *China's Second Revolution* (Washington, D.C.: The Brookings Institution, 1987), 238–44.

74. R. Sullivan, "The Nature and Implications of United States-China Trade toward the Year 2000," in *China's Global Presence,* eds. D. Lampton and K. Keyse (Washington, D.C.: American Enterprise Institute, 1988), 156.

75. K. Lieberthal, "Domestic Politics and Foreign Policy," in *China's Foreign Relations in the 1980s,* ed. H. Harding (New Haven, Conn.: Yale University Press, 1984), 63.

76. H. Harding, "China's Changing Roles in the Contemporary World," in *China's Foreign Relations,* ed. H. Harding, 194.

77. C. L. Hamrin, "China Reassesses the Superpowers," *Pacific Affairs* 56, no. 2 (1983): 209–25.

78. J. Pollack, "China and the Global Strategic Balance," in *China's Foreign Relations,* ed. H. Harding, 81–82.

79. H. Harding, "China's Changing Roles," 195.

80. C. L. Hamrin, *China and the Challenge of the Future* (Boulder, Colo.: Westview, 1990), 86.

81. R. Sutter, "Realities of International Power and China's 'Interdependence' in Foreign Affairs," *Journal of Northeast Asian Studies* 3, no. 4 (1984): 21.

82. J. Garver, "Peking's Soviet and American Policies: Toward Equidistance," *Issues and Studies* 24, no. 10 (1988): 59–60.

83. R. Sutter, *Sino-Soviet Relations: Recent Improvements and Implications for the United States,* Library of Congress, Issue Brief 86138 (1986): 9, 11.

84. N. Chanda, "Superpower Triangle," *Far Eastern Economic Review* 128, no. 13 (1985): 17–18; Chanda, "No Boat to China," *Far Eastern Economic Review* 128, no. 21 (1985): 14–15; Chanda, "Ships That Pass . . . ," *Far Eastern Economic Review* 132, no. 21 (1986): 32.

85. R. Sullivan, "Nature and Implications of U.S.-China Trade," 159.

86. H. Harding, *China's Second Revolution,* 254.

87. S. Dryden, "Banking and Credit," in *The Post-Containment Handbook,* ed. R. Cullen (Boulder, Colo.: Westview, 1990), 19.

88. See J. Baker, "From Revolution to Democracy: Central and Eastern Europe in the New Europe: *U.S. Department of State Dispatch* 1 (1990): 12–13. IMF disbursements to Czechoslovakia in 1991 totaled $1.3 billion, those from the Bank for Reconstruction and Development totaled $300 million, and disbursements from the European Community equaled $200 million. In April 1992, the IMF made a $3.3 billion loan to the CSFR, a vote of confidence in its economic reforms.

In September 1990, the United States waived the Jackson-Vanik amendment opening the way for MFN status. By the following spring, the two countries entered into a landmark bilateral trade agreement that eliminated the Jackson-Vanik requirement of annual certification of free emigration. The U.S. General Accounting Office estimated that granting MFN status to Czechoslovakia would reduce the weighted average U.S. tariff rate on dutiable products from 29.5 percent to an estimated 5.2 percent.

Economic assistance included technical aid, private sector economic assistance from a $370 million fund committed to Central and Eastern Europe, and U.S. urging of the World Bank to lend $5 billion to Central and Eastern Europe and an additional $9 billion over the following three years. By first quarter 1992, the U.S. Agency for International Development reported that assistance obligations to Czechoslovakia—primarily in the form of technical assistance—totaled $86.5 million. The U.S. State Department estimated that U.S. assistance and progress in negotiating an investment treaty helped generate about $1.5 billion in direct investment by U.S. companies during late 1991 and early 1992.

Investment guarantees and credits: Czechoslovakia was made eligible for export credit guarantees of the U.S. Export-Import Bank and Commodity Credit Corporation (for agricultural sales). In October 1991, the two countries entered into a bilateral agreement on investment that was ratified by their respective legislatures the following year.

High technology: At a June 1990 high-level meeting, COCOM limited the scope of export controls to East European destinations and moved from a policy of general denial of high-tech exports to a policy of assumed approval. In November 1990, the United States and the CSFR concluded a memorandum of understanding whereby the United States agreed to decontrol high-technology exports to the CSFR and the CSFR would, in exchange, create and implement its own system of technology controls that met the goals of COCOM. In early 1991, COCOM ratified "favorable consideration" treatment for the CSFR allowing it expeditious access to virtually all high technology in recognition of its efforts to set up national technology control systems to prevent the diversion of Western high-technology exports to proscribed destinations.

Trade and investment growth: In the years 1990 and 1991, two-way trade between the United States and Czechoslovakia increased over 50 percent from $178 million to $268 million. During the first nine months of 1992, Czech imports from the United States rose an additional 25.5 percent to $199 million, while exports to the United States jumped 74.9 percent to $139 million.

89. U.S. House, *Approval of Extension of Most-Favored-Nation Treatment to Czechoslovakia,* 101st Congress, 2d sess., 15 November 1990, 1.

90. M. Svek, "Czechoslovakia's Velvet Divorce," *Current History* 91 (1992): 376.

91. F. T. Miko, "Parliamentary Development in the Czech and Slovak Federal Republic," *CRS Review* (July 1991): 35–37.

92. R. Cupitt, "Export Controls: The Perspective of the Czech and Slovak Federal Republic," in *International Cooperation on Nonproliferation Export Controls,* eds. G. Bertsch, R. Cupitt, and S. Elliott-Gower (Ann Arbor, Mich.: University of Michigan Press, 1994), 89.

93. Ibid.

94. *CSTK,* "Document on Arms Transfers Approved" (30 January) in FBIS-EEU-92–021, 31 January 1992.

95. Svobodne Slovo, "No Objections to Total Ban on Chemical Weapons" (25 October) in FBIS-EEU-90-212, 1 November 1990.

96. "U.S., Other Nations Reach Agreement on Restricting Nuclear Weapons Exports," *International Trade Reporter* 9 (1992): 435.

CTK, "Czech Envoy Supports Global Nuclear Test Ban" (11 January) in FBIS-EEU-90-012, 17 January 1991.

97. *CTK,* "Cabinet Joins Arms Embargo, Addresses Reforms" (11 July) in FBIS-EEU-91-134, 12 July 1991.

98. Under these agreements, Czechoslovak forces would be reduced by 1,600 tanks, 2,309 armored vehicles, 2,335 artillery systems, and 24 combat airplanes, whether through destruction or export. These reductions were from an existing stock of 3,315 tanks, 4,503 combat vehicles, 3,485 artillery systems, and 446 fighter planes.

99. The Czech Republic passed such a law in early 1994, although, at that time, Slovakia had not.

100. *Mlada Fronta Dnes,* "Calfa Interviewed on Arms Trade, Policy" (5 March) in FBIS-EEU-92-047, 10 March 1992, 11–14; Cupitt, "Export Controls," 92.

101. I. Lamper and V. Mlynar, "Klondike: Czechoslovakia Trade in Arms," *Respekt* (27 January) in FBIS-EEU-92–023, 4 February 1992, 10–16; *Mlada Fronta Dnes,* 11–14.

102 *Mlada Fronta Dnes,* "Calfa Interviewed," 12.

103. *Pravda Daily,* "Meciar Concerned about Hungarian Arms Buildup" (6 January) in FBIS-EEU-93–005, 8 January 1993.

104. J. L. Graff, "Confronting a Tankless Task," *Time* (17 June 1991).

105. A. L. George, *Bridging the Gap* (Washington, D.C.: United States Institute of Peace Press, 1993), xvii.

106. D. A. Baldwin, "Inter-nation Influence Revisited," *Journal of Conflict Resolution* 15 (1971): 477.

107. Baldwin, *Economic Statecraft,* 371. Some have argued that influence attempts based on vague demands may be more successful than those based on specific demands. See T. Shelling, *Arms and Influence* (New Haven, Conn.: Yale University Press, 1966), 84–85; R. Jervis, *The Logic of Images in International Relations* (Princeton, N.J.: Princeton University Press, 1970), 123–30; and Baldwin, "Thinking about Threats," 75–76.

Part Three

Regional Conflict Resolution

5

Carrots and Cooperation: Incentives for Conflict Prevention in South Asia

David Cortright and Amitabh Mattoo

I N 1990, SOUTH ASIA may have come perilously close to the brink of nuclear war. In the midst of an intensifying wave of insurgency in Kashmir, Indian and Pakistani military officials reportedly began preparations
to equip their military forces with nuclear weapons. Richard J. Kerr, then
deputy director of the U.S. Central Intelligence Agency, called the confrontation "far more frightening than the Cuban missile crisis," the closest
the world had ever come to an actual nuclear exchange.[1] Top Indian and
Pakistani officials have denied that such a crisis took place, but at least one
former high-ranking Indian officer reported in 1995 that the possibility of
a Pakistani nuclear strike was taken very seriously at the time.[2] The last
word on the 1990 crisis has not been written, but the incident illustrates
the high stakes involved and the importance of the region to U.S. security.

Few conflicts in the world have proved as intractable and threatening to
world peace as the hydra-headed hostility between these two nuclear-capable neighbors of South Asia. The last fifty years have witnessed three major
wars and numerous incidents of heightened tension.[3] Since 1989 the two
countries have been locked in a bitter proxy war in the disputed state of
Jammu and Kashmir that has taken more than 10,000 lives and forced
300,000 residents to flee.[4] Diplomatic relations between the two countries
have been at a very low ebb, with neither New Delhi nor Islamabad willing
to make serious moves toward reconciliation. As a task force of the Coun-

cil on Foreign Relations observed, "Indo-Pakistani relations are less extensive than were those between the United States and the Soviet Union at the height of the cold war."[5] In these circumstances, the involvement of outside powers can play an important role in reducing tension and encouraging cooperation between the two countries.

This chapter outlines a series of steps that can contribute to the prevention and resolution of conflict in South Asia. It is written not as a conceptual analysis of inducement strategies in general but as a series of specific proposals for international policy, particularly U.S. policy. Historical examples are examined, but the main emphasis is on the need for a new diplomatic approach to the region. Our conclusions are unambiguous: carrots will work better than sticks. Incentives for South Asia have been effective in the past and are likely to succeed in the future. Sanctions and coercive measures have usually failed.

Incentives have been used previously to serve cold war purposes. India remained a reliable ally of the Soviet Union through the 1970s and 1980s partly due to the incentives offered by Moscow. Massive military assistance was provided on soft rupee-ruble terms (the total amount of Soviet aid from 1960 to 1993 was valued at 16.9 billion rubles), and Moscow gave consistent diplomatic support for India's position on Kashmir in the United Nations Security Council.[6] In turn, India signed the 1971 Treaty of Peace, Friendship, and Cooperation with Moscow that eroded the credibility of its nonaligned posture. Similarly, Pakistan's strategic alliance with the United States through the 1980s had much to do with the military hardware and foreign aid that Washington lavished upon Islamabad, as well as the political support given to the military regime then in power. Admittedly, other factors were also responsible for these close ties, but incentives reinforced and cemented the common interests and significantly modified the political behavior of both India and Pakistan.

Is it possible to offer incentives now that foster cooperation rather than confrontation, that seek to resolve regional tensions rather than heighten them? While recognizing that the complexities of the Indo-Pakistan conflict do not favor easy solutions, we nonetheless believe that external actors can play a vital role in building a culture of peace in South Asia. This chapter begins with a review of past influence attempts and why they have so often failed. We then examine new approaches to nonproliferation policy, both positive and negative, and present the results of recent surveys of Indian and Pakistani public opinion. Next we explore the strategy of commercial engagement with the region that we believe can become a constructive tool for enhancing cooperation. We conclude with a review of the conflict in Kashmir and a plan for preventing this disputed region from becoming the flash point of nuclear war.

Appreciating South Asia

The most important first step in forging a successful new relationship with India and Pakistan is the conceptual one. Without a new appreciation of the significance of the region, the United States can never hope to fashion a constructive relationship. As a study commission of the Asia Society recently observed: "South Asia's fate will increasingly influence the world Americans and others live in. It is a region where the issues likely to dominate international relations in the 21st century come together, and where 20 percent of humanity lives."[7] Ethnic conflict, nuclear proliferation, great power competition, extremes of poverty and underdevelopment, burgeoning population growth, environmental crisis—all of these challenges come together in the crucible of South Asia. The Council on Foreign Relations report warned that the region's combination of large, nuclear-capable armed forces and deeply rooted ethnopolitical tensions "could prove explosive."[8] The United States can no longer afford to minimize its involvement in the region or treat developments there as mere appendages of geopolitical contests elsewhere.

Despite the many problems of the region, new opportunities have emerged in recent years for constructive engagement.[9] The end of the cold war has eliminated India's diplomatic dependence on the Soviet Union and created a desire for improved ties with the West. Economic reform, market liberalization, and a more-favorable climate for private investment in both India and Pakistan have created important commercial opportunities. India's enduring democratic character and Pakistan's new, although still imperfect, commitment to democracy also augur well for a more hopeful relationship with the United States. Not since the time of Indian and Pakistani independence have the prospects for friendship with the United States been greater.

A new U.S. policy toward South Asia must rest on an appreciation of the region's distinct cultural heritage. As a country with a rich and ancient civilization dating back thousands of years, India sees itself as a great nation with a rightful claim to leadership in the world community. Both India and Pakistan forged their national identities in the long struggle against British colonialism. The humiliating and degrading experience of foreign domination, and the fight against it, have left an indelible mark on the political consciousness of the people of South Asia. The spirit of anticolonialism and resentment against attempts at external control are deeply rooted in both Indian and Pakistani culture. Any attempt to influence South Asia must be acutely sensitive to this postcolonial consciousness.[10]

Broken Sticks: Past Efforts to Influence South Asia

South Asia has not suffered from a lack of international attention. In the years since independence, India and Pakistan have been subjected to numerous influence attempts by Western nations. The United States and Canada have imposed negative sanctions against India or Pakistan at least eight times, usually with little success. While the threat of more severe measures, what might be called the "shadow of sanctions," may deter extreme steps such as a second nuclear test in India, or missile deployments and fissile material production in Pakistan, many of the specific sanctions efforts of the past have been ineffective.[11] Consider some of the cases. From 1965 to 1967, the Johnson administration imposed sanctions against India by halting the delivery of food aid under the Food for Peace program (PL480). The ostensible purpose was to pressure India into expanding domestic agricultural production, but the real objective was to change New Delhi's stance on the war in Vietnam.[12] Washington's action not only failed to alter India's strong condemnation of the U.S. war effort, but as Lawrence Veit, then U.S. Treasury attaché in New Delhi put it, "the United States reaped a harvest of Indian wrath which endured for more than a decade."[13]

In 1971, the United States unilaterally halted the delivery of $87.6 million in development loans and cut off foreign aid for India after identifying New Delhi as the "main aggressor" in the war against Pakistan. Again, the U.S. action had no impact on actual policy and did not prevent India's armed forces from routing Pakistan and helping to establish an independent Bangladesh. As one commentator pointed out: "New AID projects could be stopped. Private statements could be issued. But there was no way to favorably influence the course of major events in the subcontinent, and that presumably was the object of American policy. Mrs. Gandhi had won."[14]

In 1974, after India tested a nuclear device, Canada imposed sanctions on both India and Pakistan. The Canadians suspended all nuclear cooperation with the two countries. The nuclear programs of both countries faced some difficulties and Pakistan's program was temporarily stalled, but there was no discernable change in the long-term commitment of New Delhi and Islamabad to acquire nuclear weapons capability.[15]

Positive measures have also been applied in South Asia, although these have often been used in a coercive manner, turning carrots into sticks. India has been one of the largest recipients of foreign aid of any nation on earth, although the amounts have been relatively small when calculated on a per capita basis.[16] At one time during the 1960s, the United States provided more than half of all development assistance to India, but the levels of aid have dwindled recently to very meager levels.[17] In fiscal year 1993,

U.S. aid to India, excluding PL480 allotments, was a mere $24.7 million. This was the third-lowest amount given to any nation, with only Cyprus and Panama ranking below India.[18] Aid policy to India has also been subjected to congressional attempts to impose restrictions and conditions. In 1991, the House of Representatives passed the Lagomarsino amendment (named for the Republican Congressman from California) cutting off aid to India unless it terminated its nuclear weapons program. This provision would have extended to India the same restrictions that apply to Pakistan under the Pressler amendment, which cuts off aid unless the president certifies that Pakistan does not possess a nuclear explosive device.[19] In 1992, the House approved the Burton amendment (named for the Republican Congressman from Indiana) reducing aid to India as a punishment for New Delhi's crackdown in Punjab and Kashmir. Neither of these efforts was successful, in part because Congress was unable during these years to pass a foreign aid authorization bill. The debate was followed closely in India, however, and fueled resentment against the United States.

U.S. aid policy toward Pakistan has also been erratic and counterproductive. When Islamabad's help was needed during the 1980s to counter the Soviet invasion of Afghanistan, Washington showered Pakistan with military and economic assistance. From 1982 to 1990, the United States provided Islamabad $5.4 billion in mostly military aid.[20] The country served as a virtual launching pad for extensive covert operations and military support for the Afghan rebels. In the process, previous U.S. concerns about nuclear proliferation and human rights violations by Pakistani leaders were ignored. The Pakistani armed forces and some political elites benefited during this period, but the country as a whole suffered. Pakistan remained one of the most underdeveloped nations on earth, ranking 144 out of 170 nations on the Physical Quality of Life index, below nations such as Bangladesh and Haiti.[21]

In 1990, following Soviet withdrawal from Afghanistan, the Bush administration reversed course and refused to certify Pakistan's nonnuclear status, leading to an abrupt cutoff of aid under the Pressler amendment. The result was a serious deterioration of U.S.-Pakistani relations. A classic rally-around-the-flag effect ensued, with government spokespersons and opposition groups alike attacking U.S. policy to show their patriotic credentials.[22] The aid cutoff created a widespread sense of victimization and outrage at unequal treatment. Why was this policy directed only at Pakistan, many asked, when India has a larger and more developed nuclear program? Why were other de facto nuclear powers, most particularly Israel, ignored?

The end result of this on again, off again policy has been the alienation of many sectors of Pakistani society. The armed forces and military elites remain skeptical and suspicious of Washington. Weak civilian governments plead for a renewal of U.S. aid. The beleaguered forces of civil society are ignored in their campaigns for democratic reform. As in India, U.S. policy seems to have created the worst of both worlds—an inability to achieve the desired goals, combined with widespread resentment and animosity among domestic political constituencies.

New Approaches to Nonproliferation

Until recently, Washington's attempts to prevent nuclear proliferation in South Asia have relied primarily on negative pressures, including technology restrictions, aid cutoffs, and conditions on development assistance. Some nonproliferation experts have urged an even tougher approach, demanding that New Delhi be forced to choose between "bombs or breakfast."[23] But excessive pressures could make matters worse by provoking a right-wing upsurge. Nationalist groups such as the Bharatiya Janata Party (BJP) have gained ground recently, and they could seize upon further Western pressures to rally additional political support. The BJP emerged as the largest vote getter in 1996 national elections. Leaders of the BJP have openly advocated a nuclear weapons capability for India, and during the brief BJP-led government in May 1996, Prime Minister A. B. Vajpayee reiterated his party's intention to pursue overt weaponization.[24] Hard-line policies from the West would reinforce nationalist tendencies not only in the BJP but in the Congress Party as well.

In light of these circumstances, positive measures are likely to be more effective than continued negative pressures. We endorse the recommendation of the Council on Foreign Relations task force for a new U.S. policy of greater engagement toward India and Pakistan. The task force report criticized nonproliferation sanctions as achieving only "modest success at best" while constricting bilateral relations generally and undermining other U.S. interests in the region. "The most sensible alternative U.S. policy," according to the report, "would be to engage both countries more rather than less."[25]

Along with a change of method must come a change of direction. Washington's previous emphasis on persuading India to accede to the Nuclear Nonproliferation Treaty (NPT) was a fruitless exercise that failed to understand New Delhi's long-standing objection to the inequities of the NPT system.[26] As a subgroup of the Asia Society study mission concluded in its 1995 report on nonproliferation, "the straight NPT line has failed to make a dent in South Asia for nearly twenty-five years, and this shows no sign of changing."[27] U.S. policymakers seemed to recognize the futility of focusing on the NPT, and during discussions with India and Pakistan prior to the NPT extension conference in April-May 1995, the State Department did not insist upon accession to the treaty. U.S. officials hoped that New Delhi would sign the Comprehensive Test Ban Treaty in 1996, but a hardening of attitudes on nuclear policy left India on the sidelines (where it was joined by Pakistan). The failure to convince India and Pakistan to join these major arms control initiatives suggests the need for a new, more incremental approach to encouraging arms restraint in the region. One step in this direction might be to facilitate confidence-building measures between India and Pakistan, such as offering technology assistance for permissive action links (PALS) to prevent accidental or unauthorized use of nuclear weapons.[28] The latter step would mean acknowledging, at least temporarily, the de facto nuclear status of the region, but it could provide a measure of safety and help to build the cooperative relations that are necessary for denuclearization.

Some will object to any easing of technology restrictions on India as a setback to nonproliferation policy generally, but it is important to distinguish the proliferation problem in South Asia from the situation in such countries as Iraq.[29] India and Pakistan want friendship with the United States, not hostility. Both states fully accept the sovereignty of the other. India has shown some restraint in its nuclear program by not deploying weapons and not conducting a second nuclear test.[30] Pakistan reportedly has frozen its fissile material production and missile deployment programs and has expressed its willingness to sign the NPT if India will do the same. According to the Council on Foreign Relations task force, "it is important to recognize the considerable restraint both sides have exercised in managing their nuclear affairs."[31] These considerations suggest, according to the Asia Society subgroup, the need for "a U.S. strategy of continued, patient, and constructive engagement."[32]

The negative sanctions of the Pressler amendment have failed to prevent Pakistan from developing a nuclear weapons capability. Unilateral sanctions of this nature are rarely successful and in fact often generate counterproductive resentments.[33] The provisions of the Pressler amendment were eased and waived temporarily through the Brown amendment in 1995 to permit the delivery of a package of conventional weapons. We recommend an indefinite suspension of the Pressler amendment, in parallel with steps to lift technology restrictions to India. We are not suggesting the abandonment of efforts to encourage denuclearization in Pakistan and India. Quite the contrary. Nor do we favor the renewal of arms transfers to the region. Rather, we are proposing a policy that emphasizes positive inducements rather than negative sanctions as the most effective means of achieving nonproliferation goals and resolving regional differences. As outlined below, the lifting of trade and technology restrictions could be included in a package of incentives for resolution of the Kashmir crisis and overall conflict prevention in the region.

The Council on Foreign Relations task force similarly recommended a policy of "real incentives for both countries to restrain their nuclear weapons and missile programs."[34] The task force report argued that the prospects for reversing the de facto nuclear weapons status of the two countries is "extremely unlikely":

> The U.S. should focus instead on establishing a more stable and sustainable plateau for Indian and Pakistani nuclear relations. This would involve concentrating on persuading both countries to refrain from testing nuclear explosives, deploying nuclear weapons, and exporting nuclear weapon- or missile-related material, technology, or expertise. The United States should also urge both countries to refrain from missile deployments and cease unsafeguarded production of fissile material.[35]

We support the task force's call for greater realism and recognize the need to focus, at least over the short term, on capping rather than rolling back the two countries' nuclear weapons programs. But we believe the task force report is too pessimistic about the long-term prospects for nonproliferation in the region. The report ignores important steps that the United States can take to facilitate denuclearization, most importantly to restrain its own weapons programs and to join with other nuclear weapons states in a program of global disarmament.

It is essential for the United States to broaden the framework of South Asian nonproliferation policy to include China and Russia. It is impossible to isolate concerns in South Asia from the broader international context of nuclear policy, especially in Beijing and Moscow. The goal of U.S. policy, as one scholar put it, should be to "extract as much denuclearization from as wide a region around [South Asia] as possible."[36] The use of incentives in the region and in the broader international framework should aim toward consistent progress on continued nuclear reductions, greater transparency, and additional confidence-building measures.

Russian cooperation could be particularly valuable not only for nonproliferation policy but for general conflict resolution. Moscow's compliance with U.S. efforts to block missile technology transfers to India in 1993 indicates a willingness to cooperate with U.S. aims in South Asia. Russia still exerts considerable influence in India, despite the end of the cold war. Working together the United States and Russia could achieve much in reducing tensions in the region. If the United States and Russia were to expend now even a portion of the effort to influence Pakistan and India that was exerted in the past, the impact could be dramatic.

Part of an enlarged commitment to the region by the United States and Russia could be a package of security guarantees to India and Pakistan. In the trilateral statement in Moscow in January 1994, Russia and the United

States joined together in pledging not to use nuclear weapons against a nonnuclear Ukraine, thereby helping to clear the way for Kiev's accession to the NPT.[37] The situation is not parallel in South Asia, but similar security guarantees might nonetheless play a constructive role. The United States and Russia might join in pledging not to use nuclear weapons against India or Pakistan, in exchange for a series of specific steps (pointedly not including NPT accession) such as a verifiable halt to fissile material production and the opening of additional nuclear facilities to International Atomic Energy Agency safeguards. In addition, the two countries could offer to help guarantee a settlement in Kashmir, as proposed below.

An Explosive Package: Arms for Pakistan

One of the incentives the United States has traditionally used in relations with Pakistan is military assistance. In 1994 the Clinton administration proposed a one-time waiver of the Pressler amendment to allow the transfer of embargoed F-16 fighter jets to Pakistan.[38] The proposal was designed in part to settle a lingering dispute from the 1989 sale of F-16 fighter planes to Pakistan. Islamabad paid $658 million for twenty-eight planes at that time, but the actual transfer of the jets was blocked when the Pressler amendment was invoked in 1990. The status of the F-16 sale remained in limbo thereafter, as successive Pakistani governments demanded either delivery of the planes or return of the money. The Clinton administration's 1994 proposal called for linking the arms transfer to a "verifiable cap" on Islamabad's nuclear program. Congressional leaders refused to support the waiver, however, and Prime Minister Benazir Bhutto declared that Pakistan would "not accept any unilateral pressure . . . on our peaceful nuclear program."[39]

In 1995, the Clinton administration offered a new arms transfer proposal that won approval from the Republican-controlled Congress. The new plan called for selling the embargoed F-16s to a third party, forwarding the proceeds to Islamabad, and delivering a package of military equipment to Pakistan. The arms package included 3 antisubmarine aircraft, 28 surface-to-surface missiles, 360 air-to-air missiles, and a range of artillery, equipment, and ammunition. Authorization for the transfer was provided by the Brown amendment (named for the Republican senator from Colorado) to the 1996 Foreign Assistance Act. Approved by a House-Senate conference committee in October 1995, the Brown amendment permitted delivery of the arms package and allowed future economic aid and the provision of limited military assistance for counterterrorism and other specified purposes.[40] The reaction to the Pakistan arms transfer in New

Delhi was predictably angry, with government officials and opposition leaders alike denouncing the Brown amendment. Foreign Minister Pranab Mukherjee asserted that India would be forced to purchase additional weapons of its own in response.[41] Prime Minister Narasimha Rao charged that the arming of Pakistan would trigger a regional arms race.[42] Leaders of the opposition BJP claimed that Washington was undermining India's military security.[43]

The reaction in Islamabad, while not negative, was hardly enthusiastic. Washington's offer did little to win friends or lessen the country's zeal for nuclear capability. A parliamentary committee in Islamabad issued a report in July coinciding with the Clinton administration proposal that strongly condemned U.S. policy and recommended keeping the nuclear option open. The Foreign Relations Committee in Islamabad criticized Washington's post–cold war approach to Pakistan as "singularly punitive" and a "policy of discrimination."[44] As for the prospects of closer relations between Washington and Islamabad, the report recommended a "handshake but no embrace."[45] It concluded, "we cannot barter away our nuclear capability for the resumption of American aid."

The Clinton White House, like previous administrations, has argued that conventional arms transfers "promote regional stability in areas critical to U.S. interests, while preventing proliferation of weapons of mass destruction."[46] During the 1980s, the Reagan administration made this claim in justifying military aid to Islamabad, arguing that "our security relationship and assistance program are the most effective means available for us to dissuade Pakistan from acquiring nuclear explosive devices."[47] Yet by 1989, CIA director William Webster testified before the Senate Governmental Affairs Committee that "clearly Pakistan is engaged in developing a nuclear capability."[48] And on 23 August 1994, then Pakistani prime minister Nawaz Sharif unequivocally declared at a public meeting that "Pakistan possesses the atom bomb."[49] So much for the effectiveness of U.S. aid in preventing the Pakistani bomb program.

Arms transfers are justified as a means of promoting security, but they can have the effect of fueling regional conflicts and human rights abuses. U.S.-supplied arms comprise a significant proportion (more than 25 percent) of the weapons used in one-third of the ethnic and territorial conflicts now underway in the world.[50] The United States has supplied 44 percent of Pakistan's weapons. Much of this transfer came during a time of military dictatorship and widespread political repression in Pakistan. Washington also supplied a substantial flow of arms through covert operations during the Afghan War. Some of these weapons have since found their way into the hands of Islamic extremist forces in Kashmir and Sikh militants in Punjab.[51]

Military aid to Pakistan also has a counterproductive consequence in

India. Each attempt to provide weapons or military equipment to Islamabad has prompted an outcry from both government and opposition forces in India and has strengthened hard-line tendencies. The carrot that is offered to Pakistan is seen as a stick to India. This is a formula for certain failure. No policy toward South Asia that is seen as advancing the interests of one party to the detriment of the other will succeed in enhancing cooperation and peaceful relations. The United States must turn away from such approaches and find win-win solutions that advance the interests of both sides.

Military Cooperation: Encouraging Restraint?

Washington has sought to influence the armed forces of the two nations through military cooperation agreements. In January 1995, Defense Secretary William Perry signed a security agreement with India that called for military consultations, joint training programs, combined military exercises, and a series of weapons research and production activities.[52] According to Perry, the pact represents "a new era in our security relations" and "opens the door" to improved cooperation in other areas.[53] The State Department initially ruled out arms transfers to India on the grounds that they might "upset the military balance in the region," but a modest sales program has now begun.[54]

The United States also signed a military cooperation agreement with Pakistan in January 1995. On his way to New Delhi, Defense Secretary Perry visited Islamabad to inform Prime Minister Bhutto of the accord to be signed in New Delhi and to revive a program of consultations and joint exercises between the U.S. and Pakistani armed forces that had been suspended with the cutoff of aid in 1990. Like the agreement with India, the revived military cooperation program with Islamabad called for consultations among senior defense officials, exchanges of intelligence information, and joint exercise and training programs.

According to the U.S. State Department, these military cooperation agreements are designed to encourage greater political realism in India and Pakistan.[55] Military officials in both countries will have access to U.S. thinking and supposedly will be encouraged to strengthen procedures for civilian oversight of the military. Cooperation with the United States will also increase the self-confidence of defense officials, according to the State Department, and reduce perceived threat levels.[56] The assumption in Washington is that the new agreements will create a vested interest in the militaries of both sides to maintain good relations with the United States and that this will temper any tendency toward military adventurism.

The problem with this strategy is that providing aid for the military can have negative political consequences, bolstering the power and prestige of the military establishment at the expense of civilian forces.[57] This is a particular problem for Pakistan, where the armed forces have been and remain a dominant force in political life.[58] In India, civilian control of the military is a well-established practice and principle, but in Pakistan military dominance remains acute, especially in foreign and nuclear policy—precisely the areas where U.S. concern is greatest. Any policy that further entrenches the power of the Pakistani military will weaken the forces of civil society and jeopardize the long-term prospects for peace. Washington should use its influence with the armed forces of the two countries to encourage demilitarization, civilian control of the military, and enhanced respect for civil and human rights.

A Permanent Seat on the UN Security Council?

A number of observers have suggested offering India a permanent seat on an expanded UN Security Council as an inducement for denuclearization and cooperative behavior.[59] Because India views itself as a global power and has expectations of international leadership, the argument goes, giving New Delhi a permanent seat on the Security Council would encourage India's sense of global responsibility. In most formulations of this proposal, a seat for New Delhi would be contingent upon India's renouncing the nuclear weapons option.[60] More recently, the disincentive of ruling out a Security Council seat has been proposed as a way of deterring New Delhi from conducting a second nuclear test. Because Pakistan's reaction to a permanent seat for India might be negative, it would be important to gain specific assurances from India for the resolution of differences between the two countries. State Department officials acknowledge that the prospect of a Security Council seat could be a powerful incentive, but they caution that this can only be a vague and oblique inducement at present.[61] The prospect of changing the composition of the Security Council is an extremely complicated and thorny question with wide ramifications for the United Nations system. For the present, the option of a Security Council seat for India remains highly uncertain.

The broader appeal of a global leadership role for India is a significant inducement, however. Whether or not India is included in a restructured Security Council, New Delhi can and should be encouraged to assume greater responsibility in international affairs. India should be given a seat at the table, figuratively if not literally, so that its energies and resources can be harnessed to resolve global problems. Such a process could be used for persuading India to promote greater regional and international cooperation.

Which Incentives Are Most Popular in India and Pakistan?

Two recent surveys of elite public opinion, sponsored by the Joan B. Kroc Institute for International Peace Studies at the University of Notre Dame, provide evidence on the types of incentives and rewards that would most likely increase Indian and Pakistani support for denuclearization. The first survey was conducted by the Marketing and Research Group of New Delhi in September and October 1994. The second study, conducted by Saleem Majid Marketing of Lahore, was published in August 1996. The two surveys are the most comprehensive studies of their kind ever conducted in South Asia. They asked respondents not only about their views on current nuclear policy but also about the factors that might convince them to support alternative positions.[62]

In the Indian study, a majority of respondents (57 percent) supported New Delhi's policy of nuclear ambiguity, that is neither renouncing nor developing nuclear weapons but keeping the option open. Thirty-three percent favored an overt nuclear capability, with only 8 percent opposing the nuclear option. The results of the Pakistan study were remarkably similar: 61 percent supported the official policy of ambiguity, 32 percent favored weaponization, and only 6 percent supported nuclear renunciation. In India, the primary justification for nuclear weapons was the prospect of nuclear capability in Pakistan. When supporters of government policy were asked what could justify India's developing nuclear weapons, 48 percent identified a Pakistani nuclear test. Among nuclear advocates, 54 percent identified the threat from a nuclear Pakistan as the major concern. In Pakistan, support for the nuclear option was similarly based on fear of its neighbor. When supporters of official policy were asked what could justify Pakistan's developing nuclear weapons, the vast majority referred to a possible Indian nuclear test and to India's deployment of ballistic missiles. Among nuclear advocates, 100 percent identified "threats from India" as the major justification. The findings of the two studies confirm that the improvement of relations between India and Pakistan is the key to denuclearization. The findings give impetus to Western efforts to encourage dialogue and cooperation.

For respondents in India, the second most frequently cited justification for developing nuclear weapons was to enhance the nation's status and bargaining position in international affairs. Many Indian elites see nuclear weapons as a currency of power and favor the nuclear weapons option as a way of gaining international prestige. The fact that permanent membership in the UN Security Council is presently reserved for the five officially declared nuclear weapons states no doubt reinforces this impression. The need to dispel this troubling connection between nuclear weapons status and global leadership is an argument for reforming the Security Council to include nonnuclear states such as Germany and Japan, and for conditioning the admission of any additional powers, perhaps including India, on accession to the nuclear Non-Proliferation Treaty. It also strengthens the argument for greater efforts by the nuclear weapons states to de-emphasize the role of nuclear weapons in world affairs. As long as the United States and the other nuclear weapons states cling to these weapons as the ultimate arbiter of power, other nations will seek similar capability. A sustained commitment to denuclearization is needed to reduce and perhaps eventually eliminate the perceived nexus between the bomb and global prestige.

One of the most significant findings of both the Pakistan and India surveys was the overwhelming support among educated elites for global nuclear disarmament. In Pakistan, 97 percent of all respondents favored an international agreement eliminating nuclear weapons. Among Indians, 94 percent expressed support for such a treaty. The prospect of an international nuclear disarmament treaty would be a powerful factor in persuading Indian elites to renounce the nuclear option. When supporters of official policy and nuclear advocates in India were asked what could justify a renunciation of the nuclear option, both groups identified "a time-bound plan for global disarmament" as the most decisive factor. A global disarmament plan would do far more than any other step to convince Indian elites to renounce the nuclear option.

Many in the United States may dismiss such a policy as utopian and unrealistic, but in fact Washington has officially committed itself to this goal several times, most recently at the nuclear Non-Proliferation Treaty Extension/Review Conference in New York in May 1995.[63] As part of the agreement that led to unanimous support for indefinite extension of the treaty, the United States and other nuclear powers approved a document, "Principles and Objectives for Nuclear Nonproliferation and Disarmament," that committed them to achieving worldwide nuclear disarmament. The document reaffirmed Article VI of the NPT, which requires "good faith" negotiations for complete disarmament, and specifically promised "the determined pursuit by the nuclear weapons states of systematic and progressive efforts to reduce nuclear weapons globally, with the ultimate goal of eliminating those weapons."[64] In December 1996, General Lee Butler, former head of the U.S. Strategic Air Command, joined with dozens of other retired general officers to add the voice of military authority to the call for nuclear weapons abolition.[65] Progress toward disarmament in fulfillment of the NPT pledges would significantly advance the international nonproliferation agenda and could have a dramatic impact on ridding South Asia of nuclear weapons.

Technology Transfers: The Need for Realism

A growing number of analysts have concluded that U.S. restrictions on the export of dual-use technologies to South Asia are a significant impediment to U.S.-India friendship.[66] Both India and Pakistan have sought access to U.S. technologies, but exports have been banned for such items as high-speed computers, laser optical devices, cathode ray oscilloscopes, and telecommunications transmission equipment. Lifting these export controls would be a major step toward improved relations and could be offered as an incentive for specific steps to resolve the crisis in Kashmir. The Council on Foreign Relations task force explicitly recommended loosening U.S. constraints on certain dual-use technologies, including computers and peaceful space launch equipment.[67]

Removing technology restrictions makes sense for the simple reason that such controls do not work very well, especially when applied to a vast, diversified country like India.[68] With its large economy, relatively sophisticated scientific infrastructure, and access to markets throughout the world, India is able to acquire the technologies it wants regardless of U.S. export controls. The costs and time involved in developing advanced technologies may be greater under U.S. restrictions than it would be otherwise, but India has usually managed to accomplish its objectives. Indigenous advances in parallel processing, for example, enabled India to overcome the previous U.S. ban on the export of supercomputers. The threat of U.S. sanctions against the Soviet space agency Glavkosmos blocked the export of cryogenic rocket engines to India in 1993, but India's missile and space programs continued to make extraordinary advances.[69] The latter case is particularly instructive. India had a fairly ambitious space program before the Missile Technology Control Regime (MTCR) went into effect in 1987 and, according to Glavkosmos scientists, possessed the ability to produce cryogenic rockets even without Russian assistance.[70] The MTCR may have impeded India's missile programs slightly but it also had the effect of spurring greater self-reliance in rocket production.[71] According to one analyst, U.S. actions in the 1993 incident backfired by arousing nationalist indignation and "may have provided [India] with an excuse to become a full-fledged nuclear power."[72] New Delhi showed its response by testing a medium-range ballistic missile in February 1994. More recently the Indian space agency signed multimillion dollar commercial agreements with the world's largest space telecommunications companies for use of the satellites it will soon begin launching.[73]

We are not suggesting that nonproliferation restrictions be lifted completely. Measures such as the ban on transferring nuclear materials should be retained. The threat of future sanctions, as provided by the 1994 Nuclear Nonproliferation Act, also has some deterrent effect.[74] Under the provisions of that act, the United States would be required to suspend all financial interactions with India or any other country designated as a "nonnuclear-weapon state" if that country were to detonate a nuclear explosive or engage in other acts of proliferation. A nuclear test by India would result in an immediate cutoff of vital U.S. financing and would jeopardize several major investment projects. The potential political and economic costs involved undoubtedly act as a restraint on nuclear decision making in New Delhi. While direct nonproliferation controls remain valuable, we believe that many dual-use technology restrictions have little or no utility. A commitment to lifting these restrictions could create genuine goodwill between the United States and India and open new possibilities for conflict prevention. Specific incentives that the United States and its partners could offer include granting trade licenses similar to the General Cocom Trade (GCT) and General Cooperating Governments (GCG) licenses available to the major industrial countries. These advantages could be offered in the context of an Indo-Pakistani plan for settling the Kashmiri crisis.

The Strategy of Commercial Engagement

It has long been a tenet of liberal democratic theory that the spread of commerce creates the foundations for peace and international cooperation. The nineteenth-century British philosopher, John Stuart Mill, wrote, "It is commerce which is rapidly rendering war obsolete, by strengthening and multiplying the personal interests which are in natural opposition to it."[75] One can be skeptical of grandiose philosophical claims and still grant an element of truth to the assertion that trade creates mutual understanding and interdependence between nations and can strengthen the preference for cooperation. As the volume of commercial interaction between nations grows, so do the prospects for mutual understanding and respect. The interdependence that comes with increased trade, investment, and technology exchange can also increase the impact of incentive offers.[76] Elevating this principle to a strategy of international relations holds enormous promise for enhancing the prospects of cooperative security.

The Clinton administration has embarked on a new initiative in this area known as the Big Emerging Markets strategy. As articulated by former undersecretary of commerce for international trade Jeffrey Garten, the strategy is designed to strengthen U.S. engagement in the ten largest emerging markets among developing nations, of which India is one of the most important. The strategy aims at achieving a convergence of interests with these nations and promoting a broader world community of market economics, democracy, and cooperation.[77] In the specific case of India, the assumption is that India's growing dependence on foreign trade and investment will become an inducement for maintaining stable relations with Pakistan and other neighbors.[78] The Big Emerging Markets strategy draws its inspiration in part from the remarkable commercial interdependence and nonaggressive relations that have evolved among the European Community, the United States, and Japan in recent decades. Is it possible to broaden this "zone of democratic peace" to other parts of the world, based on the special role of regional economic giants? This is the central challenge that the new strategy seeks to address.

The Asia Society study group agrees with this approach and recommended that economic relations be the "focal point of U.S. engagement with the region."[79] The Council on Foreign Relations task force likewise urged stronger U.S. support for economic liberalization in the region.[80] Enhanced economic ties could help to moderate political differences and create greater understanding and cooperation between the United States and South Asia. The resulting economic growth in India and Pakistan would improve the lives of people in the region and begin to ameliorate some of the root causes of conflict such as population growth and poverty.[81]

There is evidence that developing nations committed to economic liberalization and market reform are more likely to favor cooperative security policies. In her study of nuclear nonproliferation, political scientist Etel Solingen found a direct relation between a commitment to economic globalization and denuclearization: "The historical record across regions suggests that where liberalizing coalitions had the upper hand, nuclear policy shifted toward more cooperative nuclear postures. Nationalist-confessional coalitions, in contrast, shied away from any commitments for effective denuclearization."[82] Looking specifically at India and Pakistan, Solingen found that government coalitions committed to economic reform were more likely to favor cooperative security policies. The previous Pakistani governments of Prime Ministers Nawaz Sharif and Moeen Qureshi made gestures toward reduced military spending and regional denuclearization, in part to attract foreign loans and investments.[83] In India, by contrast, the weak coalition government of Prime Minister P. V. Narasimha Rao slowed the pace of economic liberalization and prevented progress toward bilateral cooperation while steadily hardening India's stand on nuclear policy. Many other factors are at work in explaining these policy choices, but Solingen is correct in drawing the connection between a commitment to increased international trade and support for cooperative security policies.

Author Mitchell Reiss has made a similar case in analyzing the reasons why certain nations have decided to roll back their nuclear programs. For

Argentina, Brazil, and South Africa, the decision to temper or eliminate nuclear weapons programs was based on a belief that this would "accelerate and expand commercial interaction with other regional actors and with the industrialized West."[84] Nuclear restraint was seen in part as a strategy to "attract foreign investment and lift multilateral restrictions on sensitive technologies that could be used for economic development."[85] The strategy of commercial engagement seeks to encourage this kind of thinking in South Asia as well.

India's economic liberalization program has greatly facilitated this new approach. The loosening of government controls and the opening of markets have helped to bring about a dramatic improvement in India's economy. In 1991, economic growth was declining, foreign currency reserves plummeting, and inflation soaring. Today India is experiencing solid economic growth, and inflation has moderated. International trade is increasing, and foreign investment is on the rise. The United States has become India's largest source of foreign investment and most important trading partner.[86] According to the Asia Society, direct investment in India rose from a mere $20 million in 1990 to more than $1 billion in 1993. During that year alone, U.S. exports increased by 44 percent.[87] Table 1 shows these trends. Pakistan has also pursued market reforms, although the country's continuing economic difficulties and extreme underdevelopment make the prospects for progress more uncertain.

Pakistan's weaker economic condition suggests that the use of conditionality may be more effective here than in India.[88] The need for foreign

Table 5.1. U.S. Investment and Trade with India and Pakistan

Year	U.S. direct investment position abroad at year end ($ millions)		U.S. trade data total volume of trade exports and imports ($ millions)	
	India	*Pakistan*	*India*	*Pakistan*
1985	383	104	3804.1	1308.3
1986	421	109	3794.4	1154.7
1987	439	161	3994.5	1133.3
1988	436	186	5451.0	1552.8
1989	(D)	177	5772.2	1646.4
1990	372	184	5680.4	1752.2
1991	415	187	5192.5	1612.8
1992	484	245	5696.9	1746.3
1993	611	256	7331.8	1708.5
1994	818	280	7603.5	1729.9

D-Suppressed to avoid disclosure of individual company data.
Source: Bureau of Economic Analysis, U.S. Department of Commerce

aid and investment can serve as a powerful inducement for cooperation and military restraint. In 1992–93, the United States threatened to place Pakistan on the official State Department list of nations supporting terrorism unless Islamabad stopped its aid to Sikh militants in Punjab and reduced its support for Muslim separatists in Kashmir.[89] Such a listing would have impeded Pakistan's efforts to attract loans and investment. Islamabad responded by halting aid to the Sikhs and reducing support for the Kashmiris, although assistance for the latter was shifted to privatized channels. In February 1994, the International Monetary Fund approved a $1.4 billion credit, which was followed by a $2.5 billion loan package from the World Bank, the Asian Development Bank, and others.[90] The international donors conditioned this aid on greater progress toward economic reform and reductions in Islamabad's excessively high military budget, which is nearly two-and-a-half times greater than all health and education expenditures combined.[91] In accepting the 1994 loans and credits, Prime Minister Benazir Bhutto pledged to reduce military spending from 7.9 percent of gross domestic product to 5.4 percent.[92] Islamabad also previously agreed to freeze its uranium enrichment program in the hopes of improving economic and political ties with the United States.[93]

Perhaps the greatest effect of trade liberalization may occur in the region itself. Applying World Trade Organization rules to South Asia may open the door to greater commerce within the region. The nations of the South Asian Association for Regional Cooperation (SAARC) currently trade less than 5 percent with one another. This tragic lack of commercial interaction between India and Pakistan has not only distorted their respective economies but limited social development and compounded problems of misperception. The Council on Foreign Relations task force recommended that the United States provide "direct economic incentives," including U.S. assistance and support for India and Pakistan in international financial institutions, to speed the progress of trade liberalization.[94] If the general system of trade preferences can be fully extended to the region and trade barriers removed, the opening of commerce and communication that would result could have significant benefits, politically as well as economically. Western governments and financial institutions should continue to exert pressure for trade liberalization, especially within the region.

The use of trade preferences and financial conditionality can be an effective incentive, but it must be applied with sensitivity. Heavy-handed pressures on Islamabad or New Delhi could disrupt delicate political balances and strengthen hard-line nationalist forces. There are substantial political and economic interests in both India and Pakistan that benefit from economic reform and improved ties to the United States. These forces will continue to push in the direction of liberalization and reform, but only if they are seen as acting in the national interest, not in response to pressure from the West.[95]

Debt for Disarmament?

The most significant step the United States could take to improve the economic prospects for South Asia would be to join with other industrial nations in easing the region's debt burden. If such action were conditioned on specific steps toward demilitarization and conflict resolution, it could be a highly attractive incentive. The idea of a debt for disarmament swap for South Asia was advanced by Pakistani journalist Haider Rizvi at the Conference on Bombs, Carrots, and Sticks at the University of Notre Dame in 1994. Rizvi suggested that the G-7 nations and international financial institutions agree to write off portions of Pakistan's huge foreign debt in exchange for specific commitments to reduce the burden of military spending and halt the development of nuclear weapons.[96] The Council on Foreign Relations task force also recommended a policy of "debt reduction or forgiveness" toward Pakistan.[97] Pakistan's international debt as of 1993 totaled more than $26 billion, with annual debt service payments of more than $2.4 billion.[98] By offering to forgive part of this debt, lenders would lift a burden on the economy and free resources for human development.

We acknowledge the difficulty involved in operationalizing this concept. Debt-relief strategies are often proposed by development specialists but seldom implemented by financial institutions or governments. Some examples exist, however, suggesting that the method can be applied if the political will exists. During the Gulf War, the U.S.-led coalition was held together with the help of substantial debt forgiveness for Egypt, resulting in a $14 billion reduction of Cairo's international debt obligations.[99] On a more modest scale, debt for nature swaps are helping to preserve forests and natural habitats in Latin America. The approach we are urging would be limited and selective. It would include a pattern of reciprocity, in the manner of the Agreed Framework plan with North Korea, in which incentive measures are linked to specific reform steps.[100] Debt relief for South Asia should be conditioned on specific demilitarization measures and concrete steps to resolve the conflict in Kashmir. The money saved from reduced debt servicing should go entirely to social development. This would greatly benefit the country as a whole, giving special encouragement to democratic reform forces, while diminishing the influence of the military. In this way the proposed policy would benefit Pakistan without threatening India. Indeed such a process might be viewed positively in New Delhi.

A similar policy could be applied to India. Although New Delhi's stronger economic position gives less urgency to the need for debt relief, India nonetheless has a huge external debt (more than $91 billion in 1993) and spends large sums each year on debt servicing ($8.9 billion in 1993).[101] India could benefit greatly from being relieved of these obligations. The same stipulations would need to be applied, requiring military and nuclear restraint and specific steps toward compromise in Kashmir. The funds freed from debt servicing would have to be devoted exclusively to social development. These conditions would help to reassure Pakistan that India's armed forces would not benefit from these financial savings. Conditioning debt relief in both countries on concrete steps toward demilitarization and conflict resolution would greatly improve the security climate in the region and lay the foundation for a more peaceful and secure future.

A Plan for Kashmir

The roots of conflict in South Asia do not lie in the nuclear competition. Nuclear weapons are only the symptom of a much deeper malady. It is the fundamental political animosity between the two nations that motivates nuclear policy, not the other way around. The resolution of that underlying enmity will be necessary to achieve progress toward denuclearization. The ending of the cold war showed that a reduction of political tensions between former adversaries can pave the way for significant nuclear reduction. The same process may be possible in South Asia.

The key to resolving tensions between India and Pakistan lies in a settlement of the dispute over Jammu and Kashmir. If this bitter conflict were resolved, bilateral relations would improve dramatically. India and Pakistan went to war over the region immediately after independence in 1947, and they have remained deadlocked over the divided province ever since. The region has a Muslim majority population but also contains significant minorities of Hindus, Buddhists, and Sikhs. The troubles are centered in Indian-administered Kashmir, where a dozen militant groups are fighting for independence or accession to Pakistan. This is where efforts to resolve the crisis must begin. Once self-governance is achieved there, Pakistan would be under pressure to grant similar autonomy to its Kashmiri territory as well.

We believe that the United States and its allies can play a vital role in defusing this conflict by offering a specific package of economic and political incentives tied to a general strategy for political settlement. India and Pakistan might be prepared to act on Kashmir if offered the right combination of inducements. While Kashmir remains a deeply emotive issue for people in both countries, and India as of now is not willing to accept international mediation, both New Delhi and Islamabad recognize the need for a way out of the present deadlock. Neither side can achieve an absolute victory in Kashmir; nor for domestic political reasons is it possible for either to withdraw completely. Both countries are searching for a solution that may be short of victory but that can be achieved without severe domestic repercussions. There are groups and important individuals on both sides who want to overcome the Kashmir impasse. Inertia and the long legacy of suspicion and hate between the two countries will prevent them from acting in their own best interest. Incentives and pressures from the outside are needed to move the process forward.

We anticipate a three-phase path to peace in Kashmir. The United States and its allies would have a crucial role to play in all three phases, although this involvement should be as low profile as possible, especially in the crucial initial phases. Our vision is of a Kashmir that has been granted maximum autonomy, with soft borders and complete freedom of movement between Indian-administered and Pakistan-administered areas, where Kashmiri aspirations of "azadi," or freedom, are expressed in internationally guaranteed elections to choose their own local leaders. Any long-term settlement of the conflict must promise self-governance for the Kashmiri people, the eventual reunification of Kashmir, and a reassertion of the region's traditional syncretic culture.

Phase One: Catalyst

The United States and its Western allies must begin by offering a substantial package of incentives tied to two specific objectives. The first is to ensure that Pakistan stops providing military support and training facilities for Kashmiri militants. The second is to gain India's approval for elections that would choose Kashmiri representatives to negotiate with the federal government. The incentives to Pakistan might include agreeing to keep Islamabad off the list of states supporting terrorism, along with various kinds of economic assistance. A number of the options mentioned earlier, including debt relief, additional loans and credits, and a suspension of the Pressler amendment, could also be included. Military cooperation might be justified in this instance if it would help to appease right-wing Islamic extremist groups in Pakistan. For India the greatest incentive for granting elections would be Pakistan's decision to stop aiding the militants. Additional steps would be necessary, including the lifting of technology restrictions. The possibility of a seat on the UN Security Council (following a settlement in Kashmir) might also be considered.

Phase Two: Observer

Elections would be held to choose representatives to negotiate with India for the terms of maximum autonomy within Indian-administered

Kashmir. These would not be formal governmental elections, which would have to come later, but an initial testing of the electoral process to select political representatives for the difficult bargaining process that must precede final decisions on governance. The September 1996 balloting in Kashmir was perhaps a small step toward a revival of democracy in the region, but these elections were flawed in many respects and cannot be seen as a substitute for the genuinely free and inclusive political process that will be necessary to help resolve the crisis. To ensure that the balloting we envision is scrupulously fair and carried out without the fear of the gun, India would have to announce a cease-fire and withdraw the extra security forces it has sent to the province since 1990. Pakistan would have to assist in demobilizing guerilla groups. The demobilizations and withdrawals should be monitored by impartial international agencies and respected world leaders. The elections would need to include all sectors of Kashmiri society, with steps taken to ensure that Kashmiris who have fled the province because of the violence can vote and return home safely. The elections themselves should follow a system of proportional representation, with all organizations that get at least half a percent of the vote entitled to representation. This would ensure that Gujjars, Bakerwals, Pandits, and other ethnic groups that traditionally have been excluded are guaranteed a seat at the table. A team of eminent persons and election experts should be accredited to observe and monitor the elections to ensure their fairness.

Phase Three: Guarantor

The representatives selected through secret balloting would then conduct negotiations with the federal government to determine the exact nature of autonomy and to set a timetable for formal elections on the form and content of local governance. We believe that this autonomy should be as expansive as possible. Apart from foreign affairs and defense, the Kashmiris should have virtually complete freedom to run their affairs as they wish. Guarantees for the protection of minority rights would be needed, however, as would protections for Kashmir's traditional secular society. The United States, Russia, and the European Union, acting in concert or through the United Nations, could act as guarantors of these arrangements.

If such a process could be arranged for Indian-administered Kashmir, a similar autonomy plan would be established in Pakistani-administered Kashmir. Border controls between the two Kashmirs would then be abolished, and the region would begin to come together again as one society, still administered between two countries but no longer a source of war and conflict. Over time the proposed settlement would help to usher in a new culture of peace in the region and allow for the consideration of longer-term solutions that would be part of a more stable climate of regional cooperation and economic integration.

We do not deny the extreme difficulty of implementing this or any other plan for solving the Kashmiri crisis. Many scholars and policymakers have noted the apparent intractability of the conflict and the long record of failed attempts at resolution and mediation.[102] In many respects, the conflict has become more difficult in recent years, as the level of violent insurgency has increased and India has sent tens of thousands of additional troops to the region. We believe this is all the more reason for a concerted international campaign to find a solution. The key to resolving the crisis in Kashmir is nurturing a process of internal political legitimacy. A solution must come from within. It cannot be imposed externally. The essential requirement is to encourage a legitimate, nonviolent process of political engagement among the constituencies and political groupings within Kashmir. If the Kashmiri people, through their own internal political processes, can coalesce around this or another settlement plan, the task of outside forces would then be to convince India and Pakistan to accept it. As we have emphasized, however, the United States and its allies could play a crucial role in this regard. The major countries have many carrots to offer and could wield significant influence if they so desired.

The most effective inducement the United States can offer is the general prospect of good relations. The benefits to be gained from friendship with the United States are powerful incentives for both India and Pakistan. Despite political rhetoric to the contrary, enlightened Indians and Pakistanis recognize that the United States is the preeminent arbiter of international affairs, the most important economic and political power on earth. Neither country would gain from a flare-up in regional tensions that soured relations with Washington.[103] The major concerns of each country—economic development, regional security, status and recognition on the world and regional stages—can be significantly influenced by the policies of the United States. This desire for good relations with Washington can be used as an invaluable trump card to encourage cooperation and conflict resolution.

The problem returns to one of perception and commitment. Washington must recognize the legacy of suspicion toward outside powers that exists in the region and work to establish a long-term basis for mutual respect and cooperation. If the United States were to accord South Asia the importance it deserves and use the formidable resources available to broker a settlement, the chances of success would be considerable. By applying intensive diplomatic attention and offering substantial incentives in the form of economic assistance, political support, and security guarantees, Washington could make a significant contribution to settling the crisis in Kashmir and preventing conflict in the region.

Notes

1. Seymour Hersh, "On the Nuclear Edge," *The New Yorker*, 29 March 1993, 56.

2. See Kanti Bajpai and Amitabh Mattoo, "First Strike!" *Pioneer* (New Delhi), 23 April 1995.

3. For a review of the Indo-Pakistani wars, see Sumit Ganguly, *The Origins of War in South Asia: The Indo-Pakistani Conflicts Since 1947* (Boulder, Colo.: Westview, 1994).

4. Analyses of the Kashmir conflict are provided in Raju Thomas, ed., *Perspectives on Kashmir: The Roots of Conflict in South Asia* (Boulder, Colo.: Westview, 1992).

5. Council on Foreign Relations, *A New U.S. Policy toward India and Pakistan: Report of an Independent Task Force,* Richard N. Haass, chairman (New York: Council on Foreign Relations, 1997), 5.

6. Shahid Alam, "Some Implications of the Aborted Sale of Russian Cryogenic Rocket Engines to India," *Comparative Strategy* 13, no. 3 (July–September 1994): 291.

7. The Asia Society, *South Asia and the United States after the Cold War: A Study Mission* (New York: The Asia Society, 1994), vii.

8. Council on Foreign Relations, *A New U.S. Policy,* 23.

9. Ibid.

10. Shekhar Gupta, *India Redefines Its Role,* Adelphi Paper 293 (London: Oxford University Press for the International Institute for Strategic Studies, 1995), 66.

11. This argument was put forward by Professor Kanti Bajpai at a School of International Studies seminar, Jawaharlal Nehru University, New Delhi, India, 14 December 1995.

The eight cases include (1) the U.S. cutoff of food aid to India in 1965–67 over differences on the Vietnam War, (2) the U.S. suspension of development assistance to India in 1971 over the war against Pakistan, (3) Canada's suspension of nuclear assistance to India in 1974 after the Pokhran test, (4) Canada's termination of nuclear assistance to Pakistan in 1974–76 due to a lack of safeguards, (5) the U.S. suspension of nuclear fuel to India in 1978–82 because of insufficient safeguards, (6) the U.S. withdrawal of military aid in 1979–81 to Pakistan because of Pakistan's nuclear program, (7) the U.S. imposition of the Pressler amendment in 1990 cutting off all aid to Pakistan because of Pakistan's nuclear program, and (8) the U.S. efforts to halt Russian missile technology transfers to India in 1993 because of nonproliferation concerns. These cases are drawn in part from Gary Clyde Hufbauer, Jeffrey J. Schott, and Kimberly Ann Elliott, *Economic Sanctions Reconsidered*, vols. 1 and 2, 2d ed. (Washington, D.C.: Institute for International Economics, 1990). See also Neeraj Kaushal, "Peace(s) of Carrot(s): Urging Nuclear Restraint in South Asia," paper delivered at the Conference on Bombs, Carrots, and Sticks: Economic Sanctions and Nuclear Nonproliferation, University of Notre Dame, Notre Dame, Indiana, April 1994.

12. Harold Saunders, a member of Johnson's National Security Council, as quoted in Dennis Kux, *India and the United States: Estranged Democracies, 1947–1991* (Washington D.C.: National Defense Univ. Press, 1992), 260.

13. Ibid.

14. Wayne Wilcox, *The Emergence of Bangladesh*, Foreign Affairs Study Number Seven (Washington, D.C.: American Enterprise Institute, 1973), 52.

15. See Hufbauer et al., *Economic Sanctions Reconsidered*, vol. 2, 373–81.

16. Ira N. Gang and Haider Ali Khan, "Some Determinants of Foreign Aid in India, 1960–85," *World Development* 18, no. 3 (March 1990): 432.

17. Ibid., 433.

18. *Congressional Quarterly*, 2 April 1994, 808.

19. *Congressional Quarterly*, 21 September 1991, 2706.

20. *Congressional Quarterly*, 16 May 1992, 1352.

21. George Thomas Kurian, *The New Book of World Rankings*, 3d ed. (New York: Facts on File, 1991).

22. Haider Rizvi, "The Prospects for Carrots and Sticks in South Asia," Paper delivered at the Conference on Bombs, Carrots, and Sticks: Economic Sanctions and Nuclear Nonproliferation, University of Notre Dame, Notre Dame, Indiana, April 1994.

23. Gary Milhollin, keynote address delivered at the Conference on Bombs, Carrots, and Sticks: Economic Sanctions and Nuclear Nonproliferation, University of Notre Dame, Notre Dame, Indiana, April 1994.

24. Murli Manohar Joshi, former president of the BJP, has said on several occasions that India should develop the bomb. Lal Kishan Advani, the present BJP chief, has been more circumspect in public, but few doubt that a BJP-led government would be more favorable to nuclear development. See Varun Sahni, "Going Nuclear: Establishing an Overt Nuclear Weapons Capability," in *India and the Bomb: Public Opinion and Nuclear Options*, eds. David Cortright and Amitabh Mattoo (Notre Dame, Ind.: University of Notre Dame Press, 1996). See also Brahma Chellaney, "India's New Leader to Deploy Nukes," *Washington Times,* 16 May 1996, 1, 20.

25. Council on Foreign Relations, *A New U.S. Policy,* 4, 25.

26. Ashok Kapur, "Western Biases," *The Bulletin of the Atomic Scientists* 51, no. 1 (January/February 1995): 42.

27. The Asia Society, *Preventing Nuclear Proliferation in South Asia* (New York: The Asia Society, 1995), 27.

28. Amitabh Mattoo, "Prospects for Carrots and Sticks in South Asia," paper delivered at the Conference on Bombs, Carrots, and Sticks: Economic Sanctions and Nuclear Nonproliferation, University of Notre Dame, Notre Dame, Indiana, April 1994, 11.

29. Asia Society, *Preventing Nuclear Proliferation*, 37 (see reference 27).

30. Deepa Ollapally and Raja Ramanna, "U.S.-India Tensions: Misperceptions on Nuclear Proliferation," *Foreign Affairs* 74, no. 1 (January/February 1995): 16.

31. Council on Foreign Relations, *A New U.S. Policy,* 30.

32. Asia Society, *Preventing Nuclear Proliferation,* 37.

33. See David Cortright and George Lopez, "Economic Sanctions in Contemporary Global Relations," in *Economic Sanctions: Panacea or Peacebuilding in a Post–Cold War World?* eds. David Cortright and George Lopez (Boulder, Colo.: Westview, 1995).

34. Council on Foreign Relations, *A New U.S. Policy,* 32.

35. Ibid., 2.

36. Gupta, *India Redefines,* 46.

37. "Trilateral Statement by the Presidents of the United States, Russia, and Ukraine," reprinted in "Select Documents from the U.S.-Russian Summit," *Arms Control Today* 24, no. 1 (January/February 1994): 21.

38. R. Jeffrey Smith, "U.S. Proposes Sale of F-16s to Pakistan," *Washington Post,* 23 March 1994.

39. *Congressional Quarterly,* 9 April 1994, 851.

40. Jonathan S. Landay, "India Cries 'Tilt' after U.S. Aids Pakistan," *The Christian Science Monitor,* 31 October 1995, 1; Council on Foreign Relations, *A New U.S. Policy,* 12.

41. Voice of America broadcast, 31 July 1995.

42. Brahma Chellaney, "Arms Sales Aggravate U.S.-India Ties," *Washington Times,* 23 December 1995.

43. Landay, "India Cries," 8.

44. "Pakistan Must Have Nuclear Option, Committee Says," *Reuters News Reports,* 21 July 1995.

45. Ibid. The phrase "handshake but no embrace" was initially used by Pakistani President Zia-ul-Haq.

46. "Factsheet: Conventional Arms Transfer Policy," White House Press Office, Washington, D.C., 17 February 1995.

47. Quoted from letter to Congress from President Ronald Reagan, required under Sec. 620 E(e) of the Foreign Assistance Act (Pressler amendment), 25 November 1985.

48. "U.S. Aid Policies and Pakistan's Bomb: What Were We Trying to Accomplish," factsheet from Senate Governmental Affairs Committee, Washington, D.C., no date.

49. *The Dawn* (Karachi), 24 August 1994.

50. William D. Hartung, *U.S. Weapons at War: Arms Deliveries to Regions of Conflict* (New York: World Policy Institute, 1995), 1.

51. Ibid., 1, 18.

52. John Burns, "U.S.-India Pact," *New York Times,* 13 January 1995, A-12.

53. Ibid.

54. Interview, David Cortright with Brady Kiesling, 20 July 1995.

55. Ibid.

56. Ibid.

57. David Baldwin, "Foreign Aid, Intervention, and Influence," *World Politics* 21, no. 3 (April 1969): 438.

58. Asia Society, *South Asia and the United States*, 37.

59. Gupta, *India Redefines*, 45; Asia Society, *Preventing Nuclear Proliferation*, 37; Selig Harrison and Geoffrey Kemp, *India and America: After the Cold War* (Washington, D.C.: The Carnegie Endowment, 1993). Stephen P. Cohen has argued that India should receive a permanent Security Council seat, plus missile defense technology, in exchange for denuclearization; see *Washington Post*, 28 September 1993.

60. Asia Society, *Preventing Nuclear Proliferation*, 37.

61. Interview, Brady Kiesling.

62. *India's Nuclear Choices*, report of the Joan B. Kroc Institute for International Peace Studies, University of Notre Dame and the Fourth Freedom Forum, Goshen, Indiana, November/December 1994; and *Pakistan's Nuclear Choices,* the Joan B. Kroc Institute for International Peace Studies, University of Notre Dame and the Fourth Freedom Forum, Goshen, Indiana, August 1996. The Kroc Institute survey results and a series of essays exploring the issues examined are contained in *India and the Bomb*, eds. Cortright and Mattoo, and *Pakistan and the Bomb: Public Opinion and Nuclear Options,* edited by David Cortright and Samina Ahmed (Notre Dame, Ind.: University of Notre Dame Press, forthcoming).

63. For a review of early U.S. commitments to eliminate nuclear weapons, see David Cortright, "The Coming of Incrementalism," *The Bulletin of the Atomic Scientists* 52, no. 2 (March/April 1996): 32–36. Additional pledges after the early 1960s include the following. In the preamble to the Partial Test Ban Treaty of 1963, the United States and other signatories proclaim "as their principal aim the speediest possible achievement of an agreement on general and complete disarmament." In the preamble to the 1972 Treaty on the Limitation of Anti-Ballistic Missile Systems, the United States and the Soviet Union are pledged "to take effective measures toward reductions in strategic arms, nuclear disarmament, and general and complete disarmament." The strongest commitment to nuclear abolition is in Article VI of the 1968 Nonproliferation Treaty, which obligates the United States and other signatories "to pursue negotiations in good faith on effective measures relating to . . . nuclear disarmament, and on a treaty on general and complete disarmament under strict and effective international control." See Joseph Rotblat, "Past Attempts to Abolish Nuclear Weapons," in *A Nuclear-Weapon-Free-World: Desirable, Feasible?* eds. Joseph Rotblat, Jack Steinberger, and Bhalochandra Udgaonkar (Boulder, Colo.: Westview, 1993).

64. "Documents: Resolutions Adopted at the NPT Extension Conference," *Arms Control Today* 25, no. 5 (June 1995): 30.

65. Remarks of General Lee Butler, USAF (ret.), Washington, D.C., National Press Club, 4 December 1996.

66. Asia Society, *South Asia and the United States*, ix; Ollapally and Ramanna, "U.S.-India Tensions," 16; Kapur, "Western Biases," 42.

67. Council on Foreign Relations, *A New U.S. Policy,* 35.

68. Ollapally and Ramanna, "U.S.-India Tensions," 17.

69. Brahma Chellaney, "The Missile Technology Control Regime: Its Challenges and Rigors for India," Paper delivered to the Joint Indo-American Seminar on Nonproliferation and Technology, University of Pennsylvania, Philadelphia, Pennsylvania, 1994.

70. Alam, "Some Implications," 295.
71. Ollapally and Ramanna, "U.S.-India Tensions," 17.
72. Alam, "Some Implications," 295–96.
73. "Space Pacts Boost India," *Aviation Week and Space Technology*, 13 February 1995, 59.
74. Public Law 103–236, 30 April 1994; see Section 102(b).
75. John Stuart Mill, *Principles of Political Economy*, new ed. (London: Longmans Green, 1923), 582.
76. Martin Patchen, *Resolving Disputes between Nations: Coercion or Conciliation?* (Durham, N.C.: Duke University Press, 1988), 327.
77. John Stremlau, "Clinton's Dollar Diplomacy," *Foreign Policy*, no. 97 (Winter 1994/95): 21.
78. Ibid., 29.
79. Asia Society, *South Asia and the United States*, viii.
80. Council on Foreign Relations, *A New U.S. Policy*, 5, 40.
81. Ibid., ix.
82. Etel Solingen, "The New Multilateralism and Nonproliferation: Bringing in Domestic Politics," *Global Governance* 1, no. 2 (May–August 1995): 214.
83. Ibid., 211.
84. Mitchell Reiss, "Nuclear Rollback Decisions: Future Lessons," *Arms Control Today* 25, no. 6 (July/August 1995): 12.
85. Ibid.
86. John Burns, "U.S.-India Pact"; see also David Singer, "In India U.S. Diplomacy Is Sounding a Lot Like Economics," *New York Times*, 23 April 1995, A-12.
87. Asia Society, *South Asia and the United States*, 8.
88. James Clad, "The Aid Lever," *Far Eastern Economic Review* 150, no. 40 (4 October 1990): 24, 32.
89. Ibid., 55.
90. Shada Islam, "Bhutto's Bonus: IMF, Aid Donors Encourage Pakistan to Push Reform," *Far Eastern Economic Review* 157, no. 10 (10 March 1994): 55.
91. Jean-Claude Berthelemy, Remy Herrera, and Somnath Sen, "Military Expenditure Reductions in India and Pakistan: Analytic Perspectives," *Peace Economics, Peace Science, and Public Policy* 2, no. 3 (1995): 22; see also United Nations Development Program, *Human Development Report, 1992*.
92. Islam, "Bhutto's Bonus," 55.
93. Reiss, "Nuclear Rollback," 12.
94. Council on Foreign Relations, *A New U.S. Policy*, 40.
95. Gupta, *India Redefines*, 67.
96. Rizvi, "The Prospects for Carrots and Sticks in South Asia."
97. Council on Foreign Relations, *A New U.S. Policy*, 3.
98. The World Bank, *World Bank Data 1995*, CD Rom, 1996.
99. *The Middle East*, 8th ed. (Washington, D.C.: Congressional Quarterly, 1994), 204.
100. See Scott Snyder's analysis in chapter 3.
101. World Bank, *World Bank Data 1995*, CD Rom, 1996.
102. See, for example, Sumit Ganguly and Kanti Bajpai, "India and the Crisis in Kashmir," *Asian Survey* 34, no. 5 (May 1994): 401–16.
103. Gupta, *India Redefines*, 63.

6

Economic Incentives and the Bosnian Peace Process

Raimo Väyrynen

The Need for a Comprehensive Approach

THE IMPLEMENTATION of the Dayton accord in Bosnia-Herzegovina is a test case on the nature and extent of the international community's influence on intrastate political processes. The cease-fire in Bosnia has required a major effort by governments and international organizations. It is clearly an imposed solution on the parties, which have shown little interest in collaborating with each other and whose attitudes toward external actors depend on expected unilateral gains rather than on goodwill.

Bosnia is a test case in at least two respects: to what extent peace can be externally enforced, and how enforcement should mix constructive and coercive means of influence. My tentative conclusion is that external enforcement is, within limits, possible and even desirable, provided there are sufficient incentives to make the solution attractive, backed by credible threats of the external actors' readiness to use coercive means should the need arise. Perhaps most importantly, consolidation of an imposed peace requires an integrated strategy which takes into account long-term social and political factors and includes aid for economic reconstruction.

Both research and policy dealing with violent conflicts have been surprisingly oblivious of the need to consolidate peace by political and economic means after a cease-fire has been achieved. Instead, the focus has been on the military monitoring and keeping of peace, but even here economic and social interfaces have been largely overlooked. Peacekeeping, and the prevention and resolution of conflict, have received most of the attention in recent policy and scholarly debates. The aftermath of conflict has garnered less interest.

This is no doubt justified in the sense that an effective system for the early warning, prevention, and resolution of deadly conflict can help to save both human life and entire societies from the destruction of war. On the other hand, in the real world, the prevention and mitigation of violence often fail. Therefore, the termination of fighting and efforts to prevent it from starting again deserve serious attention. Peacebuilding, including institutional and economic reconstruction, is an important means not only to repair a war-torn society, but also to eliminate the root causes of violence. In this context it is interesting to observe that the World Bank has recently increased its loans and other forms of support to war-torn countries.[1]

Studies dealing with the termination of civil wars have barely touched upon the economic dimension. The negotiation and implementation of peace settlements have been considered largely in terms of political reconciliation and the redistribution, balancing, and sharing of power among parties to the peace agreement.[2] On the other hand, we know that civil wars and humanitarian emergencies have often been fueled by the struggle for economic resources, or expressed more broadly, for entitlements in society.[3] If the struggle for economic resources is an important cause for the outbreak of violent conflict, it can hardly be less important in the aftermath of war. An integrated approach to peacebuilding is needed that focuses not only on political issues but on economic and social strategies and their links with political and military issues. While largely neglected in the past, such strategies seem to be gaining increasing attention, as recent policy reports show.[4]

In Bosnia, interest in the military enforcement of the Dayton accord (initially the International Enforcement Force, IFOR, later replaced by the Stabilization Force, SFOR) has been much greater than in the civilian components, including the provision of international police forces and financial support for reconstruction. Resources for military enforcement have been promptly available, and political objectives have been restricted. Links with the civilian policing and economic reconstruction provisions of the peace agreement have remained limited. In fact, I argue that the multiple imbalances between the military and civilian aspects of enforcement have jeopardized the implementation of the Dayton accord.

Overcoming Aid Policy Constraints

The problems resulting from the slow and limited provision of economic support for peace settlements have been compounded in many cases by the restrictive economic policies of international financial institutions. For example, it has been suggested that International Monetary Fund (IMF) demands for structural adjustment in El Salvador, including cutbacks in public spending and real salaries, have undermined the efforts of the United Nations Observer Mission in El Salvador (ONUSAL) to consolidate the 1992 peace accords.[5] Structural adjustment programs are not the cause of civil wars, but in some countries they seem to have increased the intensity of the economic and social distress and thus have contributed to the spread of violence.[6] In Yugoslavia, the economic austerity of the 1980s was a significant factor in tearing apart the federal political structure. While the IMF cannot be directly blamed for the breakup of Yugoslavia, it is fair to say that the austerity program and the greater exposure to the global market demanded by the fund greatly contributed to the political polarization between the central bureaucracy and republican governments. This was, in turn, conducive to political polarization and escalation of the crisis.[7]

If structural adjustment initially contributes to the deepening of crisis, it can hardly be an answer to the dilemmas of postconflict peacebuilding. The least that can be required from the international community in peacebuilding is that it must develop a consistent and coherent strategy to reconstruct war-torn societies and inch them toward a more stable future. Such a strategy is particularly needed now as there is an increasing number of countries undergoing reconstruction: Angola, Bosnia, Ethiopia, Eritrea, Haiti, Mozambique, South Africa, Uganda, and even Somalia, to mention the best-known examples.

To smooth the way of postwar reconstruction, one possibility is to create an international arrangement in which countries recovering from war have a special economic status. These countries would be exempt from at least some of the obligations imposed by the IMF and other international financial institutions.[8] Such an arrangement would help eliminate the multiple and even incompatible agendas that now govern the reconstruction process in several war-torn countries.

Toward an Integrated Strategy

Economic reconstruction as part of a broader peacebuilding process has focused mostly on technical issues: how much and in which sectors resources are needed, when and for what purposes aid should be delivered. Such a "World Bank approach," while necessary, is not sufficient. Instead, external economic aid should be steered also by political needs and goals; that is, it must embody an explicit and active political strategy for peacebuilding and conflict prevention. Obviously, this suggestion runs counter to the dogma that international financial institutions must be "apolitical" in their activities. This presumption can be contested in general, but here it suffices to say that peacebuilding cannot be an apolitical process. If it is legitimate to speak of external economic assistance, sanctions, and political conditionalities to promote democracy, it must also be acceptable to incorporate political criteria into postwar aid for reconstruction.[9]

An integrated political and economic strategy of peacebuilding should be based on a careful, differentiated analysis of the target society. Violence may have been fueled by ethnic and religious animosities and struggles for political power, but almost always it also has been fostered by an unequal distribution of economic and social resources. In addition to resource imbalances, political and legal institutions may have discriminated against some groups and prevented them from enjoying their rightful entitlements. Therefore, violence has been perpetrated both as a reaction against inequities, on the one hand, and as a method of maintaining privileges, on the other.[10]

The initial inequities and privileges are seldom eliminated by war and may be increased by it. That is why a major task of peacebuilding is to make sure that the original causes of fighting, and their socioeconomic consequences, are alleviated and not maintained or even exacerbated by the peace. It has been rightly observed that not only war but also reconciliation has its winners and losers.[11] In addition to a political solution, the reconciliation process must contain an economic element. It should support the aggrieved party but also maintain the interest of the winner. Postwar reconstruction must also take into account the extent to which various social groups and regions have suffered from the war.

There is little if any basis for demanding war reparations in today's civil wars. In fact, an evenhanded economic and political treatment of all parties may make it easier to successfully push other elements of the settlement, including the punishment of war criminals, provided those criminals are tried and sentenced as individuals rather than as representatives of their ethnic or other community. However, if a party tries to obstruct the implementation of the peace agreement, the international community must be prepared to deprive it of the benefits of the postwar reconstruction.

Economic Instruments and Peace Agreements

Wolfgang H. Reinicke has suggested that international financial institutions should develop a general strategy of conflict prevention, including a system of "ethnonational assessment" (ENA). The purpose of such a strategy would be to make sure that lending and other policies of the financial institutions do not instigate violence in the target country and thus become counterproductive. A more specific and demanding strategy of conflict prevention would require intervention targeted at those groups that threaten to launch or escalate ethnonational violence.[12] While Reinicke's suggestions are in many ways useful, they do not specifically address the problem of postconflict reconstruction and the role of international financial institutions in it. Ball and Halevy are more explicit in this regard, but they fail to establish any clear linkage between the means and objectives of peacebuilding.[13] These studies suggest, however, that in the postconflict context, active and targeted economic measures would provide political levers for ensuring the implementation of the peace agreement.

Peace and cease-fire agreements may contain economic provisions concerning, for example, war reparations and mutual economic cooperation. They seldom specify whether and how economic means should be used in enforcing the agreement itself, although in some cases, economic punishments could be used as an instrument to enforce peace agreements. The discussion in the summer of 1996 on whether the United States should reimpose economic sanctions on Republika Srpska because of its reluctance to extradite indicted war criminals is an example of such a possibility. The International Criminal Tribunal has called for the imposition of economic sanctions against Republika Srpska and, in the case of noncooperation, even against Serbia.[14] The effectiveness of such sanctions would be undermined, however, by disagreements among the senders. The United States and Germany are in favor of reimposing sanctions if Republika Srpska does not collaborate, but Russia is opposed, while Britain and France are hesitant.[15]

The reimposition of economic punishments may not be a meaningful way to ensure compliance with the peace agreement. A better approach would be to reinforce the compliant behavior that produced it in the first place. Such a reinforcement can be achieved by rewarding the supporters of the treaty. Incentives to reinforce compliance with the terms of the peace agreement should not be unconditional, however. If inducements fail to produce adequate results, the senders must be able to resort to more tangible means of influence. If sanctions are employed, they should be limited to punishing the specific violations of the agreement rather than to express dissatisfaction across the board.[16] Withholding of assistance by temporarily canceling economic incentives is one of the tools for such a limited enforcement policy.

A key issue in using economic means of influence is the nature of the objectives. Are they mainly military and political, or do they also aim to ameliorate economic hardships and reintegrate the society across ethnic, religious, and other divisions? In this context one can speak of limited and comprehensive peace agreements. In recent years the tendency has been toward comprehensive agreements, including also institutional and economic reconstruction, due to the large-scale devastation of societies by civil wars.

Another key issue concerns the degree of political commitment. Does the use of economic and other instruments of enforcement signal the full commitment of the external actors to the implementation of a peace agreement? If so, what kinds of interests steer their decision making? The reasons for commitment can either spring from the actors' self-interests or more general humanitarian interests. One also must ask whether the commitments are short term or long term and how much third parties are ready to pay to make sure that the local actors comply with the provisions of the peace agreement.

"A threat is costly when it fails," Thomas Schelling has remarked, while "a promise is costly when it succeeds."[17] In the Bosnian context, the use of economic incentives to encourage the target to behave constructively engenders costs to the third parties that may be higher than the costs of threats. In the use of economic rewards, the ability to generate necessary resources and agreement to share their costs are pivotal matters. These issues are especially pertinent if economic rewards are delivered as aid rather than trade. Aid is a more costly and unilateral transaction than trade.

The use of aid as an economic incentive means that the costs for the sender(s) are higher. Lisa Martin has stressed that high, self-imposed costs by the sender increase cooperation with other senders and also make sanctions more credible on the receiving end.[18] This would lead to the conclusion that aid is a more effective instrument of enforcement than trade. On the other hand, it has been suggested that while aid sanctions are easier to coordinate, they may elicit less cooperation among the senders than trade sanctions.[19] This controversy can be resolved potentially by introducing the time span into the analysis. Over a short term, aid deliveries probably have more immediate and usually positive effects, while over a long term, import preferences, export credits, and other trade incentives become more attractive. In addition to creating a quicker impact, aid incentives can also be targeted more selectively. The downside in the use of aid as the main instrument of enforcement is that those delivering it must be initially ready to shoulder a high economic burden. As the Bosnian case shows, this requirement may become a major obstacle to the effective and balanced implementation of a peace accord.

The fundamental question in the Bosnian situation is whether there exist sufficient mutual interests, agreement, and trust between the external powers implementing the Dayton accord on the one hand and the local actors on the other. If the external powers disagree with each other, then whose voice carries most weight, and what kinds of coalitions emerge between them and local actors? Does the disagreement between the senders concern ends, means, or both, and are economic incentives the most appropriate and effective means to address the problems that arise in the implementation process? Finally, what means are available to increase the value of a compromise and to punish noncompliance?

Peace in Bosnia-Herzegovina

The use of economic instruments is nothing new in former Yugoslavia. Governments and international organizations have used both negative and positive measures to influence the behavior of the parties since the beginning of the crisis. In 1991, Western powers first used promises of economic rewards and then threats of punishment to persuade or compel the parties to solve their disputes in a peaceful manner. These early efforts had very little effect on the conflict process. During the second half of 1991, the European Community and the United States imposed more extensive economic sanctions on former Yugoslavia. In April 1992, however, they were lifted except for those against Serbia, which were tightened later on in the same year.[20]

In April 1994, Croatia was tempted by economic incentives to support the Washington Agreements, which created the Muslim-Croat federation in Bosnia. In this context, the World Bank approved a $128 million loan to Croatia and the IMF gave an additional $192 million.[21] On the other hand, the United States threatened Croatia with economic sanctions should it not show at least minimal respect for Bosnia's sovereignty. Peter Galbraith, U.S. ambassador to Zagreb, delivered a speech in February 1994 containing the message that "Croatia has a choice of joining the West economically and politically or sharing Serbia's destiny—isolation, economic collapse, and never-ending warfare."[22]

The combination of promising rewards and threatening punishments produced political results in Croatia. The success was mainly due to two factors. The choice between isolation and integration became a central issue in the debate over Croatia's future international position. The integration option gained an upper hand domestically, partly because President Franjo Tudjman felt that it would give him a place of pride in history and a stronger hand to expel Serbian troops from Croatia. The federation also promised rewards to the Bosnian government in Sarajevo, including the resumption of humanitarian aid deliveries to isolated Muslim enclaves and a more-abundant flow of arms to government troops. Belgrade did not oppose the federation, partly because it could provide a future justification to establish a closer liaison with the Serb-inhabited areas of Bosnia.[23]

The economic provisions of the Dayton accord are limited. The General Framework Agreement does not even mention the word "economic." Nor are there any specific references to economic assistance for reconstruction. Article I of Annex 10, containing an agreement on the civilian implementation of the peace plan, briefly mentions that it will "entail a wide range of activities including continuation of the humanitarian aid effort for as long as necessary; rehabilitation of infrastructure and economic reconstruction." As I will discuss in more detail below, Annex 9 of the accord contains provisions on public corporations in Bosnia-Herzegovina. These provisions have a clear-cut political rationale; by rebuilding transportation links, the preconditions for economic cooperation and mutual gains can be enhanced and possibilities for political integration strengthened.

Aid for economic reconstruction is a bargaining relationship that is informed by the political objectives of the parties. Aid may be motivated by a common morality to help the communities ravaged by war, but it also has instrumental goals. In the Bosnian case, the most important goals of aid have been to (1) remedy the destruction brought about by the war, (2) help to enforce the provisions of the Dayton accord, and (3) build a more vibrant and integrated economy in Bosnia-Herzegovina and the entire region. The two first goals are short-term, the third long-term.

The single most important political objective of the Dayton accord is to recreate Bosnia-Herzegovina within its sovereign borders as a unified, but decentralized state. To achieve this primary goal, the peace process must be able to build confidence among the parties. It must also control the flow of arms, prevent external interventions, and create a workable democratic and market-oriented society. Although Bosnian territory is currently divided into separate areas physically controlled by the Serbs and the Muslim-Croat federation, the Dayton accord establishes a variety of links between them. These links are institutional, economic, and humanitarian, founded on the principles of the free movement of people and the right of refugees to return.

Everyone recognizes that the goal of decentralized unity for Bosnia is ambitious and problematic. There are grave doubts whether the Croats and Serbs in Bosnia and their mentors in Zagreb and Belgrade are genuinely interested in holding the country together. Skepticism about the prospects for unity has prompted experts of different persuasions to conclude that the Dayton accord will be unlikely to provide a viable solution. Some even advocate its cancellation and the outright partitioning of the country. Mearsheimer and Van Evera suggest that Bosnian government troops should be equipped with heavy weapons and trained to establish a balance of power in Bosnia-Herzegovina and the entire region.[24] This is, in effect, the policy recently followed by the United States.

However, the arming-and-partitioning approach has major disadvantages. Partitioning would not only make it impossible to resettle refugees but would generate new population transfers. It would lead to a severance of economic links as well as destruction of common institutions and whatever common identities remain among different ethnic communities.

These outcomes are clearly undesirable. To avoid them, external powers have instead used political, economic, and military tools to enforce the basic objectives of the peace accord. IFOR/SFOR military actions have helped to implement its provisions on military disengagement and territorial control. These efforts have proceeded successfully in areas where the Dayton accord has created somewhat ethnically homogeneous "homelands," especially for the Croats and Serbs. Major tensions have arisen primarily in areas that either remain contested (e.g., Brcko) or where different national communities are supposed to coexist (Mostar and Sarajevo). NATO countries have been reluctant to use IFOR/SFOR military capabilities to secure the stability of contested areas in Mostar and Sarajevo, or to enforce other aspects of the Dayton accord, especially the arrest of indicted war criminals. In these cases they have resorted to diplomatic means, such as the emergency meeting among the presidents of Bosnia, Croatia, and Serbia in Rome in February 1996. Diplomacy alone is unlikely to be adequate to resolve problems of noncompliance, however, which is why the international guarantors of the peace agreement must be ready to employ material means of enforcement, including both coercive measures and incentives.

Promoting Economic Integration

As mentioned, the Dayton accord contains provisions on the establishment of a Commission on Public Corporations. It has been mandated to "examine" possibilities for founding public corporations to "operate joint public facilities, such as for the operation of utility, energy, postal and communication facilities." The accord especially stresses the need to establish a public transportation corporation to operate roads, railways, ports, and so on, for the "mutual benefit" of both entities. That corporation should provide a "model for the establishment of other joint public corporations." The creation and successful operation of public corporations requires investment capital. To make such capital available and promote the economic integration of Bosnia, international financial institutions should develop a strategic investment plan. In addition to attracting funds, such a plan could be used to reward those groups that have showed genuine commitment to implementing the peace agreement.[25]

It is especially important that both the Croat- and Serb-dominated areas be integrated with the government-held parts of the Bosnian economy. Wars have severed earlier economic connections between the ethnonational communities and tied them more closely to external actors than to each other. Economic dependencies of the Croat part of Bosnia on Croatia and of Republika Srpska on Serbia are, however, difficult to reduce both for practical and ideological reasons. These dependencies are illustrated in the widespread use (along with the D-mark) of the Croatian currency, kuna, in the Croat-controlled areas of Bosnia, and the Yugoslav dinar in Republika Srpska. The economic integration of Bosnia-Herzegovina would require the establishment of a working banking system, a common central bank, and a common customs and payments union and tax administration, as envisaged in the Dayton accord.[26]

To define the priorities and coordinate the use of aid funds, the Muslim-Croat federation has set up the fifteen-member Reconstruction Cabinet and the Coordination Board to carry out the practical work. The Serb Republic has established its own Reconstruction Agency to work on the reconstruction program within its entity.[27] Thus, there is no single organization in Bosnia-Herzegovina in which different communities would cooperate for reconstruction. As a result, the state nature of Bosnia's political subunits has steadily increased.

In addition, the combined effects of Tito's "self-managed" economic model, war, and sanctions have created artificial and distorted economies in the region. These economies are controlled by political authorities, organized crime, and other special interests. Organized crime in the form of drug trade, prostitution, and car theft has become a lucrative business, often in association with the corrupt local police. The division of Bosnia into ethnic para-states has provided a sort of protection for the criminals and permitted them to benefit from cross-border operations. The likely outcome is the establishment of a sort of frontier economy of which the so-called Arizona market of stolen and smuggled goods south of Brcko is the best example. The market is one of the few places where one can sell and buy without any regard to ethnicity or nationality.[28]

Cronies of the political leaders have benefitted from the violation of sanctions by gaining control of scarce commodities such as gasoline. They have also been awarded exclusive permits for specific economic activities giving access to foreign currency and monopoly profits. These cronies may have vested interests in undermining privatization and other efforts to convert Bosnia into a unified market economy. At a minimum, they are against liberal economic reforms, as the Serbian example shows. The end of economic sanctions has not resulted in the relinquishing of monopolistic access to economic power in favor of market-based operations.[29]

The economic assets of Republika Srpska are particularly weak. The republic, especially its eastern part, is mostly rural and in many places depopulated. It has some natural resources, such as iron ore, but processing facilities are located in the Croat-Muslim Federation. Another typical example of this weakness is the importance of Muslim-controlled Tuzla for

Republika Srpska as a source of energy, raw materials, and table salt.[30] The republic seem. to have economically only two options: either to continue its close ties with the economy of the Yugoslav Federation, or to encourage links with the Croat-Muslim Federation's economy, especially Sarajevo. Its chances of becoming a self-supporting economy are questionable at best.

Against this backdrop, promises made by Radovan Karadzic to the Bosnian Serbs are fanciful. To prop up his own political position and attract fellow Serbs either to stay in the republic or return from Bosnia, Karadzic painted lavish images of a new, ethnically homogeneous "Serb Sarajevo." The artistic embellishments of the new metropolis promised "world-class universities, a huge sports stadium, and a gold-topped Orthodox church to memorialize the war dead."[31]

Absent substantial external assistance and pressure, the economic reintegration of Bosnia is unlikely to occur. Nationalist ideologies propagating political and economic separation continue to dominate both in the Serb- and Croat-controlled parts of Bosnia-Herzegovina. Internally, there are no adequate resources to generate growth and build infrastructure that would draw the scattered pieces together. The lack of political will makes this task even more difficult. The crucial question, then, is whether the international community is able to provide incentives that can push reluctant parties to cooperate more closely with each other.

The Dayton Accord's Civilian Operations

As emphasized earlier, an integrated international strategy to implement peace agreements is needed. Such a strategy has been lacking so far for Bosnia-Herzegovina. True, both the United States and the European Union have specified the general political goals that their involvement in Bosnia should promote. However, these goals are formulated in very general terms, referring to the stabilization of democracy and market economy in Bosnia, and no specific program of action has been developed to reach these objectives by the available means.[32] In the summer of 1996, this situation started to change as more and more governments made their aid conditional on political developments, especially the arrest of war criminals.

The international community, most visibly the United States and the European Union, have made a strong commitment to peace in Bosnia by pushing through the Dayton accord, sending 60,000 troops to implement it, and becoming involved in the political reconstruction of the country, most prominently in organizing the fall 1996 elections even if preconditions for them were not yet ripe. This diplomatic and military commitment has not been matched, however, by a comparable economic program of action to underpin the political process and to keep it on track. Even though the basic importance of civilian reconstruction of Bosnia has been generally admitted, its progress has been lagging badly behind military implementation. In the spring of 1997 the World Bank said that it had used only one-third of the $1.8 billion made available for the Bosnian reconstruction because of the reluctance of the parties to initiate any meaningful economic reforms.[33]

The civilian operations are organized under the Peace Implementation Council (PIC), which has 42 states and ten international organizations as its members. The council's steering committee, comprising G-7 countries as well as Russia and the representatives of the European Union and Islamic countries, is chaired by the high representative of the European Union, Carl Bildt, who must also coordinate efforts with NATO, the Organization for Security and Cooperation in Europe (OSCE), and the United Nations High Commissioner for Refugees (UNHCR). It is difficult for such a large body to develop a coherent, long-term strategy to implement the nonmilitary aspects of the peace agreement.

That is why, in reality, the high representative, together with major governments, will have to shoulder the main responsibility. In that regard huge political problems have emerged. Several governments supporting the Bosnian Muslims have criticized Bildt for having been ineffective and too closely affiliated with the Serbs in Bosnia and Serbia. At least part of that criticism has been exaggerated and one-sided, however. It may have been due to the fact that Bildt, more than any other actor, has made efforts to use reconstruction funds as an instrument to promote the provisions of the Dayton accord and occasionally also to rein in the policies of the Bosnian government.[34]

Reconstruction efforts are not always easy to distinguish from the humanitarian operations that were carried out in Bosnia, Croatia, and Serbia during the war and still continue because of ongoing needs. Humanitarian aid cannot be continued indefinitely, and in the transition period aid structures and practices must be reviewed and local communities must be made more self-reliant, which is also one of the tasks of reconstruction. While humanitarian aid continues, it may serve as an economic incentive. Thus, aid programs for education, health, and services could be geared to make the resettlement and reintegration of people easier, and to encourage the return of skilled labor from abroad.[35]

The World Bank and International Aid

The international community has estimated in detail the needs of Bosnia's reconstruction. The standard estimate, provided by the World Bank, is that

Bosnia needs a total of $5.1 billion in external aid for reconstruction and recovery over a three-year period. The bulk of this assistance, 83 percent, is to go toward capital investment. Bosnia's gross need for external financing is estimated at $12.7 billion during the period from 1996 to the year 2000, of which international aid is expected to cover about 40 percent.

The World Bank has been designated as the lead agency in reconstructing the Bosnian economy. In January 1996 it committed $150 million of its own funds for emergency assistance and these payments have continued ever since. The delivery of aid has been slowed down, however, by disagreements over the sharing of responsibility for the debts accumulated by the old Yugoslavia. Bosnia's external debt at the end of 1995 amounted to $3.2 billion and waits for settlement. Unless debt relief can be worked out, the Bosnian government would use 15 percent of the external financing for servicing its debt from now to the year 2000.[36]

The World Bank is under political pressure to move ahead quickly in funding Bosnian reconstruction. In April 1996, it launched three long-term programs for transportation, agriculture, and water supply (since then programs have been expanded to housing, electricity production, demining, and the demobilization of soldiers). They were approved in three months, in contrast to the average of one year that a similar process usually takes. James D. Wolfensohn, president of the World Bank, stated that the bank's first priority is to create in Bosnia 300,000 new jobs by public works programs and targeted assistance to farmers and small businesses.[37]

According to the bank, more than $500 million are needed for each of the following areas: transportation, electrical power, telecommunications, and health. The needs in these and other fields are interconnected. For example, the damage to water and sewage networks is causing health problems, while without a working transportation system industrial production cannot recover. In fact, the World Bank has developed in a short time very specific sectoral plans for the reconstruction of Bosnian society.[38]

The rebuilding of the Bosnian economy has been slow to start, however. It has been delayed by the lack of adequate funding from the main donors to recruit staff for the operations. In Carl Bildt's estimate, by the beginning of March 1996, donors had paid only some 60 percent of the $550 million pledged for initial reconstruction projects.[39] Almost as a sign of desperation, in April 1996, Bildt requested NATO to provide military engineers from IFOR to restore communication links, water supplies, and power stations in Bosnia-Herzegovina.

In the first international donors meeting of December 1995 the participating governments made a commitment to provide $550 million by the end of March 1996. However, the European Union was the only donor that, by and large, lived up to its promises, paying close to $100 million. In the United States, Bosnian aid money became a hostage of the budget battles between the White House and Congress. President Clinton made repeated efforts to convince Congress of the need to pay at least some of the money pledged. On Capitol Hill there has been a strong feeling that it was enough for the United States to fund its 20,000 IFOR troops. However, U.S. companies campaigned early to receive a major share of the reconstruction contracts in Bosnia.[40] In the second donors' meeting of April 1996, the United States pledged to deliver $200 million of aid to the Bosnian reconstruction effort.[41]

Inadequate International Leadership

In the Bosnian reconstruction there is a real problem of international leadership. The importance of the "demonstrative aspect" of leadership can be seen in the tendency of other governments to follow the U.S. example. If the United States fails to deliver its share of funds for reconstruction efforts, this will encourage "free-riding" on the part of other potential donors. The political targeting of aid requires "directional leadership." Such leadership influences targets "by molding their interests, values and beliefs, rather than coercing or alluring them to do things they would rather not have done."[42] The United States must provide both demonstrative and directional leadership if the Bosnia reconstruction plan is to have any chance of success.

In Bosnia, criticisms of U.S. policy are mounting on both counts. Washington has been blamed not only for its failure to provide funds for reconstruction, but also for not acting more forcefully to integrate Mostar. Washington has been criticized as well for its efforts to deliver weapons and military aid to the Bosnian government.[43] The European Union objects to U.S. plans to "equip and train" the Bosnian government army, urging instead a greater emphasis on civilian reconstruction and rebuilding relations with Serbia. In March 1996, a donors conference was organized in Ankara in which Washington contributed $100 million toward the rearmament program of $800 million.[44] The European Union so strongly disagreed with the United States that its member governments decided to boycott the Ankara meeting. In July 1996, Bosnia and the United States signed an agreement that committed Washington to deliver a total of $400 million of military aid by the end of the year.

Japan wants to avoid the situation in which it was caught during the Gulf War, when it had no other option than to contribute $13 billion to fund the war. Now Tokyo wants to become fully involved in international decision making to defend its own interests. It feels that Bosnia's reconstruction is more of a European and U.S. responsibility. In Tokyo's opinion, Japan's contributions to Bosnia should, at a minimum, be linked with the U.S. and European funding of oil deliveries and light-water reactors to North Korea in the effort to stop its nuclear weapon program.[45]

The role of Islamic countries in the reconstruction of Bosnia has far-reaching political implications. By late 1996, these countries had provided 15 percent of the total funds for reconstruction. In November 1996, the Organization of the Islamic Conference and representatives from twelve countries held a meeting in Sarajevo to discuss the provision of humanitarian, economic, and military aid to the Bosnian government.[46]

An integrated economic strategy to steer the implementation of a peace agreement is impossible if adequate funds are not made available. This has been clearly a problem in Bosnia, where the main donors have lacked a mutual agreement on their roles and responsibilities. The United States thinks that its military investment in IFOR/SFOR and the rearming of the Bosnian government should be its main contribution, with the World Bank and the European Union bearing the brunt of the economic reconstruction. Europeans prefer a more balanced sharing of the economic burden, partly because of the possibility that they will have to take a greater responsibility for military operations as well after the potential withdrawal of U.S. troops. The Japanese commitment to aid Bosnia is and will probably remain quite limited.

Problems in funding and burden-sharing weaken the directional leadership that both the United States and the European Union should exercise. Such a leadership should link means (i.e., financial resources), and goals (i.e., the integration and pacification of Bosnia). The lack of leadership is evident in the inability of leading NATO and EU powers to keep their ally, Greece, in check. The Greek telecommunication company OTE is using some $260,000 to develop civilian and military telecommunication links solely between Republika Srpska and Belgrade. This amounts to separatism, which is incompatible with the basic goal of a unified Bosnia.[47]

To explore further the role of economic incentives and directional leadership in the implementation of the Dayton accord, I will focus in the remaining pages on three critical areas in Bosnia where peace and stability have faced difficulties: Banja Luka, Mostar, and Sarajevo.

Three Test Cases

Banja Luka

Banja Luka, in northwestern Bosnia with 240,000 inhabitants, is the largest and most developed city in Republika Srpska. It is also ethnically very homogenous because its Muslims were, at Radovan Karadzic's behest, thoroughly terrorized and forced to flee in the summer of 1992.[48] It is a paradox that while Muslims continue to be evicted from their homes, the politics of Banja Luka's Serbs have been at the same time somewhat more liberal than those of the leadership in Pale. Banja Luka has closer relations than Pale with both Belgrade and Western powers. The former prime minister of Republika Srpska, Rajko Kasagic, used Banja Luka as his power base in his efforts to influence internal and external affairs of the Republika.

Banja Luka has been rewarded for this political independence. Most of the external aid for reconstruction goes to the Croat-Muslim federation, partly because the Bosnian Serbs refused to participate in the donors conference in April 1996. Some money however, has trickled to the Banja Luka region, for instance, to open a power station and a coal mine. External political support has been manifested by the decision of the EU high representative to set up an office in Banja Luka and spend time there.[49] These economic and political measures of support were intended to split the Bosnian Serbs by rewarding the "good" guys of Banja Luka and punishing the "bad" ones of Pale. Bosnian Serb hard-liners resisted these efforts, however, and fired Kasagic from the post of prime minister because he had, in Karadzic's words, "considerably harmed the Republika Srpska" by suggesting that all provisions of the Dayton accord, including the detention of war criminals, should be implemented.[50]

The international community applied political pressure on the Pale leadership to keep Kasagic in power. For example, Javier Solana, NATO's secretary general, traveled to Banja Luka to show his support. These political gestures ultimately failed, however, and the Bosnian Serb Parliament sacked Kasagic by a vote of 84 to 43. Thus, the selective use of incentives to support a more moderate leadership was blocked by a power move of Bosnian Serb hard-liners. While international political pressure was unable to prevent this move, the jury is still out. The leadership of Banja Luka continues to follow an independent line in opposition to Pale.

Mostar

In 1991 the Mostar area had a population of 120,000 people, of whom 35 percent were Muslims, 34 percent Croats, and 19 percent Serbs (although in many cases the mixed ethnicity made these categories meaningless). In April 1992, Serbs attempted to gain control of the valley in which Mostar is located to block Bosnian access to the Adriatic Sea. The Croats and Muslims joined forces against the attack and were able to defend the city, although the Serbs retained control of some of the surrounding territory. The alliance did not last long, however, and the Croat troops started attacking Muslims in May 1992, taking over the western side of Mostar. The fighting left about 2,000 dead.

By 1993 the city was devastated, and most of the Muslims were pushed to its eastern districts. The ancient bridge, Stari Most, connecting Mostar across the Neretva River, was destroyed by both Croat and Serb shelling. The Croats, linked politically and economically to independent Croatia, started an intensive hate campaign against Mostar's Serbs and especially its Muslims. The arrival of rural refugees from other parts of Bosnia-Herzegovina exacerbated its demographic dislocations and brought mountain people in contact with city dwellers, fueling tensions. Croat-controlled western Mostar has been characterized as a frontier city where the mafia rules, while the Muslim eastern part more resembles a ghetto.[51]

Indeed, the military and political organizations in the Croatian part of Bosnia have assumed a direct economic role by taxing local communities and confiscating production facilities. An example is the $650 million aluminium plant just outside Mostar which should be the property of the Croat-Muslim federation, but which has been taken over by the local Croat leadership.[52] It is difficult to change by external punishments and incentives the behavior of a nondemocratic elite whose survival depends on the resistance to any change in the political situation.

In Mostar, economic incentives were adopted early. In July 1994, after the United States had arranged a shotgun marriage between Bosnia's Croats and Muslims, the European Union took the responsibility of integrating Mostar as a way of cementing the federation. Hans Koschnick, the former mayor of Bremen, was appointed to head the European Union Administration (EUAM). In 1995, a total of $100 million was earmarked by the union for the rebuilding and integration of Mostar. More than 60 medium-sized and 450 smaller companies have received financial support. Water and power supplies have been repaired and houses and bridges have been rebuilt.[53] To ensure the stability needed for the reconstruction effort, the European Union deployed police forces in Mostar.

Reintegration of the city is one of the goals of the Dayton accord. In February 1996, Koschnick presented a plan in which Mostar was to be organized into seven administrative districts: three of them to be controlled by the Croats, three by the Muslims, while the large central area that includes the airport, train station, and water works was to be jointly administered. This solution did not satisfy the Croats, who considered the central district too large. As a result several hundred of them stormed the EUAM headquarters, and, later on, an attempt was made on Koschnick's life. A main reason for the Croat resistance to Mostar's unification is that it is the only viable candidate to become the capital of the self-proclaimed Republic Herceg-Bosna.[54]

To support Koschnick, Klaus Kinkel, the German foreign minister, actively twisted President Tudjman's arm. Because of their historical political connections and economic leverage with the Croats, the Germans had a

certain credibility for this task. In 1994, 36 percent of all foreign investments in Croatia came from Germany. Kinkel threatened to reimpose economic sanctions, to end support for Croatia's membership in the Council
of Europe, and to block its cooperation with the European Union.[55] Kinkel's pressure on Zagreb was nothing new, as Germany had throughout
the Bosnian crisis tried to convince the Croatian government to end the
ethnic division of Mostar.[56]

Germany's threats lessened Zagreb's support for Mostar's Croats, but
they were not sufficient to prevent the Croatian hard-liners from prevailing
in the dispute. In a compromise reached in the Rome meeting on 17–18
February 1996, a joint Croat-Muslim police force was established for
Mostar and the size of its central district was made smaller than originally
suggested by Koschnick.[57] This is a sobering reminder of the limits of
political and economic diplomacy, even if exercised by the leading European power. It is also a reflection of the lack of effective leadership from
the United States and other major powers, which did not give sufficient
economic and political support to this effort.

Partly as a result of this setback, Koschnick resigned from his post as the
head of the EUAM. His decision was also a protest against the permissive
attitude toward Zagreb of Britain and Italy, and to a lesser extent France.
With the United States standing on the sidelines, the European powers
have been unable to develop a unified strategy toward Croatia and the
future of Mostar. The inability to reintegrate Mostar gains particular relevance if one believes in the maxim that "as goes Mostar—toward reintegration or final disintegration—so will go the federation and thus all of
Bosnia."[58] Disagreements between Croats and Muslims have pushed the
latter to seek new allies among the Serbs of the region who have been
isolated both from Pale and Banja Luka. In particular, the economic cooperation between Muslims and Serbs has started to expand.[59]

Neither economic incentives nor threats of punishment have been able
to alter the basic course of developments in Mostar. Local interests and
identities so far have had a stronger impact on the shape of events than
external means of influence. The European Union has consistently advocated that Mostar and Sarajevo should remain undivided, but this goal will
be difficult to accomplish without a much greater commitment of economic and political resources.[60] The difficulties faced in the reintegration
of Mostar have been amplified by developments since the elections held in
Mostar in June 1996, which resulted in a victory for the ethnic parties
deepening the division of the city. The prounification Muslim List of Citizens won 48 percent and the Croatian Democratic Community (HDZ)
45 percent of the vote. In early 1997, there were repeated clashes between
Croats and Muslims and even against international military and civilian
personnel working in Mostar. In February 1997, plainclothes Croatian

police fired on an unarmed Muslim group attempting to visit a cemetery in the city's west side. In the face of such unremitting ethnic hostility, international enforcement efforts have been unable to unify the city.

Sarajevo

The restoration of Sarajevo's multiethnic nature has proven to be equally difficult. During the return of federal control in the spring of 1996, only a few thousand Serbs stayed on in the neighborhoods of Grbavica and Ilidza, while 50,000 others left for Republika Srpska, some voluntarily, others under pressure. The pressure from Serb extremists in some cases went so far as to include kidnapping children from their homes, with the children returned only after the parents agreed to leave the suburbs. Where Serb extremists failed to expel residents from their homes, Muslim thugs came and pressured people to leave. Those Serbs who wanted to remain in Sarajevo were squeezed between two extremist forces and had few alternatives other than to leave.

Sarajevo has been united under Bosnian government control, as envisaged in the Dayton accord, but the price has been very high. The fleeing Serbs took with them everything that could be transported by trucks and burned the houses. Factories were stripped, and their machinery was taken to Republika Srpska. In all, millions of dollars' worth of property was destroyed. The forced departure of Serbs from Sarajevo has been used by the Serbs elsewhere as an argument against the right of Muslims to return to their homes. In the present atmosphere, the chances for ensuring a genuinely multiethnic Sarajevo are slim. The international community has done very little in the early phases of implementing the Dayton accord to promote this goal. The timeline has been too short for economic incentives to have an impact. The United Nations was also slow in deploying the promised 1,721 international police officers to protect minorities (the Americans were the main defaulters).[60] In early 1996, it was even difficult to avoid the impression that IFOR was abetting ethnic cleansing as its troops guided the flight of Serbs out of Sarajevo rather than protecting their homes.

It may not be too late, however, to employ economic incentives to restore Sarajevo's historical multiethnic nature. There are, for instance, middle-class professionals (doctors, engineers, teachers, etc.) among the Serbs whose interests would be served by returning to Sarajevo. Their employment opportunities are in cities rather than in the rural villages of Republika Srpska. When the most intense passions die down, it would be important to try to attract these professionals back to Sarajevo and other major cities of Bosnia. For instance, multiethnicity should be a main criterion in recruiting faculty to the Bosnian universities whose reconstruction is about to start. The international community has leverage to promote goals that support pluralism and integration in Bosnia, for instance, through the Tempus program, the European Union's major instrument for the development and restructuring of higher education in Central and Eastern Europe.[61] It has been also suggested that in places like Sarajevo, international science and technology centers should be established. Such centers would keep the local experts employed through external grants and would connect them with the international scientific community.[62] Guaranteeing the multiethnic composition of the staff should be one of the guiding ideas behind the establishment of such a center.

Conclusion

By 1997 the annual income per capita in Bosnia had dropped to $500 and the rate of unemployment stood at nearly 70 percent. The total population of the country was a million less (3.4 million) than in 1990. In light of the urgent need for reconstruction, international aid efforts have started to make progress in improving the living conditions of the people, especially in areas controlled by the Sarajevo government. After several delays, the expected amounts of funds have been pledged for the initial reconstruction effort. It also seems that, despite delays, international economic aid has provided political support for the Bosnian government. Military aid from the United States and Islamic countries is restoring the military balance within Bosnia-Herzegovina, but it is also strengthening the state nature of the Islamic part of Bosnia.

International economic aid has not been systematically integrated with the political goals of the peace process, with the exception of some specific cases. This has been especially difficult in Herzeg-Bosna and Republika Srpska, in part because the amounts of aid involved have been minimal. In effect, the major powers have decided not to create an economic lever to influence the politics of these entities. International agencies have preferred to influence the politics of Bosnian Croats and Serbs through Zagreb and Belgrade, respectively. This may be a reasonable solution, since the influence of these capitals on their ethnic kin in Bosnia is considerable, although less so in Belgrade's relations with Pale.

It is a moot point whether larger amounts of aid would have persuaded the Bosnian Croat and Serb leaders to pursue more integrationist policies. To date, efforts to influence them have been based primarily on threats of punishments rather than economic inducements. The experiences in Banja Luka and Mostar suggest, however, that economic rewards also have their limitations. Ethnonationalism has been a dominant motive, putting politics rather than economics in command. Even in Sarajevo the impact of aid money seems to have been limited. President Alija Izetbegović and his Party of Democratic Action have sharpened the Islamic character of the Bosnian government and have opposed efforts to restore its multiethnic nature.

The enforcement of the civilian provisions of the Dayton accord has so far failed to achieve the goal of creating a multiethnic peaceful society in Bosnia-Herzegovina. Agreements calling for freedom of movement, the right of refugees to return home, freedom of association, and the detention of war criminals have been ignored or implemented to a very limited degree only. This failure is due less to the impossibility of achieving these goals than to the inadequacy of international enforcement efforts. If success is to be achieved in Bosnia-Herzegovina, or in other future cases, international involvement will require a more integrated strategy, greater unity among the external actors, and a larger commitment of political and economic resources.

Notes

1. Since 1993 the World Bank has given $175 million to Lebanon, $150 million to Bosnia, $134 million to Angola, $128 million to Croatia, $100 million to Cambodia, $50 million to Rwanda and West Bank/Gaza each, and $26 million to Eritrea. U.S. critics of this lending argue that it is too much steered by the political interests of the United States and may weaken the bank's credit rating; see Paul Blustein, "A Loan Amid the Ruins: World Bank Shifts Aid to Rebuilding War-torn Countries," *Washington Post,* 13 February, 1996,

2. See the case studies in Roy Licklider, ed. *Stopping the Killing: How Civil Wars End* (New York: New York University Press, 1993); and I. William Zartman, ed. *Elusive Peace: Negotiating an End to Civil Wars* (Washington, D.C.: The Brookings Institution, 1995).

3. An important new strand of research is emerging on how the society's resources and access to them are redistributed in protracted military and humanitarian crises; see Mark Duffield, "The Political Economy of Internal War: Asset Transfer, Complex Emergencies and International Aid," in *War and Hunger: Rethinking International Responses to Complex Emergencies,* edited by Joanna Macrae and Anthony Zwi (London: Zed Books 1994), 50–69.

4. See for example Nicole Ball and Tammy Halevy, *Making Peace Work: The Role of the International Development Community,* Policy Essay no. 18 (Washington, D.C.: Overseas Development Council, 1996). The report by Ball and Halevy considers the reconstruction strategies perhaps too much in terms of development aid, overlooking other economic strategies. It also assumes the donor community to be a rather homogenous whole.

5. See chapter 7 in this volume. See also Alvaro de Soto and Graciana del Castillo, "Obstacles to Peacebuilding," *Foreign Policy* 94 (1994): 69–83. A more positive assessment of the role of external economic assistance is provided by Yvon

Grenier, "Foreign Assistance and the Market Place of Peacemaking: Lessons from El Salvador," Working Paper Series (Halifax, Nova Scotia: Centre for Foreign Policy Studies, Dalhousie University, 1995). The peace process in El Salvador also faces other problems, including the functions of the new civil police and the reintegration of former combatants in society; see Alvaro de Soto, "Implementation of Comprehensive Peace Agreements: Staying the Course in El Salvador," *Global Governance* 1, no. 2 (1995): 189–203.

6. A. B. Zack-Williams, "The Deepening Crisis and Survival Strategies," in *Beyond Structural Adjustment in Africa: The Political Economy of Sustainable and Democratic Development,* edited by Julius E. Nyang'oro and Timothy N. Shaw (New York: Praeger, 1992), 149–68.

7. See Susan Woodward, *Balkan Tragedy: Chaos and Dissolution after the Cold War* (Washington, D.C.: Brookings Institution, 1995), 47–81.

8. This proposal was made by Stephen John Stedman in a symposium, "World Order, Global Justice, and the Perils of Anarchy," at Michigan State University, 29–31 March 1996.

9. Larry Diamond, *Promoting Democracy in the 1990s: Actors and Instruments, Issues and Imperatives* (Washington, D.C.: Carnegie Commission on Preventing Deadly Conflict, 1995), 48–59.

10. For a discussion on the role of entitlements in social conflicts, see Raimo Väyrynen, "Toward a Theory of Ethnic Conflicts and their Resolution," Occasional Paper 6:OP:3, Joan B. Kroc Institute for International Peace Studies, University of Notre Dame, Notre Dame, Ind., 1994, 14–19.

11. Stephen John Stedman, "The End of the Zimbabwean Civil War," in Licklider, *Stopping the Killing,* 159–60.

12. Wolfgang H. Reinicke, "Can International Financial Institutions Prevent Internal Violence? The Sources of Ethno-National Conflict in Transitional Societies," in Preventing Conflict in the Post-Communist World. Mobilizing International and Regional Organizations, edited by Abram Chayes and Antonia Handler Chayes (Washington, D.C.: Brookings Institution, 1996), 312–27. While international economic actors have started paying attention to the need for military reforms and conflict resolution in the recipient countries, their concrete measures have been rather timid so far; see Nicole Ball, "International Economic Actors," in *Coping with Conflict After the Cold War,* edited by Edward A. Kolodziej and Roger E. Kanet (Baltimore: The Johns Hopkins University Press, 1996), 168–97.

13. Ball and Halevy, *Making Peace Work,* 28–46.

14. OMRI report, *Pursuing Balkan Peace* 1, no. 23 (11 June 1996).

15. Laura Silber, "Shadow of Sanctions Adds to Serbian Woes," *Financial Times,* 30 May 1996, 3; Laura Silber, "Sanctions Option to Neutralize Karadzic," *Financial Times* 19 June 1996, 5; and Raymond Bonner, "U.S. to Tell Serbs That They Risk New Economic Sanctions," *New York Times,* 17 July 1996, A6.

16. Various objectives of sanctions are discussed by Jürg Martin Gabriel, "Wirtschaftssanktionen: Begriffe, Faktoren, Theorien," no. 184 (Institut für Politikwissenschaften, Hochscule St. Gallen, Beiträge und Berichte, 1992), 17–19.

17. Thomas C. Schelling, *The Strategy of Conflict* (Cambridge, Mass: Harvard University Press, 1980 [1960]), 177.

18. Lisa L. Martin, *Coercive Cooperation: Explaining Multilateral Economic Sanctions* (Princeton, N.J.: Princeton University Press, 1992).

19. Edward D. Mansfield, "International Institutions and Economic Sanctions," *World Politics* 47, no. 4 (1995): 580–81.

20. Hanns W. Maull, "Germany in the Yugoslav Crisis" *Survival* 37, no. 4 (1996): 100–101; and Susan L. Woodward, "The Use of Sanctions in Former Yugoslavia: Misunderstanding Political Realities," in *Economic Sanctions: Panacea or Peacebuilding in a Post–Cold War World?* edited by David Cortright and George Lopez (Boulder, Colo.: Westview Press, 1995), 141–51.

21. Reinicke, "Can International Financial Institutions Prevent Internal Violence," 317.

22. Laura Silber and Allan Little, *Yugoslavia: Death of a Nation* (New York: TV Books, 1996), 322.

23. Ibid., 319–23; see also David Owen, *Balkan Odyssey* (New York: Harcourt Brace & Co., 1995), 268–69.

24. See John J. Mearsheimer and Stephen Van Evera, "When Peace Means War," *The New Republic*, 18 December 1995, 16–21. A more-balanced, but still skeptical evaluation of the chances of peace is provided in Michael Ignatieff, "The Missed Chances in Bosnia," *New York Review of Books*, 29 February 1996, 8–10.

25. On strategic investments in reconstruction, see Melanie H. Stein, "Conflict Prevention in Transition Economies: A Role for the European Bank for Reconstruction and Development?" in Chayes and Chayes, *Preventing Conflict in the Post-Communist World*, 361–65.

26. For the (slow) progress in implementing these goals, see *Bosnia and Herzegovina, Toward Economic Recovery* (Washington, D.C.: The World Bank, 1996), 28–33; and Anthony Robinson, "The Uphill Track to Recovery," *Financial Times*, 13 June 1996, 11.

27. World Bank, *Bosnia and Herzegovina*, xvii–xviii, 13–14.

28. Chris Hedges, "Finally, a Unity Force in Bosnia: Making Money," *New York Times*, 17 October 1996, A4, and Chris Hedges, "Gangs Descend, to Pick Bosnia's Carcass Clean," *New York Times*, 27 October 1996, A6.

29. Mark M. Nelson, "Overseas Investors Find Serbian Leaders Corralling Economy," *Wall Street Journal*, 2 February 1996, A1, A10; Jane Perlez, "Serbian Chief Moves on Opposition: Milosevic Also Tries to Reassert State Control of Economy," *New York Times*, 4 March 1996, A6; and Jane Perlez, "Balkan Economies Stagnate in Grip of Political Leaders," *New York Times*, 20 August 1996, A1, A4.

30. See Robinson, "The Uphill Track to Recovery," 11; (see note 26); see also William Finegan, "Letter from Tuzla: Salt City," *New Yorker*, 12 February 1996, 52.

31. As described by Kit R. Roane, "Serb Dreams of New City in Bosnia," *The New York Times*, 24 February 1996, A4.

32. See for example Foreign Affairs Council of Ministers, "Policy Paper on Former Yugoslavia," The European Union, Brussels, BIO/95/403/1 (6 November 1995).

33. See for example Michael Dobbs and Dana Priest, "Now the Real Work

Begins: In Bosnia, The Civilian Tasks May be More Difficult Than the Military Ones," *Washington Post National Weekly Edition,* 18–24 December 1995, 14; see also Barbara Crossette, "Civilian Effort for Peace in Bosnia Seen Lagging," *New York Times,* 3 January 1996, A5; George Moffett, "Peace in Bosnia Hinges on Postwar Rebuilding," *Christian Science Monitor,* 20 December 1995, 1 and 18; and "Ein Kleiner Marshall-Plan für Bosnien," *Frankfurter Allgemeine Zeitung,* 12 April 1996, 2. Chris Hedges, "For Bosnia, Peace is Coming Empty-Handed," *New York Times,* 18 May 1997, A3.

34. *OMRI Daily Digest,* no. 229, 26 November 1996.

35. See Commission of the European Union, "Humanitarian Aid to the Former Yugoslavia: Prospects and Guidelines," Brussels, [COM(95) 564] (17 November 1995), 5; and Commission of the European Union, "Humanitarian Assistance in Favour of the Victims of the Conflict in the Former Yugoslavia," memo/95/137 (12 December 1995).

36. World Bank, *Bosnia and Herzegovina,* 61–66.

37. Richard W. Stevenson, "World Bank Gets Bosnia Aid Role," *New York Times,* 18 April 1996, A6. Contrary to the criticism expressed in this paper, it has been stressed that "by international aid standards, action has been swift"; see Grep Ip, "Trying to Make Peace Pay," *The Globe and Mail,* 1 July 1996.

38. See Central Europe Department of the World Bank and the European Bank for Reconstruction and Development, "Bosnia and Herzegovina: Priorities for Recovery and Growth," Discussion Papers Nos. 1, 2, and 3, prepared with the active cooperation of the IMF for the first donor's meeting to be held in Brussels on 21–22 December 1995.

39. Craig R. Whitney, "In Bosnia, Securing a Peace Depends on Roads, Refugees and Elections," *New York Times,* 26 March 1996, A6. The preface to a technical World Bank report states that "timing is critical. For the people of Bosnia and Herzegovina to feel the benefits of peace, quick and visible results on the ground are needed. In order to generate concrete results before the autumn elections—to sign contracts, begin procurement, and commence construction before the construction season—pledges need to be translated into concrete commitments for programs and projects without delay." See *Projects in Support of the Priority Reconstruction Program in Bosnia and Herzegovina* (Washington, D.C.: The World Bank, 10 May 1996).

40. Mark M. Nelson and Carla Anne Robbins, "Companies Jockey for Share of Effort to Rebuild Bosnia," *The Wall Street Journal,* 24 November 1995. The corporate interest in aid money can also be seen in the strong presence of business executives in Secretary Ron Brown's tragic trip to Bosnia in April 1996. Largely the same companies followed Brown's successor, Mickey Kantor, on his trip to Bosnia in July 1996.

41. Stevenson, "World Bank Gets Bosnia Aid Role," A6.

42. Raino Malnes, "'Leader' and 'Entrepreneur' in International Negotiations: A Conceptual Analysis," *European Journal of International Relations* 1, no. 1 (1995): 93.

43. This criticism is spelled out, for instance, in the dispatch by the Oslobodjenje Agency from Sarajevo on 9 March 1996.

44. Lionel Barber, Harriet Martin, and Laura Silber, "Transatlantic Row Looming over Bosnia," *Financial Times*, 15 March 1996, 3.

45. Hijiri Inose, "Japan Promises Bosnia Aid—To a Limit," *Nikkei Weekly*, 26 February 1996, 2; see also chapter 3 in this volume.

46. *OMRI Daily Digest*, no. 229, 26 November 1996.

47. In general, the Greek government is assisting Republika Srpska to the tune of $100 million to help its industrial development; see *OMRI Special Report: Pursuing Balkan Peace* (21 May 1996); see also Kerin Hope and Harriet Martin, "Athens Attacked for Work on Bosnian Serb Telecom Project," *Financial Times*, 4 June 1996.

48. Silber and Little, *Death of a Nation*, 245–46.

49. *The Economist*, "Bosnia: Tender Shoots," 18 May 1996, 33–34; see also Scott Peterson, "Bosnia Serbs Feel West's Cold Shoulder," *The Christian Science Monitor*, 15 May 1996, 6.

50. OMRI Special Report, *Pursuing Balkan Peace*, 21 May 1996.

51. For detailed reports, see Kenneth Brown, "Mostar, Without Bridges, Without Light." *Mediterraneans*, no. 7 (1995): 12–31; and Michael Dobbs, "The Misery of Mostar," *Washington Post National Weekly Edition*, 25 September–1 October 1995, 25.

52. Xavier Bougarel, "L'économie du conflit bosniaque: entre prédation et production," in *Economie des guerres civiles*, edited by François Jean and Jean-Christophe Rufin (Paris: Hachette, 1996), pp. 256–62, and Chris Hedges, "On Bosnia's Ethnic Fault Lines, It's Still Tense, but World Is Silent," *New York Times*, 18 February 1997.

53. "The European Union Administration of Mostar" (London: International Crisis Group, 13 June 1996) In all, the European Union spent $150 million for Mostar.

54. "Mostar: Jagt den Deutschen davon," *Der Spiegel*, 12 February 1996, 124–26.

55. "German Politicians Express Support for Embattled EU Administrator in Mostar," *The Week in Germany* (New York: The German Information Center, 16 February 1996): 1.

56. Owen, *Balkan Odyssey*, 201–2.

57. "Bosnia-Hercegovina: Rome 'Mini Summit,' " *Keesing's Record of World Events: News Digest for February 1996* (London, 1996): 40961–62.

58. Anthony Borden, "Moving Dayton to Bosnia," *The Nation*, 25 March 1996, 20.

59. Rémy Ourdan, "La rapprochement entre Serbs et Musulmans à Mostar pourrait préfigurer la réconciliation de tous les Bosniaques," *Le Monde*, 29 March 1996.

60. Owen, *Balkan Odyssey*, 238–39.

61. Barbara Crossette, "U.N. Is Slow in Deploying Bosnia Police," *New York Times*, 21 March 1996, A6.

62. Burton Bollag, "Educators Begin the Difficult Task of Rebuilding Bosnian Higher Education," *The Chronicle of Higher Education*, 3 May 1996, A44.

63. Glenn E. Schweitzer, "A Multilateral Approach to Curbing Proliferation of Weapons Know-How," *Global Governance* 2, no. 1 (1996): 38–40.

7

Incentives and the Salvadoran Peace Process

Geoff Thale

A REVIEW OF INTERNATIONAL diplomatic efforts to bring an end to the twelve-year civil war in El Salvador and to support the implementation of the peace agreements, signed 16 January 1992 in Mexico, offers a number of instructive examples of the use of incentives as a diplomatic tool. Inducement strategies, along with a variety of other more traditional tactics, were used by the United States, and later by multilateral actors, to move the Salvadoran government—and, in interesting ways, its opponents, the rebel Farabundo Marti National Liberation Front (FMLN)—to accept the principle of a negotiated solution to the conflict, to engage in constructive negotiations, to reach outcomes in those negotiations desired by the outside actors, to implement various elements of the peace agreements, and to engage in reconciliation and reconstruction.

International actors had mixed successes in achieving their goals, and the effectiveness of incentives as a tool of diplomacy varied considerably. As this chapter will show, the effectiveness of particular incentives depended on a number of factors. These factors included the nature of the desired outcome and its fit within the constellation of goals aspired to by the various international actors, the consistency of the offering of incentives, the type of follow-up, and the presence of internal forces who supported the outcome.

During the course of the war itself, the United States pressed a counter-insurgency strategy on the Salvadoran government. That strategy involved persuading the Salvadoran armed forces to adopt new military tactics to combat the rebels, encouraging the government and the armed forces to respect human rights while prosecuting the war, and persuading the government to implement agrarian reform as a way of undercutting support for the rebels. In pressing the elements of this strategy on the Salvadorans, the United States employed several kinds of incentives along with more traditional diplomatic tools. Washington was not entirely successful in achieving these goals, however, and this failure forms the backdrop to subsequent efforts to support a negotiated end to the conflict. Therefore, this paper briefly reviews the history of U.S. efforts to support agrarian reform and improve the Salvadoran government's human rights record during the war.

The war in El Salvador settled into a stalemate in the mid-1980s. The guerilla offensive of 1989, while a military failure, changed the political dynamic and forced all the parties involved in the Salvadoran conflict to reevaluate their commitment to a military solution. At the same time, the changing regional climate sparked by the Esquipulas peace process and decreasing East-West tensions gave the parties more room to reevaluate.[1] In this context, the United States, the United Nations, and other Latin American and European countries offered a number of incentives, both to the government and to the FMLN, to encourage the two sides to negotiate an end to the war. These were perhaps the most successful of the incentives offered in the peace process. The chapter discusses these efforts, and why and to what extent they were successful.

Once the Peace Accords were signed in 1992, the United Nations, the United States, and other international actors helped to ensure that the accords were actually implemented. The UN, as the party responsible for verifying that implementation, rendered judgments about the state of the peace process; both sides sought its approval. In addition, at key moments, the United States and the European Community offered financial incentives and imposed some financial sanctions. This chapter briefly reviews the UN efforts, and the international incentives and sanctions used to move the implementation process forward.

The chapter also looks briefly at the process of postwar reconstruction and the role of international incentives in that process. In the final pages, the chapter considers the declining international interest in El Salvador today, and the fewer and less-effective incentives the international community has to offer as a result. It speculates on the lessons this suggests for international involvement in peace processes, and some of the limits on the interests and the power of various international actors.

The Nature of Incentives

It is useful, in thinking about the effectiveness of various forms of incentives, to define more precisely the kinds of incentives that are being offered and the context in which they are offered. In its simplest form, an incentive is an offer by a sender to provide a good that the recipient desires, if the recipient engages in some specified behavior. Another more complicated form of incentive exists when the sender government offers a good directly related to the desired outcome—when, for example, a sender offers to fund postwar reconstruction programs on the condition that the recipient design and implement such programs. In this case, the recipient government may not desire, or at least not strongly desire, the "good" being offered, but may engage in the desired behavior because it is relatively costfree to the recipient. This will greatly influence the strength of the recipient's commitment to carry out the desired behavior when the inevitable problems and complications occur.

There are several other variants. A sender may offer some good to a recipient without identifying a particular behavior it seeks in response. In this form of incentive the sender seeks some unspecified influence on the recipient's behavior. In another variant, the sender (or a multilateral actor) already provides aid or assistance or some other benefit to the recipient and decides to urge the recipient to engage in a particular behavior, hoping that the aid it provides will permit it to influence the recipient's decision-making process. How explicitly the sender country links the continuance of its already existing aid to the recipient's compliance with the request varies, depending on the importance of the desired behavior to the recipient country, and the relative importance of the desired change in behavior in relation to the other goals of the sender. This variant is significantly different from the simple form, because in this case the "good" that the sender country has to offer is tied to more than one goal, and those goals may be related to each other in complicated ways. In such cases, the sender country is already providing assistance for one set of reasons, and is now threatening to condition that assistance on another set of reasons. The effectiveness of the incentive will be determined by the interplay between the sender's goals. This is more typical of the real world, and certainly more typical of the El Salvador case. An important factor to analyze in studying the effectiveness of particular incentives, therefore, is whether the incentive is linked to a single goal, or is tied to multiple objectives.

In reviewing the use of incentives in the peace and reconstruction process in El Salvador, it will be important to look at these factors—how important to the sender is the desired outcome, how that outcome fits into

the sender's broader set of goals and objectives, and how strongly the recipient desires the good being offered.

From War to Peace in El Salvador

Open civil war broke out in El Salvador in late 1980 and continued until
a peace agreement was signed on 16 January 1992. The war was fought
between the Salvadoran government and a coalition of five rebel groups,
the FMLN. Although rooted in the poverty and inequality of El Salvador,
the war was perceived by all parties as taking place within the cold war
context. The Salvadoran oligarchy, a group that was strongly resistant to
reform, and the military that was allied with it, viewed all opposition as
Communist inspired, and sought its forcible repression. The Carter administration began a military buildup in El Salvador to confront what it
said was "left-wing terrorism supported covertly with arms, ammunition,
training, and political and military advice by Cuba and other Communist
nations."[2] The Reagan administration portrayed El Salvador as a key part
of a world struggle, "a global issue because it interjected the war of national liberation into the Western Hemisphere," in the words of Secretary
of State Alexander Haig.[3]

The rebels for their part sought the support of Cuba, Nicaragua, and
the Soviet Union. While they described the goal of the revolutionary
movement as national and democratic, all five guerilla groups came, over
the course of time, to describe themselves as "Marxist-Leninists."

The location of the war in El Salvador in this larger geostrategic context
made the search for a negotiated solution, and even for an improvement
in the human rights situation, extremely difficult. Both the parties to the
conflict and their international backers saw military victory as imperative,
and all other considerations (including human rights) were viewed as sub-
ordinate. At the same time, this international dimension to the conflict
meant that other governments had extensive contact with all the parties in
El Salvador. When international conditions changed, and the international
mood favored negotiated solutions, the foreign actors were able to exert
influence on the domestic actors for resolution of the conflict.

The Salvadoran war was particularly bloody. Especially in the early years
of the war, paramilitary death squads targeted guerilla sympathizers and
opposition political activists for death. Possessed of only rudimentary intelligence about how the revolutionary opposition was structured, and inclined to see all political disagreement as armed revolutionary opposition,
the death squad apparatus, with the conscious support of significant sectors of the military, the security forces, and the government, captured,
tortured, and killed more than 30,000 people in the first two years of the

war, including trade union activists, Christian base community leaders, community organizers, and others. While the numbers of killings declined in the later years of the war, and the killing became more selective, the Salvadoran extreme right, through the course of the war, never abandoned the strategy of counterrevolutionary terror.[4]

In the second half of the 1980s, the imperative for victory at any price diminished. The Esquipulas peace process helped create a less-polarized climate, and encouraged the search for peace. Cold war tensions began to diminish. As this happened, the United States and other actors began to move more effectively to improve the human rights situation and bring the war to a negotiated conclusion. The Salvadoran guerillas proposed negotiations to end the war as early as 1981, and the two sides conducted a number of high-level meetings to discuss the possibility of a negotiated solution in the mid-1980s, but the negotiations failed to break the stalemate.[5]

In the late 1980s, a number of changes took place. Leaders on both sides of the conflict in El Salvador itself began to express more flexibility, as the social and economic costs of the prolonged war were felt more strongly. The failed rebel offensive of 1989 changed the way the parties viewed the military and political situation on the ground. Also important were the end of the cold war, and the accession to power in Washington of a less hard-line Bush administration. Serious negotiations now became conceivable.

The UN began to play an active role in the peace process in 1989. It had been in informal contact with the parties previously, and in December of that year both sides contacted UN officials to request their involvement. In 1990, the UN began to actively facilitate a negotiations process, and in April 1990, the "Four Friends" of the UN secretary-general (Mexico, Columbia, Venezuela, and Spain) agreed to assist the parties in seeking a solution. When the FMLN and the government agreed on an agenda and a time line for the negotiations, peace talks formally began. The U.S. also signaled its support for the principle of a negotiated solution. The Bush administration quietly informed the Salvadoran military that, because of budget pressures, aid would be gradually reduced over the next several years, although it would not pressure the military for a specific solution.[6] Meanwhile, a majority in the U.S. Congress voted to reduce military aid to El Salvador and to create a series of incentives for a negotiated solution. The ups and downs of U.S. military assistance to El Salvador over the next year would influence developments at the negotiating table.[7]

By early 1991, it was clear that a negotiated solution was inevitable. The United States began, with the Salvadoran government, to plan for postwar reconstruction, and the international community began to consider the kinds of support and incentives it might offer for postwar development.

Steps taken by the United States and the international community helped shape the specifics of the Peace Accords and the postwar reconstruction plans.

Peace was reached with the signing of accords on 16 January 1992. The next three years saw the international community actively involved in supporting the implementation of those agreements, and in supporting the reconstruction process. U.S. and international financial incentives for the implementation and reconstruction process were vital to moving the process forward.

Reform and the Use of Incentives during the War

U.S. counterinsurgency strategy in El Salvador called for strengthening the military against the rebels while winning the political support of the civilian population. To this end, the United States urged increased respect for human rights and agrarian reform on the Salvadoran government. Human rights became an important issue, not only because it was an aspect of counterinsurgency, but because it was a key element in the domestic U.S. debate on El Salvador. Repression was the traditional method of coping with political opposition in the country, and the Salvadoran extreme right employed this method as the revolutionary movement began to grow in the mid and late 1970s. When the Carter administration began to increase military aid to El Salvador in late 1979, human rights and antiwar activists, along with their allies in the Congress, began to raise concerns about the kind of government the United States was supporting in El Salvador. Human rights became the axis around which the question of military aid for El Salvador was debated in the United States in the early 1980s.[8]

With the growth of military aid to El Salvador, and the dispatching of U.S. military advisors, the United States formed a strategic relationship with the Salvadoran armed forces. The Salvadoran military, on its own, was clearly committed to defeating the guerilla opposition. The United States offered the money and the training to do so successfully. The United States, determined to defeat "Soviet-sponsored aggression," was eager to equip and train the Salvadoran military, and sought to influence the strategy and tactics the military employed in order to achieve victory.[9]

The power and the political influence of the Salvadoran military grew dramatically during the war, expanding fivefold from a force of 12,000 to 60,000 by the war's end. Its officers reaped personal rewards from corruption, many of them becoming rich over the course of the war.[10] The Salvadoran elite, which had previously seen the military as its servant, began to treat the armed forces as an independent force with political views and interests of its own. That increase in power and influence was based in part on the military's position as the bulwark of defense against the insurgency, and also on the resources that the Salvadoran military came to command, particularly the inflow of U.S. dollars and equipment.

The United States thus had the potential for substantial leverage over the Salvadoran military. It was supplying the financial assistance, training, and equipment that the armed forces needed to fight the war. Through its aid program and the presence of U.S. military advisors, the United States was able to signal its approval and support for particular officers or sectors of the military. The increased political power of the military as a whole, and the prestige of senior military officers depended ultimately on the resources that the United States was providing for the war. The United States was offering a number of "goods" that the Salvadoran military desired, and it was in a position to condition the delivery of those goods on changes in the behavior of the military.

The United States used its influence to persuade key officers in the Salvadoran military to adopt a counterinsurgency strategy based on winning hearts and minds. The United States also increased the effectiveness of some, though probably not the majority of Salvadoran military fighting units, and it converted some officers into close U.S. allies.[11] But the United States failed to get the Salvadoran military to adopt overall the small unit strategy it was propounding, and, most dramatically, it failed to get the Salvadoran security apparatus to improve its human rights performance.[12]

Incentives for Human Rights Improvement

The Reagan and Bush administrations sought to improve the human rights performance of the Salvadoran military and its allies for two reasons. First, they needed to appease congressional Democrats who were attempting to condition or cut U.S. assistance; second, they believed that continuing human rights violations undercut Salvadoran popular support for the military, which was critical to the counterinsurgency strategy that the United States was pushing in El Salvador. The White House applied various diplomatic and political pressures to seek human rights improvement in El Salvador, but it opposed conditioning U.S. military assistance on such improvement. For the administration, human rights improvement was always subservient to the goal of winning the war. After the brief lull in U.S. aid in December 1980 and January 1981, following the murder of the four North American churchwomen on 2 December 1980, no U.S. administration cut off aid to the Salvadoran military until the passage of the Dodd-Leahy legislation in October 1990. This was despite a human rights record that a Pentagon-commissioned study described as one "no truly democratic and just society could tolerate."[13]

Although the U.S. Congress sharply debated the issue of military aid to El Salvador in the early 1980s, it consistently compromised by allowing continued military assistance, while conditioning such aid on presidential "certifications" that the human rights situation was improving. The Reagan administration provided that certification four times. The certification requirements were dropped by the Congress in 1984, after the election of centrist José Napoleon Duarte as president of El Salvador.

The United States was not, in general, successful in persuading the Salvadoran government to respect human rights during the course of the war, although congressional pressure probably set some limits on what the government and the armed forces did. Much of the human rights improvement that did take place was because of shifting military strategies by the two sides, rather than because the Salvadoran government and military changed their human rights policies.[14]

The U.S. efforts failed for several reasons. First, the Salvadorans believed (correctly, as it turns out) that the United States had prioritized winning the war over respect for human rights, and that it would not cut off military assistance, whatever rhetorical statements it made. Thus, there was no real incentive for improvement.[15] Second, the administration and the Congress had different emphases, so that the United States was not speaking with a single voice. Third, the U.S. effort to improve human rights was directed at a government, ruling group, and military that were more or less unified in not caring about human rights. No significant power bloc in the country was committed to seeing the situation improve and therefore there were no internal factions whose power in the country was strengthened by U.S. or international intervention.

Incentives for Agrarian Reform

U.S. advisors were convinced that agrarian reform was critical for gaining the approval of the civilian population. The United States offered the Salvadoran government a number of incentives to implement a land reform program. In 1979 and 1980, USAID (United States Agency for International Development) and USAID contractors prepared concept papers on land reform and offered technical advice to the Salvadoran government on the development and implementation of land reform programs. From 1980 through 1985, the United States gave the Salvadoran government $137 million, in six separate USAID projects, for agrarian reform. The largest of these provided credit to cooperatives and farms formed in the early stages of the land reform movement.[16] The United States also helped establish the Salvadoran Institute for Agrarian Transformation, and helped with the implementation of the initial phases of the agrarian reform project.

But the project ran into tremendous resistance from Salvadoran elites. They saw, correctly, that their power base and their way of life were being threatened. The proposed land reform process was rapid, with little time to adjust. Because the properties taken would be paid off in long-term bonds, there was no immediate financial incentive.[17] Landed elites resisted forcefully. The reformers in El Salvador had a very thin power base; their position was bolstered by U.S. support (which helps explain why any land reform was accomplished), but they did not have the power to see the program through. The U.S. incentives were not effective or powerful enough to overcome political resistance to land reform. What the United States had to offer (funding, technical assistance, and political support for a land reform program) helped reduce the costs of land reform, but these were not sufficiently attractive to the landed oligarchy to overcome their opposition. In the end, the United States reached the limits of its influence. The most far-reaching part of the land reform program, which would have affected midsize coffee farms, was suspended by the Salvadoran National Assembly.

The land reform was not meaningless. A significant number of landless peasants received titles to small properties. And when the Salvadoran National Assembly tried to suspend the "land to the tiller" program, threats by the U.S. Congress to suspend aid to El Salvador led the assembly to quickly reinstate the program. But larger landholdings were not affected.

Incentives for Negotiations

International incentives played an important role in the peace negotiations in El Salvador. The first talk of negotiations took place in October 1981, when Nicaraguan president Daniel Ortega read an FMLN proposal for negotiations to the General Assembly of the United Nations. At that early stage of the war, however, both sides were intent on military victory. Both sides thought they could win, and in the context of the cold war, neither side saw other options. In late 1984, the two sides met for talks, but again there was no movement.[18]

In 1987, the situation began to change. Prompted by the Esquipulas process, the two sides met twice in October 1987, although the talks broke off after those rounds. Sporadic rounds of dialogue continued until the guerilla offensive of 1989, but the dialogue did not advance because neither party sought to negotiate seriously.[19] Nonetheless, internal changes were under way in both camps. In the beginning of 1989, the rebels made an offer to participate in the political process if elections were postponed. While this offer was made as the rebels prepared to launch a major military offensive later that year, the offer represented a significant shift in their position. According to Salvadoran analysts, while the rebels did not expect the government to accept the offer, they were prepared to follow through if the government responded.[20] In fact, the Bush administration urged the Salvadoran government to seriously consider the proposal. The rebels had never previously offered to accept key elements of the electoral system and the current constitution.

This evolution in FMLN thinking was sparked by a number of factors, including the Esquipulas process, but also by developments within the rebel leadership. In 1988, several prominent civilian allies of the FMLN returned to El Salvador to take part in the political process. They led small social democratic political parties and were preparing to take part in the 1989 elections. They had played an important role in the rebels' international diplomatic efforts, through their links with social democratic parties in Europe and Latin America, and because of their relatively moderate image. Their diplomatic work had brought the FMLN a certain level of legitimacy, and allowed them to make their case to the international community. When the civilians returned to El Salvador, rebel leaders had to take on more direct diplomatic responsibilities themselves. In visits to Latin American and European capitals in 1988, FMLN leaders were strongly urged to seek a negotiated solution to the conflict.[21] At the same time, Soviet officials were reported to have warned the Salvadoran Left that, in the event of a rebel victory, the Salvadoran guerillas should not expect that the Soviet Union would offer them substantial economic aid.[22] These signals generated pressure for a new strategy. They also paralleled emerging differences within the FMLN. Some of the organizations in the FMLN were more open to negotiating with the Salvadoran government, while others were committed to a decisive military victory.[23] The Latin American and European trip functioned as a kind of incentive to move FMLN thinking toward negotiations.

A number of factors led to the beginning of the actual negotiations process. The waning of the cold war and the steps toward peace in Nicaragua created new conditions for both the FMLN and the Salvadoran government, and for the United States as external sponsor. The 1989 offensive jumpstarted the process, helping to convince the two sides that neither could completely defeat the other militarily. In December 1989, a month after the rebel offensive, the U.S. assistant secretary of state for inter-American affairs, Bernard Aronson, first spoke publicly of support for a negotiated end to the war, a position reaffirmed by Secretary of State James Baker in February 1990.[24] In early 1990, administration officials reportedly told the Salvadoran armed forces that, while Washington would not push the government into negotiations, U.S. military assistance would likely decline over the next two years.[25] That year for the first time the U.S. Congress actually cut aid to the Salvadoran military. Spurred by the FMLN offensive, and especially by the murder of six Jesuit priests along with their housekeeper and her sixteen-year-old daughter by U.S.-trained government troops, Congress approved legislation (the Dodd-Leahy bill) to halve military aid. This complex bill was provisionally approved by the House of Representatives in June and finalized by the Senate in October 1990. The bill, crafted by Senators Christopher Dodd and Patrick Leahy, both Democrats, was explicitly designed to provide incentives for negotiations. It cut military aid in half, threatened to cut it to zero if the government did not negotiate in good faith, and threatened to restore it entirely if the guerillas launched another offensive. The Salvadoran military saw for the first time that U.S. assistance could actually be cut, and this served as another powerful spur to negotiations.

The Bush administration's commitment to a negotiated peace was unclear and equivocal. Washington expressed its desire for a negotiated solution without any specific vision of what the terms might be. David Holiday and Bill Stanley have argued that the United States at that time was "only cautiously supportive of the negotiations."[26] In fact, in early February 1991 unnamed State Department officials criticized Alvaro de Soto, the UN mediator, in remarks to the *New York Times*. But as the FMLN changed its negotiating position toward accepting a formula that preserved the institutionality of the government's armed forces, "the minimum requirement of U.S. policy had been met," and the Bush administration became more strongly supportive of the negotiations process.[27]

U.S. support for the peace negotiations was also complicated by differences between the Congress and the administration. In October 1990, over the objections of the Bush administration, the Senate decisively approved the Dodd-Leahy legislation. Half of the military aid appropriated for fiscal 1991 was set aside for postwar demobilization and the transition to peace. But in January 1991, that aid was restored to the military. After the rebels downed a U.S. helicopter, and apparently executed the two surviving U.S. servicemen, President Bush used a waiver provision in the legislation to reinstate the military aid. A Salvadoran army spokesperson said, "The vote of confidence the Congress had taken away from the armed forces has been restored."[28]

The pace of the negotiations was affected by the flow of U.S. aid. After the Senate approved the aid cut in October 1990 the bargaining process moved ahead. When President Bush released the aid in January 1991, the negotiations slowed down. In August 1991, when congressional Democrats showed that they had the votes for even deeper cuts in U.S. assistance, the "administration began to take a significantly more active role in supporting the negotiations," and the process moved quickly to its conclusion.[29] The key agreements of the final accords were reached in September 1991.

Incentives for the FMLN

One of the most interesting aspects of the Salvadoran peace process was the impact on the FMLN of direct U.S. contact, and the way in which the legitimacy this seemed to confer served as a powerful incentive in encouraging the rebels to accept a negotiated solution.

Throughout the war, there had been behind-the-scenes contacts between the United States and negotiators who represented the FMLN. But a key moment came in July 1991, when Representative Joe Moakley, a Democrat, traveled to the rebel-held town of Santa Marta, over the objections of State Department officials. He was accompanied by a reluctant U.S. ambassador, William Walker. A month later, Ambassador Walker returned to El Salvador, accompanied by Mark Hamilton, the commander of U.S. MilGroup, and Dick McCall, a senior staffer on the Senate Foreign Relations Committee. They met with a top rebel commander.[30] These two visits had a powerful effect. The FMLN perceived the visit as "signaling a new U.S. willingness to treat the rebels as legitimate participants in Salvadoran political life."[31]

In a broader sense, U.S. support for the negotiations process offered some form of recognition to the FMLN, and this was clearly an important incentive. Contacts with the FMLN became more serious after Ambassador Walker visited Santa Marta, culminating in the breakfast encounter that Assistant Secretary of State Aronson "accidentally" had with the FMLN negotiators during the final stages of the negotiation. The U.S. message that it would live with the FMLN as a legal opposition political party was a clear incentive to the rebel leadership, and encouraged them in the negotiations process.

Incentives during the Negotiations

Along with offering incentives that encouraged the parties to negotiate, U.S. and UN officials provided incentives to facilitate the bargaining process itself. During the peace negotiations, the UN embraced the idea of a new civilian police force and actively encouraged the parties to accept it. UN advisors drafted the proposals for the police reform sections of the Peace Accords, as well as the proposed accompanying legislation. The United States privately briefed negotiators on each side about the kinds of training and assistance it could offer a new force after a peace agreement was reached.[32] As the negotiations moved forward, the United States and other senders also offered incentives that affected both the government and the FMLN, offering to fund particular postwar programs and showing both sides drafts of the kind of programs they could provide.[33] The parties hoped that additional international support would materialize for a number of aspects of the Peace Accords, including reconstruction, the new police, and land reform. Many of the agreements were negotiated in the expectation that the international community would provide the necessary support. But in fact there were very few concrete commitments made by the international community during the negotiations process, which later caused real problems in the accords implementation phase. The expectations of support eased the negotiations process, but they proved to be unrealistic.[34]

Accords Implementation

Predictably, the implementation of the Peace Accords has been a difficult and complicated process. The United Nations Observer Mission in El Salvador (ONUSAL) and its successors (United Nations International Mission in El Salvador [MINUSAL] and United Nations Verification Mission [ONUV]) played a key role in monitoring the implementation process, helping the parties mediate disputes about the meaning of the accords, and overcoming the periodic recalcitrance of the parties. Incentives were key to these international community efforts.

Three examples illustrate the ways in which incentives facilitated the implementation process. Under the terms of the accords, a three-member Ad Hoc Commission was empowered to review the records of Salvadoran military officers, particularly on human rights grounds, and to recommend the transfer or discharge of any officer it reviewed. The government was then given sixty days to implement the commission's recommendations. The commission was widely expected to order the symbolic dismissal of a few officers. But to everyone's surprise, the commission's report, delivered to the United Nations 23 September 1992, called for 102 officers to be dismissed or transferred, including most members of the senior officer corps.[35]

The Salvadoran armed forces balked at complying with the recommendations of the commission. Senior military officers publicly criticized the report as a leftist plot. In late October 1992, Salvadoran president Alfredo Cristiani announced that he would postpone action on the commission's recommendations until the FMLN completed its demobilization. While some organizations within the FMLN were apparently willing to negotiate delays in the resignation of some senior officers in return for new reintegration programs for midlevel guerilla commanders, the UN took a firm stand that the ad hoc commission's recommendations were binding and nonnegotiable.[36] The UN continued to press the Salvadoran government on this issue, and in early 1993 the United States suspended the delivery of some military aid in the pipeline to El Salvador. It made clear to the Salvadoran military that aid would not be released until there was an agreement to accept the recommendations of the ad hoc commission. This created a powerful incentive for the military, particularly for younger officers who saw their force being threatened by the intransigence of older officers. When it became apparent in March 1993 that the Truth Commission created by the Peace Accords would also name senior officers as responsible for human rights violations, President Cristiani informed the UN that the remaining officers would resign from active duty by 30 June. The power of the UN's position, the incentive created by the slowdown in U.S. military assistance, and the differences within the officer corps created a situation in which all the identified senior officers were compelled to leave.

Another long and difficult issue was the implementation of the agreement to transfer small plots of land to former combatants of both sides, as well as to about 25,000 FMLN supporters. Because of changes in El Salvador's economy and investment structure during the war, the economic elite were less committed to maintaining the traditional patterns of landholding than they had been in the early 1980s.[37] As a result, the government was able to negotiate a land transfer agreement as part of the Peace Accords. But implementing the agreement proved difficult. There were serious legal and bureaucratic complications in the transfer process, as well as tremendous political resistance by some landholders and by those on the political right who remained committed to the oligarchic order.[38] The UN and the United States both played critical roles in moving this issue forward. The United States, through USAID, provided about 85 percent of the funding for the transfer of land to FMLN ex-combatants and their supporters, making the program relatively costfree to the Salvadoran government.[39] Both USAID and the UN Mission treated the land transfer program as a high priority, focusing attention on it, and reporting publicly on its status.

The ultimate success of the land transfer program resulted from a number of factors.[40] First, USAID obviously provided a powerful incentive by offering to fund the whole program. The financial cost to the Salvadoran government of compliance was low, and foreign financing meant that the government could not plead the excuse of lack of funds. Second, the role that USAID and the UN played in encouraging and offering incentives for the program strengthened those forces in the Salvadoran government who wanted to see the program completed. U.S. and international actions supported them in internal power battles.[41] Ultimately continued external pressure and substantial funding from USAID made it possible for the program to be completed.

The third example of the role of incentives in the implementation of the Peace Accords centers on the 1994 elections. Dubbed the "elections of the century," the 1994 balloting was the first in which the FMLN rebels participated, and the first elections in fifteen years to select political leadership at all levels—municipal, legislative, and presidential. The 1994 voting was to be one of the key elements of the peace process. All parties agreed that the elections had to be perceived as open and honest. International legitimacy was key to gaining access to the aid dollars promised for postwar reconstruction and development. International approval was important in securing the World Bank loans that would finance the revamping of the Salvadoran economy.

Reforms to the electoral system were mandated in the Peace Accords. A new electoral code was approved in January 1993, eight months behind schedule. The UN Mission in El Salvador opened an electoral office in July 1993. The United Nations Observer Mission in El Salvador was widely viewed as the arbiter of international legitimacy, and it was thus important for the Salvadoran government to maintain the approval of the UN.[42] The Salvadoran government thus had powerful incentives to comply with UN recommendations on the voter registration and election process.

The United States also had an interest in the success of the electoral process. The newly inaugurated Clinton administration had policy concerns that the process be free and fair. In addition, pressure from Democratic members of Congress who had long followed El Salvador had an impact on USAID and on U.S. embassy officials. The election pitted Ruben Zamora, an opposition figure known to many in Washington, against Armando Calderon Sol, the mayor of San Salvador and candidate of the rightist ARENA Party. Although President Cristiani and the ARENA Party had led the country into peace negotiations with the rebels, the party's origins in the extreme right made many, including some Democratic members of Congress, uncomfortable. In the spring of 1993, key congressional staffers warned U.S. government officials that they would employ administrative mechanisms at their disposal to hold up the release of economic aid to El Salvador if there was not sufficient progress on voter registration.[43]

The Salvadoran Supreme Electoral Tribunal—the government agency charged with registering voters, maintaining the voter rolls, and conducting elections—began the voter registration process that spring, but it did not approve a formal registration plan until the summer. International observers and opposition political parties began to voice concerns about the tribunal's competence and its very commitment to registering new voters.[44] In July 1993, Democrats in the House of Representatives held up the release of $70 million in economic assistance to El Salvador. This was a substantial portion of the $110 million intended for balance of payments assistance to the Salvadoran government in fiscal 1993. At the urging of congressional Democrats, the aid was withheld until after the elections themselves in March 1994.

The suspension of U.S. aid was explicitly linked to progress in voter registration. In an August letter to USAID administrator Brian Atwood, House Foreign Operations Subcommittee chairman David Obey, a Democrat, wrote that "we need to create further incentives" to "conduct a successful voter registration campaign in El Salvador."[45] In September, the administration wrote Obey to say that disbursement of the funds "would be linked to . . . satisfactory progress by the Tribunal, first in registering voters, and second in issuing the necessary voter cards."[46]

This created powerful incentives for the Salvadoran government. The now-suspended assistance had been earmarked for meeting balance of payment needs, providing the Salvadoran government with access to U.S. dollars. While the government had some access to dollars through newly opened World Bank channels, and thus was not as dependent on direct U.S. aid as it had been during the war, it still needed the funds. The pressure on the Electoral Tribunal to register more voters increased significantly. President Cristiani convened a meeting with the tribunal and all political party leaders to resolve this issue.

At the same time, the UN Mission began to assist the tribunal in carrying out the registration process. UN staffers provided transportation for election registrars, assisted in planning and troubleshooting registration campaigns, etc. The combination of the UN's on-the-ground assistance, the government's need for UN approval, and the pressure from the U.S. aid suspension overcame the obstacles. In the end, voter registration reached about 85 percent.[47] While registration rates were probably lower in zones that had historically been guerilla controlled, and while election-day procedures disenfranchised some properly registered voters, the elections were generally fair, and the results, with some local exceptions, were broadly representative. The ARENA Party presidential candidate Armando Calderón Sol, won an overwhelming victory with 66 percent of the vote in a runoff in the second round. In the national legislature, the Arena Party gained 39 of the 84 available seats, compared to 21 seats for the FMLN, which emerged as the second largest party in the assembly. The elections were quite an accomplishment, given the obstacles that existed in mid-1993. International pressures and incentives made a crucial difference in this success.[48]

As noted earlier, both the Salvadoran government and the FMLN were strongly motivated by the desire to have the UN Mission's approval. The

UN reports on the peace process mattered a great deal to both parties, and were perceived as linked to the flow of international assistance. Both sides had strong incentives, at least in the first three years of the peace process, to behave in ways that won UN legitimacy and approval.

Postwar Reconstruction and Reconciliation

In addition to the accords implementation itself, the international community has played an important role in supporting postwar reconstruction in El Salvador. USAID and the Salvadoran government started reconstruction planning in 1991, when it became clear that a peace agreement might be signed.[49] USAID, because of its technical assistance capabilities and its capacity to commit funds, played an important role in this process. The most significant issues in the reconstruction process concern the coordination of the reconstruction plan between the two parties, and the degree of implementation by international donors.

The international community expressed a desire for the reconstruction plan to be developed in a "concerted" fashion. In March 1992, shortly after the Peace Accords were signed, the World Bank convened a consultative group meeting of potential donors to El Salvador, including interested governments and international financial institutions. In the preparations for the meeting, donors made clear to both the Salvadoran government and the FMLN that their support for reconstruction "depended less on the [plan's] development content, and more on demonstrated broad political support." Donors expected both parties to come in with a commonly agreed plan for postwar reconstruction and for international assistance.[50]

This was a powerful incentive, but it played itself out in a complicated fashion. The government and the FMLN had distinctly different visions of the reconstruction process, based in part on conflicting economic and ideological conceptions, and in part on the need to channel reconstruction assistance to different political and social bases. Under the circumstances, it was difficult for the two to negotiate a common reconstruction plan. In addition, the government, with a relatively sophisticated technical apparatus, and with assistance from USAID, had a far more elaborate, detailed, and convincing proposal than did the FMLN, whose technical capacity was limited. In negotiations early in 1992, the government made a few concessions to the FMLN, including vague language on FMLN and NGO participation in the planning process. But the conceptions of the two sides were still far apart as the date of the consultative group meeting approached. Both parties worried about the risk of losing international aid and about being blamed politically for such a failure, if they could not endorse a single plan. In the end, the FMLN reluctantly endorsed the government plan.[51]

Once the consultative group met, the actual shape of the reconstruction plan depended on the individual funding decisions of particular donors. Pledges made at the consultative group were not binding, and subsequent negotiations between the individual donors and the Salvadoran government reshaped many commitments. There was no formal international monitoring mechanism established for this process.[52]

For the third meeting of the consultative group in June 1995, Salvadoran nongovernmental groups, as well as the FMLN, organized themselves to question the development and implementation of the reconstruction plan, comparing it to the goals outlined in the 1992 consultative group meeting. They prepared a written critique and made proposals to incorporate the nongovernmental sector in the planning and evaluation of the National Reconstruction Plan. The groups also lobbied various donor governments and agencies, seeking support for their position. They found a surprisingly receptive audience, and at the consultative group meeting, a number of donors spoke out strongly to urge the Salvadoran government to involve NGOs more fully in the process. There was little organized follow-up on the part of the international donors, however, and many of the Salvadoran NGOs moved on to other issues rather than sustaining their interest. The success of the consultative group mechanism in creating effective incentives was thus limited by the lack of specific follow-up mechanisms.[53]

Declining International Influence

By late 1995, international interest in El Salvador had declined significantly. Although some important elements of the peace process were still unfinished, and there was still debate about postwar reconstruction, international attention moved elsewhere. In large measure, this was because El Salvador was no longer in crisis, and no longer a threat to regional stability. The war had ended, and the FMLN had demobilized, made the transition to political life, and participated in elections in 1994. The Salvadoran government had won an important measure of international legitimacy.

While El Salvador continues to receive substantial amounts of international assistance (U.S. economic aid, though drastically below wartime levels, is still higher than aid to most of Latin America), there is less aid than there once was, and the Salvadoran government is less dependent on that aid. The international community's ability to exercise influence and offer incentives has thus diminished.

One striking example of this is the case of electoral reform. Following the 1994 elections in El Salvador, the winning presidential candidate and his defeated opponent called jointly for a series of electoral reforms to address the irregularities that had occurred in that election. Later that year, a commission composed of all the political parties in the country endorsed a specific set of reform proposals. By July 1996, not one of those proposals had been implemented. The reforms would have weakened the power of local mayors and weakened the patronage opportunities available to two smaller political parties. The ARENA Party, just three votes short of a majority in the National Assembly, refused to advance the reforms.

The international community weighed in strongly on this issue. The United Nations Mission in El Salvador reported on the problems of electoral reform. The United Nations Development Program offered technical assistance, and tried to coordinate donors to pressure the Salvadoran government. Secretary of State Warren Christopher publicly called on the assembly to approve the reforms in a speech in February 1994.[54] And USAID held up the disbursement of $10 million in economic support funds pending progress on the reforms. But none of these pressures and incentives moved the assembly or the ARENA Party to overcome internal opposition and approve the legislation.[55]

Because there are unfinished elements of the peace process, and because there are continuing debates about the postwar reconstruction process, international donors interested in supporting the peace process will need to coordinate their efforts more effectively in the coming years if they want to offer meaningful incentives in El Salvador.

Lessons

The El Salvador case suggests several conclusions about incentives. First, the incentives (or disincentives) created by international funding (or nonfunding) can have a powerful impact. In 1988, the Soviet Union warned the FMLN not to expect the kind of assistance that the Sandinistas had received, and this clearly had an impact on the FMLN's willingness to entertain the possibility of a negotiated solution. In 1989, and more forcefully in 1990, the Bush administration warned the Salvadoran military that military aid levels would decline over time. The U.S. Congress followed up by cutting aid appropriations. This strongly influenced the military's willingness to negotiate an end to the war.

Second, the impact of these incentives is often felt over the medium-to-long term. Neither the FMLN nor the Salvadoran military accepted the notion of a negotiated settlement overnight, and neither the United States nor the Soviet Union demanded that they do so. But as the parties sorted out internally the implications of the changes in international assistance, the U.S. and Soviet messages began to sink in.

Third, incentives work when sender nations are serious about their intentions. During the war, the United States never really intended to cut aid, and the Salvadorans knew it. The impact of the passage of the Dodd-Leahy bill was profound. The United States actually cut aid to the Salvadoran armed forces, and threatened to cut even more if certain conditions were not met.

Fourth, international legitimacy matters greatly. This is especially true for groups that have been on the outside. The FMLN was strongly influenced by the messages from friendly Latin American governments in 1988, and was decisively influenced by the prospect of recognition or acceptance from the United States in 1991. Both the FMLN and the government sought the approval of the UN Mission in El Salvador.

Fifth, international incentives are more effective when they are perceived to strengthen particular views in an internal debate. Progress was achieved in the implementation of land reform because U.S. financial assistance enhanced the position of those within the Salvadoran government who favored such reform, enabling them to withstand opposition from landed elites. Recognition and encouragement for FMLN advocates of a negotiated solution influenced the evolution of policy within the rebel movement.

Sixth, incentives policies may require senders to make substantial commitments to monitoring compliance. Incentives often work as broad tools of national policy where their impact is general and long term. On those occasions when the international community has sought more detailed compliance with specific conditions, it has had to develop specialized monitoring and follow-up mechanisms to verify compliance. The UN Observer Mission played this role in the Peace Accords process and in the elections. No such mechanism was established for the reconstruction plan, and the incentives were far less effective. Compliance can often require a level of involvement, follow-up, and supervision that most international donors are unwilling or unable to provide. Such involvement can also draw the international community into domestic political battles, where the results can be problematic.

Seventh, incentives are more effective when international actors speak with a single voice. When there are perceived divisions in the sender country, as was the case with the U.S. Congress and the administration over human rights issues, or when there is lack of coordination among sender countries, as in the inadequate delivery of postwar reconstruction aid, incentives policies will be less successful. Consistency and coherence of policy are essential for incentives strategies as they are for all arenas of international affairs.

Notes

1. On 7 August 1987 in a meeting in Esquipulas, Guatemala, the Central American presidents agreed to a peace plan proposed by Costa Rican president Oscar Arias. The plan, backed by Spain and Germany, focused on Nicaragua but encouraged a peace process throughout Central America, including El Salvador. This drew Europeans and Latin American leaders together. Although it did not herald a total end to the conflict, it generated a formula and the momentum needed for future agreements. See Jack Child, "The Arias Plan: 1987–1988 Summits," in *The Central American Peace Process, 1983–1991* (Boulder, Colo.: Lynne Rienner Publishers, 1992), 45–59.

2. Tommie Sue Montgomery, *Revolution in El Salvador, From Civil Strife to Civil Peace* (Boulder, Colo.: Westview Press, 1995), 146.

3. Ibid., 14.

4. As late as September 1990, Americas Watch could begin a human rights report on El Salvador by saying, "Despite a decade of promises by government officials to bring to justice those responsible for gross violations of human rights in El Salvador, the impunity of military officers and death squad members remains intact." They ended the report with "[A]ll indications point to a continuation of the total impunity with which the Salvadoran Armed Forces commit extrajudicial execution, torture, and massacre" (El Salvador, *Impunity Prevails in Human Rights Cases* [New York: Americas Watch, September 1990].)

5. Oscar Martinez Penate, *El Salvador: Del Conflicto Armado A La Negociacion* (Ontario, Canada: Bandek Enterprises, 1995), 91–95.

6. George R. Vickers, "The Political Reality after Eleven Years of War," in *Is There a Transition to Democracy in El Salvador?* Joseph S. Tulchin with Gary Bland (Boulder, Colo.: Lynne Rienner Publishers, 1992), 39.

7. Terry Lynn Karl, "El Salvador's Negotiated Revolution," *Foreign Affairs* 71, no. 2 (Spring 1992): 156.

8. For a discussion of the U.S. debate on El Salvador aid in the early 1980s, see Cynthia J. Arnson, *Crossroads, Congress, the President, and Central America, 1976–1993* (University Park, Penn.: Pennsylvania State Univ. Press, 1993).

9. Montgomery, *Revolution in El Salvador*, 148–50.

10. For a discussion of corruption and personal enrichment on the part of Salvadoran military officers, see Joel Millman, "El Salvador's Army: A Force Unto Itself," *New York Times Magazine*, 10 December 1989.

11. A. J. Bacevich, James Hallums, Richard White, and Thomas Young, *American Military Policy in Small Wars: The Case of El Salvador* (Washington, D.C.: Pergamon Brassey's International Defense Publishers, 1988), 68.

12. Hugh Byrne, "The Problem of Revolution: A Study of Strategies of Insurgency and Counter-Insurgency in El Salvador's Civil War, 1981–1991" (Ph.D. diss., University of California, Los Angeles, 1995), 174–76, 291.

13. Benjamin C. Schwarz, "American Counter-Insurgency Doctrine and El Salvador: The Frustrations of Reform and the Illusion of Nation-Building," (Santa Monica, Calif.: National Defense Research Institute, RAND Corporation, 1991), 23.

14. For a discussion of the different periods of human rights violations, see *De*

la Locura a la Esperanza: La Guerra de Doce Anos en El Salvador, Report of the Truth Commission for El Salvador (New York: United Nations, 1993), 17–39.

15. Schwarz, "American Counter-Insurgency Doctrine and El Salvador," vii.

16. Jim Leach, George Miller, and Mark Hatfield, *U.S. Aid to El Salvador: An Evaluation of the Past, A Proposal for the Future. A Report to the Arms Control and Foreign Policy Caucus* (Washington, D.C., 1 February 1985), 11.

17. Elizabeth Wood, "Economic Structure, Agrarian Elites, and Democracy: The Anomalous Case of El Salvador" (Paper prepared for the Latin American Studies Association conference, Washington, D.C., 26–30 September 1995).

18. Penate, 95.

19. Karl, 150.

20. Personal communication, interviews with Salvadoran business and religious leaders, January 1989.

21. Karl, 151.

22. Child, 73.

23. Tom Gibb and Frank Smyth, *El Salvador: Is Peace Possible? A Report on the Prospects for Negotiations and U.S. Policy* (Washington, D.C.: Washington Office on Latin America, 1990), 5–11.

24. Karl, 153.

25. Vickers, 37.

26. William Stanley and David Holiday, *Under the Best of Circumstances: ONUSAL and Dilemmas of Verification and Institution Building in El Salvador* (Paper delivered at Peacekeeping Conference, sponsored by North-South Center, Miami, Florida, 12 April 1996), 9.

27. Ibid., 10.

28. Karl, 157.

29. Ibid., 159.

30. Arnson, 260–61. For a somewhat different view of the meeting, and of the relationship between the United States government and the FMLN, see Joseph G. Sullivan, "How Peace Came to El Salvador," *Orbis* (Winter 1994): 87–88.

31. Arnson, 261.

32. Sullivan, 88. See also William Stanley, *Protectors or Perpetrators? The Institutional Crisis of the Salvadoran Civilian Police* (Washington, D.C.: Washington Office on Latin America and Hemisphere Initiatives, 1996), 5–6.

33. Stanley and Holiday, 12–13.

34. Alvaro de Soto and Graciana Del Castillo, "Obstacles to Peacebuilding," *Foreign Policy* (Spring 1994): 73.

35. Montgomery, 241–42.

36. Stanley and Holiday, 21–23.

37. See Wood, 7–9.

38. For a discussion of the land transfer program and its political complexities, see Jack Spence, George Vickers, and David Dye, *The Salvadoran Peace Accords and Democratization, A Three Year Progress Report and Recommendations* (Cambridge, Mass.: Hemisphere Initiatives, 1995), 13–17.

39. The United States had intended to support land transfer programs for demobilized soldiers of the Salvadoran military as well, but suspended the program because of concerns about corruption.

40. "Success" here is measured by the number of ex-combatants who received title to property. Many of these newly landed small farmers will, over the next few years, fail economically, because of the small size of their plots, problems with technical assistance, credit, and marketing, and because of the Salvadoran economy's policy orientation toward the export market. They will not be successfully integrated into the economy, and they may lose the land they have acquired.

41. Spence, Vickers, and Dye, 17.

42. Stanley and Holiday, 11.

43. In a meeting the author attended in June 1993 with Democratic staffers for the House Foreign Operations Subcommittee to report on a delegation visit to El Salvador, a senior staffer gave assurances that this message had been communicated to administration officials.

44. See Madalene O'Donnell, Jack Spence, and George Vickers, *El Salvador Elections 1994, The Voter Registration Triangle* (Cambridge, Mass. Hemisphere Initiatives, 1993), for an account of the first concerns about the Salvadoran elections raised by international observers and the United Nations.

45. Letter, Rep. David R. Obey to J. Brian Atwood, 5 August 1993.

46. Letter, J. Brian Atwood to Rep. David R. Obey, 23 September 1993.

47. U.S. Citizens Election Observer Mission, *Free and Fair? The Conduct of El Salvador's 1994 Elections* (Washington, D.C., June 1994), 4.

48. For a good, brief discussion of the electoral process, the role of the UN, and the outcome of the elections, see Tommie Sue Montgomery, "Getting to Peace in El Salvador: The Roles of the United Nations Secretariat and ONUSAL," *Journal of Interamerican Studies and World Affairs* 37, no. 4 (Winter 1995).

49. Sullivan, 94. See also Stewart Lawrence, *Postwar El Salvador: An Examination of Military Issues Relating to Reconstruction* (Cambridge, Mass.: Unitarian Universalist Service Committee, October 1991).

50. Peter Solis, *Reluctant Reforms: The Cristiani Government and the International Community in the Process of Salvadoran Post-War Reconstruction* (Washington, D.C.: Washington Office on Latin America, June 1993), 4.

51. Ibid., 3–5.

52. James Boyce et al., *Adjustment toward Peace: Economic Policy and Post-war Reconstruction in El Salvador* (San Salvador: United Nations Development Program, May 1995), 76–78.

53. The author participated in a series of meetings with a group of Salvadoran NGOs and North American counterparts to prepare for the Consultative Group, then met with U.S. AID officials to present the critique the Salvadorans had drafted.

54. U.S. Department of State, Office of Spokesman, address by Secretary of State Warren Christopher before the Legislative Assembly of El Salvador, delivered 26 February 1996, Legislative Assembly, San Salvador, El Salvador.

55. Latin America Working Group, *El Salvador Delegation Report, June 1996* (Washington, D.C.: Latin America Working Group, June 1996), 8–9.

8

Incentives and Domestic Reform in South Africa

Jeffrey Herbst

INTERNATIONAL ATTEMPTS TO prompt a settlement of South Africa's domestic problems have a long history. While sanctions had been used by the international community since the United Nations imposed an arms embargo in 1963, many believed that successive white regimes in South Africa could not simply be bludgeoned into submission. The dismal record of the universal sanctions imposed on Southern Rhodesia (now Zimbabwe) in 1965 after Ian Smith declared a Unilateral Declaration of Independence had demonstrated the limited utility of trade restrictions. South Africa seemed even less vulnerable to sanctions because it had a more advanced economy, its exports were primarily composed of high-value, low-volume minerals, and there were grave doubts that economic pressure alone would prompt Afrikaner leaders to dismantle the racist system they had so painstakingly constructed. Indeed, in the early 1980s, a series of leaders, notably Ronald Reagan's assistant secretary of state for African affairs, Dr. Chester Crocker, but also Prime Minister Margaret Thatcher, argued, against the growing cacophony for comprehensive sanctions, that incentives would have to be used by the international community in conjunction with punitive measures to promote change in South Africa.

By 1986, the use of incentives had been overwhelmingly rejected as Congress enacted the Comprehensive Anti-Apartheid Act over President Reagan's veto, marking only the second time since World War II that a

U.S. president had been unable to sustain a veto on a foreign policy issue (the other was the enactment of the War Powers Act over President Nixon's veto). Any position taken toward Pretoria that was not overtly hostile was widely seen in the United States as racist. Understanding why incentives in the end proved to be unsustainable in the South Africa case is thus particularly important.

Preventive Diplomacy and Constructive Engagement

Given the current attention devoted to preventing conflicts, it is sometimes implied that diplomacy in the past was entirely crisis driven without a preventive aspect. In the South African case, as in many others, this notion is incorrect. It was widely recognized for decades throughout the world that change was coming in South Africa and that it was essential that actions be taken before the country plunged into a full-fledged race war. As the Study Commission on U.S. Policy toward Southern Africa noted in its aptly named 1981 report, *South Africa: Time Running Out,* "The final battle lines have not yet been drawn in South Africa. Fundamental political change without sustained, large-scale violence is still possible, although time is running out."[1] The commission also took the sensible position, adopted by almost all other observers, that while apartheid could only be eliminated by the South Africans themselves, the United States was not without influence.

American administrations since Kennedy had applied some mixture of sanctions, incentives, and diplomacy in their dealings with South Africa. However, the debate over the use of incentives versus sanctions came to the fore at the start of the Reagan administration. The new Republican administration came to power with a much better defined, and more controversial, policy than had been the case with its immediate predecessors, although Crocker would belatedly stress the continuities between the policy he championed and that of previous administrations.[2] Previous administrations had appealed for change in South Africa to varying degrees but never had a policy with much clarity, much less one that calibrated the use of sanctions and incentives. In his 1980 *Foreign Affairs* article, "South Africa: A Strategy for Change," which would become the architectonic analysis for American policy toward South Africa during the next eight years, Crocker laid out what he called "a strategy for change." Crocker argued that then prime minister P. W. Botha and his colleagues were carrying out the "equivalent in Afrikaner nationalist terms of a drawn-out coup d'etat."[3] In his view, the "modernizers" "do not have an ideological blueprint. They have a set of attitudes—pragmatic, flexible, determined—and a concept of strategy defined as the continuing process of matching ends and means."[4] In Crocker's view, the Afrikaner elite was

> edging toward a model featuring an economically unified confederation (coded "constellation") and a high degree of political decentralization. Political power would be "divided" (not "shared") among a wide range of units: "independent black states," a projected white-Coloured-Asian government (or governments), and a series of "autonomous" and "self-governing" black municipalities located in the "white areas."[5]

Crocker was obviously sympathetic toward this solution but never indicated if it would be acceptable to the black majority. Indeed, he admitted that "the black political arena is an increasingly complex puzzle for outsiders to measure and for participants to operate in."[6]

Crocker was quite clear on the limits of American influence. Still, pointing out that external pressure had always been a part of South African politics, he sketched out several anchors for American diplomacy. Especially important was his description of the importance of the encouraging role that the U.S. government could play: "An important role of official U.S. policy is to lay down guidelines, help create a climate supportive of constructive engagement by other Western governments, and encourage our diverse and pluralistic society to engage with, not turn away from, a changing South Africa."[7] He continued by noting that:

> Publicly expressed encouragement and support of positive steps is another important tool of policy. When South Africa's limited but real policy changes and its obvious political flux are continuously described by Western officials as "the status quo"—and when our officials speak only the language of ticking clocks and time bombs—it is not likely that we will be taken seriously by the leadership there. A tone of empathy is required not only for the suffering and injustice caused to blacks in a racist system, but also for the awesome political dilemma in which Afrikaners and other whites find themselves. . . . Support for evolutionary change implies sensitivity to the concerns of local actors, and is nothing for us to be reticent about. Such a stance also gives us a little-noted source of leverage because of the certainty that if we cease supporting it, no one else will take our place.[8]

While encouragement and a tone of empathy might not normally be considered strong incentives, they were salient in the case of South Africa because the country had already gone through close to three decades of approbation (including the arms embargo and effective expulsion from the Commonwealth) and its relationship with America had been deteriorating for many years.

The policy of constructive engagement was in sharp contrast to the sanctions approach favored by other governments. The policy derived its potential influence precisely from this distinction. A commitment not to sanction was in effect an incentive. The South Africa case thus presents a novel form of the interrelationship between carrots and sticks. It also illustrates how the mere fact of engagement in a setting of diplomatic hostility can be an incentive. This form of incentive was also present in the case of the U.S. dialogue with North Korea from 1993 to 1994 described in chapter 3. Whereas engagement (along with material benefits) brought success in the case of North Korea, the Reagan administration's engagement with the apartheid regime in South Africa proved unsuccessful.

Crocker's display of empathy for the Afrikaners, and his high hopes for them, were already unusual in the early 1980s and quickly became anachronistic. While it is easy to parody constructive engagement (a phrase that Crocker would later regret coining), many of the immediate and subsequent criticisms of the article, and of the policy in general, were incorrect. Crocker was no apologist for apartheid and he had nothing but disdain for the "slick hucksters of the status quo peddling a message of krugerrands, the Cape route and chrome reserves."[9] Nor did Crocker dismiss the use of "pressure," which he distinguished from "punishment." In a critical passage, he noted: "Pressure also has a role to play in a policy of constructive engagement. Pressure in both the public and diplomatic channels can strengthen the hand of official modernizers and other agents of change, adding to the far more important forces at work within South African society."[10] Importantly, Crocker endorsed sanctions, such as the ban on arms sales and the refusal to use South African defense facilities, that had been adopted by previous administrations.

The prospects of a coordinated policy toward South Africa were further strengthened by the appearance of other leaders with similar sentiments. Prime Minister Thatcher did not share the Foreign Office's view that more pressure be applied on South Africa and she certainly did not agree with many in the Commonwealth that mandatory sanctions be applied immediately. Indeed, she would later recall that "the worst approach was to isolate South Africa further. Indeed, the isolation had already gone too far, contributing to an inflexible, siege mentality among the governing Afrikaner class."[11] She also argued, "What I wanted to achieve was step-by-step reform—with more democracy, secure human rights, and a flourishing free enterprise economy able to generate wealth to improve black living standards. I wanted to see a South Africa which was fully reintegrated into the international community."[12]

Chancellor Helmut Kohl of West Germany—the other Western leader of importance to white South Africa—also held no brief for sanctions. While France, especially under the leadership of François Mitterrand, was more antagonistic toward South Africa, it had limited interests in the

Southern Africa region where there were no French speakers. Therefore, in the early 1980s, there was as much consensus in Western capitals about how to approach South Africa as there probably could be on a difficult issue. Further, the United States had, in Crocker, an official who was concerned not just about diplomacy but that the use of incentives and sanctions be analytically informed.

The Travails of Constructive Engagement

Constructive engagement to promote domestic reform in South Africa failed. Not only did it not promote political reform in a foreign country—a task that is always difficult—but it produced significant collateral damage by weakening the Reagan presidency and, arguably, by causing a deterioration in race relations in the United States. Prime Minister Thatcher's endorsement of a mixed approach to South Africa also caused her tremendous diplomatic problems, especially with the Commonwealth. The mixed use of sanctions and incentives failed for several reasons, many arguably beyond the control of those who were implementing the policy. As the travails of U.S. policy toward South Africa have already been documented at considerable length, I will here concentrate on the major reasons for failure rather than again presenting the complex diplomatic record.[13]

Disparity between Means and the Desired End

The major problem that the Reagan administration and other interested foreigners faced when trying to promote change in South Africa was that their policy tools were not commensurate with the magnitude of the changes they were demanding from Pretoria. Apartheid, it must always be remembered, was a system that had its origins in South Africa's industrial development beginning in the mid–nineteenth century and indirectly in the relationship that the arriving Europeans established with the local African populations starting in the mid–seventeenth century. While there were many aspects to apartheid, its fundamental purpose was to protect white standards of living by segmenting blacks into specific parts of the labor market so that they could not compete with white workers and thereby lower white wages. To segment the labor market, it was necessary to physically separate racial groups and to keep as many Africans as possible in the homelands that were created at the peripheries of white South Africa. Over decades, especially after the Afrikaner political victory in 1948, a nightmarish bureaucracy was created that sought to regulate almost every aspect of the lives of black people: where they lived, what jobs they could have, whom they married and slept with, and what they could read or listen to.

Education, health, and other social services were provided to blacks at third-world levels while whites enjoyed a first-world lifestyle.

It is thus clear what apartheid was not: It was not the policy of one or two bad leaders. It was not the adoption of policies by an aberrant government that did not really reflect society. Nor was it the implementation of policies that benefited a small ruling clique. Finally, it was not a foreign policy gambit that, while perhaps important to the leaders, was not central to the lives of the population. Rather, apartheid was a system that benefited millions of whites that had been developed over decades. Nowhere is the nature of apartheid clearer than in comparing the system to the plight of blacks in the United States. While American blacks had been traditionally treated extremely poorly, they could demand their rights, especially in the 1960s, by arguing that amendments to the U.S. Constitution already protected them but that racist local leaders were discriminating against them. What was needed was enforcement of their rights and a diminishment of the powers of local officials. In South Africa, blacks, especially Africans, by law did not have many rights. Thus, the African demand for an end to apartheid was not a civil rights question, as black demands for justice in the United States had been, but rather a revolutionary threat to the entire system.

Indeed, the great irony of the Reagan administration's constructive engagement policy was that, in other areas, it was sensitive to the distinction between governments which systematically interfered with the everyday lives of their citizens and those that were more simply authoritarian. Professor Jeane Kirkpatrick, in the article that would raise her to prominence, wrote that "traditional autocrats," in contrast to totalitarian regimes, "leave in place existing allocations of wealth, power, status and other resources . . . they do not disturb the habitual rhythms of work and leisure, habitual places of residence, habitual patterns of family and personal relations."[14] She concluded by sharply criticizing the assumptions that many in the Carter administration held about reform of totalitarian regimes and argued that those countries could not be expected to liberalize their politics except through extraordinary means.

Of course, using Kirkpatrick's definitions, South Africa was not a traditional authoritarian regime but a totalitarian one. To a breathtaking extent, it interfered with the daily lives of blacks; indeed, it made policy in all of the areas that Kirkpatrick argued that traditional authoritarian regimes did not bother with. Crocker's argument that South Africa was changing quickly under the lead of modernizers was therefore not only factually controversial but put him analytically at odds with one of the chief architects of the Reagan administration's foreign policy. Such analytic confusion was not only telling, it also was a hint of the policy confusion that was to come.

Critically, there was no set of incentives that the U.S. administration could offer the South African government to change its system of rule as long as it perceived that it was still benefiting from it. The inducements offered by Crocker and Thatcher above, mainly reintegration into the world economy and better treatment by the world powers, paled in comparison to the benefits apartheid provided to the white population. In the early 1980s, apartheid still seemed militarily defensible; indeed, the security threat to the white regime was extraordinarily low given the resentment and grievances of the black majority. The economy was booming due to the sharp increase in the price of gold. The Botha administration had resigned itself to poor treatment from the international community and was increasingly claiming to enjoy its polecat status.

Crocker was well aware of the lack of U.S. influence. As a result, he proposed that U.S. influence be "carefully husbanded" and applied to concrete instances of change. That such a policy might involve the United States in only the "amelioration" of apartheid did not bother Crocker as long as the process was open-ended and consistent with a nonracial order.[15] Analytically, this stance made a great deal of sense. However, practically, it was too clever by half. First, precisely because abolishing apartheid would be a long, drawn-out process, there would inevitably be many instances where it was not clear if a concrete measure (say, repealing the ban on mixed marriages) was an end in and of itself or part of a process. Indeed, many in the white regime wanted to make no more than cosmetic changes and would inevitably use the American stance to defend their actions and argue that they need not move faster. The sheer complexity of apartheid and its mutifaceted intrusiveness into so many lives gave Pretoria many potential concessions to make that would not fundamentally alter the system. Second, since the ability to influence is finite, supporting small changes in the hope that leaders are going down the right road will inevitably cause the exhaustion of political capital, perhaps long before the desired end result is reached.

Finally, and most importantly, the black majority viewed apartheid as a system and was not that interested in small changes that were doled out by Pretoria in a miserly manner. Indeed, the African National Congress (ANC) and other black organizations (whose views were never accorded the same importance as those of the white government by Crocker) were vociferously opposed to granting Pretoria credit for small, incremental changes because they did not believe that real change was coming and because they did not feel that apartheid as a system could be overturned until the majority could elect its own leaders. The Reagan administration routinely got itself into trouble by championing South African actions that many in the black majority perceived as little more than cosmetic. For Crocker's policy of husbanding limited influence to work, he would have had to get all participants on board and convince them all that such "con-

fidence-building measures" were important in and of themselves. However, such diplomatic work with the various black organizations was never
attempted and would have undoubtedly failed if tried.

The impact of U.S. incentives was further reduced because domestic
reform in South Africa was not the only issue of policy concern. Although
Crocker had claimed in his article that movement toward Namibian independence was "inexorable,"[16] achieving independence for Africa's last col-
ony in exchange for the removal of Cuban troops from Angola quickly
became the Reagan administration's highest priority in Southern Africa.
The threat posed by Cuban troops in Angola attracted the attention of the
new conservative administration while many African leaders saw resolving
the wars in Namibia and Angola as the region's highest priority.[17] Much
of the limited political capital that the United States had vis-à-vis South
Africa was exhausted during negotiations over the regional settlement. Indeed, one of the incentives that the United States used in pressuring Pretoria to cooperate in the regional negotiations was the promise of better
relations with the United States. The same carrot could then not be used
effectively again to promote domestic reform. There were simply too many
targets and not enough bullets.

The American-brokered negotiations between the South Africans, Angolans, and Cubans are notable because in that case, as opposed to demanding domestic reform, an incentive (the removal of Cuban troops)
was provided to the South Africans that was concomitant with the demand
being made (Namibian independence). Crocker noted in his memoir that
the linkage he established would

> offer a major, visible, and strategic quid pro quo for agreeing to implement
> the Namibian decolonization plan: the reversal of South Africa's lonely hu-
> miliation in 1975; the removal of the SADF's [South African Defense Force]
> only conventional equal; the likely reduction of Communist influence in the
> region; a serious constraint on SWAPO [South West African People's Orga-
> nization] and a likely boost for UNITA [National Union for the Total Inde-
> pendence of Angola].[18]

Similarly, the Angolans, in exchange for the Cubans leaving, were being
promised the extraordinary incentive of the removal of their major adversary from their border, one who had consistently intervened in their country and caused great damage. Still, even with these very large carrots, the
deal took eight years to strike and was eventually consummated, in part,
because of the unpredicted rise of Mikhail Gorbachev and the totally unex-
pected development of cooperative diplomacy between the superpowers
that was designed to solve major regional disputes across the world.

To say that the incentives the world could provide South African leaders were not concomitant with what was being asked does not imply that there was any other set of policies that would have made Pretoria's leaders act in a more deliberate manner. In the early 1980s, or later, sanctions such as the world was willing actually to apply to South Africa would not have inflicted enough harm to provoke a move toward political reform.[19] Indeed, the increasingly hostile rhetoric from the Carter administration had produced a hardening of attitudes in South Africa. When sanctions came, they were adopted less because of a calibrated view of how pressure might affect South Africa's leaders than as a visceral response to the horrors of apartheid combined with a large dose of purely American politics.

That incentives, or sanctions, or some mix of the two did not provide enough leverage to force a change in another country's domestic policies is hardly unusual. Seldom will the international community have recourse to policy instruments that will be able to successfully influence an in-grained set of domestic institutions and policies given the powerful social forces at work in most countries. However, the prominent use of incentives may be especially problematic in cases of limited leverage because the likely inability to declare the policy a success makes the United States or other countries demanding change look weak and opens the door to charges of appeasement. Thus, the use of incentives might, even more so than sanctions, profitably be limited to cases where there are well-defined demands that are actually commensurate with the incentives being offered.

Certainly, one way that incentives can be used in a calibrated manner is if there is a well-defined schedule of demands that can be met in an observable manner. For instance, incentives may not only work but be publicly palatable in the case of nuclear proliferation because deadlines can be set around the production or destruction of material and significant resources are devoted to oversight. This is the pattern established in the 1994 Agreed Framework with North Korea, as Scott Snyder elaborates in chapter 3. A well-defined roadmap makes it clear when incremental concessions amount to the disavowal of a nuclear weapons capacity. Similarly, the American kowtowing toward Syrian president Assad during each hostage release from Lebanon was viable because it was clear that the kind words for the dictator were linked to each hostage release and would end when there were no more hostages. On the other hand, the open-ended process of reforming apartheid was arguably a particularly bad venue for the prominent use of incentives because it would not be clear when the always unpopular need to publicly reward racists would be over.

Diplomatic Dilemmas Posed by Incentives

If it were to work, the kind of strategy envisioned by Crocker would have put enormous strains on the diplomatic resources of the United

States. Crocker envisioned a complex mix of incentives and sanctions that would have allowed the United States to move in a nuanced manner "to maintain a close, ongoing watch on the situation while carefully assessing our own bargaining position."[20] However, even if the power of incentives had matched the demands, the Reagan administration simply was not up to this degree of nuanced diplomacy in an obscure part of the world. As Crocker details in his memoirs at considerable length, conservative elements in the administration who were unabashedly pro-Pretoria worked systematically to destroy his nuanced policy of incentives and sanctions. To take only the most grievous example, when the administration's South Africa policy was falling apart in mid-1986 as Congress demanded greater sanctions, conservative elements managed to defeat Crocker and position the administration in a manner that seemed to be defending South Africa when the township violence and associated repression was being featured on television screens nightly. Crocker critiques President Reagan's key 22 July 1986 speech (when the president tried and failed to make the case for a continuation of his policy) as follows: "But Botha must have particularly enjoyed hearing that he could choose which blacks to talk to: 'the South African Government is under no obligation to negotiate the future of the country with any organization that proclaims a goal of creating a Communist State—and uses terrorist tactics to achieve it.' "[21]

The incoherent policy of the Reagan administration actually speeded the adoption of sanctions and the disavowal of incentives. The choice many in Congress faced was between opting for sanctions and an unambiguous disavowal of apartheid or siding with an administration that could not clearly state how it felt about developments in the racially divided country.

When using incentives, or some mix of incentives and sanctions, it may be particularly important for the United States, or other governments, to be clear on the limits of those incentives. Dissension in the ranks may also encourage elements in the target country to think that they can get more for less. Indeed, in a world where government officials can jet overnight anywhere, target countries may devote considerable energy to developing and exploiting dissension among key members of the country demanding change. South African officials, for instance, were often in the United States to meet their allies outside of the State Department, often helped in their end runs by the Heritage Foundation and other groups that were not sympathetic to the pressure aspects of constructive engagement.

Incentives and Domestic Politics

South Africa was an incendiary issue in American politics because of apartheid's resonance with America's own troubled civil rights history. Indeed, as early as 1948, U.S. foreign policy toward the anticommunist

South African regime was complicated by the National Party's (NP) adoption of racist policies at a time when the American racial practices were coming under greater domestic and international scrutiny.[22] It was also recognized early on that U.S. policy toward South Africa and domestic civil rights issues were linked and could be exploited by those who did not find American policy tough enough against Pretoria. For instance, Undersecretary G. Mennen Williams wrote to Secretary of State Dean Rusk in 1963:

> We have reached the point where we must take a more vigorous stand against apartheid. In African opinion we can no longer rest our case on a condemnation of apartheid. We must be ready to back our condemnation with some form of meaningful action. . . . We confront this African pressure for action at a time when powerful forces in our own society are demanding action on racial inequalities at home. The two forces are inter-related and, as [the recent conference in] Addis showed, Africans are as aware of the inter-relationship as those who are opposing segregation in the United States.[23]

South Africa became an even more controversial issue in the 1980s because of the Reagan administration's backtracking on a number of civil rights issues and because of the increasing brutality of the South African authorities as they attempted to crack down on the still limited opposition. Further, Randall Robinson of TransAfrica and his colleagues in the Free South Africa Movement succeeded in using the South African issue as a club to hurt the Reagan administration more generally. By beginning a series of highly publicized sit-ins at the South African Embassy in Washington in November 1984, Robinson focused the public's attention on the failures of constructive engagement and repeatedly charged that the administration was appeasing the white regime. Of course, Robinson was, in addition to publicizing the new township violence in South Africa, hoping that the demonstrations would serve to reenergize the African American population. In the 1984 presidential elections, African Americans had voted overwhelmingly for a candidate (Mondale) who had suffered one of the greatest defeats in American electoral history. The protests at the embassy were not only a way of highlighting the evils of apartheid, they were also a way of putting race back as an issue the administration had to deal with in domestic politics.

Thus, while the demonstration movement mushroomed faster than anyone could have imagined (in part because the South African authorities foolishly decided to press charges against the original demonstrators), it was always clear that South Africa was not just another domestic policy issue. Much like the issue of Cuban troops abroad (a particularly sensitive issue to the vocal Cuban Americans in this country), South Africa was in many ways a domestic issue as much as a foreign policy concern. Clear evidence of the true nature of the South Africa issue for America was the involvement of many interest groups usually associated with domestic politics (e.g., much of the civil rights movement) in the sanctions campaign. Apartheid was therefore an issue that did not lend itself to the prominent use of incentives because the risk of appearing soft was so much greater than in most diplomatic issues that are handled outside of the public's gaze.

Indeed, the diplomatic history suggests that the Reagan administration was all but obsessed with how to manage the public diplomacy surrounding the controversy over apartheid and constructive engagement. As a classified memo from the U.S. ambassador to South Africa, Herman Nickel, to Chester Crocker noted, "Our major challenge is to change the terms of the public debate, moving it beyond universal condemnation of apartheid and ways of signaling American disapproval to the more constructive question of how we can best use what influence we have to help South Africans achieve a more just and stable order."[24] Nickel clearly understood that providing even empathy to the South African regime was problematic: "every time we recite the evidence of change, we risk sounding like South African Government apologists and invite our critics to cite all the remaining unresolved grievances—notably South African Government's unwillingness to relinquish control and transfer power to the black majority. Anything less is dismissed as cosmetic and peripheral."[25] As a result, the Reagan administration committed itself to a coordinated public relations campaign to convince broad segments of American society that the incentives integral to constructive engagement did not amount to support of apartheid.[26]

However, it was in the end impossible for the administration to win the battle over public diplomacy. The case Crocker was trying to make was extremely nuanced. As per his 1980 *Foreign Affairs* article, Crocker argued that he was not against sanctions per se, but that each sanction had to be analyzed separately to understand its punitive impact.[27] However, this nuanced approach simply fell apart under the weight of the deteriorating situation in South Africa in the mid-1980s. Congressman Howard Wolpe, Crocker's major nemesis while he was chair of the House Subcommittee on Africa, summed up the feeling of many when he asked at one hearing:

Mr. Secretary, could you explain once again how we are, as you say in your testimony, an increasingly effective force for change . . . when, in the last 18 months, over 1,300 people have been killed, mostly by security forces; 36,000 have been arrested for political reasons, including over 2,000 children; torture remains rampant; and the gap between black and white leaders in South Africa has visibly widened?[28]

Indeed, as Nickels sensed, the Crocker policy failed, in large part, because the policy failed to convey the moral outrage against apartheid that an increasing share of the American public felt was necessary. Crocker repeatedly noted that while the United States was justified in expressing moral indignation about apartheid "moral indignation by itself is not foreign policy" and that a policy of mixed incentives and sanctions was required.[29] However, even those who usually could be counted on to support the Reagan administration found that, at a time when the United States was not even claiming that it could be a major influence on events, that the expression of moral outrage was perhaps the only useful action the United States could take. For instance, Senator Mitch McConnell, Republican from Kentucky, critiqued constructive engagement by arguing that only a focus on the injustices of apartheid made for a viable policy. He concluded by saying that he agreed that "indignation alone is not a strategy" but neither, he suggested, was "wishful thinking."[30]

Incentives are used perhaps most effectively when the issues involved are not widely publicized so that policymakers can avoid the charge of appeasement. One of the reasons that incentives may have figured so prominently in issues of nuclear proliferation is that, despite the issue's innate importance, the public has only the most limited tolerance for the technical issues surrounding reactors and weapons. Similarly, while the linkage between Namibian independence and the removal of Cuban troops from Angola generated a great deal of criticism in the specialized literature, such incentives were possible because the public was not attuned to the issue of Namibian independence. On the other hand, apartheid was an immediate, visceral issue that Americans were especially sensitive to because of our own poor record of civil rights.

In retrospect, assigning the policy a name, much less the term "constructive engagement," was a particularly self-defeating act. The name gave something opponents could rally around, attracted considerable publicity, and could be parodied with ease ("destructive engagement" was only the most popular takeoff). Adopting policies that use incentives but that cannot be described, and therefore derided, with a simple name would be sensible.

The issue of appeasement was particularly salient during the debate over apartheid because the South Africans allowed the world's television cameras to film, at length, the carnage associated with the township uprisings between 1984 and 1986. Many people in the United States and elsewhere had the impression that South Africa was in flames when most of the township violence was actually highly compartmentalized and none of it touched the white areas. Indeed one of the more amusing parts of the Crocker memoir is his railing against the idiocy of the South African authorities for allowing the press to cover the uprisings at length.[31] His condemnation of the actual human rights violations in South Africa are seldom more pointed, in part because it was the South African public spectacle that caused the Reagan administration so many problems. More technical issues that can be handled outside of the spotlight might, again, lend themselves better to the use of incentives.

Finally, countries other than the United States may be able to use incentives in their foreign policies in a less-controversial and more-constructive manner. The degree to which diplomacy in the United States is managed in public and, in particular, by Congress, is without parallel. Nowhere else, for instance, would the spectacle be found of an administration official of the rank of Crocker being repeatedly humiliated in public hearings called by Congress. Nor do the structures of even other Western democracies provide as many opportunities for opponents to oppose and (in the case of the sanctions override in 1986) actually repudiate foreign policy measures adopted by the executive. While there are inevitably trade-offs between secrecy and accountability, it is a simple reality that incentives may sometimes be easier for countries whose foreign policies are open to less public scrutiny.

The End of Apartheid

White rule was overthrown in South Africa quicker than most could have imagined and managed to a far greater extent than thought possible by a white leader. The cataclysm of revolutionary violence that had been central to so many scenarios did not occur. While the exact cause for the ending of apartheid will be debated for many years, by the late 1980s there was growing realization within the official white community that grand apartheid was not viable. This evolution came about, in part, because, while the security forces waged an extraordinarily successful campaign against the ANC throughout Southern Africa during the 1980s, there was little doubt after the 1984–86 township uprisings that the country was less secure than ever before. The international sanctions, refusals by foreign banks to roll over loans, and the sports and cultural boycotts also made it clear to white leaders that they would never be accepted internationally until minority rule ceased. Perhaps most importantly, there was an acknowledgment within the government that the very structures of apartheid were imploding. Even in Botha's famous 1985 Rubicon speech—widely viewed as a reaffirmation of apartheid—there was an admission that influx controls (the set of laws and practices that kept many Africans from migrating to the white cities), the very core of grand apartheid, were too costly to operate.[32] Or as F. W. de Klerk would later admit, "If our old policy, which was so unpopular in many circles, could work, then we would have surely clung to it. But as responsible leaders charged with the government of the country, we came to the conclusion that the policy we had planned could simply not work."[33] While some of these trends were visible when Crocker was writing in the early 1980s, it was the deterioration of South Africa after constructive engagement began that was critical to the white leadership's change of mind.

Indeed, two events in 1989 caused a fundamental change in the white vision of a minimally acceptable future that would allow for minority rule. First, F. W. de Klerk came to power after P. W. Botha had a stroke. De Klerk carried none of the baggage associated with Botha: he was from a later generation of Afrikaners confident of their position and not scarred by the long battles with the English; he apparently took a dim view of the security forces that Botha (a former minister of defense) had integrated into the highest levels of government; and he was not so personally associated with the defense of apartheid and the State of Emergency. This is not to say that de Klerk came to power as a reformer. In fact, de Klerk was from the more conservative wing of the National Party (NP) and there was little in his background as an almost classic Afrikaner politician and as the son of a leading NP politician to believe that he would quickly move to dismantle apartheid. However, the leadership change at least opened up the possibility of a different white negotiating stance. Indeed, de Klerk began his critical 2 February 1990 speech to Parliament (when the ANC was unbanned) on a strikingly different tone from Botha's talk of a total onslaught: "[there is] the growing realization by an increasing number of South Africans that only a negotiated understanding among the representative leaders of the entire population is able to ensure lasting peace."[34]

The second critical development was the collapse of Communism worldwide, symbolized by the fall of the Berlin Wall in November 1989. De Klerk understood, before almost anyone else, that Communism's failure would have a profound effect on the ANC's project of overturning white rule. In the same 2 February 1990 speech, de Klerk actually analyzed the changes in the world before turning to events in his own country. De Klerk argued that

> The collapse, particularly of the economic system in Eastern Europe, also serves as a warning to those who insist on persisting with it in Africa. Those who seek to force this failure of a system on South Africa, should engage in a total revision of their point of view. . . . Southern Africa now has an historical opportunity to set aside its conflicts and ideological differences and draw up a joint programme of reconstruction.[35]

De Klerk argued that the fall of Communism created "a new scenario." As a result, there was "a window of opportunity [for South Africa] which, if not seen and used, would have been a major blunder."[36] Indeed, the massive failure of Communism gave de Klerk considerable confidence that the radicals had, in his words, been "castrated."[37] He seemed certain that the ANC would be prevented from engaging in some of the more radical policies that it had always been associated with, notably the nationalization of the banks and the mines, and that what redistribution did occur would be moderated significantly by the new realities of the international economy.

At the same time, the ANC realized by the late 1980s that its maximalist demands could not be met. During the 1980s, the ANC's guerillas had been pushed out of their bases in Mozambique and Angola. The township violence between 1984 and 1986, while unprecedented, had not directly threatened the white regime although the riots made the specter of the country hurtling toward ungovernability and race war clearer to all. Nelson Mandela came to understand that the government could not be overthrown and that the attempt to mobilize the population for armed struggle would only lead to disaster. In an important 1989 letter to Botha from jail, which set the stage for negotiations, Mandela wrote:

> I am disturbed, as many other South Africans no doubt are, by the specter of a South Africa split into two hostile camps; blacks . . . on one side and whites on the other, slaughtering one another; by acute tensions which are building up dangerously in practically every sphere of our lives, a situation which, in turn, preshadows more violent clashes in the days ahead. This is the crisis that has forced me to act.[38]

Further, Mandela defined ANC interests in a way that allowed for negotiations. In his 1989 letter to Botha, Mandela took the important first step by stating that the two fundamental issues for him were majority rule in a unitary state and the establishment of safeguards for the white majority.[39]

Having independently come to the conclusion that they could not win outright but that the other side was weak enough to cut an acceptable deal, the white government and the African National Congress initiated a series of delicate negotiations in 1990 that culminated in the 1994 elections for a new, nonracial government. It appears unlikely that any set of policies adopted by external powers could have significantly altered the pace or contours of the negotiations. The eventually successful negotiations were driven in good part by the strategic assessments of two men as to how the internal dynamics of the country were evolving. Both de Klerk and Mandela probably had to go through the events of the 1980s to reach their settlement in the 1990s. The settlement was forged from the remnants of ANC/NP policies and protest politics, allowing both sides to have a winning hand. There were also extraordinarily fortuitous events, like Botha's stroke and the fall of the Berlin Wall, which had profound ramifications but which could not have been predicted or accelerated.

Conclusion

While constructive engagement probably did little to help South Africa, it also did little harm to that country. Rather, almost all of the damaging aspects of the policy were felt at home, in good part because of the incentives that were an aspect of the policy. While any American administration that was in power in the 1980s would have been under severe pressure to "do something" about South Africa, the prominent use of incentives in an administration that seemingly did not have a clear understanding of its own policy served as a lightening rod for not only direct criticism but also the promotion of all kinds of other agendas that were irrelevant to South Africa but quite important to various groups of Americans. The South African case is therefore probably most instructive in the ways not to use incentives.

Notes

1. Study Commission on U.S. Policy toward Southern Africa, *South Africa: Time Running Out* (Berkeley: University of California Press, 1981), xxiv.
2. U.S. House, Chester Crocker, "Testimony of Chester Crocker," Subcommittee on International Economic Policy and Trade, and on Africa, *The Anti-Apartheid Act of 1985,* 17 April 1985, 53.
3. Chester A. Crocker, "South Africa: A Strategy for Change," *Foreign Affairs* 59 (Winter 1980): 334.
4. Ibid., 337.
5. Ibid., 339.
6. Ibid., 342.
7. Ibid., 350.
8. Ibid., 351.
9. Ibid., 324.
10. Ibid., 351.
11. Margaret Thatcher, *The Downing Street Years* (Great Britain: Harper Collins, 1993), 513.
12. Ibid.
13. For a good review of U.S. policy, see Pauline H. Baker, *The United States and South Africa: The Reagan Years* (New York: The Ford Foundation, 1989).
14. Jeane Kirkpatrick, "Dictatorships and Double Standards," *Commentary* 68 (November 1979): 44.
15. Crocker, "Strategy for Change," 327.
16. Ibid., 323.
17. Chester A. Crocker, *High Noon in Southern Africa: Making Peace in a Rough Neighborhood* (New York: W.W. Norton, 1992), 74–75.
18. Ibid., 67.
19. Certainly, Randall Robinson is simply incorrect in stating that de Klerk

released Mandela largely because of the sanctions adopted by the U.S. government. Like the incentives previously offered, the sanctions by themselves were not enough to change the basic calculus of the South African government. See Randall Robinson, "Preface," in *South Africa and the United States: The Declassified History,* ed. Kenneth Mokoena (New York: The New Press, 1993), xvi.

20. Crocker, "Strategy for Change," 351.

21. Crocker, *High Noon in Southern Africa,* 323.

22 Thomas Borstelmann, *Apartheid's Reluctant Uncle: The United States and Southern Africa in the Early Cold War* (New York: Oxford University Press, 1993), 103.

23. G. Mennen Williams, "Memorandum for Secretary Dean Rusk," reprinted in *South Africa and the United States,* ed. Mokoena, 54.

24. Herman Nickel, "Our Public Diplomacy Initiative: The Theoretical Framework," in *South Africa and the United States,* ed. Mokoena, 85.

25. Ibid., 86.

26. See "National Security Decision Directive 187: United States Policy toward South Africa," in *South Africa and the United States,* ed. Mokoena, 96–97.

27. Chester Crocker in response to questions, Subcommittee on International Economic Policy and Trade, and on Africa, *The President's Report on Progress toward Ending Apartheid in South Africa and the Question of Future Sanctions,* 5 November 1987, 22.

28. Howard Wolpe, statement in Subcommittee on International Economic Policy and Trade, and on Africa, *Legislative Options and United States Policy toward South Africa,* 9 April 1986, 65.

29. Chester Crocker, "Testimony of Chester Crocker," Subcommittee on International Economic Policy and Trade, and on Africa, *The Anti-Apartheid Act of 1985,* 17 April 1985, 51.

30. Mitch McConnell, remarks in Committee on Foreign Relations, *U.S. Policy toward South Africa,* 24 April 1985, 3.

31. Crocker, *High Noon in Southern Africa,* 259.

32. "Extracts from South African President P. W. Botha's Speech," *Reuters North European Service,* 16 August 1985.

33 "De Klerk Interviewed on Talks with ANC," *BBC Summary of World Broadcasts,* 9 May 1990, part 4.

34. F. W. de Klerk, "Address by the State President," reprinted in Robert Schrire, *Adapt or Die: The End of White Politics in South Africa* (New York: Ford Foundation, 1991), 160.

35. Ibid., 162.

36. Arnaud de Borchgrave, "De Klerk sees Open Society in Six Months," *Washington Times,* 14 June 1990, 1.

37. "Interview with F. W. de Klerk," *Foreign Broadcast Information Service— Africa,* 7 September 1993, 17.

38. Nelson Mandela, "Statement to President P. W. Botha," in *Mandela, Tambo and the African National Congress,* eds. Sheridan Johns and R. Hunt Davis (New York: Oxford University Press, 1991), 218.

39. Ibid., 225.

Part Four

Multilateral Application

9

Gaining Leverage for International Organizations: Incentives and Baltic-Russian Relations, 1992–1994

Heather F. Hurlburt[1]

T HE END OF A BIPOLAR ORDER saw a rise in expectations both that international organizations could step in and keep peace and that, through incentives or other tools, conflict could be prevented. However, the limited abilities of international organizations to guarantee or develop peace and stability have been a major disappointment in recent years. The dashing of post–cold war hopes for a new internationalism has become the cliché of the moment, replaced with a sour, pessimistic withdrawal. International bodies are left with fewer resources to carry out tasks assigned to them, thus making failure and further disappointment even more likely. Large-scale sanctions or enforcement actions become less feasible, though challenges to the authority of international regimes have scarcely decreased.

International organizations and states seeking to affect situations considered too sensitive or too marginal for full engagement will have to find methods of influence that draw on resources they already possess. The question of preventive incentives arises from this rubric quite naturally; how can a state be persuaded to do the right thing in advance?[2] The scarcity of resources has taken its toll on the traditional incentives countries could be offered, however. Foreign assistance levels have declined in the

United States and other major countries, and governments therefore must rely on other tools for exerting influence.

International organizations in particular have been asked to meet ever-increasing challenges with resources and procedures designed for quieter times. Within the broad range of policy options that can be held out as incentives, international organizations can use their own legitimacy-conferring powers (and any concrete benefits that may accompany them) as incentives. One method that has been tried is conditioning membership, status, and benefits normally associated with such organizations on adherence to specified norms of behavior or resolution of particular conflicts. Such incentives require less investment of national will and resources than do punitive measures such as sanctions or enforcement. They also can be employed preventively, and if successful, they may have an additional positive effect on the prestige and authority of the organization responsible. International organizations and states not directly involved in a conflict may thus find incentives particularly useful tools.

This study examines the use of incentives by international organizations and concerned states to influence the resolution of two contentious issues between Russia and its Baltic neighbors between 1992 and 1994: the withdrawal of Russian troops based in Estonia, Latvia, and Lithuania, and the evolving nationality and citizenship policies of the three states. Western states, the Council of Europe, and the Organization for Security and Cooperation in Europe (OSCE) joined forces to ensure withdrawal of ex-Soviet troops from the Baltic states and resolution of concerns over citizenship for nonethnic Balts.[3] Their efforts combined national financial assistance and political pressure with the moral and actual support, as well as the privileges of membership, that international organizations could offer. Examined closely, these methods suggest potential for carefully coordinated use of international organizations to avert conflicts through positive incentives. However, the Baltic experience also suggests limitations connected to political will, credibility, and follow-through.

Emergence of a Potential Conflict

The three Baltic states had enjoyed a relatively privileged position in the West during the period of their incorporation into the Soviet Union (between 1940 and 1991). Their status as Soviet republics was never officially recognized by the United States and many other Western governments. Active émigré groups were successful in giving them a level of public visibility closer to that of Poland or Hungary than of the other Soviet republics. The visibility of Baltic independence movements began in the late 1980s, setting the stage for high levels of Western concern and involvement in the process that led to their early declarations of independence, Soviet military crackdowns in 1991, and achievement of independence later that same year.

Even so, the West did not move immediately to grant them security guarantees, extensive tariff breaks, or massive financial and military assistance in 1991. The several reasons for this reluctance—concern over the Soviet response, fiscal parsimony at home, the countervailing demands of German unification—have been extensively analyzed and debated. But the West was keenly interested in the security of the Baltic states. Efforts to work within the existing fiscal and diplomatic parameters gave rise to creative uses of incentives: targeting of aid to domestic flash points, and marshaling the resources offered by existing international organizations to provide incentives to shape Baltic—and Russian—behavior. Most concerned were the United States, Canada, Germany, and Great Britain—with the North Atlantic Treaty Organization (NATO) and the European Union (EU) in their wake—and the Nordic countries. This group of "friends of the Baltics" found ways to use already-existing procedures and the standards of international organizations as reinforcement for bilateral initiatives and as incentives in their own right.

This method of influence was one with which European states had some experience in the field of human rights. The European Union had used human rights benchmarks in attempts to press for improvements in Spain, Portugal, and Greece when they were candidates for membership.[4] However, the particular phenomena of Baltic-Russian relations were so novel in 1992 that considerable room for experimentation existed. Thus, several new instruments or new uses of old instruments were tested, with some success, in the Baltic case.

By mid-1992, initial Russian acquiescence or even support for the statehood of three small neighbors was turning to hostility, presenting the international community with a new dilemma. A substantial element of the Russian elite and Russian military remained unresigned to the loss of strategic ports on the Baltic Sea. The moves and rhetoric of the newly independent Baltic state to repudiate the preceding forty years of Soviet dominance, which included resentment toward the population brought from Russia, reinforced Russian concerns. Russia began to turn to international organizations—chiefly the United Nations and the Organization for Security and Cooperation in Europe—with allegations of human rights violations in Baltic policies toward ethnic Russian or Russian-speaking residents.

Russian politicians were not long in seizing on this issue; the Russian Parliament threatened Estonia with sanctions as early as July 1992.[5] Debates over eligibility for citizenship, voting rights, and permanent residence, particularly in Estonia and Latvia, brought long-repressed nationalist sentiments to the fore on both sides. Latvia had only a plurality of ethnic Latvian residents, and Estonia and Lithuania were both home to sizable Russian-speaking minorities. Ensuring primacy of the national language and culture was a priority across the Baltic political spectrum, with extremist elements calling for the expulsion of Soviet-era settlers, particularly those with military or security service connections. Ex-Soviet troops remained in all three countries, as did large numbers of support staff, retired soldiers, and defense industry workers. In addition to the problem of encouraging the parties to reach agreement on the forces' withdrawal, the status of individuals who wanted to remain—or who had already retired—was hotly contested. The two issues were thus conflated, even without efforts to use one for leverage on the other.

Inevitably, the relationship became a potent issue in domestic politics on all sides. Even moderate Russian politicians could not hear with equanimity the calls of some Baltic politicians for the expulsion of ethnic Russians. More nationalist Russians responded with calls for the reoccupation of the states, or at least for the application of strong nonmilitary pressures. Russian president Boris Yeltsin halted the troop pullout first in December 1992, attempting to strengthen his nationalist credentials. The Baltic response—intensified calls for assistance from and ties to NATO and other Western institutions—increased Russian resentment. This cycle had clear potential to reinforce extremists on both sides. One victim was moderate Latvian foreign minister Janis Jurkans, whose "weak" nationalist credentials forced his resignation during late 1992 debates between moderates and hard-liners over the troop withdrawal negotiations.

Western governments viewed the problem as one of ensuring peace and the long-term survival of the Baltic states without stirring up dangerous nationalist pressures in Russia that might jeopardize Yeltsin's moves toward democracy. Initial hopes that the West would commit itself militarily to the Baltics' defense were dashed; only Carl Bildt, then prime minister of Sweden, even alluded to such a possibility.[6] Left with a limited arsenal, international organizations and governments worked together to offer several different incentives, which became salient features of the international community's response. Membership in or association agreements with European organizations—the Council of Europe, the OSCE, and the European Union—were conditioned on Baltic adoption of liberal citizenship laws and residence procedures for nonethnic Balts. The need for Russia to limit its attempts to influence Baltic policies as it, too, strove for Council of Europe acceptance and Western financial support was also made clear. Assistance with housing was offered to Russia in exchange for the withdrawal of Russian forces. Western governments promised to remain involved in monitoring the issue to help Estonia and Latvia make the difficult compromises necessary to defuse the crisis. These policies helped to produce some significant results. Russian troops withdrew completely from the Baltic countries, and problematic citizenship and naturalization laws in Estonia and Latvia were altered.

Before analyzing the use of incentives in these circumstances, a few caveats must be introduced. Incentives did not operate in a vacuum. For brevity's sake, this study will not investigate the role of Russian threats in influencing Baltic policies, nor can it deal comprehensively with the internal debate surrounding policy choices in Estonia and Latvia.[7] It could be argued that the presence of these other dynamics made incentives more useful, by giving officials a more positive reason for "doing the right thing." The international success of incentives in this case did not come without a cost. The pressure accompanying the incentives has led some Estonian and Latvian officials to criticize international organizations for one-sided and undue attention to their countries' "minor" problems. Simultaneously, the underlying Western support for the Baltic states' independence and sovereignty, led Russia to criticize the West and the international organizations for "indifference" to their concerns and for a "cold war mentality" in refusing to condemn the policies of the Baltic states. This particular variety of moral hazard is, of course, endemic to bodies that attempt to mediate between two strongly held positions. Whether the organizations' credibility and effectiveness with the Baltics and Russia are damaged remains to be seen.

Structural Incentives—Getting Western Approval

In Western haste to express support for their new independence, the Baltic countries were granted almost immediate admission to the OSCE and the United Nations in autumn 1991. The Council of Europe, however, only initiated its admission process at that time. As had been the case with previous applicants, it instituted a program of visits, reports, and inspections of laws, to ensure that the three measured up to its extensive standards. Russia seized on the Council of Europe review, and the ongoing possibilities to raise human rights issues provided at the OSCE and UN, to protest "human rights violations" in proposed requirements for naturalization and the exclusion of noncitizens from elections in the Baltics. Estonia, the first of the three Baltic states to bring citizenship proposals before its legislature, was persuaded to invite an OSCE rapporteur mission visit—a procedure designed to foster international scrutiny of human rights cases and situations.[8] This was the first time a state had agreed to subject itself to this intrusive procedure, a milestone for international scrutiny of such internal matters as citizenship laws. The mission itself reported that the "Constitution of Estonia as well as other laws examined by the mission meet the international standards for the enjoyment of human rights."[9] This assurance gave the OSCE credibility within Estonia, and gave the Estonian government a positive reference to use in dealing with the UN, the Council of Europe, and numerous other international as well as Russian interlocutors. Simultaneously, however, the report noted developments that aroused concern, related to citizenship and naturalization policies. The OSCE established a permanent presence in Estonia in February 1993 "to promote stability, dialogue and understanding between the communities in Estonia."[10] Thus, Russia also had results to point to in domestic and international debate. This dual result gave the OSCE an entrée to both parties, as each had gained from the mission.

With the OSCE on the ground, and Council of Europe consideration ongoing, the international community was well placed when tensions rose over citizenship requirements and a draft law on the status of aliens. The Council of Europe was able to insist that changes be made in existing and proposed laws before Estonia would be accepted. The exclusion of noncitizens (most of the Slavic population) from voting in national elections was strongly questioned, and the eventual acceptance of Estonia included the following stipulation: "[The council] expects the Estonian authorities to base their policy regarding the protection of minorities on the principles laid down in Recommendation 1201 (1993) on an additional Protocol on the rights of minorities to the European Convention on Human Rights."[11]

The alien law in its initial form left numerous elements of its application and implementation unspecified, and required that noncitizens obtain work and citizenship permits within two years or face deportation. The Council of Europe expressed concern. Max van der Stoel, the OSCE high commissioner on national minorities, bluntly noted that the lack of clear procedures, avenues for appeal, and promises of citizenship to preindependence residents could raise concerns "to such an extent that it could lead to a destabilization of the country as a whole" and urged their reconsideration.[12] Influenced by statements and high-level diplomatic interventions from Western governments (as well as interruption in the flow of natural gas from Russia), Estonian president Lennart Meri refused to sign the law and asked the Estonian Parliament to revise it. The revisions clarified some of its vagaries and assured ethnic Russians that they would not arbitrarily be deported while unemployed.

It seems clear that international support and the threat of its withdrawal, as well as efforts to direct Western assistance to ease intercommunity friction, made the internal decision to withdraw and revise the law easier for President Meri and the Parliament. Heightened Western interest in Estonia included the direction of U.S. credits toward enterprises in Russian-populated regions and promises of additional credits in the future. This helped to soothe the Russians and gave the Estonian government a card to play with its own hard-liners.[13] On the Russian side, the high profile of international involvement, and international willingness to criticize the Estonian proposals, allowed the Russian authorities to claim something of a success.[14] Estonian government officials did likewise.[15] The international incentive structure of norm-based membership, which brought with it tangible and intangible rewards, had, in this case, functioned well.

Tensions rose to a similar level in Latvia the following year, with the promulgation of a draft law on citizenship. In the Latvian case, the lack of a citizenship law had already led the Council of Europe to postpone Latvia's admission. When a draft law passed its first reading 25 November 1993, including quotas limiting annual naturalization of residents to a percentage of the growth rate of the Latvia population, the international community became actively involved. The Council of Europe criticized the text as "vague," "arbitrary," and "not in line with European standards."[16] The OSCE high commissioner said:

> If the overwhelming majority of non-Latvians in your country is denied the right to become citizens, and consequently the right to be involved in key decisions concerning their own interests, *the character of the democratic system in Latvia might even be put into question. In this connection I refer to the 1990 CSCE Copenhagen Document, which states that the basis of the authority and legitimacy of all governments is the will of the people.*[17] (Emphasis added)

Shortly thereafter, the troop withdrawal negotiations also hit a rough patch, and the success of Vladimir Zhirinovsky and his heavily nationalist party in Russia's December 1993 elections caused the West to look on Baltic-Russian tensions with greater concern.

Western nations, notably the United States and the Nordic countries, began to coordinate policy. Swedish pressure on both the troop withdrawal and minority rights issues was backed up by U.S. intervention at key moments. Nordic and U.S. representatives took the lead in keeping the issues alive before the OSCE and Council of Europe.[18] Most explicitly, Council of Europe officials went on record in spring 1994 with their belief that the draft law disqualified Latvia from membership. Gentle reminders that the Council of Europe standards would also be applied to applicants to the European Union had an effect as well.[19] When, despite these pressures, the Latvian Parliament passed the citizenship law in June 1994, the ground was well laid for international involvement. The OSCE high commissioner, the Council of Europe, and the European Union again reviewed the statute and again suggested that it did not meet European standards. Phone calls from Nordic leaders were followed by the fortunate timing of President Clinton's visit to Riga on 6 July. Clinton promised to speed the establishment of enterprise funds for the Baltic states and called on Latvians to heed "the better angels" of their nature and make peace with Russian residents.[20] The sequence of events that followed was similar to the Estonian case: Latvian president Guntars Ulmanis refused to sign the law. Although the resulting debate in Parliament broke up the ruling coalition, the quotas were removed and other changes made. The revised law was signed on 11 August. Latvia was then admitted to the Council of Europe in early 1995. Again, the immediate results were favorable, but some longer-term costs had been incurred. One analyst wrote:

> The major disagreements between Latvia and Russia have been resolved, but neither side is completely happy. Russia still believes that the citizenship law is too harsh but realizes that its complaints will no longer elicit a response from the international community. Many Latvians believe that the West forced its (sic) government to grant too many concessions. . . . but recognize that they were needed to overcome Russia's intransigence.[21]

The two countries' place in European organizations—and their right to that place, and to their aspirations toward eventual European Union, if not NATO membership—had been secured. The establishment of that place as a reward for modifications in laws also preempted many further Russian challenges. Indeed, while Russia has not stopped accusing the two states of human rights violations, Russian attempts to condemn them or lower their status at international bodies decreased after these incidents. The use of international organization affiliation as an incentive may have increased the confidence, and thus stability, of both Latvia and Russia.

Financial Incentives—Getting the Troops Out

As has already been noted, the elaboration of citizenship and alien laws proceeded in parallel with tendentious negotiations over the withdrawal of Russian (formerly Soviet) forces from the Baltic countries. In July 1992, the three countries and the West succeeded in wringing from Moscow, in the context of an OSCE summit meeting, an acknowledgment that the troops' presence "without the required consent of those countries" constituted "a problem from the past" and a commitment to an "early, orderly and complete withdrawal" of the troops.[22] The inclusion of this particular section, over which Lithuania had held the entire summit document hostage for inclusion of a reference to the troops' illegal status, was an early taste for the Baltic countries of the power and benefits conferred through the international organizations and was regarded as a major triumph for them. The stage for longer-term international involvement was thus set.

Lithuania's inclusive citizenship policies had won it some favor with Moscow; reflecting this better relationship, a troop withdrawal agreement was signed on 8 September 1992. The withdrawal was completed on schedule, although not without some hiccups, on 31 August 1993.[23] However, negotiations with Estonia and Latvia were less fruitful, bogging down over Russian objections to the residence and citizenship policies of the two states as well as Russian demands regarding the fate of specific military installations. Russia halted withdrawals in December 1992, and threatened to do so repeatedly, while pressing in bilateral and international fora for recognition of a direct link between the pace of withdrawal and adoption of citizenship and residency regulations more to Moscow's liking.

The Nordic countries and the United States attempted to replicate the earlier U.S.-German policy of funding housing construction for Russian units departing from eastern Germany. Denmark and Norway came forward with offers in December 1992, in response to Russia's halting the withdrawal. Sweden offered assistance in retraining officers, noting that as cooperation and aid programs were developed, Sweden and Russia "needed to solve the problems that had tarnished their relations in the past" and specifically to set a deadline for Russian withdrawal from the Baltic states.[24] The United States appropriated six million dollars in 1993 and offered five to seven thousand housing units to Russia for returning soldiers in the hope that, as in the German case, military unrest would be blunted.[25] The provision of housing took on an additional use in the Baltic case—dissuading Soviet army officers from remaining in the Baltic countries out of fear that Russia held nothing for them.

Even these incentives proved insufficient to dissipate Russia's remaining political concerns, or to provide sufficient political cover for Russian leaders, who had seen "mistreatment" of Russians in the Baltics become a useful domestic issue for mainstream and nationalist politicians. Concerned that the climate in Russia was moving toward neo-imperialist views, European governments began to look for ways to make compromise palatable to the Estonian and Latvian governments. This was a tough sell. As with citizenship, the Estonian and Latvian governments had domestic opposition that vociferously opposed any compromise with Russia and particularly any admission of the rights or permanent status of ethnic Russians and former officers of the Soviet army. The Baltic governments also complained vigorously that they were singled out for undue pressure by the international organizations, when many others—particularly Russia—were committing far worse "violations" of human rights.[26]

With money already tight in Western ministries, and Russia apparently unmovable, the international organizations had precious little to offer. The impasse was overcome through the introduction of outside involvement in the withdrawal process. This proposal had surfaced initially in 1992, but Russia had refused to accept international oversight, and the NATO countries had declined to press the point. The idea resurfaced in 1994, in much-watered-down form, and was used to break crucial blockages in the withdrawal negotiations. Latvia was promised use of an OSCE mission to monitor and carry out subsequent inspections of the destruction of the Soviet radar site at Skrunda, which the Russians had hoped to keep.[27] Also, inclusion of an OSCE representative in joint Latvian-Russian deliberations to oversee allocation of permanent resident status and civil rights to Russian military pensioners and their families was held out as a sweetener for Latvian acceptance of pensioners remaining in Latvia.

When an agreement was finally signed on 30 April 1994, Latvians, Russians, and the Western press alike pointed to the crucial role of outside pressure in reaching an accord.[28] What had been made clear by the length of the negotiations, and the strength of domestic feeling was that pressure alone would not have worked; the Latvian side had to emerge from the negotiations with palpable gains and assurances for its domestic constituencies. The offer of international oversight, while less important per se than bilateral pressure from the United States and Sweden, served as a carrot to counter that pressure. In response to the 1993 deadlock, the United States had been able to bring to the 1994 discussions in Latvia and Estonia an appropriation of 160 million dollars to assist the withdrawal, specifically to build housing for Russian officers and their families but also to assist in dismantling the Skrunda radar system in Latvia.[29]

Recognizing the role Sweden in particular had played, Russian foreign minister Kozyrev urged that it exert a similar influence on Estonia.[30] The Estonian situation continued to escalate, however, with human rights charges and countercharges being made throughout May and June 1994. Estonia's neighboring Nordic states established, at Russian urging, a Baltic Council Commissioner on Democratic Rights and Institutions for the region. Coming as it did at the end of a meeting where Kozyrev again linked troop withdrawal and rights for ethnic Russians, the appointment of the commissioner was perceived as a Russian victory, an admission that a problem with democratic rights and institutions existed. Perhaps more important, it gave the Russian foreign ministry a triumph to claim for domestic consumption—although it also laid Western diplomacy open to the criticism that it cared more for placating Russian nationalists than for serious appraisals of the region's problems. However, the symbolic nature of this step was underlined when Ole Espersen, the incumbent Baltic Council commissioner, was not involved in the last-minute negotiations that followed. He presented his first report only to the Baltic Council meeting the following year and has been little heard from since. The Baltics and their Western supporters had crafted his mandate in such a way that he was not directly involved. Moreover, the last phases of the talks were staged to avoid the circuslike atmosphere of international fact-finding missions. Pressures and incentives for democratic rights were offered more quietly through local ambassadors and calls and visits from capitals.

Estonia finally reached a compromise agreement with Russia on 26 July 1994. Substantial Western involvement and pressure had been applied on both sides. Estonia had received both the reassurance it sought and a final push for compromise during a Baltic summit with President Clinton (the first U.S. president to visit the independent Baltic states) in Riga on 6 July. The summit rhetoric, stressing U.S. and Western commitment to the maintenance of Baltic independence, was backed up with quiet support and continuing pressure from international organizations.[31] An environment was created in which the Estonian government could finally face down its own hard-liners and make concessions sought by Moscow, chiefly permitting military pensioners to receive residence permits as well as granting Russia extra time to dismantle military reactors at the Paldiski submarine base. These concessions, which had been the last sticking point of the talks, were further eased by the assignment of an international oversight and mediation role to the OSCE mission, which was given a place on the commission established by the Estonian government to make recommendations on residence permits for Soviet military retirees.

In both the Latvian and Estonian cases, the deliberative bodies established to monitor and implement the agreements have functioned with OSCE participation, although not without controversy. The efforts of the OSCE representatives—and the Baltic governments' reactions to their suggestions—have periodically appeared on the agenda of OSCE sessions since 1994. Estonia in particular has complained bitterly of "interference" by international representatives, while in Latvia, OSCE officials have had difficulties with Russian obstruction. However, Russian troops were completely withdrawn from Latvia by the 31 August 1994 deadline, and the Skrunda radar was first downgraded to observatory purposes and then destroyed.

International Organizations and Incentives in a Time of Scarcity

The reader may demur that the tactics described above are not particularly innovative; that states have been offering carrots as well as sticks to each other since statecraft began. But the characteristics that led to the successful use of incentives in this situation may be expected to recur often in an era where no state or group of states has the will or power projection capability to resolve conflicts by fiat. Key aspects of this situation include the following:

- Interested third parties (NATO and the Nordic countries in this case) lack the political will or the unilateral strength to take the side of one party unequivocally and with military means if necessary.
- The parties to a dispute or potential conflict are members of, or at least profoundly affected by, multilateral regimes that have goods to offer or deny participants.

What made these incentives successful in the Baltic case? The countries involved had the ability to offer appropriate incentives. There was authority and coordination among the actors responding, and the incentives offered had the desired effect in a timely fashion.

First, states and international organizations reacted in a coordinated and innovative manner as challenges arose. An informal "friends of the Baltics" group had emerged at OSCE conferences well before Baltic independence.[32] After independence the process of consultation among these countries provided a natural forum for melding their desire for stability in the region with moral and political support for Baltic independence. Sufficient thought and resources were devoted to create incentives that responded to the very real needs and desires of the recipient states. Many of the incentives were framed, as we have seen, as assistance rather than compellence. Their perception as such by recipient governments and domestic constituencies was a crucial factor in their acceptance.

A striking contrast can be found in the roundtable discussions growing out of the European Union Stability Pact, proposed in 1993 to iron out differences on minority rights among states aspiring to EU membership. The EU created roundtables for the sets of countries concerned—the Baltics and Russia, Hungary and Slovakia, and Hungary and Romania—to negotiate agreements on minority status. The Baltic "table" failed to produce any agreement for the May 1995 concluding summit, and the Hungarian-Romanian talks missed that deadline as well. The Hungarian-Slovak treaty was not ratified by the Slovak side until March 1996 and was accompanied by an interpretation squarely at odds with the Hungarian view.[33] Perhaps more important, the situation in the countries concerned did not stabilize as a result of the talks, which in some cases stirred up domestic discontent among minority and majority extremist groups.[34] Certainly, the Slovak-Hungarian Treaty became a sore point in Slovak domestic politics and has, to date, had little if any concrete impact on the lives of ethnic Hungarians in Slovakia. Nor, as noted above, has it provided a common basis for Slovak-Hungarian relations to develop. The governments participating in the roundtables were often only lukewarm about the pact, construing it as another hurdle to EU membership without any associated benefits. In contrast to the supportive incentives offered to the Balts during the troop withdrawal and residential status discussions, the

EU Stability Pact stoked Baltic fears of being "left alone" with the Russians, thus lessening their incentive to cooperate.[35] For both Balts and Russians, the EU roundtable negotiating forum was hostile ground. Neither was a member of or had much leverage over the convening body. The Stability Pact forum offered the key players neither concrete incentives nor an equal place at the table—important reasons for its Baltic failure.

The OSCE/Council of Europe process succeeded because concrete rewards were offered and the participating parties had credibility with the recipients. Extensive aid programs already existed, serving both as unspoken incentives and as assurances that the governments concerned were truly supportive. The would-be benefactors had status in the eyes of all sides. The Latvian and Estonian governments recalled the support of Western states and human rights bodies during the struggle for independence. Moreover, their strategic situation made survival dependent on retaining powerful friends in the West. The West's broad and deep engagement in Baltic sovereignty made pressure through incentives more acceptable than would have been the case had they been coupled with sanctions. To the Russians, the international organizations offered the possibility to scrutinize and comment upon the human rights situation in the Baltics (very useful for domestic politicking) and the threat of further separation from a Europe that spoke in unison against violence and threats in the Baltics.

International organizations helped the Baltics and Russia have it both ways. International organizations could act as "fall guys" or surrogates for national governments by offering both carrots and sticks to any or all parties. They used a baseline of standards to which all the states involved had freely committed themselves and a process over which each state exercised veto power. Their ongoing presence also served as a lightning rod for criticism and a source of assistance even to nonstate entities, from which all parties could take comfort or political ammunition. But their powers were created and guaranteed by national governments which provided the necessary funds and political support. Without the strong support of the United States, including its insistence on compliance with international norms, the organizations would have been far less powerful.

Effective involvement of the international community and favorable preconditions would not on their own have been enough to bring success, however. Promised incentives had to be delivered. The Baltic countries entered the Council of Europe, and promptly began to use both it and the OSCE to advance their foreign policy objectives. Extra monitors did arrive from the OSCE to oversee troop withdrawals and subsequent citizenship and resident-status discussions. Housing for ex-Soviet officers and their families came but more slowly. Only in August 1995 did Germany succeed in completing the program it had negotiated for Soviet troop withdrawals, which had begun five years earlier. The status of some of the promised

U.S. funds for the housing of Russian troops remains in doubt. By all indications, officers who suffer under this slowness are extremely disgruntled. However, as noted, the speed with which promised money was in fact allocated by the U.S. and Scandinavian governments served as a pledge of sincerity and determination during the negotiations themselves. Thus, the immediate purpose was served, but Russian willingness to accept similar promises again is far less clear.

While ranking this use of incentives as a success, we must also look at what was not achieved. Baltic-Russian relations remain troubled, with citizenship and discrimination issues particularly contentious. The Estonian and Latvian authorities have obtained Western approval and Russian acquiescence, but little more. Incentives alone changed neither the nature of the relationship, nor the geopolitical situation of Estonia, Latvia, and Lithuania. The small states still must face a large and uneasy Russia without any guarantee of Western intervention in future conflicts. Russia's acceptance of international scrutiny of Baltic nationality policies and Western assistance for the eventual withdrawal of troops has not stopped the flow of anti-Baltic and anti-Western rhetoric. Indeed, certain extremist groups have made propaganda points from the withdrawal (much as they did on the earlier withdrawal from Germany and the former Warsaw Pact states), presenting it as an abdication of Russia's sphere of influence without adequate compensation or sufficient concern for the "compatriots" left behind. On 28 July 1995, the upper house of the Russian Parliament again postponed ratification of the troop withdrawal agreement, after the lower house had done so (and well after the last troops were withdrawn).

The status of the OSCE and Council of Europe may have suffered in the Baltic states as a result of the compromise nature of the outcome. Even the details of ongoing international involvement are still challenged by the parties. Estonia complained, for example, that the OSCE delegate to the Estonian commission on residence permits had overstepped his mandate by proposing the establishment of an international commission to resolve differences of interpretations.[36] Both Estonia and Latvia have made no secret of their desire to be done with OSCE presences and OSCE scrutiny. In Russia, damage to institutional credibility seems to have been less, as indicated by Moscow's admission of an OSCE team to observe and assist in resolving the conflict in Chechnya. On both sides, future cooperation with international organizations is likely to be decided on the merits, with recognition of both the positive and negative sides of past interactions.

The OSCE and Council of Europe have attempted to carry out similar mediating and advice-giving functions elsewhere, with only limited success. Where influential member states have not had vital interests they were willing to defend, OSCE efforts have been marginalized.[37] Another limiting factor has been the perception by states involved in disputes that their interests at stake were more vital to national (or political) survival than any benefits incentives could provide.[38] When political will and resources are such that the strongest incentives that can be offered are the fruits of cooperation with international organizations, and the accompanying membership status, incentives cannot be counted upon to resolve or prevent a conflict. They can, however, be a helpful part of a package of bilateral and multilateral responses to an incipient conflict—if the overall response to the parties is one of positive, long-term engagement that does not stress punitive actions but rather holds out real hopes for inclusion in a community of prosperous and secure nations. The sheer amount of interest, resources, and coordination that made the use of international incentives effective in the Baltic states, and the limited definition of success applied, should prompt second thoughts before incentives-based policies are recommended as a panacea for low-intensity, low-resource conflict prevention and resolution. Nonetheless, creatively designed incentives and the commitment of international coalitions can pay off—if, as for other forms of conflict resolution, political will and the means of follow-through are present. In these circumstances, incentives can be used to help frame a political settlement and create a culture of tolerance.

Notes

1. This article was prepared while the author was on staff at the Carnegie Endowment for International Peace. The views expressed are those of the author alone and do not represent official U.S. government policy.

2. Incentive is here used to mean the promise of a reward in return for taking, or failing to take, some action. Success can then be measured by the completion or avoidance of the relevant action.

3. Then the Conference on Security and Cooperation in Europe. For simplicity, OSCE will be used throughout.

4. See Andrew Moravcsik, "Explaining International Human Rights Regimes," *European Journal of International Affairs* (June 1995):166–68.

5. Vitaly Portnikov, "Russian Parliament Defends Ethnic Russians in the Baltics," *Nezavisimaya Gazeta,* 18 July 1992, 3.

6. On 11 August 1992, Carl Bildt wrote in the Swedish newspaper *Svenska Dagbladet* that Vladimir Zhirinovsky "wants to put pressure on Finland, Estonia, Latvia and Lithuania and preferably reconquer them all. Who could assert that automatic neutrality should be Sweden's line in such a situation?" Because of ongoing domestic debate about Sweden's security policy, this was taken in the region as a strong statement of nonneutrality. See Tony Austin, *The Reuter Library Report,* 11 August 1992.

7. Lithuania, where politics took a different course and conciliatory citizenship policies were adopted with little reference to the international community, will be left aside entirely.

8. An explanation of the procedure can be found in the Commission on Security and Cooperation in Europe, Report on the Moscow Meeting of the Conference on the Human Dimension of the CSCE, Washington, D.C., 1992.

9. Available from the OSCE Secretariat as *Report of the CSCE Office for Democratic Institutions and Human Rights Mission on the Study of Estonian Legislation Invited by the Republic of Estonia,* Prague, 1993.

10. Mission mandate available from OSCE Secretariat, Prague, The Czech Republic, as Annex 1 to CSCE/19 CSO/Journal No. 2.

11. Parliamentary Assembly of the Council of Europe, Opinion No. 170 (1993), *On the application of the Republic of Estonia for membership of the Council of Europe.* Text adopted 13 May 1993; paragraph 5. The protocol referred to contained the set of minority-rights provisions binding on Council members at that time. It has since been expanded but, even in 1993, put its adherents at a level of obligation far above UN or other regional documents. Its overlap with OSCE commitments was extensive but not complete.

12. Max van der Stoel letter to Estonian foreign minister Velliste, available from the OSCE Secretariat as *CSCE Communication No. 192,* 1993.

13. Anatol Lieven, *The Baltic Revolution: Estonia, Latvia, Lithuania, and the Path to Independence,* (New Haven, Conn.: Yale University Press, 1993), 379.

14. See Russian commentary reported in Ann Sheehy, "The Estonian Law on Aliens," RFE/RL Research Report no. 38 (24 September 1993): 10.

15. Estonia's foreign minister claimed victory in the propaganda war over the issue in March 1993. See Andrus Park, "Ethnicity and Independence: The Case of Estonia in Comparative Perspective," *Europe-Asia Studies* 46, no. 1, (1994): 83.

16. Comments of the Council of Europe experts are reproduced in the Parliamentary Assembly of the Council of Europe, *Report on the application by Latvia for membership of the Council of Europe* (Rapporteur: Mr. Espersen), Doc. 7169, 6 October 1994, 9.

17. Max van der Stoel letter to Latvian foreign minister Georgs Andrejevs, 10 December 1993, Reference No. 1463/93/L; available from the OSCE Secretariat.

18. Dov Zakheim, "When Bildt Came to Call," *Washington Times,* 8 December 1993, A17 (*supra,* fn. 10) and the journals of the 24th, 25th, and 27th CSCE Committees of Senior Officials, 1993 and 1994.

19. Steven Erlanger, "Latvia Amends Harsh Citizenship Law that Angered Russians," *New York Times,* 24 July 1994, sec. 1, p. 3.

20. Thomas Friedman, "Clinton Makes Appeal to Latvia to Accept Its Russian Civilians," *New York Times,* 7 July 1994, sec. 1, p. 1.

21. Saulius Girnius, "Relations between the Baltic States and Russia," *RFE/RL Research Report no.33* (26 August 1994): 31.

22. Paragraph 15 of the Helsinki Summit Declaration, *CSCE Helsinki Document 1992: The Challenges of Change.* This section relies upon the recollection of the author and her colleagues at the Helsinki and subsequent CSCE negotiations.

23. Saulius Girnius, "Progress in Withdrawal of Troops from Lithuania?" *RFE/RL Research Report no. 34,* 28 August 1992; and Girnius, "Relations between the Baltic States and Russia."

24. "Swedish Premier Arrives in Moscow," *ITAR-TASS* (news service), 8 February 1993.

25. "President Clinton Meets with Baltic Presidents," *U.S. Department of State Dispatch* 4, no. 40: 688.

26. There is no doubt that for some Estonian and Latvian officials this was a debating point rather than a personal conviction, but Estonian officials were calling for international investigations into the situation in Russia's Caucasus region almost a year before the Russian invasion of Chechnya.

27. As it happened, destruction was carried out in 1995 (by a U.S. contractor), but Russian officials prevented the OSCE envoy from being present.

28. Girnius, "Relations between the Baltic States and Russia"; "Sweden's Baltic Bulwark," *The Economist*, 9 July 1994, 53; and Denis Perkin, "Russia Wants Sweden to Mediate Talks with Estonia," *TASS*, 5 May 1994.

29. Information provided by the Joint Baltic-American National Council. It is worth noting that, although the quick appropriation of funds in 1993 and 1994 established the seriousness of U.S. intentions in a useful and timely way, spending the money has not been so easy. Difficulties and uncertainties regarding the complete availability of the money continue.

30. Perkin, "Russia Wants Sweden to Mediate Talks."

31. Clinton said, just before appealing for tolerance for ethnic minorities, "we will rejoice with you when the last of the foreign troops vanish from your homelands." Remarks in Riga, Latvia, on 6 July 1994; reprinted in *U.S. Department of State Dispatch* 5, no. 31 (1 August 1994): 513.

32. See, for example, the Helsinki Commission's "Report on the Geneva Meeting of Experts on National Minorities," Washington, D.C., 1991.

33. The best chronicle of events leading to the ratification of the treaty and both sides interpretation of it can be found in *OMRI Daily Reports* for the period (Prague, The Czech Republic: Open Media Research Institute).

34. A short primer on the European Union Stability Pact, including its linkage to EU membership, can be found in *The Economist*, 18 March 1995, 55. For reporting on subsequent debate in Hungary, Slovakia, and Romania see Sharon Fisher, "Treaty Fails to End Squabbles over Hungarian Relations," *Transition*, 9 June 1995, 2–7.

35. From the author's conversations with Estonian officials.

36. Communication with OSCE delegate.

37. The OSCE's struggle with competing Russian mediation in Moldova and Nagorno Karabakh is detailed in my "Russia, the OSCE, and European Security Architecture," *Helsinki Monitor* 6, no. 2 (1995). For a more recent example, see Lee Hockstadter, "Russians Push to End Chechyn War before Vote," *Washington Post*, 24 March 1996, 1.

38. The many efforts at mediation in the Greek-Macedonian name dispute comes most forcefully to mind.

10

The Role of International Financial Institutions in Preventing and Resolving Conflict

Nicole Ball, Jordana D. Friedman, and Caleb S. Rossiter

The Problem: Militarization as an Obstacle to Development

The Opportunity: The Value of International Financial Institution Incentives

INDUSTRIALIZED COUNTRIES such as the United States, France, and Great Britain are ironically both the largest exporters of arms to the developing world and among the major providers of foreign aid and loans through bilateral and multilateral agencies, including the international financial institutions (IFIs).[1] While arms exports by themselves do not cause violent conflict, the constant flow of weapons to trouble spots has indisputably fueled violence, decimated communities, and destroyed economies in Afghanistan, Haiti, Lebanon, Liberia, Rwanda, and other countries. Donor governments and the multilateral aid and lending institutions they control by virtue of holding a majority voting share have a particular responsibility to help stem the flow of arms to developing nations and curb other destructive activities. Their leverage resides in the fact that they supply approximately $60 billion worth of economic aid and loans to the developing world each year.[2] Sustainable development, broadly based participation in the political process, and peace and security are closely related.

High levels of military spending and arms imports, the inability to resolve conflicts within and among states, and the use of security forces to prevent the emergence of representative political systems can severely reduce opportunities for development and further erode security. In the coming years, the great threat to security in most parts of the world will arise from internal conflicts generated by the inequitable distribution of political and economic resources, by the unwillingness of political elites (including the security forces) to share power, and by the efforts on the part of one segment of the population to dominate another segment based on characteristics such as ethnic, regional, religious, or clan affiliations.

Although it has long been evident that many developing country governments have accorded significantly greater priority to building up the military establishment than to promoting political, economic, and social development, the international aid and lending community largely ignored the trade-off between military spending and development during the cold war. In countries such as El Salvador and Nicaragua, the major powers often provided economic assistance to enable developing country governments to maintain their military budgets and arms imports at levels that could not be sustained using domestic resources alone. While this attitude began to change with the demise of the Soviet Union in 1991, the major powers have yet to press consistently for behavioral changes that will enhance both security and development.

Due to their considerable financial resources, technical assets, and global presence, the IFIs have the capacity to assist in maintaining or recreating an environment of peace and stability. This chapter examines the ways IFIs can, and in some cases have sought to, prevent or resolve conflicts by influencing such variables as a potential recipient's level of military spending, the quality of its governance (including the transparency of its military budget and degree of military involvement in the civilian economy), its adherence to democratic methods (both in elections and judicial systems) and other international human rights standards, and its cooperation with international and regional security agreements. It shows how IFIs have funded and even helped implement measures aimed at building and maintaining peace in postconflict settings, including troop demobilization and reintegration, community reconstruction, and land mine removal.

The prevention of conflict requires the involvement and leadership of national governments, political parties, nongovernmental organizations, the United Nations, and regional security bodies. But the IFIs have a crucial and unavoidable role to play in helping to establish the social and economic conditions conducive to conflict prevention and conflict resolution. Indeed, IFI policies are most effective when pursued in association with confidence-building measures and security guarantees established by participating political actors.

Outline of the Chapter

The first section describes the range of demilitarization tools available to the development community. Although these tools are typically applied in concert and influence each other, they are divided here for the purpose of analysis into three methods: *persuasion,* technical and financial *support,* and indirect and direct *pressure,* which is often referred to as conditionality. This section then gives examples of situations in which IFIs can and have pursued policies aimed both at conflict prevention and at conflict resolution.

The second section presents a case study of the role of IFIs in preventing conflict. This section describes how World Bank pressure was brought to bear on the government of Malawi to encourage the transition in the 1990s from an unaccountable, authoritarian regime to a more democratic and open form of government. The third section presents two case studies of World Bank engagement in the process of conflict resolution. First, it examines the World Bank's assistance to the West Bank and Gaza Strip during the Arab-Israeli peace process, starting in 1993. Second, it describes support for a demobilization process in Uganda that began in 1992.

The chapter ends in section four by recommending that the World Bank and other IFIs vigorously employ the entire range of tools at their disposal in support of peacebuilding and demilitarization in the coming years. Active IFI involvement could help bolster the growing international consensus that successful economic and social development is deeply dependent on political liberalization, a shift in priorities away from the military sector, and a strong commitment to the peaceful resolution of conflicts.

Summary of IFI Tools: Persuasion, Support, and Pressure

International financial institutions may use any combination of persuasion, support, or pressure to effect changes in a country's security policy and the behavior of its armed forces. In public, representatives of the World Bank, the IMF, and the regional development banks have claimed that they are barred by their charters from considering such "political" criteria when making aid and lending decisions, but this diplomatic fiction has long been dispensed with in loan negotiations. As Albert Hirschman observed in his classic study *National Power and the Structure of the State,* decisions to provide loans and credits to other nations are inherently political and cannot be separated from the larger policy framework of international relations.[3] The IFIs are intensely, and unavoidably, political institutions whose policies are determined solely by the majority vote of shareholders—meaning in nearly all cases the consensus of the developed nations. The difference between "political" and "economic" criteria is undefined in the charters of these institutions, and throughout their histories they have consistently raised political- and security-related concerns under the rubric of the good governance and predictable investment standards that economists agree are needed for sound economic development.[4]

Persuasion

Persuasion has taken a number of forms. The first involves public statements by the senior management of development cooperation agencies expressing displeasure with high military spending levels, drawing correlations between high military expenditure and lower rates of development, and hinting that borrower countries will be looked upon more favorably if they pursue efforts to reduce military budgets and redirect resources to the social sector. Persuasion also takes place in private consultations that are part of the overall policy dialogue with an individual recipient country. Development officials may inform a country that they consider certain military policy decisions such as spending levels to be of economic as well as political and strategic import. They may suggest that it is in the country's best interest to reexamine such policies as high military spending, lack of transparency in the reporting of military budgets, arms exports to unstable states, major arms procurement, or excessive military involvement in political affairs.

The World Bank, through its public expenditure reviews (PERs), and the IMF, in its Article IV consultations, have begun in recent years to draw the connection between development and reduced military spending and to collect information on recipient countries' military expenditures. In 1989, the managing director of the IMF, Michel Camdessus, and then World Bank president, Barber Conable, began speaking out about the inherent conflict between unproductive military spending and the development financing that indirectly subsidizes it.[5] This perspective was reinforced by the 1991 publication of the United Nations Development Program's *Human Development Report,* which linked the widespread poverty in developing nations to excessive levels of military spending and argued for a shift from military to social priorities as a development strategy.[6]

It is clear that persuasion has played an integral role in efforts by IFIs to effect changes in military expenditure levels of recipient countries. However, the quality of information collected on military budgets often remains, in the words of Camdessus, "opaque."[7] Operational level staff at the IFIs have been unable to translate the intentions of their superiors into specific actions that would improve the quality of the information, such as independent audits of military budgets and military involvement in the economy.[8]

Obviously, persuasion is a policy tool of limited use, particularly if it amounts to empty rhetoric rather than to actual policy reform. Nevertheless, the power of persuasion should not be discounted, particularly when recipient countries begin to see a consensus developing among groups of donors such as the Development Assistance Committee (DAC) of the Organization for Economic Cooperation and Development (OECD) or the Group of Seven (G-7). The G-7 countries alone account for a majority of voting shares in the IMF and the World Bank, and so can determine policy at these institutions. Signs of such consensus among these powerful members of the IFIs are growing. In December 1993, member states of the OECD's Development Assistance Committee (DAC) approved a document highlighting the connection between excessive military spending and conflict, and urged nations to reduce military budgets. The OECD has also advocated dialogue between lenders and recipients and greater transparency of military budgets and programs. The *DAC Orientations on Participatory Development and Good Governance* state that:

> DAC Members recognise the importance of peace and security for development. When military expenditure is excessive, it can result in conflict and repression, contribute to instability in the region and divert scarce resources away from development needs. DAC Members emphasize the importance of establishing and maintaining the primacy of the role of civilians in political and economic affairs and the significance they attach to avoiding or reducing excessive military expenditure.[9]

The 1995 G-7 Communiqué contains the following paragraph on reducing military spending and increasing social investment: "We will work with others to encourage relevant multilateral institutions to: take trends in military and other unproductive spending into account in extending assistance (and) . . . direct a substantially increased proportion of their resources to basic social programmes and other measures which attack the roots of poverty."[10]

Donor persuasion, like support and pressure, might be expected to work best when it is directed toward poorer countries, such as many in sub-Saharan Africa, that rely most heavily on concessional aid. These countries are more likely to feel an obligation to heed donor advice since they are dependent on external financing for a large percentage of their external income. Donor persuasion is also more likely to succeed when it is applied to countries that recognize it to be in their own national interest to demilitarize, stop weapons testing, or sign a nonproliferation agreement. On the other hand, the moral appeal of donor persuasion is undercut by the excessive military spending or weapons trafficking activities of the largest donor countries, including the United States.

Support

Development cooperation agencies, including the IFIs, can provide positive incentives, or carrots, to potential recipient countries in the form of financial, technical, or diplomatic support. The offer of financial support for the implementation of policy reform in the security sector or for specific demilitarization activities can influence a borrower country's decision to undertake radical change. In Central America, Nicaragua and El Salvador were assisted in their demilitarization processes by financing from a broad range of donors, including the United States Agency for International Development (USAID) and the European Union. World Bank financing has helped to facilitate troop demobilization and reintegration in such countries as Cambodia, Mozambique, and Uganda.[11]

Technical support from donors places skilled manpower and equipment in the hands of countries that would otherwise not be able to afford or gain access to them. Countries such as Cambodia and Angola have relied upon skilled labor and equipment provided by the international development cooperation community to clear land mines, destroy surplus weapons, and plan for the demobilization and reintegration of soldiers into the civilian economy. IFIs have also supplied some limited technical assistance in such seemingly mundane but critically important areas as defense-sector accounting and budgeting. For example, Argentina, which has undertaken efforts to reduce military spending and rationalize its armed forces over the last decade, has also requested World Bank assistance to analyze its military expenditures.

The international lending community can complement efforts to provide diplomatic support to settle conflicts by promising economic assistance to support the implementation of peace agreements. All of these forms of support—or carrots—can help induce parties to a conflict to come to the negotiating table, advance through further stages of postconflict reconciliation, agree to maintain a cease-fire, comply with an international treaty, demonstrate transparency in military budgeting, or pursue a policy of reduction in the size of the armed forces.

Pressure and Conditionality

Placing pressure on a recipient government is often referred to as "conditionality," meaning that policy change is a precondition for the provision of assistance. International financial institutions may apply pressure both indirectly and directly. Indirect pressure, which is applied *without* explicit conditions on the policies in question, can have the same goals as explicit, direct pressure. This indirect pressure can be exerted through a tool like the World Bank's Structural Adjustment Lending (SAL) program. As part of a SAL program, the World Bank can put implicit pressure on a country's military budget by setting targets for expenditure in social and economic sectors that will squeeze out military spending. The IMF can also indirectly affect the military sector by setting targets for cutting fiscal deficits that make it difficult for recipient countries to avoid reductions in military expenditures.

Direct pressure is defined as the linking of particular policy reforms or actions to the provision of financial resources. The IFIs have long set explicit conditions for lending based on a country's economic policies and performance. The IMF and the World Bank, for example, require specific policy reforms of countries receiving economic stabilization and structural adjustment financing. While such conditioned lending often leads to changes in policy, countries sometimes prove unable or unwilling to undertake all the necessary reforms. Evaluations of IMF and World Bank adjustment lending demonstrate that economic conditionality works best in countries where the government is convinced of the need for change.

In addition, economic conditionality is nearly always combined with persuasion to convince the government of the desirability of reform and financial support to defray some of the costs associated with those reforms. This point is particularly critical given the recent tendency of the donors to institute other forms of policy conditionality. Increasingly over the last decade, the bilateral donors have required recipient countries to demonstrate their commitment to such goals as the eradication of poverty, protection of human rights standards, promotion of democracy, preservation of the environment, and reduction in military spending.[12] The addition of multiple policy objectives makes the use of economic conditionality more problematic. Donor nations may differ in their commitment to the objectives, and recipient countries may find it more difficult to adapt multiple policy reforms. As with other tools of diplomacy, the success of aid conditionality depends on sender nations maintaining a sustained and focused commitment to specific objectives.

In terms of reducing the potential for violent conflict, conditionality allows a donor to threaten to reduce or withhold aid if the recipient country does not comply with such conditions as shifting funds from the military to the social sector, or allowing free campaigning for public office and the setting of an election by a specific date. Cases where IFIs have used such conditionality abound (particularly as a result of pressure from its most influential member governments), although this tool is more widely used by bilateral donors. The United States prevented the World Bank from loaning to Vietnam in the 1970s and 1980s, with Congress going so far as to require a letter of confirmation from World Bank president Robert McNamara before appropriating additional funds for the bank.[13] South Africa was discouraged from approaching the IMF during the waning years of apartheid because of the storm of political protest that accompanied its successful application to the IMF for financing in 1983. The United States, other bilateral donors, and the World Bank limited aid to Kenya in 1991 and to Malawi from 1992 to 1994 until elections had taken place in those countries.[14] The United States voted to oppose or abstain from voting on thirteen IFI loans to China during a three-month period in 1995 because China did not adhere to basic human rights standards, although the loans all went through because the United States failed to persuade other executive directors at the various IFIs to oppose them.[15]

Conditionality can be helpful in bringing about changes in human rights standards or military policies. This in turn can foster a national and even regional environment conducive to conflict resolution and peace. However, conditionality is a controversial tool that can have counterproductive effects. Just as economic sanctions can generate a "rally-around-the-flag" effect that entrenches a targeted regime's resistance to external pressure, heavy-handed inducement efforts and excessively rigid conditionality can foster resentment.[16] Nationalist leaders may rail against external efforts to "bribe" the country, vowing that the nation is "not for sale." Such sentiments often greet general conditionality policies related to structural adjustment. Many of the developing nations that are subject to such pressures criticize them as an infringement of national sovereignty.[17] These concerns reflect deeply felt objections to the continuing disparities in international power and wealth. Countries subjected to nonproliferation pressures from the United States may also resent the double standard of being asked to forgo weapons programs that the United States and the major powers retain. When conditionality is perceived as maintaining disparities of wealth and power rather than fostering development and peace, it will be ineffective. Such sensitivities are important because subjective factors significantly influence the potential effectiveness of incentives.

The paradox of conditionality is that when standards are applied rigidly, without regard to the traditions and political dynamics within a recipient nation, they may produce the opposite effect intended, perhaps weakening reform groups and inadvertently strengthening hard-line factions in the recipient nation.[18] If financial assistance is to advance the process of reform and conflict prevention, the procedures for applying conditionality must be transparent and respectful.[19] The relationship should be one of positive inducement rather than negative compulsion. Donors must have a thorough understanding of cultural traditions and political concerns within the recipient country and should avoid statements or acts that could enflame nationalist resentments. Dialogue will enable lenders on both sides to design exchanges that are mutually beneficial.[20] If blended with sensitivity, openness, and support for democratic reform, conditionality can be an effective tool in shaping the behavior of recipient nations.

The policies of the international financial institutions derive from the voting power of the member states, which is determined by economic clout. Japan and Germany, as the world's second- and third-largest economies, thus have enormous influence on the direction of World Bank and IMF policy. They are also the countries that took some of the earliest steps to link economic assistance to military restraint in their bilateral lending policies. In 1991, Japan announced that lending decisions henceforth would factor in such considerations as military spending levels, nonproliferation policy, and arms transfers. These principles were codified in Japan's official development assistance charter in June 1992. Tokyo has been cautious in applying these criteria, however.[21] Japanese officials have preferred negotiations and dialogue to abrupt changes in assistance levels. They have used lending policies more as an incentive to promote positive behavior than as a coercive measure to punish wrongdoing. In a number of cases, though, Japan has threatened to or actually reduced aid because of violations of nonproliferation norms. In May 1995, Japan threatened to cut back aid to China if that country continued either its underground nuclear tests or its tests of long-range mobile intercontinental ballistic missiles. By late August, when China had not suspended its testing program, Japan announced that it would freeze most of its grant aid to China, excluding a portion designated for emergency relief measures and humanitarian aid.[22]

In 1991, the German Ministry for Economic Cooperation and Development approved policy guidelines for evaluating the impact of a recipient's military policy as a criterion for aid policy. The criteria that German development officials have specifically identified include reductions in military spending, compliance with nonproliferation norms, greater transparency of military budgets and programs, and democratic accountability in police and military forces.[23] Germany has applied these standards to both its international lending and foreign aid programs with uneven outcomes, however, because foreign policy and trade considerations routinely take precedence over the commitment to military reform. This is a problem faced by most bilateral aid donors.

Despite much discussion, lending nations and international financial institutions have been reluctant to push hard for military reform in practice.[24] In the *Orientations on Participatory Development and Good Governance,* DAC member governments agreed that when seeking reductions in military spending, donors should focus first of all on dialogue and "positive assistance" and should consider conditioned aid "as a last resort."[25] The United States has refused to adopt such criteria, and even Germany and Japan have been reluctant to apply these standards consistently to all aid recipients. In fact, Washington and other major donor governments supply weapons and political backing to many of the regimes that have engaged in military abuses. The development cooperation agencies in the major donor countries are acutely aware that inconsistency in their countries' own policies is a major impediment to donor efforts to reform the security sector in recipient countries. The OECD Development Assistance Committee has noted:

> The approach outlined here by DAC members recognizes that to advance the complex agenda of participatory development, good governance, human rights and democratisation, their own countries must accept a number of responsibilities . . . not least, they must work for coherence in the policies and practices of their own governments, individually and collectively. An obvious example . . . is that efforts to promote reduced military expenditure lose credibility and effectiveness when at the same time other agencies of governments may be actively promoting increased arms exports to the same developing countries.[26]

Despite the hesitancy of lender nations and financial institutions, economic assistance has enormous potential for advancing the agenda of international peace and conflict prevention. A concerted international effort to use financial assistance to promote military spending restraint, transparency, conflict resolution, and nonproliferation could have an enormous impact on world security. There are solid economic reasons, in addition to the security benefits, for adopting such a policy. The instability and uncertainty that come from war, repression, and weapons proliferation increase risks and limit the opportunities for investment and trade. A stable and peaceful security environment is essential for achieving economic development and enhancing world trade.

IFIs and Conflict Prevention: The Transition to Democracy in Malawi

From 1992 to 1994 World Bank pressure—in coordination with aid suspensions by major bilateral donors—helped a remarkable citizens' protest movement in Malawi topple one of Africa's oldest and toughest dictatorships and establish a democratic form of government. The transition in this country of ten million with an annual per capita income of $100 was swift and, to both Malawians and outside observers, stunning.[27] "Life President" Hastings Kamuza Banda and his Malawi Congress Party had run a virtual police state for thirty years, silencing opposition through censorship, detention, torture, and assassination.[28] When an incipient citizens' movement formed in 1992, spurred by Malawi's Roman Catholic bishops' public attack on the government's human rights abuses and by protests from other religious leaders, President Banda initially tried to silence the movement and the government perpetrated even greater human rights abuses. In May 1992, the World Bank, as the leader of the donors' Consultative Group, issued a rare, explicit call to donors to suspend aid programs for six months.[29] Great Britain and other governments followed suit and cut off financial support.

A motivating factor for the clear and aggressive stance of the World Bank was the Malawi security forces' violation of the bank's traditional diplomatic privileges. Malawian forces had entered World bank offices and inspected documents without bank approval.[30] Similarly, Great Britain was a leading force in sanctioning Malawi, due in part to the incarceration of a Malawian religious leader married to a British citizen.[31] Beyond these particular incidents, the overriding motivation of the World Bank was clearly that governance and sound growth were becoming difficult to sustain in this deteriorating human rights environment.[32]

While the World Bank did not itself suspend any loans, and indeed continued to make new loans, its public call and private statements to government officials helped to convince the government of Malawi that, in the words of a Malawian who was a close observer of the transition to democracy, the "handwriting was on the wall."[33] Rather than risk civil war or financial disaster in a country that was heavily aid dependent, President Banda reversed his policy of repression and scheduled a national referendum to determine whether the Malawian people desired a multiparty system. He also repealed edicts that permitted the detention of political opponents without trial, and released seventy long-term detainees.[34]

Even though the Malawian government controlled the media and the administration of the referendum, the people of Malawi voted overwhelmingly in June 1993 for a transition to multiparty elections. The first free elections were held in May 1994 with the presence of international monitors.[35] President Banda's few attempts to intimidate his political opponents were publicized and criticized by the international and national media who were finally able to operate freely. Seven registered political parties put up candidates and campaigned for the presidency and the Parliament. Only three parties emerged as dominant players: Banda's Malawi Congress Party (MCP); the Alliance for Democracy, led by human rights activists and former exiles; and the United Democratic Front (UDF), composed of political refugees, many of whom had fallen out of favor with the MCP, the ruling party. UDF won a narrow majority in the legislature and its leader, Bakili Muluzi, overwhelmingly won the presidential sweepstakes.

Banda's legacy still overshadows the new government of Malawi as it tries to build democracy in a country with no tradition of democratic politics. The civil institutions that are emerging are fragile and often easily influenced by politicians. Aid has been reinstated, but the declining prices of Malawi's exports, the devaluation of the currency, the drought of 1992–93, and the temporary aid suspension have combined to lower standards of living.[36]

Malawi has taken an important step along the road from dictatorship to democracy without suffering the scourge of civil war. This occurred in part because the IFIs and bilateral donors not only threatened to suspend aid if certain conditions were not met but in some cases actually carried out the threat. In a country as aid-dependent as Malawi, both the suspension of aid and the threat of suspending even more were instrumental in forcing the Banda government to hold free and fair elections. The temporary suspension of aid was an effective tool, although it was also a rather blunt instrument, as evidenced by the decline in the quality of life for the country's poorest inhabitants. Now that Malawi is launched on the road toward democracy, the IFIs and bilateral donors should consider providing the country with special supplementary aid packages that could help alleviate the economic hardship experienced by the Malawian people during and after the events of the period of 1992 to 1994. In addition, the IFIs can provide technical assistance to the executive and judicial branches of government as they try to regain control of the resources Banda and his allies diverted during his rule.

Case Studies of the Conflict Resolution Role of International Financial Institutions

The West Bank and Gaza Strip

Since the September 1993 signing of the Israeli-Palestinian Declaration of Principles, international financial and technical assistance to the West Bank and Gaza Strip has been regarded by both the international community and the Palestinian Authority as an integral part of the Arab-Israeli peace process.[37] In October 1993, the World Bank held a meeting of IFIs and bilateral aid agencies as a follow-up to the Israeli-PLO peace accord.[38] The donors pledged over $2 billion (later $2.5 billion) to promote economic and social development in the West Bank and Gaza and to strengthen the institutional capacity of the Palestinian Authority (PA), the new administrative body overseeing political, social, and economic decisions in the territories formerly under Israeli control. As Rex Brynen notes, the ambitious promise of $2.5 billion of aid to the West Bank and Gaza over a five-year period from 1994 to 1998 represents one of the most compelling examples ever of peacebuilding through international donor assistance.[39]

The participation of the IFIs and many bilateral donors in the Israeli-PLO peace process was significant because these bodies saw themselves as having not only an economic development function but also an important supporting role to play in the establishment and nurturing of political and social institutions in Gaza and the West Bank.[40] The international community hoped that by helping to rebuild the West Bank and Gaza both politically and economically it could encourage the Palestinian people and leadership to become more politically and psychologically engaged in the peace process. As Warren Christopher, U.S. secretary of state, said at the October 1994 donors meeting, "We must demonstrate the tangible benefits of peace, and we must do so quickly if the advocates of peace are to be strengthened and the enemies of peace to be discredited."[41]

After some delay and as a result of pressure from the United States, the World Bank took control of the overall donor assistance process in the West Bank and Gaza. It did so against the wishes of the European Union, which sought to exercise some independence in the provision of its aid program.[42] Two principal bodies were created to coordinate the multilateral aid effort for the West Bank and Gaza Strip: the Ad-Hoc Liaison Committee (AHLC) and the Consultative Group. The World Bank, along with the United States and the European Union, has played a particularly influential role in both the Consultative Group and the AHLC. The role of the Consultative Group in the West Bank and Gaza has been to garner support and financing for specific assistance strategies.

As the leading provider of financial and technical assistance in the West Bank and Gaza, the World Bank has played a major role in developing special project proposals with the Palestinian Authority and presenting them to the different donor groups. For example, the World Bank presented the Emergency Assistance Program for the Occupied Territories to the first Consultative Group meeting in December 1993. The Emergency Assistance Program outlined sectoral needs and priorities during the period from 1994 to 1996 at a projected cost of $1.2 billion.[43] The World Bank also developed its own more detailed aid program entitled the Emergency Rehabilitation Program. This $128 million program identified 117 smaller projects throughout the West Bank and Gaza. The World Bank provided $30 million through its concessionary aid agency, the International Development Association (IDA), with the rest of the financing coming from bilateral donors.[44] The International Finance Corporation (IFC), another World Bank lending institution, also provided loans for private sector investment in the area.

The World Bank has been responsible for managing two specialized funds, the Technical Assistance Trust Fund and the Holst Fund, named after Johan Jorgen Holst, the late foreign minister of Norway, who was instrumental in negotiating the September 1993 Declaration of Principles.

The $25 million Technical Assistance Trust Fund primarily financed the growth and cultivation of technical and administrative infrastructure.[45] In November 1994, donors to the West Bank and Gaza Strip pledged $60 million to the Holst Fund, the aim of which was to support the operating costs of the Palestinian Authority and its development arm until tax income increased substantially.[46] The Holst Fund was meant to provide an emergency aid package for the Palestinians from November 1994 to March 1995. By 1 March, 1995, however, the Holst Fund was practically broke, with only $4,000 remaining in its coffers. Donors had failed to honor pledges totaling $37 million.[47] The donor community's inability to honor its commitments repeatedly forced the World Bank and Norway to serve as emergency fundraisers and put them in the unusual role of cheerleaders seeking funds from weary and skeptical donors.

Problems of underfunding, inefficiency, and poor aid coordination have existed ever since the West Bank and Gaza development program was conceived in late 1993. In 1994, poor donor coordination and the Palestinian community's inability to process the aid contributed to many delays in the provision of assistance. That year, only $228 million out of $800 million pledged was actually delivered.[48] Many felt that the lack of available funds to cover the Palestinian Authority's staff costs jeopardized the success of the Israeli-Palestinian agreement. They reasoned that for the peace process to succeed, the twenty-four thousand employees of the Palestinian Authority had to know that their livelihoods and the Palestinian political and administrative apparatus would be secure.[49]

In 1995, the failure of would-be donors to fulfill their pledges to the Holst Fund became a source of considerable tension among the different aid bodies. The inability of the Holst Fund to cover a $136 million Palestinian Authority budget deficit also touched off conflict between the authority and the international donor community. The Palestinians construed the shortage of aid funding as a form of punishment, just as they interpreted ongoing delays in the development process as an oblique manifestation of donor pressure. For their part, many of the donors were distrustful of how the Palestinian Authority dispersed the funds, despite the existence of donor controls requiring transparency and accountability in PA disbursement records.[50]

In April 1996, Arafat held talks with James Wolfensohn, World Bank president, to express concern about what he perceived as the failure of the Holst Fund and other donor efforts in the region.[51] In response, Wolfensohn announced that an additional $20 million would be extended to the Palestinian Authority that day and promised $70 million more over the next two months.[52] The World Bank commitment was prompted in part by the financial crisis in the Palestinian autonomous areas resulting from Israel's decision in March 1996 to close its borders with the West Bank and Gaza following terrorist attacks. The loss of jobs in the West Bank and Gaza due to the border shutdown and the ongoing Palestinian fiscal crisis left two-thirds of the Palestinian workforce unemployed. The link between development assistance and the success of the peace process was made explicit by Wolfensohn: "The sense of urgency is clear. Peace will only be assured in that area if you can get jobs for those people."[53]

The example of international aid for the West Bank and Gaza offers lessons, both cautionary and hopeful, on the role of development assistance in fostering an environment conducive to cooperation and peace. Clearly, donors should not make pledges of funding that they cannot honor. They must strive to coordinate their activities so that aid is delivered quickly and efficiently and high-priority peacebuilding projects are fully funded before other less-urgent ones are initiated. In a situation of uncertainty and dramatic political and economic transition like the one taking place in the West Bank and Gaza, the local community may interpret a reversal or delay in the provision of aid as a form of punishment or the brandishing of a stick. This can harden attitudes and unnecessarily complicate the peace process. Donors also must establish effective controls to ensure that the disbursement of funds is conducted in a transparent and accountable manner. Another lesson of the development assistance program in the West Bank and Gaza is that long-term development programs may need temporarily to take a backseat to programs with short- to medium-term political payoffs, such as the provision of recurrent costs for administrative salaries. In particular, support for the staffing needs and institutional requirements of emerging political authorities may be an urgent priority in transition societies.

On balance, despite the problems of coordination and delays in the provision of promised assistance, the World Bank-led effort in the West Bank and Gaza has contributed to and been an essential element of the Israeli-Palestinian peace process. The World Bank and its collaborators have demonstrated that even in the highly charged political setting of the Middle East, development assistance can help to create the preconditions for peace. Arafat gave voice to this argument in late April 1996 when he told a National Press Club audience in Washington, "It is most important to increase foreign investment and to improve the quality of life for Palestinians who are supporting the peace process."[54]

Uganda

In 1986, following fifteen years of civil war, nearly 30 percent of the Ugandan government's operating budget and nearly 20 percent of its capital budget was allocated to the armed forces. Over the next five years, as defeated opponents were incorporated into the National Resistance Army

(NRA) and the NRA began a process of professionalization, these figures rose to 43 and 38 percent respectively.[55] Under strong pressure from several major aid donors, the government and the NRA decided in May 1992 to reduce significantly the size of the armed forces in order to increase the amount of public funding available for social and economic development.

With the support and financing of the donor community, including the World Bank, the government of Uganda established the Veterans Assistance Program (VAP) to help the demobilized soldiers make the transition from active military duty to civilian life.[56] The government recognized that these soldiers were a "specially vulnerable group" requiring financial and other assistance. Years in the NRA had left them with little civilian experience, no savings, and limited vocational skills with which to facilitate their reintegration into everyday life.

Funding for the VAP came almost entirely from external donors, including the World Bank and bilateral aid agencies. The NRA designated candidates for demobilization, disarmed them, and transported them to discharge centers. The Ugandan Veteran Assistance Board (UVAB) then facilitated their reintegration into civilian society by providing assistance to veterans and their dependents for a period of six months under the VAP. Each veteran was given a plot of land, school fees for children, an agricultural starter package, materials for house-building, and an allowance for food, clothing, and health care. The VAP has also offered some longer term reintegration assistance, including social services, job counseling, educational opportunities, and vocational training. Special funds have been earmarked by donors for such programs as AIDS counseling (15 percent of veterans are ill, many of them with AIDS) and health care for the disabled. In the mid-1990s, a number of income-generating projects came on stream, and efforts have increasingly been made to incorporate veterans and their wives as beneficiaries.[57]

The demobilization and reintegration process began in December 1992. By April 1993, 23,000 troops had been successfully demobilized. By 1995, nearly 36,400 soldiers had been released from the NRA.[58] The relative success of the demobilization effort was due to the fact that it was being implemented by a clearly established and stable government aided by external financing. By contrast, unstable and divided political regimes in Angola or Somalia have been less successful in making the transition from war to peace. Although the original intent of the demobilization program in Uganda was to reduce military spending levels, immediate savings have not been realized because one of the aims of the demobilization program was to create a more professional standing army, which required raising the salaries of the soldiers who remained on active duty. However, military spending has fallen as a percentage of government expenditure, and it is continuing to decrease.[59]

Despite the successful demobilization of soldiers in Uganda, there is concern among donors including the World Bank that some Ugandan military veterans are training militia or local defense units in the use of arms against remaining rebel groups. Some of these veterans are paid by district governments and act as civilian police forces, causing donors to suspect that the Ugandan government is merely replacing some official military spending in the 1980s with unofficial spending on covert military activity in the 1990s. It has also been difficult for donors to know exactly how resources are being spent in the security sector because the Ugandan government has been reluctant to open its military budgets to external examination. The World Bank's policy in Uganda has been to accept de facto the Ugandan government's figures for its military budget and to respect its desire not to disclose detailed military spending information.

The World Bank and other donors also face a difficult decision about the duration of their support for reintegration in Uganda. They do not want to create a permanent bureaucracy for managing the country's veterans' programs and hope to phase out the UVAB in 1997. The World Bank's policy is to ensure that when the UVAB is disbanded, veterans will have access to existing rural programs for education, health, and the provision of credit. Unfortunately, these programs are relatively new, and it is not yet possible to evaluate how effectively they will serve the special needs of veterans and their dependents. On balance, though, the World Bank's involvement in demobilization and reintegration in Uganda has been valuable and has generated support from the bilateral donors and UN agencies.

Recommendations and Conclusions

As the development cooperation community recognizes, achieving sustainable economic development in the post–cold war years requires systematic attention to the process of peacebuilding, both prior to and after conflicts. To date, the IFIs have tiptoed around the political controversies inherent in linking development to demilitarization criteria, and the result has been a confused and sporadic effort. The IFIs have not yet fully implemented the many statements and reports emanating from the policy level that have addressed the connections between poverty and excessive military expenditures. A greater commitment by the IFIs would enable these powerful institutions to use the tools of persuasion, support, and conditionality to advance the potential for economic development by reducing the chances of deadly conflict.

The IFIs should take steps to ensure that their assistance supports such critical objectives as full transparency of military budgets, an end to military ownership of civilian enterprises, a functioning judicial system that can identify and punish corruption and human-rights abuses, and a democratic political system that permits citizens to choose their leaders and express their views peacefully.[60]

U.S. law already requires U.S. executive directors at the IFIs to address some of these issues before approving loans. Under a 1994 law, they must take into account the transparency of military budgets and the recipient's efforts to reduce military spending and end military involvement in the civilian economy. Under a 1996 law, U.S. officials in these institutions must oppose loans after three years to governments not conducting a civilian audit of their military budget.[61]

To be fully effective, the IFIs' strategies must be integrated with regional confidence-building and security initiatives. Such integration will require greater project and policy coordination by IFI staff with the United Nations and regional political bodies such as the Organization of African Unity.

Where possible, persuasion and support are preferable to pressure. The IFIs should offer increased economic assistance to countries making efforts to reduce military spending, destroy their surplus weapons stockpiles, resolve political disputes by peaceful democratic means, and adhere to international arms agreements. Positive reinforcement based on the provision of a reward is more likely to result in desired changes in behavior and should always be tried as a first step. The IFIs are facing cuts in their lending operations, due in part to the reluctance of the U.S. Congress to fund foreign aid programs, so additional funding for countries that are demilitarizing and promoting political stability will inevitably lead to indirect pressure on other recipients. However, if persuasion, support, and indirect pressure are not sufficient to induce the desired policy changes, then the only effective tool at the disposal of the IFIs will be direct conditionality. If the IFIs shy away from wielding it, they will undercut the entire process of conflict prevention that is so essential to global economic growth.

In the realm of conflict resolution and postconflict reconstruction, where the IFIs have a longer and clearer track record than in conflict prevention, the IFIs should dramatically increase their technical and financial involvement. To date, the few IFI programs in this area have had a largely positive impact, and the creation of a Post-Conflict Unit can be seen as a positive step. More advice and money, though, will not be sufficient. The IFIs have often avoided directly linking their programs with the policies of the bodies directing the political side of peace processes, such as peacekeeping operations headed by special representatives of the UN secretary general. While the IFIs must, of course, bring their unique, economically oriented perspective to bear, they should be more willing to adjust their operations to the overall political goals established by the international community. This could lead them, for example, to relax temporarily financial standards and budget targets if they threaten the peace progress.

In addition, the IFIs must, as a matter of strategy in implementing such programs, react more quickly to delays and bottlenecks in the coordination and delivery of assistance. Political support for a peace process can be weakened by the failure of the implementing parties to honor promises of economic improvement in a timely manner. The World Bank has a comparative advantage in leveraging contributions from other donors and in managing trust funds. As the manager of Consultative Groups, the bank also has considerable experience in the area of donor coordination.[62] These attributes can be put to good use in postconflict environments.

The problems that have confronted early IFI efforts to support peacebuilding should not be overstated. On the whole, the IFIs bring tremendous optimism to peace processes when they can promise sufficient resources. While they, along with the entire development community, need to adjust their operating procedures to bring them into line with the needs of peacebuilding, the IFIs have gained valuable experience in postconflict transitions in recent years. With clear guidance from their directors, meaning the development of a new, more aggressive consensus among major shareholders and supportive developing countries, the IFIs can and should play an increasingly important role in conflict prevention and resolution.

Notes

1. The IFIs include the World Bank, the International Monetary Fund (IMF), and the four major regional development banks—The African Development Bank, the Asian Development Bank, the European Bank for Reconstruction and Development, and the Inter-American Development Bank.

2. Organization for Economic Cooperation and Development (OECD), Development Assistance Committee, *Development Cooperation, 1995 Report* (Paris, 1996), Statistical Annex, Table 21, A37.

3. Albert Hirschman, *National Power and the Structure of the State,* expanded ed. (Berkeley, Calif.: University of California Press, 1980).

4. For a full treatment of the argument about political and economic criteria at the IFIs, see Lawyers Committee for human rights, *The World Bank: Governance and Human Rights,* New York, August 1993, and Caleb Rossiter, *The Financial Hit List and Human Rights: The Carter Record, the Reagan Reaction,* parts 1 and 2 of a series on human rights and the IFIs, Center for International Policy, Washington, D.C., 1984.

5. See Nicole Ball, *Pressing for Peace: Can Aid Induce Reform?* ODC Policy Essay no. 6 (Washington, D.C.: Overseas Development Council, 1992; distributed by Johns Hopkins University Press), 50–53.

6. As reported in the *Far Eastern Economic Review,* 13 June 1991, 20–21.

7. Personal communication, Michel Camdessus, 19 May 1996.

8. Personal communication, Michel Camdessus, 19 May 1996.

9. OECD, Development Assistance Committee, *DAC Orientations on Participatory Development and Good Governance,* OCDE/GD (93) 191 (Paris, 1993), 19.

10. *Halifax Summit Communiqué,* Halifax, Nova Scotia, Canada, June 1995, paragraph 28, 5.

11. Sarah Keener, Suzanne Heigh, Luiz Pereira da Silva, and Nicole Ball, "Demobilization and Reintegration of Military Personnel in Africa: The Evidence from Seven Country Case Studies" (Washington, D.C.: The World Bank, Africa Regional Series, October 1993), vi. Nat J. Colletta, Markus Kostner, and Ingo Wiederhofer, "The Transition from War to Peace in Sub-Saharan Africa." Directions in Development, The World Bank, Washington, D.C., 1996. Information on Cambodia from personal communication with World Bank staff.

12. For a detailed treatment of aid conditionality, see Joan M. Nelson and Stephanie J. Eglinton, *Global Goals, Contentious Means: Issues of Multiple Aid Conditionality,* ODC Policy Essay no. 10 (Washington, D.C.: Overseas Development Council, 1993; distributed by Johns Hopkins University Press).

13. Center for International Policy, *The Financial Hit List: Part I of a Series on Human Rights and the International Financial institutions,* Washington, D.C., 1984, 5.

14. Lawyers Committee for Human Rights, *The World Bank: Governance and Human Rights,* 56–60.

15. *International Financial Institutions' Quarterly Transactions Opposed by the United States on the Basis of Human Rights Considerations* (1 July 1995–30 September 1995), Enclosure 2.

16. Ivan Eland, "Economic Sanctions as Tools of Foreign Policy," in *Economic Sanctions: Panacea or Peacebuilding in a Post–Cold War World?* eds. David Cortright and George Lopez (Boulder, Colo.: Westview Press, 1995), 32–33.

17. Nelson and Eglinton, *Global Goals,* 24.

18. Etel Solingen, "The New Multilateralism and Nonproliferation: Bringing in Domestic Politics," *Global Governance* 1, no. 2 (May–August 1995): 220–21.

19. Jorgen Dige Pedersen, "The Complexities of Conditionality: The Case of India," *The European Journal of Development Research* 5 (1993): 101.

20. Peter A. van Bergeijk, *Economic Diplomacy, Trade, and Commercial Policy: Positive and Negative Sanctions in a New World Order* (Aldershot, England: Edward Elgar, 1994), 68.

21. Nicole Ball, "Development Aid for Military Reform: A Pathway to Peace," *Policy Focus,* Overseas Development Council, no. 6 (1993).

22. Reuters, "Japan Freezes Grant Aid to China," *The Washington Post,* 30 August 1995.

23. Klemens van de Sand, paper delivered at the Conference on Bombs, Carrots and Sticks: Economic Sanctions and Nuclear Nonproliferation, University of Notre Dame, Notre Dame, Indiana, April 1994.

24. Mulan Ashwin and Jordana Friedman, "Development Versus Defense: Aid as a Tool for Peace," *Research Report,* Council on Economic Priorities (March/April 1995).

25. Development Assistance Committee, *Orientations,* 21.

26. Ibid., 9.

27. U.S. Department of State, *Country Reports on Human Rights Practices 1995,* April 1996, 157.

28. "Current Events Malawi: Doing Life," *Africa Events,* February 1993, 16–17.

29. Lawyers Committee for Human Rights, *The World Bank: Governance and Human Rights,* New York, August 1993, 59.

30. Personal communication, World Bank official, Washington, D.C., 1993.

31. Personal communication, religious leader in Lilongwe, Malawi, 1994.

32. Closing Statement, Malawi Consultative Group, 13 May 1993. See Lawyers Committee for Human Rights, *The World Bank.*

33. Personal communication, Mwiza Munthali, TransAfrica Forum, Washington, D.C., 1996.

34. U.S. Department of State, *Country Reports on Human Rights Practices for 1993,* April 1994, 166.

35. Ibid., 164–86, and U.S. Department of State, *Country Reports on Human Rights Practices for 1995,* April 1996, 156.

36. U.S. Department of State, *Country Reports 1995,* 156.

37. James Vicini, "Donor Nations Prepare Palestine Investment Plan," *Reuters,* 12 June 1995.

38. See *Middle East International,* no. 460, 8 October 1993.

39. See Rex Brynen, *The (Very) Political Economy of the West Bank and Gaza: Learning Lessons about Peacebuilding and Development Assistance,* Montreal Studies on the Contemporary Arab World, Montreal: Inter-University Consortium for Arab Studies, March 1996.

40. Ironically, oil-rich Saudi Arabia turned down a U.S. request to make a significant financial contribution to the post–peace accord development process. Its post-Gulf War purchases of high-technology American weaponry—aggressively promoted by American arms-exporting corporations and personally requested of the Saudi leadership by Presidents Bush and Clinton—had left it without cash reserves. Saudi Arabia's expensive preoccupation with its military buildup is just another example of how militarization can thwart the process of economic development.

41. See Remarks by United States secretary of state Warren S. Christopher, "Building Peace and Prosperity in the Middle East and North Africa: The Role of a Regional Development Bank," presented at an Experts Meeting on the Middle East Development Bank, Washington, D.C., 10 January 1995.

42. Edmund Blair, "The Rewards of Peace," *MEED Middle East Business Weekly,* 15 April 1994, 5.

43. See Andrew Spurrier, "Going for Growth," *MEED Middle East Business Weekly,* 7 January 1995, 5, and Edmund Blair, "Seeking a Mandate for Palestine," *MEED Middle East Business Weekly,* 3 June 1994, 3.

44. Brynen, *The (Very) Political Economy,* 4.

45. Ibid., 5–6.

46. Joel Greenberg, "Failure by Pledged Donors Drains Gaza-Jericho Fund," *New York Times,* 13 March 1995, A6.

47. Reuters North American Wire, 1 March 1995.

48. Joel Greenberg, "Donor Group Agrees to Speed Aid to Palestinian-Run Zones," *New York Times,* 1 February 1995, A8.

49. Greenberg, "Failure by Pledged Donors."

50. Henry L. Hinton, Jr., "Foreign Assistance—PLO Ability to Help Support Palestinian Authority is Not Clear: Report to the Chairman, Committee on International Relations, U.S. House of Representatives," Federal Document Clearing House, Inc., GAO Reports, 1995.

51. Agence France Presse, 31 March 1996.

52. "World Bank President Says Massive Loan Lined Up for Palestinians" Dow Jones Wire, 20 April 1996. Forty subprojects were expected to be funded by this loan. Thirty-three were for rehabilitation and improvement of village access and municipal roads. Other projects involved expanding water supply and waste water disposal facilities.

53. Ibid.

54. "Arafat Seeks Financial Help from U.S., World Bank," Dow Jones Wire, 1 May 1996.

55. Nat J. Colletta, Markus Kostner, and Ingo Wiederhofer with the assistance of Emilio Mondo, Taimi Sitari, and Tadesse A. Woldu, *Case Studies in War-to-Peace Transition: The Demobilization and Reintegration of Ex-Combatants in Ethiopia, Namibia, and Uganda,* World Bank Discussion Paper no. 331, Africa Technical Department Series (Washington, D.C.: The World Bank, 1996), 219.

56. Ibid.

57. All of these activities are discussed in detail in Colletta et al., *Case Studies,* 237–74.

58. The initial target had been 50,000. For several reasons, including renewed unrest in northern Uganda, this target was not met.

59. Colletta et al., *Case Studies,* 327–28.

60. Ensuring that the work of the IFIs promotes objectives such as democratization is not the same as asking the IFIs to implement democratization programs.

61. The 1994 law is contained in the section "Military Spending by Recipient Countries: Military Involvement in the Economics of Recipient Countries" in the Foreign Operations Appropriations Act for Fiscal Year 1995. The 1996 law is contained in the section "Transparency of Budgets" in the Foreign Operations Appropriations Act for Fiscal Year 1997.

62. Other donors sometimes complain that World Bank staff do not so much coordinate as seek to dominate the donor decision-making process. To maximize the collaborative spirit among donors, it is critical that the institution in charge of effecting coordination be sensitive to the concerns of its partners.

Part Five

Conclusions and Lessons Learned

11

Incentives Strategies for Preventing Conflict

David Cortright

A S THE CASE STUDIES in this volume amply illustrate, incentives are powerful means of influencing political behavior.[1] Economic, political, and security inducements can be highly effective in deterring nuclear proliferation, preventing armed conflict, defending civil and human rights, and rebuilding war-torn societies. Conventional political analysis focuses predominantly on coercive instruments such as military force and economic sanctions, but the practice of diplomacy usually involves a significant element of inducement. By calling attention to the unique characteristics of incentives, this chapter seeks to highlight their special contribution to conflict prevention.

Incentives most often appear in combination with sanctions. The case studies in this book emphasize the use of incentives, but each episode also involves a mix of carrots and sticks. Incentives are not a policy unto themselves but are simply one part in a larger mix of policy instruments. The combination of carrots and sticks, of inducements and coercive measures, defines the success of diplomacy.

As Alexander George and others have pointed out, conventional theory has placed too much emphasis on the threatened or actual use of military force, while largely ignoring approaches that reduce tensions.[2] Attempts at international influence have tended to rely excessively on threats rather than on the more flexible use of carrots and sticks.[3] The dominant view seems to be that of Machiavelli: "It is much safer to be feared than loved."[4] Roger Fisher has observed that during the cold war the United States created elaborate means for delivering threats but developed "no comparable sophistication regarding the making of offers." Offering rewards is an important way of exerting influence, according to Fisher, for which there has been "far too little organized consideration."[5] Alexander George and Richard Smoke echo these sentiments in calling for the development of an "inducement theory" to supplement traditional deterrence theory.[6] This chapter and indeed the entire volume attempt to answer that call.

The pages that follow identify the variables that account for the success or failure of inducement policies. The chapter examines the nature of the issues involved, the players and their relationship, and the characteristics of incentives instruments themselves. It concludes with observations about the role of military assistance, foreign aid, and international trade. The chapter begins with a broad assessment of incentives strategies and the emerging model of global cooperation.

The Model of Cooperative Democratic Development

Examples of successful incentives strategies are many and varied. This volume reviews recent efforts to contain the nuclear threat from North Korea, to denuclearize Ukraine and other states, to prevent conflict in South Asia, to facilitate the Salvadoran and Bosnian peace processes, and to encourage negotiations and conflict settlement in the Middle East, South Africa, and the Baltic states. There are many other examples. One of the least recognized but most important came in the years after World War II, when Germany and Japan were integrated into the Western security system and persuaded to remain nonnuclear by security guarantees and economic assistance from the United States.[7] In the Middle East, financial assistance and political assurances have played a crucial role in encouraging the peace process—from the Camp David accords and resulting Israeli-Egyptian Peace Treaty of 1979 to the Israeli-Palestinian Declaration of Principles in 1993.

If the flawed Munich agreement of 1938 was the defining experience for Western strategists for much of this century, the German-Soviet treaty of 1990 serves as a successful counterexample.[8] The failure of appeasement in the 1930s had a profound influence on scholars and policymakers during the cold war and still casts a shadow today, helping to account for the preeminence of coercive deterrence theory.[9] The lesson of Munich was that conciliation does not work, that threats are superior to offers as guarantees of security. The peaceful ending of the cold war suggests another message. Conciliatory gestures helped to defuse decades of political tension and create a new, more cooperative basis for security. In 1990, NATO declared that the Soviet Union was no longer an enemy and gave assurances against the first use of force. Bonn provided Moscow with 15 billion DM in financial assistance (most of it to house returning troops) and agreed to renounce weapons of mass destruction and significantly reduce its armed forces. Moscow accepted the unification of Germany, long considered anathema to Soviet leaders, and agreed to withdraw all of its troops from eastern Germany. A package of economic and security inducements and mutual concessions thus ended a dangerous forty-five-year standoff in the heart of Europe. Perhaps the lessons from Germany in 1990 can temper the lessons learned there in 1938 and give new credibility and impetus to the use of inducement strategies.

There are many particular forms of incentives, but the most powerful inducement for peaceful relations in the world today is access to the emerging system of political cooperation and economic development among the major states. A zone of relatively prosperous democratic peace now stretches from Japan and Australia to North America and through much of Europe. The states in this zone are characterized by economic cooperation and development, democratic governance, and peaceful relations. While one can be critical of the inconsistencies and inequalities within and among these nations and their exploitation of others, the fact remains that access to this system of peaceful cooperation is an attractive inducement for many countries. The promise of improved political and economic relations with the major powers, especially the United States, has often served as an inducement for cooperation. In central and eastern, Europe governments are practically turning themselves upside down to become members of the club. Many nations in Africa, Asia, and Latin America are also aspiring to achieve economic prosperity, democracy, and peaceful security, often in cooperation with Western nations. Conditioning access to this system of cooperative development on the observance of agreed rules of behavior can be a powerful inducement for the prevention of conflict.[10] Paul Schroeder has described this process as "association-exclusion," contrasting it with traditional "compellence-deterrence."[11] The greatest hope for a more cooperative future lies not in the power to punish, according to Schroeder, but in the creative use of association to reward those who abide by civilized standards of behavior while excluding those who do not.

There are many examples of the unfolding of this process. In the early 1990s, the Baltic states and Russia placed greater value on membership in the European Union and the hope for economic cooperation with the West than on nationalist concerns over citizenship rights of Russian minorities and the withdrawal of Soviet troops. When European institutions insisted on a settlement of these disputes as a condition of membership, the two sides were able to arrive at an agreement (see chapter 9). In South Asia, India and Pakistan have begun to taste the benefits of improved economic interaction with the West and may be willing to temper their political animosities to realize greater opportunities for trade and investment (chapter 5). Brazil and Argentina opted to curb their incipient nuclear weapons programs in order to improve economic and political relations with the United States and their neighbors in Latin America.[12]

As the world's greatest military and economic power, as an embodiment of democratic ideals, and as the dominant influence on global culture, the United States is in a preeminent position to shape the course of world affairs. At times Washington has abused its power, especially when it has placed excessive emphasis on coercive policies (most egregiously during the Vietnam War). An incentives-based strategy offers the promise of a more constructive approach to international affairs. The United States can use its power as a positive influence for international harmony by consistently promoting equitable development, democratic governance, and peaceful relations, and by offering economic, diplomatic, and security benefits for those who follow these principles.

Many nations, especially in the developing world, are not enthusiastic about closer relations with the West and its model of cooperative development.[13] They may share the goal of a more prosperous, democratic, and peaceful future, but their past experience with colonialism and Western domination makes them skeptical of great power intentions today. Many developing nations are concerned about the enormous power imbalance in the world and believe that a greater commitment is needed in the West to equity, transparency, and consistency in relations with other states. They would agree that incentives strategies can be important in providing the means for peaceful development, but they question why Western assistance and political engagement with the poorest nations, especially in Africa, has declined. The appeal of a narrowly European or American model is limited. But if the concept of cooperative democratic development can be universalized and the zone of prosperity and peace widened, the strategy of inducements for democratic cooperation can be an effective means of enhancing world peace.

Reciprocity and Beyond

Incentives strategies can be both conditional and nonconditional. Cooperation theorists have emphasized what might be termed the power of positive reciprocity, the ability of cooperative gestures to induce similar behavior in others. Robert Axelrod and others have found that the simple tit-for-tat process, in which one party responds in kind to the gestures of the other, is a highly stable form of cooperation.[14] Incentives policies go beyond the concept of narrow reciprocity, however. Inducements are sometimes offered as part of a long-range process in which no immediate response is requested or expected. This is the so-called pure form of incentives in which there is little or no explicit conditionality.[15] Their purpose is to establish the basis for cooperative relations in the future. They may also help to rebuild a society ravaged by war in the hope that this will prevent a renewal of bloodshed, or encourage a process of dialogue and negotiation. An emphasis on inducements can change the entire setting in which interaction occurs and may even alter the recipient's image of self and of potential adversaries.[16] Whether in their pure form or in a more strictly conditional mode, incentives strategies attempt to address and shape the subjective motivations that determine policy preferences. As such they are essential to the art of diplomatic persuasion.

The history of the cold war confirms the benefits of incentives in generating a positive response. In relations between the United States and the Soviet Union, conciliatory gestures often led to reduced tensions, while hard-line policies usually produced a mirror response of heightened animosity. Lloyd Jensen found in his review of American-Soviet arms talks that concessions by one side tended to be reciprocated by the other.[17] William Gamson and André Modigliani examined eight episodes in which Western nations made conciliatory gestures to the Soviet Union from 1946 to 1963. In seven out of the eight cases, the Soviet Union reciprocated with cooperative behavior. By contrast, there was a tendency toward "refractory" actions and increased belligerence when one side was confronted by hostile actions from the other.[18] Martin Patchen's review of the literature on this subject found that "the usual tendency is for one side in a dispute to reciprocate the [conciliatory] moves of the other, to match incentives if offered with return incentives."[19] Patchen and Jensen concluded that, on balance, promises are more effective than threats in producing desired changes in another nation's behavior.[20]

Perhaps the most dramatic recent case of positive reciprocity occurred in September 1991 when President George Bush announced the unilateral demobilization of U.S. tactical nuclear weapons from ships and submarines and the removal and dismantlement of nuclear artillery and short-range missiles in Europe.[21] This bold initiative was promptly reciprocated by Soviet president Mikhail Gorbachev, who announced a similar and even more sweeping withdrawal and dismantlement of tactical nuclear weapons from Soviet land forces and naval vessels.[22] These reciprocal reductions resulted in the largest single act of denuclearization in history, removing some 13,000 nuclear weapons from deployment.[23] Contrary to the conventional concept of arms control, unilateral initiatives proved to be highly effective in reducing the nuclear danger.

This example illustrates Charles Osgood's important concept of GRIT, graduated and reciprocated initiatives in tension-reduction.[24] The GRIT strategy goes beyond simple tit-for-tat reciprocity and employs a more sophisticated series of conciliatory measures that are designed to reduce tensions and distrust.[25] The initiating side announces a series of accommodating steps and continues even in the absence of a reciprocal response. If the other side exploits the situation or acts in a hostile manner, the initiating side responds in kind, although only to the limited extent necessary to restore the status quo. If the other side reciprocates positively, the pace of conciliatory action is accelerated. The Bush-Gorbachev nuclear reductions and other mutual concessions at the end of the cold war partially followed the GRIT strategy, and helped to dispel the decades-long clouds of fear and distrust that obstructed East-West understanding. These examples corroborate the wisdom of offering concessions as a strategy for enhancing cooperation. As Alexander Wendt has observed, positive reciprocation can foster a sense of common identification and help to create mutual interests between former adversaries.[26] Deborah Welch Larson has similarly emphasized the importance of conciliatory action as a way of reducing distrust and establishing the foundations for cooperative behavior.[27]

Shaping an Incentives Policy

Strategic Design

Incentives policies are most effective when they identify and attempt to ameliorate the root causes of conflict. Whether the primary needs are economic, political, or security-related, incentives should be packaged and delivered in ways that meet those needs and lessen the likelihood of conflict. This is an important way in which incentives differ from sanctions. Where sanctions take away or deny resources to contending parties, incentives add benefits. The key to the strategic use of incentives is adding the right combination of rewards for overcoming the underlying sources of conflict. When Russian army officers and their families complained of the lack of housing at home and began to resist the rapid pace of troop withdrawals from eastern Germany, officials in Bonn fashioned a targeted economic assistance program that not only paid the cost of transporting the troops home but financed the construction of new housing facilities. This policy cleared the way for troop withdrawals while simultaneously helping to assuage the concerns of a highly vocal and potentially troublesome political constituency within Russia. As Geoffrey Thale describes in chapter 7, the U.S. Agency for International Development paid for most of the costs of the land transfer program that was an essential part of the Salvadoran peace process. This not only facilitated the government's implementation of the program but helped to overcome the resistance of the landholders and those on the political right seeking to defend the traditional oligarchic order. Foran and Spector show in chapter 2 that Ukraine's commitment to denuclearization was encouraged by security assurances from the United States and Great Britain that helped quiet nuclear hard-liners in Kiev.

A lack of strategic design has been evident in the civilian peacebuilding provisions of the Dayton peace accords, as Raimo Väyrynen documents in chapter 6. While the military components of the agreement have been fully funded and staffed, the civilian elements of the plan have suffered from a lack of coordination and resources. Insufficient emphasis has been given to mediation services and other programs that could encourage reconciliation within former Yugoslavia's war-torn society. Strategies for addressing underlying resource and employment imbalances among the different ethnic-religious communities have been lacking. Of course, conflict prevention efforts are much more complex and difficult in multiparty settings. When there are so many countervailing claims and interests, as in Bosnia, it may not be possible to craft an effective strategy for addressing the needs of all parties. In such circumstances, sender nations must often pick sides, choosing a particular party to favor and designing incentives strategies accordingly. This seems to have been the case in Bosnia, where the benefits and conditions of the Dayton accords have tended to favor the Muslim-Croat federation over Republika Srpska.

Care must be taken to avoid incentives policies that unintentionally exacerbate regional animosities. Mattoo and I note in chapter 5 that this is a concern in South Asia, where incentives for Pakistan may be viewed as a threat in India, and vice versa. The Brown amendment arms package to Islamabad in 1996 was intended to develop cooperative relations and encourage Pakistan's role as a moderate Islamic state. But this assistance aroused strong nationalist resentments in India, thereby stoking political animosities in the region. A carrot for one side should not be seen as a stick by the other. In cases of dyadic disputes, it is often necessary to provide incentives for both sides. In the Baltic states international assurances were offered to Russia as well as to Estonia and Latvia. The best approach is a win-win strategy that provides rewards to both sides and uses incentives to encourage cooperation between the two adversaries.

Value

To be successful, an incentive offer must have sufficient value to induce a recipient to change policy. In economic theory, an incentive is calibrated to increase the value of the option preferred by the sender over what the recipient would otherwise choose. An incentive seeks to raise the opportunity cost of continuing on the previous course of action by changing the calculation of cost and benefit. The scale of the incentive depends on the magnitude of the desired change in behavior. The greater the change, the larger the required inducements. Increasing the scale of an incentive beyond the point of sufficient magnitude, however, does not affect the behavior of the recipient.[28] Indeed, offering an incentive that is perceived as excessive for the given circumstances can be counterproductive, in part because it may lack credibility within the recipient nation.[29]

In the area of nonproliferation policy, Foran and Spector have developed the concept of a "reservation price," which they define as the lowest price a potential proliferator will accept for giving up its nuclear program (see chapter 2). This reservation price includes the sunk costs already invested in the nuclear program. For a country such as India, which has invested a vast quantity of scarce economic resources and a huge amount of political capital in its nuclear program over a period of more than thirty years, the reservation price is likely to be spectacularly high. In the case of North Korea, on the other hand, where the nuclear program was only partially completed when the crisis broke in 1993, the sunk costs were much lower and could be matched by the United States and its South Korean and Japanese partners. According to Foran and Spector, the magnitude of the incentives package must be commensurate with the proliferator's sunk costs. This is not meant in strictly economic terms but in a broader psychological and political sense. The sender must make an offer that roughly matches the recipient's level of commitment to the objectionable policy. This raises the importance of detecting and addressing potential proliferation problems at an early stage, before the country or group involved has invested enormous resources.

Access to advanced technology is a highly valuable inducement, especially for developing countries. In his study of trade policy and bilateral cooperation, Long found that access to technology raised the perceived value and utility of an incentives offer.[30] Because technology is so crucial to both economic development and military capability, it has value to the most fundamental objectives of government. The "atoms for peace" program was an effective inducement in the 1950s and 1960s because the United States at that time had a virtual monopoly over nuclear technologies and materials that other countries considered important to their industrial development. As the economic and environmental costs of nuclear power rose, however, the value of this inducement declined. Restrictions on high-speed computers and other technologies have been applied against India in the name of nonproliferation policy, although the effectiveness of such measures is debatable.[31] Because of the high value placed on access to such technologies, a lifting of these controls could be an effective incentive.

The value of incentives may also derive from the simple fact of membership or association. In the disputes over citizenship rights in the Baltic states, the promise of participation in multilateral institutions such as the

Council of Europe was an important inducement. The hope of more concrete benefits in the future may have been a factor in this process, but the immediate motivation was a desire for the legitimacy and recognition that participation would confer.

Little research has been conducted into a recipient's subjective calculation of value. Tuomas Forsberg has argued that quality is more important than quantity.[32] One of the most important studies into the subject of value is Eileen Crumm's analysis of Indo-Soviet relations.[33] As Crumm notes, Moscow was quite successful in establishing cooperative relations with New Delhi and securing India's support for many of its international policies. Crumm's analysis found that certain types of incentives were more effective than others. Nondurable goods have high value because their short life leads to a continuous demand for them. Oil and military spare parts were particularly valuable to India. By contrast, the provision of capital goods from Russia declined in value as India's own manufacturing and capital goods industry began to emerge in the 1960s.[34] Petroleum products and military hardware were highly desirable because New Delhi did not have easily available alternatives. These were also fungible goods that could be used flexibly in a variety of settings.[35] According to Crumm, the lack of available alternatives and the fungibility of the goods were key factors in India's perception of value.

Delivery

The effectiveness of an incentives policy depends on the manner in which it is delivered. Sensitivity to the cultural and historical traditions of the recipient nation is essential. Clarity regarding the nature of the offer is also important. Other factors that are important for establishing the credibility of an offer include a detailed plan for implementation, a demonstrated ability to deliver the promised reward, and a reputation for fulfilling pledges.[36] A concrete offer is much more likely than a vague promise to break through the noise of other forms of communication and to be taken seriously by the recipient nation.[37]

On the other hand, perceptions of double standards and unequal enforcement can undermine the legitimacy and credibility of an incentives policy. As noted in chapter 5, U.S. policy toward Islamabad has suffered from abrupt shifts in direction that have left many Pakistanis uncertain about Washington's intentions. Pakistanis also question why the United States has applied intense pressures on their relatively modest nuclear program, when fewer pressures have been directed against the much larger and more sophisticated Indian nuclear capability.

A related question concerns the packaging of incentive offers. Should incentives be provided in a large-scale package all at once, or doled out incrementally over time? Again, little scholarly research is available on these questions. Dumas has suggested that the packaging of incentives depends upon the goal. If the objective is limited and easily achievable, it may be appropriate to offer the entire package all at once. If the purpose is to create longer-term cooperation and a general climate of improved relations, a more gradual and low-key approach may be preferable.[38] The case of German financial assistance to speed Soviet troop withdrawals is an example of the former approach, where a clear, achievable objective warranted an overt and substantial offer of incentives. On the other hand, the challenge of establishing improved relations between the United States and India falls into the latter category, where a more gradual approach will be necessary.

Promptness in delivering a promised reward is important to the effectiveness and credibility of an incentives policy. The swift fulfillment of a pledge increases the influence of the promised reward and raises the likelihood of positive reciprocation.[39] If a trade concession or other form of incentive is promised, it will bring cooperation and compliance more effectively if the offer is delivered quickly. Delays in the implementation of an incentive will impede cooperation. As Nicole Ball and her colleagues note in chapter 10, the failure of international lenders to deliver on the financial pledges made at the time of the 1993 Israeli-Palestinian accords has contributed to political problems and delays in the implementation of the peace process in Gaza and the West Bank.

Research has shown that promises fulfilled far in the future have a less-potent effect on compliance.[40] These findings are consistent with cooperation theory, which emphasizes the importance of a quick response to conciliatory gestures as a way of assuring additional cooperative actions. According to Axelrod, the shorter the response time, the more stable the relationship and the more enduring the cooperation.[41] Quick response, whether to defection or cooperation, speeds the pace of interaction. When the response is friendly, a prompt reply promotes positive reciprocity and builds confidence in the prospect of future cooperation.

Timing

The effectiveness of an inducement depends not only on how it is presented but when it is presented. Seemingly irresolvable deadlocks sometimes become "hurting stalemates" in which the parties are ready to consider compromise.[42] This is when incentives policies are most likely to be effective. Determining exactly when a crisis reaches this stage of ripeness is difficult, however. Simply waiting is not a solution, for a crisis can also become "rotten" and degenerate into worsening violence. Ripeness develops when the parties in a dispute begin to show signs of weariness or when domestic or external conditions change in ways that make sustaining the previous policy more difficult. According to William Zartman, a country will be more likely to settle if it fears that the situation could get worse, or if it believes that unilateral solutions are no longer feasible.[43] In these circumstances the timely application of incentives may assist in settling the conflict and preventing violence. This is close to Roger Fisher's concept of a "yesable proposition."[44]

A well-timed offer to a party weary or wary of continued conflict can make a virtue out of necessity and ease the process of compromise. The Salvadoran settlement described in chapter 7 is a classic case of a well-timed peace initiative. The decline of external support to both sides resulting from the end of the cold war and a mutual exhaustion and recognition of the limits of unilateral military action brought the parties to the bargaining table and created a situation ripe for incentives-based diplomacy. Timing was also a factor in the negotiation of the Dayton accords. This may have been the case in former Yugoslavia. The offer to lift sanctions and provide economic assistance to Belgrade coincided with the Milosevic regime's calculation of diminishing returns for Serbian policy and helped to bring about the November 1995 Dayton accords.

Timing also relates to the nature of the issue. One of the more successful arenas for incentives policies has been nuclear nonproliferation. Traditionally nonproliferation has been associated with the use of sanctions and export controls, but many of the successes in recent decades—South Korea, Taiwan, Argentina, Brazil, Ukraine, Kazakhstan, and North Korea—also have involved the use of incentives. Proliferation cases are amenable to an incentives approach because the process of acquiring weapons of mass destruction requires an enormous amount of time and effort. It can take up to ten years for a country to develop a nuclear weapons capability, which affords ample time for the international community to detect such activity and to enter into dialogue with the offending party. It also allows time to craft and execute an appropriate diplomatic response employing carrots and sticks. As Scott Snyder documents in chapter 3, it took more than a year and a half of difficult bargaining for diplomats to find a package of inducements that could restrain Pyongyang's nuclear ambitions. The successful nuclear dissuasion efforts with South Korea and Taiwan in the 1970s and with Ukraine and Kazakhstan in the 1990s also involved lengthy diplomatic exchanges and the offering of assurances and inducements. Time is necessary for the delicate probing that is essential to effective diplomacy and for the crafting of an appropriate carrots and sticks policy that can influence the other party's behavior.

Avoiding the Risks of Appeasement

The greatest concern about incentives is that conciliatory policies may sometimes give the appearance of rewarding evil. Cooperative gestures may be seen as a sign of weakness or appeasement that can lead to additional acts of aggression. Concerns may be raised about providing rewards for a transgressor to follow norms that others accept willingly without payment.[45] In the North Korea case, critics charged that the Agreed Framework was a reward for wrongdoing that would encourage other states to engage in similar transgressions in the hope of obtaining like rewards. Opponents also expressed concern that the agreement contained no assurances against future violations. Analysts have leveled similar criticisms at U.S. trade preferences for China. A policy praised as creative engagement in the 1970s has faced increasing skepticism, as U.S.-Chinese policy differences widen over nonproliferation and trade issues even as the volume of commercial interaction between the two steadily increases.

One approach to minimizing moral hazards is to package incentives in a step-by- step reciprocal process that conditions the delivery of rewards on specific concessions by the recipient. The incentives package can be broken down into pieces, with each item delivered in response to specific commitments and actions from the other side. This model is followed in the Agreed Framework accord with North Korea. Under the terms of the 1994 plan, each incentive award from the United States and its partners is tied to clearly delineated, observable steps toward denuclearization by North Korea. The process is stretched over several years, allowing the sender states numerous opportunities to assess the compliance of the other side before delivering the next element in the incentives package. When the incentives policy relies in this manner on a long series of discrete steps, it is unwise to offer too much at the outset. The better approach is one that begins with small steps and builds steadily toward larger and more significant gestures as the process of reciprocity becomes more established.

Researchers have also found that incentives work best when they are offered from a position of strength rather than weakness. There may be a tendency for states to employ incentives when coercive options are lacking, but this temptation should be resisted.[46] If compromises are offered pusillanimously as a substitute for decisive action, the recipient may indeed attempt to exploit the situation and engage in further aggression. According to Martin Patchen, conciliatory gestures work best when they flow from strength and are accompanied by a latent threat capacity.[47] Russell Leng has observed similarly that offers "are more likely to be effective when the influencer has the requisites for the effective use of negative inducements as well."[48] In other words, when carrots are mixed with sticks, or at least the threat of sticks, the dangers of appeasement and encouraging wrongdoing can be diminished.

There are some situations where the use of incentives is simply not appropriate, either morally or as an instrument of effective policy. Incentives may be counterproductive if employed in the face of armed conflict and overt military aggression. Conciliatory gestures to tyrants can send a message of acceptance or consent that encourages wrongdoing. Incentives strategies are also inappropriate in cases of gross violations of human rights. This was the case with the Reagan administration's "constructive engagement" policy toward South Africa, as Jeffrey Herbst notes in chapter 8. The abuses of the apartheid system activated a constituency throughout the world that made an incentives-based policy politically unacceptable. The antiapartheid movement, which was very active in the United States, pursued an alternative sanctions-based approach toward the South African government and mounted a successful divestment campaign that helped to bring about the peaceful transition to a nonracial democracy.[49]

Mixing Carrots and Sticks

As noted at the outset, incentives often appear in combination with sanctions. It is difficult at times even to differentiate between the two, since the lifting of a sanction can be an incentive and the withdrawal of incentives a sanction. The promise to lift sanctions against former Yugoslavia was an effective incentive in gaining the support of Slobodan Milosevic in the Dayton peace accords. In the case of North Korea, the offer of economic and diplomatic incentives was accompanied by the movement of U.S. military forces in and around the Korean Peninsula. This simultaneous coercive message no doubt enhanced the appeal of the proposed inducements. Incentives may increase the effectiveness of sanctions. According to George, deterrence is most effective, especially for crisis prevention, when it includes inducements for cooperation as well as punishments for resistance.[50] What the stick cannot achieve by itself may be accomplished by combining it with a carrot.[51]

Deciding whether to emphasize incentives or sanctions in a given situation is related to the challenge of avoiding moral hazards. The proportion of carrots and sticks to be applied in a particular situation depends on the nature of the problem and the objectives being served. When the issues involved have a long-term horizon and do not pose an immediate threat to peace, incentives policies can be highly effective. When there is a more urgent crisis, however, incentives may not be appropriate. Especially if the conflictual situation involves mass suffering or poses grave dangers to international security, a more forceful and coercive response may be necessary. When the targeted policy is perceived as exceptionally heinous (apartheid in South Africa) or the transgression is considered a threat to peace (Iraq's invasion of Kuwait), incentives must give way to a more coercive strategy.

Lloyd J. Dumas has suggested an important distinction between sanctions and incentives.[52] Coercive measures are more appropriate and effective for addressing crises of overt aggression and deadly conflict. Inducement strategies are preferable for creating the long-term foundations for peace and cooperation and thus ameliorating conflicts before they reach the crisis stage. One approach addresses the immediate crises of violent conflict, the other creates the long-term conditions for reducing the likelihood of such conflict.

 Even in the most difficult cases, it is important to hold out at least the promise of benefits as an inducement for effective negotiation. A totally coercive policy implies the willingness to destroy or subdue the other party completely, to impose unconditional surrender. This is a costly and dangerous approach that is rarely if ever appropriate or morally justified. Successful diplomacy requires a give and take interaction that depends on the presence of both sanctions and incentives. Even if the incentive is the limited one of a promise to lift sanctions or cease coercive measures, the offer of a potential benefit can usually contribute to the prevention of conflict.

The Players and Their Interests

The Relationship

The relationship between sender and recipient influences the potential effectiveness of incentives. When relations between the parties are distant or highly conflictual, it may be difficult to create an effective incentives policy. The communication and bargaining aspects of an inducement process are more uncertain when the two sides are hostile and distrustful of each other. At the opposite end of the spectrum, where the relationship between the parties is more cordial and offers promise of cooperation, incentives will be easier to initiate and sustain. As Arnold Wolfers has noted, inducements tend to be more effective in cooperative contexts, where relations between the actors are friendly.[53] In hostile environments cooperation is more problematic.

Research into Soviet policy toward India from the 1950s into the 1980s confirms the importance of relational norms in establishing and maintaining the value of incentives. One of the keys to Moscow's success in gaining Indian friendship, according to Crumm, was its adherence to principles of noninterference, mutual benefit, and peaceful coexistence.[54] By pledging not to interfere in India's internal affairs and then sticking by that promise, Moscow established an important reservoir of goodwill and trust. When the Soviet Union provided aid to private firms in India early in the relationship, this reduced uncertainties about Moscow's willingness to respect a mixed economy and seemed to confirm the commitment to noninterference. When a communist-led government came to power in the southern state of Kerala in 1959, Moscow refrained from aiding the local leaders and continued to deal exclusively with the central authorities in New Delhi. This also calmed anxieties among Indian officials. These actions reinforced the proclaimed norms of noninterference and enhanced the value of Soviet incentives, thereby creating a firmer foundation for cooperative relations.

Conversely, unfriendly or exploitative relations between countries can make the application of incentives less effective. The patterns of mistrust and animosity that characterize troubled relations are not easily repaired even by the most generous offer of assistance. Patchen examined a number of studies that illustrate this pattern. When the sender state had a previous relationship of coercion or exploitation toward a recipient, the use of incentives was ineffective in gaining compliance.[55] The recipient nation tended to be suspicious of the sender's motives because of the previous history of exploitation. In such circumstances, a longer-term, more gradual process was found to be necessary to establish a basis for trust and cooperation.

Even where there are troubled political relations, however, incentives can be successful if they are carefully calibrated to the political and economic needs of the recipient. Few countries were more hostile and distant from one another than the United States and North Korea prior to 1994, yet the two were able to negotiate a successful compromise to the nuclear crisis with the aid of incentives. As detailed in chapter 3, the negotiations fared poorly at first as the two sides traded ultimatums and threats, but a more constructive atmosphere eventually emerged. The bargaining that led to the Agreed Framework was greatly aided by the mission to Pyongyang of Jimmy Carter in June 1994, which helped to break the diplomatic ice between the two countries and opened the door to high-level dialogue. It may be hard to get started when relations between two countries have been adversarial, but once the process of dialogue begins, mutual accommodation becomes possible. Even in the most contentious circumstances a commitment to effective diplomacy and a willingness to address the needs of the other side can bring success.

The Sender

Incentives can be offered either by a single state such as the United States, or a multilateral institution such as the Council of Europe. Each approach has both advantages and disadvantages that can affect potential effectiveness. A single nation can usually decide upon and implement an incentives strategy more effectively than a coalition. A single actor also may be better able to deliver on a promised reward and communicate a coherent objective. On the other hand, coalitions or multilateral institutions have more market power and a greater potential for offering security assurances. Multilateral participation is especially important in peace implementation and postconflict reconstruction. The enormous costs associated with rebuilding countries such as Bosnia or Angola make it impossible for any single country to shoulder the burden alone. The increasingly significant role of the World Bank and other international financial institutions in such efforts is a reflection of this need for multilateralism. An international organization also has the ability to offer membership or recognition as an inducement. In the Baltic states the promise of membership was a relatively low cost but effective incentive for resolving civil rights and troop withdrawal issues. An advantage of this approach is that it may strengthen the international organization itself through the addition of new members.

A major disadvantage of coalitions or international institutions is that sustaining a coherent policy commitment over time is more complex. Especially if the inducement strategy involves security assurances or financial assistance, maintaining the required levels of support among all the participating nations will be difficult. Another problem is that multilateral processes often result in general, vaguely defined objectives, which in turn can cloud the function and purpose of incentives. Differences among the senders can also result in confused or contradictory implementation of a policy.

The economic and military power of the sender are important to the effectiveness of an incentives offer. The larger the market power of the sender, the greater its potential for offering economic incentives. The sender's military capabilities also influence its ability to provide security assurances. These factors help to explain the leadership role of the United States and other major industrial nations. While these considerations of power are important, however, they are not sufficient. Reliability, political will, and the soundness of the underlying policy are more important to success than raw capabilities. Moreover, as emphasized elsewhere in this chapter, the effectiveness of an incentives policy depends on many other factors, including the nature of the issues, the degree of urgency, and the extent of external and domestic constraints.

The United States plays a leading role as both an individual sender and a major player in multilateral coalitions and institutions. Most of the major cases of incentives policy involve the United States acting either alone or in partnership with others. Many argue that leadership from the United States is indispensable to effective multilateral policy. Whether in fashioning the incentives package for resolving the nuclear crisis in North Korea, initiating and sustaining the Dayton peace process for Bosnia, or guiding the multilateral negotiations in the Middle East, American leadership has been decisive.

U.S. predominance is not always beneficial, however. In some circumstances Washington will do better to remain in the background and assume a less-visible role. This was the case with the December 1991 nuclear restraint agreement between Argentina and Brazil, where Germany rather than the United States assumed the leading role in promising the two countries economic benefits.[56] The United States has encountered difficulty when its credibility as a peacemaker is subject to challenge. Some of the countries subjected to nonproliferation pressures question the credibility of U.S. policy when Washington remains the world's leading exporter of weapons and military technology. Nonetheless, even with the limitations and contradictions of U.S. policy, American leadership remains essential. The challenge for the United States is to use its power consistently to promote genuine cooperation and conflict resolution.

The Sender's Options

The choices available to a sender nation vary greatly and are significantly shaped by external constraints. In the case of North Korea, multilateral economic sanctions were problematic because of Chinese and Japanese reluctance, although they remained a backup threat. The use of military force was seen by many as too risky. In this context incentives were the preferred option. In the Bosnian conflict, by contrast, when incentives and diplomacy were unable to prevent armed violence, sanctions were imposed as the most acceptable choice short of war, and eventually air strikes and NATO troop deployments were also authorized. The availability of options varies in each crisis, and the choice of one approach over another depends on the political and historical circumstances of the situation.

The ability to offer and sustain an incentives policy is also influenced by domestic factors. Incentives differ significantly from sanctions in their impact on domestic constituencies within the sender states. Where sanctions often cause hardships for industries or communities adversely affected by a cutoff of trade, incentives policies provide economic advantages for groups that stand to gain from the opening of trade or the provision of technological assistance. William Long emphasizes in chapter 4 that the use of trade and investment policies benefit market sectors and political constituencies within the sender. This can play an important role in mobilizing and sustaining support for the incentives policy.[57] The hardships and lost trade resulting from sanctions can undermine political support for such a policy.[58] The expanded opportunities and benefits that flow from trade incentives often generate increased support for inducement strategies.

On the other hand, the domestic political support accompanying an incentives policy can become an impediment when conditions require a change in policy. This has become the case with U.S. trade policy toward China. As Long notes, the opening of trade with China in the 1970s was part of a broader diplomatic initiative to gain Beijing's geopolitical cooperation, especially in containing the Soviet Union.[59] Over the years commercial interaction with China expanded rapidly, creating a large constituency in the United States dependent on the continuation of favorable trade relations. In 1995, according to the Business Coalition for U.S.-China Trade, the United States exported more than $12 billion in goods and services to China, sustaining 200,000 American jobs.[60] As political relations between Beijing and Washington deteriorated, however, in response to disagreements over human rights, nonproliferation policy, and trade issues, demands for a withholding of trade benefits increased. The annual presidential decision on extending most-favored-nation trade status to China became a focal point for those urging a shift toward more coercive policies to signal disapproval of Beijing's increasingly noncooperative behavior. The White House has responded by arguing that continued engagement is the best means of encouraging reform in China. Whatever the merits of that argument, the fact is that economic dependency on trade with China has made it extremely difficult to adjust policy in response to changing circumstances.

Objectives

The nature of the objectives sought is one of the most important variables affecting the potential effectiveness of incentives. Scholars have long recognized the link between goals and success in the use of economic sanctions.[61] Sanctions can destabilize a government or achieve modest changes in policy, but they are often unable by themselves to halt aggression or impair military capabilities.[62] With inducement strategies as well, it is easier to achieve modest change than wholesale political transformation. Arnold Wolfers has argued that incentives are likely to be most effective in the area of "low politics," where national sovereignty and territorial integrity are not at stake.[63] It is much more difficult to persuade a state to trade territory or national security for economic benefits. On the other hand, if security assurances and the benefits of political association are included in the inducements package, even far-reaching political compromises may be achievable. Denuclearization successes in Ukraine and Kazakhstan were facilitated not only by economic inducements but by broader security and political assurances. The pursuit of major political objectives may be possible, but in such cases larger and more comprehensive inducements will be necessary.

The most successful incentives strategies are those that are focused on a single objective and consistently sustained over time. The relative effectiveness of nonproliferation efforts results from the enormous legitimacy and importance attached to preventing the spread of weapons of mass destruction. Few principles of international behavior are more widely shared or intensely felt than this one. While nuclear black marketing has not been eliminated, international pressures and controls on such activities are steadily expanding. The nonproliferation norm is embodied in the Nuclear Nonproliferation Treaty (NPT) of 1968 (indefinitely extended in 1995 and now signed by 183 states) and related regimes such as the Missile Technology Control Regime and the Nuclear Suppliers Group. The United States has described nonproliferation as the number one priority of its foreign and military policy. While there are exceptions and inconsistencies in this nonproliferation commitment, the objective of preventing the spread of nuclear weapons is a nearly universal norm within the present international system. This singularity of purpose greatly enhances the chances of success.

In many cases, incentives strategies are impeded by multiple and con-flicting objectives. Shifting interests and competing purposes often lead to confusion and can undermine the effectiveness of the stated policy objectives. U.S. policy toward Pakistan offers a classic case of conflicting and inconsistent purposes, as noted in chapter 5. In the late 1970s, nonproliferation was the major priority. This was quickly dropped in the 1980s, however, when Islamabad's cooperation was needed in the struggle against the Soviet invasion of Afghanistan. U.S. aid and arms poured into Pakistan, despite clear evidence of an active nuclear weapons program. In 1990, as the Soviet army withdrew from Afghanistan and Pakistan's assistance was no longer needed, nonproliferation resurfaced as the priority, and aid was abruptly cancelled. In response, anti-American recrimination rebounded across the political spectrum.

Multiple objectives may also exhaust the available inducements and deprive senders of the ability to influence policy. In South Africa, the Reagan administration attempted to promote domestic reforms in the country's racial system, while seeking Pretoria's cooperation in policy toward Namibia and Angola. Washington offered the promise of improved diplomatic relations to gain cooperation on the regional conflicts issue, but this inducement was then no longer available to press for domestic reforms. As Jeffrey Herbst notes in chapter 8, there were "too many targets and not enough bullets."

Competing interests are a particular problem in the application of aid conditionality by international financial institutions, as Ball and her colleagues observe in chapter 10.[64] The World Bank has emphasized structural adjustment policies, which often require reductions in public sector spending, but the bank has also made commitments to alleviating poverty, which may necessitate major public investments in infrastructure, job creation, and social welfare. Structural adjustment policies may also conflict with military demobilization programs such as those in Mozambique, Uganda, and elsewhere. The joblessness and economic hardship caused by adjustment policies can make employment more difficult to find for demobilized combatants.

The Recipient

The success of incentives depends on the nature of the recipient. It is easier to influence a single actor than multiple parties. This helps to account for the relative success of nonproliferation efforts, which usually involve influencing the decisions of a single government entity. Denuclearizing Ukraine required a concentrated effort in Kiev. Preventing conflict in the Middle East, by contrast, involves complex interactions with officials in many capitals and a constant balancing of concerns from one country to another. The problem of multiple players is even more complicated in cases of intrastate conflict. Väyrynen shows in chapter 6 how the international community is faced in former Yugoslavia with a complex interaction among Serbs, Croats, and Bosnian Muslims as well as differences between Serbian authorities in Belgrade and in Pale. In these circumstances it is hard to craft coherent incentives strategies and harder still to determine their impact on the contending parties. In situations where state authority has collapsed and political power has splintered, incentives will have little or no impact.

A minimum requirement for the success of incentives or any other attempt at external influence is a coherent recipient regime. Governments that are in disarray and deeply divided or that lack effective control within their boundaries will be unable to respond to offers no matter how attractive the incentives may be. Such concerns are especially relevant in countries riven by civil conflict. This is precisely the setting where much of the deadly violence of recent years has occurred. The lack of government coherence in such circumstances can be an important limiting factor on the effectiveness of inducement strategies. Similar problems can arise in attempts to influence revolutionary regimes, which often behave in unconventional ways or which may not have full control over rapidly changing circumstances. Insurgent regimes such as Iran and Nicaragua in the 1980s tended to follow the dictates of doctrine rather than the norms of conventional statecraft. Such regimes may be relatively impervious to the usual calculations of cost and benefit.

The effectiveness of incentives also depends on the needs of the recipient. If the recipient is desperate for international recognition or financial support, incentives are likely to have a positive effect. Ukraine, Belarus, and Kazakhstan were eager for Western diplomatic support and financial assistance in the years immediately following the dissolution of the Soviet Union, and they were willing to trade the nuclear weapons on their soil for relatively low-cost economic and security commitments from the West.[65] A particularly successful example of this process was "Project Sapphire," in which the United States negotiated the secret removal from Kazakhstan of 1,300 pounds of highly enriched uranium in exchange for the relatively modest payment of $100 million and an American pledge to secure the material against potential smuggling or diversion.[66] The deal was possible because Kazakhstan did not really want the bomb-grade material in the first place and shared U.S. and Russian concerns that the material be securely stored.

The perceived urgency of an issue depends on its origins. When a troublesome situation is inherited and does not fit the objectives of a regime, accommodation to the concerns of sender states will be easier. Ukraine, Kazakhstan, and Belarus had no real plans or capability for becoming nuclear weapons states, notwithstanding assertions to the contrary from Ukrainian politicians. When the United States offered political assurances and financial support for the removal of these weapons, the post-Soviet republics were ready to part with their nuclear inheritance.[67] By contrast, India and Pakistan have developed their de facto nuclear capabilities by dint of enormous effort and sacrifice, and they view the nuclear option as crucial to national security and prestige. They are unlikely to give up their nuclear programs for any price, or at least not without exacting very substantial political and economic commitments from the West. If the recipient country feels deeply about the issue in dispute, accommodation to the demands of sender states will be more difficult, and the scale of the incentive offer will need to be increased accordingly.

Internal Dynamics

The likelihood of success depends greatly on social and political effects within the recipient nation. Because of the importance of internal dynamics in the process of political change, external attempts to change policy must be able to influence the political preferences of important actors within the recipient country. As William Long has emphasized in chapter 4 and elsewhere, incentives can appeal to groups and constituencies within the recipient nation who are willing and able to mobilize on behalf of the reforms sought by senders.[68] Long argues that incentives policies will be most effective when they target their benefits to these stakeholders and potential allies who can influence the recipient government toward accommodation.

Offering preferential trade benefits may be a particularly effective means of encouraging reform within recipient countries. Political scientist Etel

Solingen has observed a linkage within some developing countries between support for trade liberalization and acceptance of cooperative security and nuclear nonproliferation goals. The political constituencies committed to economic globalization, according to Solingen, are less inclined to favor overt nuclearization and assertive nationalism.[69] Conversely, groups endorsing greater protectionism are more likely to refrain from active denuclearization. Solingen's hypothesis may be true generally, but there are exceptions. In India, Prime Minister A. B. Vajpayee's short-lived BJP government of May 1996 declared support for continued trade liberalization while also asserting a commitment to the overt development of nuclear weapons.[70] Even if the connection between economic globalization and nonproliferation is less certain than Solingen suggests, her recommendation for incorporating this linkage into future incentives policies is sound: "Coalitions favoring steps toward denuclearization could be rewarded with a variety of trade benefits, investments, selective removal from export control lists, debt relief, and the like."[71]

An example of the successful application of targeted incentives to influence the internal political dynamics of a recipient was the U.S. offer of $10 billion in loan guarantees to Israel in 1992. The Bush administration indicated that Washington's financial support would be contingent on Israel limiting settlements in the occupied territories. This interaction occurred in the midst of an election campaign in Israel in which the opposition Labor and Meretz platforms favored the U.S. conditions while the existing Likud government did not. Officially, Washington expressed no preference in the election outcome, but the implications of its position were clear. As Solingen has noted, the U.S. stance helped the Labor-Meretz coalition expose the consequences of Likud policies in a very concrete, and ultimately successful, manner.[72]

Attempting to achieve targeted influence in this way is a delicate matter. It is always better to frame incentives as assistance rather than compellence. Overt influence attempts can backfire if they are perceived as interference or manipulation. Offering incentives that influence domestic politics requires finesse and aplomb, and a keen sensitivity to the traditions and culture of the recipient nation. Just as sanctions can generate a "rally-around-the-flag" backlash, inducement efforts may spark nationalist resentment and denunciations of attempts to "bribe" the recipient nation.[73] At times "irrational" concerns about national pride can override utilitarian calculations of cost and benefit. As with sanctions, incentive policies must consider the possibility of unpredictable subjective responses within the recipient nation.

Patchen has argued that incentives efforts work better in influencing domestic politics if the recipient nation is democratic and political factions can engage in open debate, but there is some uncertainty on this point.[74]

At times a concentrated or authoritarian leadership can make policy adjustments more readily than a government that must contend with multiple factions and democratic pressures. A representative society may be more difficult to persuade if the policy being addressed has deep public support. A great deal also depends on the previous relationship between the sender and recipient. American efforts to influence Israel have worked without generating a nationalist backlash, but equivalent attempts to induce changes within India would undoubtedly prompt loud cries of indignation. Both Israel and India are democratic, but they have had contrasting relationships with the United States (Israel friendly, India distant) and different historical experiences with external domination (India's long struggle against British colonialism resulting in a stronger sense of postcolonialism). The degree of democracy within a recipient may be less important to the success of external influence attempts than a sophisticated understanding of that country's internal social and political dynamics. Effective incentives policies require that senders have a thorough knowledge of the culture, historical traditions, and internal political processes of the recipient country.

Ultimately the success of an incentives policy depends on subjective factors within the recipient nation. As economist Denis Goulet has observed, "an incentive system can only sway a subject who is disposed to respond."[75] Moral and cultural considerations can be as important to the success of an incentives offer as purely material factors. Baldwin has made the same point in noting that the value of an incentive depends on a recipient's perceptions of the situation and the baseline of previous expectations.[76] The intended beneficiaries of an incentive will always be the final judge of its effectiveness, which makes the assessment of a recipient's subjective feelings all the more important to the prospects for success.

Incentives policies can have unanticipated negative consequences if senders are insensitive to these internal dynamics. Incentives delivered to military forces or to corrupt elites can weaken the standing of constituencies seeking democratic reform and thereby undermine the long-term prospects for cooperative behavior.[77] Understanding the likely internal consequences of inducements and targeting benefits to empower the supporters rather than the opponents of reform are key elements in the strategic design of incentives policy.

Goulet has proposed an approach to incentives policy that encourages popular participation as the key to mobilizing political support within the recipient nation.[78] This approach differs from strategies that target rewards to elites. The difference lies in the nature of the recipient's internal political dynamics. If there is popular concern about selling out to foreign influence, or a recalcitrant leadership that refuses to reform, a non-elite strategy may be preferable. Making an offer that is appealing and acceptable to the vast majority can help to minimize concerns about external interference.[79] Crafting proposals that benefit popular movements rather than narrow elites may empower such constituencies to overcome obdurate leaders. Goulet illustrates his theory with examples of development projects in Brazil where aid policies benefited social groups that adopted innovative approaches to sustainable development. A similar model could be applied in the area of security policy, with inducements directed toward groups and constituencies that are most favorable to policies of demilitarization and international cooperation. By enhancing the involvement of nonelite groups and empowering them to acquire political and economic rights, this new approach targets assistance to those who often need it most, while providing concrete inducements for domestic constituencies to mobilize on behalf of reform and cooperation.

Policy Issues

Military Assistance: A Two-Edged Sword

Military assistance is a major component of U.S. foreign policy and is one of Washington's most influential incentives tools. The United States maintains military missions, sells weapons or military services, and engages in training or joint operations with many countries throughout the world. This chapter is not the place for a detailed assessment of this phenomenon, but a few general observations are in order.

The lure of military assistance is undeniable. Access to U.S. military technology and cooperation is a powerful inducement that has been used frequently to achieve Washington's political objectives. Arms transfers are a major element of this policy for the United States and other industrialized nations. The emphasis on weapons transfers has intensified since the end of the cold war, as arms manufacturers attempt to compensate for declining domestic orders with increased sales abroad. Many of these weapons are exported to developing nations, where they may contribute to regional conflict and instability. In Somalia and elsewhere, U.S. armed forces have experienced the "boomerang effect" of being fired upon by American-made weapons.[80] Arms transfers can have negative economic consequences for the developing nations that purchase them. As Ball and her colleagues note in chapter 10, international financial institutions increasingly recognize excessive expenditures on weapons and military forces as an impediment to sustainable development.

The prevalence of military inducements in U.S. foreign policy can have other negative consequences. It reinforces a bias toward the use of military force to solve complex political problems, and it devalues the search for more nonviolent, civilian-oriented approaches to conflict prevention. Military assistance can also enhance the power of those in recipient regimes who are most hostile to democracy and thereby exacerbate the problems that often lead to armed conflict.

The example of Pakistan again illustrates this concern, as noted in chapter 5. U.S. policy toward Pakistan has relied heavily on arms transfers and military assistance. By bolstering the institutional power of the armed forces, however, these policies have strengthened those who already have too much power (and who have overthrown elected governments in the past), while weakening the fragile forces of democracy and civil society. In countries such as Pakistan, where military authority is excessive and civilian government weak, an emphasis on security assistance and military cooperation may be antithetical to the cause of promoting greater democracy.

In El Salvador as well, the use of military aid as the primary source of U.S. influence during the 1980s had the effect of strengthening the very forces responsible for repression and death squad abuses. Thale explains in chapter 7 that this greatly complicated implementation of the 1992 peace agreements, which called for a restructuring of the security forces and their more effective subordination to civilian control. The difficulties encountered in carrying out these provisions of the accords are in part attributable to the excessive power and independence which lavish and largely unconditional U.S. military assistance allowed the security forces to acquire. On the other hand, the threat to cut off this American assistance, which had become the lifeblood of the Salvadoran military, proved to be effective in convincing the security forces to accept a negotiated settlement and the beginnings of reform. Military assistance is thus a two-edged sword. It can weaken or undermine the forces of civil society, but it can also be used as a powerful tool for convincing the security forces in a recipient country to accept political reform.

Foreign Aid: The Neglected Incentive

When the Republican-dominated Congress voted in 1995 to slash international assistance spending and abolish the principal agencies responsible for foreign aid, including the Agency for International Development and the United States Information Agency, the White House condemned the legislation as "the most isolationist proposal to come before Congress in the last fifty years" and vetoed it.[81] While the legislation was indeed more draconian than earlier foreign aid bills, it merely reflected a trend of diminishing political support for foreign aid that has been underway in the United States for years. Similar reductions have occurred in other nations.

The U.S. foreign aid budget of $13.5 billion in 1995 represented less than 1 percent of the federal government budget, and 1994 overseas development assistance was barely 0.15 percent of gross national product. As Table 11.1 indicates, the United States spends the least amount on foreign assistance, measured as a percentage of gross national product, of any industrialized nation.

Even these figures are inflated, for much of what passes as foreign aid is actually military assistance. In the early 1990s, more than half of U.S. foreign aid was in the category of "security assistance," which provides financing for foreign military forces and economic support for security programs.[82] The Clinton administration has attempted to give greater emphasis to development aid and humanitarian assistance within the foreign aid budget, but these efforts have been hampered by congressional efforts to restrict the overall level of foreign aid. The cutbacks in foreign assistance affect more than direct concessional aid. They also reduce the U.S. contri-

Table 11.1. Overseas Development Assistance (ODA) as a Percentage of Gross National Product and Government Budget, 1994

	ODA *(hundreds of millions, U.S. dollars)*	*ODA* *Percent of GNP*	*ODA* *Percent of government budget*
Australia	1,088	0.35	1.19
Austria	655	0.33	n/a
Belgium	726	0.32	n/a
Canada	2,250	0.43	1.36
Denmark	1,446	1.03	2.34
Finland	290	0.31	0.96
France	8,466	0.64	n/a
Germany	6,818	0.34	1.93
Ireland	109	0.25	0.64
Italy	2,705	0.27	0.49
Japan	13,239	0.29	1.27
Luxembourg	59	0.40	1.15
Netherlands	2,517	0.76	n/a
New Zealand	110	0.24	n/a
Norway	1,137	1.05	1.86
Portugal	308	0.35	n/a
Spain	1,305	0.28	0.88
Sweden	1,819	0.96	2.57
Switzerland	982	0.36	2.96
United Kingdom	3,197	0.31	1.19
United States	9,927	0.15	1.36

Source: Development Cooperation: 1995 Report, Organization for Economic Cooperation and Development, Paris, 1996

bution to the World Bank and other international financial institutions and thereby weaken multilateral lending programs as well.

It is easy to dismiss foreign aid as unpopular and inefficient, but the negative political consequences of allowing this program to decline deserve mention. The neglect of foreign aid robs the United States of an important tool of foreign policy. As Hans Morgenthau observed, the United States has interests abroad that cannot be secured by military or other instruments of policy, where a lack of foreign aid means that American objectives cannot be supported at all.[83] In Morgenthau's conception, foreign aid is an important part of the toolbox of international policy. Along with sanctions, the use of military force, and various forms of incentives, foreign aid is one of the "weapons in the political armory of the nation."[84] The emasculation of foreign aid becomes a form of unilateral disarmament that takes away a vital instrument of policy.

Foreign aid can be used positively as an inducement for cooperation, or it can be applied coercively through the cutoff of assistance as a sanction against wrongdoing. In cases of military aggression or gross violations of human rights, aid cutoffs have been used often as a readily available, inexpensive, and swift form of signaling disapproval and applying pressure on the offending government. As Thale documents in chapter 7, the reduction of U.S. aid to El Salvador was used effectively as both a sanction and incentive for advancing the peace process. During the Carter administration, aid cutoffs to repressive regimes in Latin America and elsewhere became an effective means of promoting human rights and democratic governance.[85] If the recipient government is heavily dependent on such aid flows, the impact of an aid cutoff can be significant. Some scholars have challenged the effectiveness of aid cutoffs, but David Baldwin's analysis of these studies (based on cases from the late 1940s through the early 1970s) has shown that aid cutoffs enjoy a success rate equal to or greater than that of other foreign policy instruments, including the use of military force.[86] If there is little or no foreign aid to begin with, however, the cutoff option is not available. Here again the diminished levels of U.S. foreign aid limit Washington's options for asserting its international interests.

American foreign aid has not always been as penurious as it is now. In the years immediately following World War II, at the time of the Marshall Plan for Western Europe, international assistance spending in the United States reached 2.4 percent of gross national product.[87] The Marshall Plan was based on the assumption that economic improvement would enable countries outside the Soviet orbit to remain independent and that U.S. aid could be conditioned on cooperation for mutual benefit.[88] It was possible at that time for United Auto Workers president Walter Reuther, reflecting a substantial body of educated opinion, to advocate a program of sustained large-scale foreign assistance at the level of 4 percent of gross national product for a century.[89] Reuther and others like him argued that such international aid would benefit the United States by encouraging worldwide economic development and consequent demand for U.S. products, and by creating stable conditions for sustained peace and cooperation. Such ideas have been out of favor in Washington in recent years. Only in relation to the Middle East, where the United States continues to spend more than $5 billion a year on foreign assistance to Israel and Egypt (justified in part as an incentive to the peace process), is there a recognition of the potential value of foreign aid. For the rest of the world, U.S. policymakers have few foreign aid resources with which to encourage cooperation. The result is a self-imposed limitation on the ability to assist sustainable development and provide incentives for conflict prevention.

The Power of Trade: A Global Strategy

With the decline of foreign assistance, trade and investment policy has assumed an increasingly prominent role in international relations.[90] The privatization of government has now extended even to the conduct of foreign affairs, as the activities of private corporations have become a major tool of overseas policy. This can be a worrisome trend if it means that public interests are subordinated to private profit, as occurred in earlier decades when American "dollar diplomacy" overthrew governments and fomented wars in Central America and elsewhere to protect private investments and trade monopolies. Today as well multinational companies sometimes focus too narrowly on their own profitability and ignore larger issues of social responsibility, as evidenced by the continued support of Royal Dutch Shell and other multinational oil companies for the military junta in Nigeria.

Yet the spread of commerce and economic interdependence can also create the foundations for a more peaceful and cooperative global system. In *The Rise of the Trading State,* Richard Rosecrance has argued that increased trade and commercial interaction reinforce preferences for peace and make war less likely.[91] The classical liberal theory of international relations holds that expanded free trade reduces the likelihood of war, while protectionism and autarky lead to greater conflict.[92] Immanuel Kant argued at the end of the eighteenth century that the power of trade could be a potent force for peace:

> It is the spirit of commerce which cannot coexist with war, and which sooner or later takes hold of every nation. For, since the money power is the most reliable among all the powers subordinate to the state's power, states find themselves impelled (though hardly by moral compulsion) to promote the

noble peace and to try to avert war by mediation whenever it threatens to break out anywhere in the world.[93]

The beneficial impact of trade was a crucial element in Kant's concept of "perpetual peace." He believed that prosperous democratic nations that become economically interdependent are less likely to wage war on one another. The nineteenth-century British philosopher John Stuart Mill argued similarly that "the great extent and rapid increase of international trade [is] the principal guarantee of the peace of the world."[94]

One can be dubious of these sweeping philosophical generalizations and yet grant the important kernel of insight they contain. As Dumas has emphasized, equitable and mutually beneficial trade relations among nations can create understanding and interdependence and strengthen the preference for cooperation over conflict.[95] While commercial interdependence does not prevent conflict, it does create incentives and mechanisms for settling disputes amicably. According to Dumas, "generating sustained economic development is one of the most important elements in creating greater security."[96]

As the pace of trade, investment, communications, and technological interaction has accelerated in recent decades, the potential influence of commercial policy as a conflict prevention strategy has increased.[97] Israeli prime minister Yitzhak Rabin believed that the expansion of trade could be a force for peace in the Middle East, and he urged "a process that turns economics into the moving force that shapes the regional relations instead of national interests."[98] In keeping with Rabin's dream, the Israeli stock market and international financial institutions have shown a marked preference for conciliation over confrontation, for what Yaron Ezrahi has termed "economy over ideology."[99] In South Asia, the liberalization of commerce and the lifting of trade restrictions is leading to greater economic interaction with the world and hopefully will generate greater dialogue and exchange as well. This in turn may help to ease the animosities that have plagued the two nations since independence and may create the foundations for future political cooperation.

The new Emerging Markets policy of the Clinton administration is an attempt to generalize this principle as a strategy for international cooperation. First articulated by Jeffrey Garten, former undersecretary of commerce for international trade, the policy seeks to encourage U.S. commercial engagement in key developing countries to promote market economics, democratic governance, and peaceful relations.[100] In effect this strategy attempts to broaden access to the system of economic interdependence and nonaggressive relations that has evolved among the European Community, the United States, and Japan. The goal is to expand this "zone of democratic peace" to other parts of the world through a strategy of regional economic development and integration.

The emerging markets strategy is essentially a long-term concept for preventing conflict and building cooperative relations. It is not a program for inducing short-term accommodation or immediate reciprocity. The time horizon is more distant and the strategy for encouraging improved relations more gradual. Providing preferential trade privileges and supporting investment and commerce in emerging markets are means of building the foundations for future cooperation.[101] Prosperous regional powers integrated into the world economy can serve as models for other nations, while helping to isolate pariah regimes.[102] Growing prosperity may also help emerging nations restrain tendencies toward rebellion and secession within their own borders, hopefully stemming the rising tide of civil conflict. As the economic pie grows larger in these developing nations, governments may be able to offer inducements to internal factions for the peaceful settlement of political differences.[103]

This emphasis on the power of trade reinforces the importance noted at the outset of encouraging access to the emerging global system of cooperative democratic development. Access to trade, technology, and investment can be an attractive inducement to countries seeking economic development. Many countries aspire to partake of that "spirit of commerce" that Kant evoked, and to achieve a level of economic and political development that can bring stability and peace. A strategy that offers integration into the system of economic development in exchange for compliance with norms of international cooperation may be the most powerful tool available for creating the long-term conditions for a more stable and secure world.

This strategy requires that the major developed countries apply for themselves the norms they promote to others. The prosperity and peaceful relations that prevail in the developed world cannot come at the expense of impoverishment and oppression among developing nations. The flow of weapons to world trouble spots cannot be stemmed when arms exports remain a major priority for the United States, France, and other industrial nations. Convincing threshold states to abandon the nuclear option requires the major powers to work toward the continued reduction and eventual elimination of their own arsenals. The price of peace for the United States and its partners is a greater commitment to military restraint for themselves and a preference for conciliation over confrontation as the primary approach to international affairs.

Notes

1. I express thanks to colleagues who read early manuscripts of this chapter and provided substantive comments and suggestions, especially to Alexander

George, Lloyd J. Dumas, George Lopez, William J. Long, Bruce Jentleson, Janice Gross Stein, and Tom Leney.

2. Alexander L. George and Richard Smoke, *Deterrence in American Foreign Policy: Theory and Practice* (New York: Columbia University Press, 1974), 2, 33. For a thorough discussion of inducement strategies in the context of differing theories of international relations, see Tuomas Forsberg, "The Efficacy of Rewarding Conflict Strategies: Positive Sanctions as Face Savers, Payments, and Signals," Paper prepared for the annual meeting of the International Studies Association, San Diego, California, 16–20 April 1996.

3. George and Smoke, *Deterrence*, 2, 590; see also Alexander L. George, David K. Hall, and William R. Simons, *The Limits of Coercive Diplomacy: Laos-Cuba-Vietnam* (Boston: Little Brown and Company, 1971), 243.

4. Niccolo Machiavelli, *The Prince* (Cambridge: Cambridge University Press, 1988), 59.

5. Roger Fisher, *International Conflict for Beginners* (New York: Harper and Row, 1969), 106.

6. George and Smoke, *Deterrence*, 606–7.

7. I am grateful for this insight to Karl Kaiser, visiting scholar at the Center for International Affairs at Harvard University, during remarks at the 27 October 1995 meeting of the Carnegie Commission on Preventing Deadly Conflict.

8. I am indebted to Tuomas Forsberg for this analogy and the discussion of German unification. See Forsberg, "The Efficacy of Rewarding Conflict Strategies," 2–3, 23–28.

9. Deborah Welch Larson, *Origins of Containment: A Psychological Explanation* (Princeton, N.J.: Princeton University Press, 1985), 57; George and Smoke, *Deterrence*, 590.

10. Remarks of Karl Kaiser.

11. Paul W. Schroeder, "The New World Order: A Historical Perspective," *The Washington Quarterly* 17, no. 2 (Spring 1994): 35.

12. Mitchell Reiss, *Bridled Ambition: Why Countries Constrain Their Nuclear Capabilities* (Washington, D.C.: The Woodrow Wilson Center Press, 1995), 52, 60.

13. I am indebted for the insights in this paragraph to Olara A. Otunnu, president of the International Peace Academy and former Ugandan foreign minister, during remarks at the 27 October 1995 meeting of the Carnegie Commission on Preventing Deadly Conflict.

14. Robert Axelrod, *The Evolution of Cooperation* (New York: Basic Books, 1984); see also Russell J. Leng and Hugh G. Wheeler, "Influence Strategies, Success, and War," *Journal of Conflict Resolution* 23 (December 1979): 655–84.

15. George and Smoke, *Deterrence*, 608–9.

16. Forsberg, "The Efficacy of Rewarding," 17–18.

17. Lloyd Jensen, "Negotiating Strategic Arms Control, 1969–1979," *Journal of Conflict Resolution* 28 (1984): 535–59.

18. William Gamson and André Modigliani, *Untangling the Cold War* (Boston: Little Brown and Company, 1971).

19. Martin Patchen, *Resolving Disputes between Nations: Coercion or Conciliation?* (Durham, N.C.: Duke University Press, 1988), 262.

20. Ibid., 263.

21. "An Assault on Nuclear Arms," *U.S. News and World Report,* 7 October 1991, 24–28.

22. "Nuclear Weapons: Going, Going," *The Economist,* 12 October 1991, 54.

23. Center for Defense Information, Interview with Kathryn Schultz, 6 August 1996.

24. See Charles E. Osgood, *An Alternative to War or Surrender* (Urbana, Ill.: University of Illinois Press, 1962).

25. See Alexander George's analysis in *U.S.-Soviet Security Cooperation: Achievements, Failures, Lessons,* eds. Alexander L. George, Philip J. Farley, and Alexander Dallin (New York: Oxford University Press, 1988), 705–7.

26. Alexander Wendt, "The Anarchy Is What States Make of It: The Social Construction of Power Politics," *International Organization* 46, no. 2 (Spring 1992): 420–22.

27. Deborah Welch Larson, "Crisis Prevention and the Austrian State Treaty," *International Organization* 41, no. 1 (Winter 1987): 27–60.

28. George Tsebelis, "Are Sanctions Effective? A Game-Theoretic Analysis," *Journal of Conflict Resolution* 34, no. 1 (March 1990): 14.

29. Patchen, *Resolving Disputes,* 267.

30. William J. Long, *Economic Incentives and Bilateral Cooperation* (Ann Arbor, Mich.: University of Michigan Press, 1996).

31. See Deepa Ollapally and Raja Ramana, "U.S.-India Tensions: Misperceptions on Nuclear Proliferation," *Foreign Affairs* 74, no.1 (January/February 1995): 17.

32. Forsberg, "The Efficacy of Rewarding," 20.

33 Eileen M. Crumm, "The Value of Economic Incentives in International Politics," *Journal of Peace Research* 32, no. 3 (1995): 313–30.

34. Ibid., 324.

35. Ibid., 324–25.

36. Fisher, *International Conflict,* 119–23.

37. Patchen, *Resolving Disputes,* 267.

38. Interview, David Cortright with Lloyd J. Dumas, 11 July 1995.

39. Fisher, *International Conflict,* 124.

40. Patchen, *Resolving Disputes,* 267–68.

41. Axelrod, *Evolution of Cooperation,* 185.

42. See I. William Zartman, *Ripe for Resolution: Conflict and Intervention in Africa* (New York: Oxford University Press, 1985).

43. Ibid., 122–23.

44. Fisher, *International Conflict,* 15–26.

45. Karl Deutsch, "On the Concepts of Politics and Power," *Journal of International Affairs* 21, no. 2 (1967): 233.

46. This question was posed by Janice Gross Stein at the Panel on Preventing Deadly Conflict, Annual Meeting of the American Political Science Association, San Francisco, California, 31 August 1996.

47. Patchen, *Resolving Disputes,* 271.

48. Russell Leng, "Influence Techniques among Nations," in *Behavior, Society,*

and International Conflict, Volume 3, eds. Philip E. Tetlock et al. (Oxford: Oxford University Press, 1993), 115.

49. Jennifer Davis, "Sanctions and Apartheid: The Economic Challenge," in *Economic Sanctions: Panacea or Peacebuilding in a Post–Cold War World?* eds. David Cortright and George Lopez (Boulder, Colo.: Westview Press, 1995), 173–84.

50. George and Smoke, *Deterrence,* 608.

51. Alexander L. George, *Forceful Persuasion: Coercive Diplomacy as an Alternative to War* (Washington, D.C.: United States Institute of Peace, 1991), 11.

52. Interview, Lloyd J. Dumas.

53. Arnold Wolfers, "Power and Influence: The Means of Foreign Policy," in *Discord and Collaboration: Essays on International Politics* (Baltimore, Md.: Johns Hopkins University Press, 1962), 107–8.

54. Crumm, "The Value of Economic Incentives," 319.

55. Patchen, *Resolving Disputes,* 269.

56. Reiss, *Bridled Ambition,* 63 and 70.

57. William J. Long, "Trade and Technology Incentives and Bilateral Cooperation," *International Studies Quarterly* 40, no. 1 (March 1996), 81.

58. Gary Clyde Hufbauer, Jeffrey J. Schott, and Kimberly Ann Elliott, *Economic Sanctions Reconsidered* (Washington, D.C.: Institute for International Economics, 1990), 12.

59. Long, "Trade and Technology Incentives," 90–94.

60. Robert S. Greenberger, "China Moves Press U.S. into a Corner," *Wall Street Journal,* 8 February 1996, A10.

61. Hufbauer et al, *Economic Sanctions Reconsidered,* 49.

62. Ibid., 94–95.

63. Wolfers, "Power and Influence," 107–8.

64. See Joan M. Nelson and Stephanie J. Eglinton, *Global Goals, Contentious Means: Issues of Multiple Aid Conditionality* (Washington, D.C.: Overseas Development Council, 1993).

65. For a detailed analysis of these cases see William C. Potter, "The Politics of Nuclear Renunciation: The Cases of Belarus, Kazakhstan, and Ukraine," Occasional Paper No. 22 (Washington, D.C.: The Henry L. Stimson Center, April 1995).

66. *New York Times,* 23 November 1994, A1.

67. For a firsthand account of the successful U.S. efforts to assist and encourage denuclearization in the former Soviet Union, see James Goodby, "Averting Nuclear Chaos: The Tasks before Us," *U.S. Department of State Dispatch,* vol. 4, 11 October 1993, 704–7; see also "Averting Nuclear Chaos: A Challenge of Preventive Diplomacy," Statement of Ambassador James Goodby, Conference on Bombs, Carrots, and Sticks: Economic Sanctions and Incentives and Nuclear Nonproliferation, University of Notre Dame, Notre Dame, Indiana, April 1994.

68. Long, "Trade and Technology Incentives."

69. Etel Solingen, "The New Multilateralism and Nonproliferation: Bringing in Domestic Politics," *Global Governance* 1, no. 2 (May–August 1995): 214.

70. Vajpayee stated in a radio broadcast that his Hindu nationalist government "will exercise the option to induct nuclear weapons as a deterrent." Brahma Chella-

ney, "India's New Leader to Deploy Nukes," *Washington Times,* 16 May 1996, 1, 20.

71. Solingen, "The New Multilateralism," 218.

72. Ibid., 219.

73. See Ivan Eland, "Economic Sanctions as Tools of Foreign Policy," in *Economic Sanctions,* Cortright and Lopez, 29–42.

74. Patchen, *Resolving Disputes,* 135.

75. Denis Goulet, *Incentives for Development: The Key to Equity* (New York: New Horizons Press, 1989), 11.

76. David Baldwin, "The Power of Positive Sanctions," *World Politics* 24, no. 1 (October 1971): 23.

77. Hans Morgenthau, "A Political Theory of Foreign Aid," *American Political Science Review* 56 (June 1962): 308.

78. Goulet, *Incentives for Development,* 145, 159–61.

79. Forsberg, "The Efficacy of Rewarding," 10.

80. For a critique of weapons trafficking, see William D. Hartung, *And Weapons for All* (New York: Harper Collins, 1994).

81. *Congressional Quarterly,* 17 January 1995, 1760–63; and *Congressional Quarterly,* 20 May 1995, 1437. See also *Congressional Quarterly,* 27 May 1995, 1513.

82. Paul Ferrari, "U.S. Security Aid in a New World Order," *Policy Focus,* Overseas Development Council, no. 2 (1991).

83. Morgenthau, "Political Theory of Foreign Aid," 301.

84. Ibid., 309.

85. See Lars Schoultz, *Human Rights and United States Policy toward Latin America* (Princeton, N.J.: Princeton University Press, 1981), 139–45 and 195–209.

86. Klaus Knorr, *The Power of Nations: The Political Economy of International Relations* (New York: Basic Books, 1975), 181. See also David Baldwin, *Economic Statecraft* (Princeton, N.J.: Princeton University Press, 1985), 318–19.

87. Ibid., 296.

88. Herbert Feis, *The Diplomacy of the Dollar: The First Era, 1919–1932* (Baltimore: Johns Hopkins University Press, 1950), 72.

89. *New York Times,* 19 July 1950.

90. Long, *Economic Incentives.*

91. Richard Rosecrance, *The Rise of the Trading State* (New York: Basic Books, 1987).

92. See also the discussion in Neil R. Richardson, "International Trade as a Force for Peace," in Charles W. Kegley, Jr., ed., *Controversies in International Relations Theory: Realism and the Neoliberal Challenge* (New York: St. Martin's Press, 1995), 284–85.

93. Immanuel Kant, "Essay on Eternal Peace," reprinted in Appendix to Carl Joachim Friedrich, *Inevitable Peace* (Cambridge: Harvard University Press, 1948), 264–65.

94. John Stuart Mill, *Principles of Political Economy,* new edition (London: Longmans Green, 1923), 582.

95. Lloyd J. Dumas, "Economics and Alternative Security: Toward a Peace-keeping International Economy," in *Alternative Security: Living without Nuclear Deterrence*, ed. Burns Weston (Boulder, Colo.: Westview Press, 1990), 140–41.

96. Ibid., 163.

97. Patchen, *Resolving Disputes*, 327.

98. Report from Rabin's office, quoted in Amy Dockser Marcus, "Israel Moves to Build Tighter Economic Ties to its Arab Neighbors," *Wall Street Journal*, 3 August 1995.

99. Yaron Ezrahi, "In Israel, Peace Means Prosperity," *New York Times*, 21 January 1997.

100. John Stremlau, "Clinton's Dollar Diplomacy," *Foreign Policy*, no. 97 (Winter 1994–95): 21.

101. Interview, Lloyd J. Dumas.

102. Stremlau, "Clinton's Dollar Diplomacy," 31.

103. Ibid.

Acronyms

AEC	Atomic Energy Commission
AG	Australia Group
AHLC	Ad-Hoc Liaison Committee in the Middle East
AID	Agency for International Development
ANC	African National Congress
APEC	Asia-Pacific Economic Cooperation Group
ARENA	Nationalist Republican Alliance Party (El Salvador)
ASEA	Allmannä Svenska Electriska Aktiebolaget, then the Swedish civilian nuclear power industry, now part of ABB (Asea Brown Boveri, Ltd., Swiss/Swedish multinational corporation)
BJP	Bharatiya Janata Party (India)
CCP	Chinese Communist Party
CENTO	Central Treaty Organization
CIA	Central Intelligence Agency
COCOM	Coordinating Committee for Multilateral Export Controls
CSCE	Conference on Security and Cooperation in Europe, now Organization for Security and Cooperation in Europe (OSCE)
CSFR	Czech and Slovak Federal Republic
DAC	Development Assistance Committee of the Organization for Economic Cooperation and Development (OECD)
DIA	Defense Intelligence Agency
DPRK	Democratic People's Republic of Korea
ENA	Ethno-national assessment
EU	European Union
EUAM	European Union Administration
FMLN	Farabundo Marti National Liberation Front (El Salvador)

G-7	Group of Seven
GATT	General Agreement on Tariffs and Trade
GCG	General Cooperating Governments license
GCT	General COCOM Trade license
GRIT	Graduated and reciprocated initiatives in tension-reduction (strategy developed by Charles Osgood)
HDZ	Croatian Democratic Community
HWR	Heavy water reactor
IAEA	International Atomic Energy Agency
IDA	International Development Association (World Bank)
IFC	International Financial Corporation, a lending institution of the World Bank
IFI	International financial institution
IFOR	International Enforcement Force in Bosnia, later the Stabilization Force, SFOR
IMF	International Monetary Fund
KEDO	Korean Peninsula Energy Development Organization
KEPCO	Korean Electric Power Company
LWR	Light-water reactor
MCP	Malawi Congress Party
MFN	Most-favored-nation trading status
MINUSAL	United Nations International Mission in El Salvador
MTCR	Missile Technology Control Regime
NATO	North Atlantic Treaty Organization
NGO	Nongovernmental organization
NP	National Party in South Africa
NPT	Non-Proliferation Treaty
NRA	National Resistance Army (Uganda)
NSG	Nuclear Suppliers Group
ODA	Overseas Development Assistance
ODC	Overseas Development Council
OECD	Organization for Economic Cooperation and Development
OMRI	Open Media Research Institute
ONUSAL	United Nations Observer Mission in El Salvador
ONUV	United Nations Verification Mission to El Salvador
OSCE	Organization for Security and Cooperation in Europe
OTE	Hellenic Telecommunications Organization
PA	Palestinian Authority
PALS	Permissive action links
PERs	Public expenditure reviews of the World Bank
PLO	Palestine Liberation Organization
PRC	People's Republic of China
ROK	Republic of Korea

SAARC	South Asian Association for Regional Cooperation
SADF	South African Defense Force
SAL	Structural Adjustment Lending Program (World Bank)
SFOR	Stabilization Force
START	Strategic Arms Reduction Treaty
SWAPO	South West African People's Organization
UDF	United Democratic Front in Malawi
UNHCR	United Nations High Commissioner for Refugees
UNITA	National Union for the Total Independence of Angola
UNSC	United Nations Security Council
USAID	United States Agency for International Development
USSR	Union of Soviet Socialist Republics
UVAB	Ugandan Veteran Assistance Board
VAP	Veteran's Assistance Program (Uganda)

Bibliography

Books

Anti-Defamation League. *Beyond the White House Lawn: Current Perspectives on the Arab-Israeli Peace Process*. New York: Anti-Defamation League, 1994.

Arnson, Cynthia J. *Crossroads, Congress, the President, and Central America, 1976–1993*. University Park, Penn.: Pennsylvania State University Press, 1993.

The Asia Society. *South Asia and the United States After the Cold War: A Study Mission*. New York: The Asia Society, 1994.

———. *Preventing Nuclear Proliferation in South Asia*. New York: The Asia Society, 1995.

Axelrod, Robert. *The Evolution of Cooperation*. New York: Basic Books, 1984.

Bacevich, A. J., James Hallums, Richard White, and Thomas Young. *American Military Policy in Small Wars: The Case of El Salvador*. Washington, D.C.: Pergamon Brassey's International Defense Publishers, 1988.

Baker, J. *From Revolution to Democracy: Central and Eastern Europe in the New Europe*. Washington, D.C.: Bureau of Public Affairs, U.S. Department of State, 1990.

Baker, Pauline H. *The United States and South Africa: The Reagan Years*. New York: The Ford Foundation, 1989.

Baldwin, David A. *Economic Statecraft*. Princeton, N.J.: Princeton University Press, 1985.

Bertsch, G., R. Cupitt, and S. Elliott-Gower, eds. *International Cooperation on Nonproliferation Export Controls*. Ann Arbor: University of Michigan Press, 1994.

Blackwill, Robert D., Rodric Braithwaite, and Akhiko Tanaka. *Engaging Russia.* New York: The Trilateral Commission, 1995.

Borstelmann, Thomas. *Apartheid's Reluctant Uncle: The United States and Southern Africa in the Early Cold War.* New York: Oxford University Press, 1993.

Botti, Timothy J. *The Long Wait: The Forging of the Anglo-American Alliance, 1945–1958.* New York: Greenwood Press, 1987.

Brynen, Rex. *The (Very) Political Economy of the West Bank and Gaza: Learning Lessons about Peacebuilding and Development Assistance.* Montreal Studies on the Contemporary Arab World. Montreal: Inter-University Consortium for Arab Studies, March 1996.

Brzezinski, Z. *Power and Principle: Memoirs of the National Security Advisor, 1977–1981.* New York: Farrar, Straus, and Giroux, 1983.

Bupp, I. C., and J. Derian. *Light Water.* New York: Basic Books, 1978.

Burn, D. *The Political Economy of Nuclear Energy.* London: The Institute of Economic Affairs, 1967.

Chayes, Abram, and Antonia Handler Chayes. *Preventing Conflict in the Post-Communist World: Mobilizing International and Regional Organizations.* Washington, D.C.: Brookings Institution, 1996.

Clawson, P. *How Has Saddam Hussein Survived?* Washington, D.C.: National Defense University, 1993.

Coleman, James S. *Foundations of Social Theory.* Cambridge, Mass.: The Belknap Press, 1990.

Congressional Quarterly. *The Middle East.* 8th ed. Washington, D.C.: Congressional Quarterly, 1994.

Cortright, David, and George A. Lopez, eds. *Economic Sanctions: Panacea or Peacebuilding in a Post–Cold War World?* Boulder, Colo.: Westview Press, 1995.

Cortright, David, and Amitabh Mattoo, eds. *India and the Bomb: Public Opinion and Nuclear Options.* Notre Dame, Ind.: University of Notre Dame Press, 1996.

Coulum, R., and R. Smith, eds. *Advances in Information Processing in Organizations.* Greenwich, Conn.: JAI Press, 1985.

Crocker, Chester A. *High Noon in Southern Africa: Making Peace in a Rough Neighborhood.* New York: W.W. Norton, 1992.

Cullen, R., ed. *The Post-Containment Handbook.* Boulder, Colo.: Westview Press, 1990.

Brito, Dagobert, Michael Intrilligator, and Adele Wick, eds. *Strategies for Managing Nuclear Non-Proliferation.* Lexington, Mass.: Lexington Books, 1983.

Diamond, Larry. *Promoting Democracy in the 1990s: Actors and Instruments, Issues and Imperatives.* Washington, D.C.: Carnegie Commission on Preventing Deadly Conflict, 1995.

Doxey, Margaret. *Economic Sanctions in Contemporary Perspective.* New York: St. Martin's Press, 1987.

Feis, Herbert. *The Diplomacy of the Dollar: The First Era, 1919–1932.* Baltimore: Johns Hopkins University Press, 1950.

Fieldstein, J. S., and J. R. Freemen. *Three-Way Street: Strategic Reciprocity in World Politics.* Chicago, Ill.: University of Chicago Press, 1991.

Fisher, Roger. *International Conflict for Beginners.* New York: Harper and Row, 1969.

Foran, Virginia I., ed. *Missed Opportunities? The Role of Security Assurances in Nuclear Non-Proliferation.* Washington, D.C.: Carnegie Endowment for International Peace. Forthcoming.

Gamson, William, and André Modigliani. *Untangling the Cold War.* Boston: Little Brown and Company, 1971.

Ganguly, Sumit. *The Origins of War in South Asia: The Indo-Pakistani Conflicts Since 1947.* Boulder, Colo.: Westview Press, 1994.

Garenta, J. *Power and Powerlessness.* Urbana, Ill.: University of Illinois Press, 1980.

George, Alexander L. *Forceful Persuasion: Coercive Diplomacy as an Alternative to War.* Washington, D.C.: United States Institute of Peace, 1991.

———. *Bridging the Gap: Theory and Practice in Foreign Policy.* Washington, D.C.: United States Institute of Peace, 1993.

George, Alexander L., David K. Hall, and William R. Simons. *The Limits of Coercive Diplomacy: Laos-Cuba-Vietnam.* Boston: Little Brown and Company, 1971.

George, Alexander L., and Richard Smoke. *Deterrence in American Foreign Policy: Theory and Practice.* New York: Columbia University, 1974.

George, Alexander L., P. J. Farley, and A. Dallin, eds. *U.S.-Soviet Security Cooperation.* New York: Oxford University Press, 1985.

Gibb, Tom, and Frank Smyth. *El Salvador: Is Peace Possible? A Report on the Prospects for Negotiations and U.S. Policy.* Washington, D.C.: Washington Office on Latin America, 1990.

Gleditsch, N. P., and O. Njølstud, eds. *Arms Races: Technological and Political Dynamics.* Oslo, Norway: International Peace Research Institute, 1990.

Goulet, Denis. *Incentives for Development: The Key to Equity.* New York: New Horizons Press, 1989.

Hamrin, C.L. *China and the Challenge of the Future.* Boulder, Colo.: Westview Press, 1990.

Harding, H. *China's Second Revolution.* Washington, D.C.: The Brookings Institution, 1987.

———, ed. *China's Foreign Relations in the 1980s.* New Haven, Conn.: Yale University Press, 1984.

Harrison, Selig, and Geoffrey Kemp. *India and America: After the Cold War*. Washington, D.C.: The Carnegie Endowment, 1993.

Hartung, William D. *And Weapons for All*. New York: Harper Collins, 1994.

————. *U.S. Weapons at War: Arms Deliveries to Regions of Conflict*. New York: World Policy Institute, 1995.

Hirschman, Albert. *National Power and the Structure of the State*. Expanded edition. Berkeley, Calif.: University of California Press, 1980.

Hufbauer, Gary Clyde, Jeffrey Schott, and Kimberly Ann Elliott. *Economic Sanctions Reconsidered: History and Current Policy*, vols. I and II, 2d ed. Washington, D.C.: Institute for International Economics, 1990.

Janis, I. L., and L. Mann. *Decision-Making: A Psychological Analysis of Conflict, Choice, and Commitment*. New York: Free Press, 1977.

Jasper, James. *Nuclear Politics: Energy and the State in the United States, Sweden, and France*. Princeton, N.J.: Princeton University Press, 1990.

Jentleson, Bruce W. *With Friends Like These: Reagan, Bush, and Saddam, 1982–1990*. New York: W.W. Norton, 1994.

Jervis, R. *The Logic of Images in International Relations*. Princeton, N.J.: Princeton University Press, 1970.

Karp, R. Cowen, ed. *Security with Nuclear Weapons: Different Perspectives on National Security*. Stockholm: Stockholm International Peace Research Institute and Oxford University Press, 1991.

Keener, Sarah, Suzanne Heigh, Luiz Pereira da Silva, and Nicole Ball. *Demobilization and Reintegration of Military Personnel in Africa: The Evidence from Seven Country Case Studies*. Africa Regional Series. Washington, D.C.: The World Bank, October 1993.

Keohane, Robert. *After Hegemony: Cooperation and Discord in the World Political Economy*. Princeton, N.J.: Princeton University Press, 1984.

Knorr, Klaus. *The Power of Nations: The Political Economy of International Relations*. New York: Basic Books, 1975.

Kolodziej, Edward A., and Roger E. Kanet, eds. *Coping with Conflict After the Cold War*. Baltimore: The Johns Hopkins University Press, 1996.

Kriesberg, Louis. *International Conflict Resolution: The U.S.-USSR and the Middle East Cases*. New Haven, Conn.: Yale University Press, 1992.

Kurian, George Thomas. *The New Book of World Rankings*. 3d ed. New York: Facts on File, 1991.

Kux, Dennis. *India and the United States: Estranged Democracies, 1947–1991*. Washington D.C.: National Defense University Press, 1992.

Larson, Deborah Welch. *Origins of Containment: A Psychological Explanation*. Princeton, N.J.: Princeton University Press, 1985.

Lauren, Paul Gordon, ed. *Diplomacy: New Approaches in History, Theory, and Policy*. New York: Free Press, 1979.

Lawyers Committee for Human Rights. *The World Bank: Governance and*

Human Rights. New York: Lawyers Committee on Human Rights, August 1993.

Leyton-Brown, D., ed. *The Utility of International Economic Sanctions*. New York: St. Martin's Press, 1987.

Licklider, Roy, ed. *Stopping the Killing: How Civil Wars End*. Case Studies. New York: New York University Press, 1993.

Lieven, Anatol. *The Baltic Revolution: Estonia, Latvia, Lithuania, and the Path to Independence*. New Haven, Conn.: Yale University Press, 1993.

Litwak, Robert S. *Détente and the Nixon Doctrine*. Cambridge: Cambridge University Press, 1984.

Long, William J. *Economic Incentives and Bilateral Cooperation*. Ann Arbor, Mich.: University of Michigan Press, 1996.

Lukes, S. *Power: A Radical View*. London: Macmillan, 1974.

Machiavelli, Niccolo. *The Prince*. Cambridge: Cambridge University Press, 1988.

Macrae, Joanna, and Anthony Zwi. *War and Hunger: Rethinking International Responses to Complex Emergencies*. London: Zed Books, 1994.

Mandela, Nelson. *Mandela, Tambo and the African National Congress*. Edited by Sheridan Johns and R. Hunt Davis. New York: Oxford University Press, 1991.

Martin, Lisa L. *Coercive Cooperation: Explaining Multilateral Economic Sanctions*. Princeton, N.J.: Princeton University Press, 1992.

Mazarr, Michael J. *North Korea and the Bomb: A Case Study in Nonproliferation*. New York: St. Martin's Press, 1995.

Mendl, Wolf. *Deterrence and Persuasion: French Nuclear Armament in the Context of National Policy, 1945–1969*. New York: Praeger Publishers, 1970.

Mill, John Stuart. *Principles of Political Economy*. New ed. London: Longmans Green, 1923.

Mokoena, Kenneth, ed. *South Africa and the United States: The Declassified History*. New York: The New Press, 1993.

Montgomery, Tommie Sue. *Revolution in El Salvador, From Civil Strife to Civil Peace*. Boulder, Colo.: Westview Press, 1995.

Nelson, Joan M., and Stephanie J. Eglinton. *Global Goals, Contentious Means: Issues of Multiple Aid Conditionality*. Washington, D.C.: Overseas Development Council, 1993.

Nyang'oro, Julius E., and Timothy N. Shaw. *Beyond Structural Adjustment in Africa: The Political Economy of Sustainable and Democratic Development*. New York: Praeger, 1992.

O'Donnell, Madalene, Jack Spence, and George Vickers. *El Salvador Elections 1994, The Voter Registration Triangle*. Cambridge, Mass: Hemisphere Initiatives, 1993.

Ok-nim, Chung. *Five Hundred Eighty-Eight Days in North Korea's Nuclear*

Program: The Tactics and Strategy of the Clinton Administration (in Korean). Seoul: Seoul Press, 1995.

Osgood, Charles E. *An Alternative to War or Surrender*. Urbana: University of Illinois Press, 1962.

Owen, David. *Balkan Odyssey*. New York: Harcourt Brace & Co., 1995.

Patchen, Martin. *Resolving Disputes between Nations: Coercion or Conciliation?* Durham, N.C.: Duke University Press, 1988.

Penate, Oscar Martinez. *El Salvador: Del Conflicto Armado A La Negociacion*. Ontario, Canada: Bandek Enterprises, 1995.

Peres, Shimon, with Arye Naor. *The New Middle East*. New York: Henry Holt and Co., 1993.

Peters, Joel. *Building Bridges: The Arab-Israeli Multilateral Talks*. London: Royal Institute of International Affairs/Chameleon Press Ltd., 1994.

Princen, Thomas. *Intermediaries in International Conflict*. Princeton, N.J.: Princeton University Press, 1992.

Qingshan, T. *The Making of U.S. China Policy*. Boulder, Colo.: Lynne Rienner Publishers, 1992.

Quester, George. *Nuclear Diplomacy: The First Twenty-Five Years*. Cambridge, Mass.: Dunellen, University Press of Cambridge, 1970.

———. *The Politics of Nuclear Proliferation*. Baltimore, Md.: Johns Hopkins University Press, 1973.

Reiss, Mitchell. *Without the Bomb: The Politics of Nuclear Nonproliferation*. New York: Columbia University Press, 1988.

———. *Bridled Ambition: Why Countries Constrain Their Nuclear Capabilities*. Washington, D.C.: The Woodrow Wilson Center Press, 1995.

Rogers, Peter, and Peter Lydon, eds. *Water in the Arab World: Perspectives and Prognoses*. Cambridge, Mass.: Harvard University Press, 1994.

Rosecrance, Richard. *The Rise of the Trading State*. New York: Basic Books, 1987.

———, ed. *The Dispersion of Nuclear Weapons*. New York: Columbia University Press, 1964.

Rossiter, Caleb. *The Financial Hit List and Human Rights: The Carter Record, the Reagan Reaction*. Parts 1 and 2 of a series on human rights and the international financial institutions. Washington, D.C.: Center for International Policy, 1984.

Rotblat, Joseph, Jack Steinberger, and Bhalochandra Udgaonkar, eds. *A Nuclear-Weapon-Free-World: Desirable, Feasible?* Boulder, Colo.: Westview Press, 1993.

Rothgeb, John M. *Defining Power: Influence and Force in the Contemporary International System*. New York: St. Martin's Press, 1993.

Schelling, Thomas C. *Arms and Influence*. New Haven, Conn.: Yale University Press, 1966.

————. *The Strategy of Conflict.* Cambridge, Mass: Harvard University Press 1980 [1960].

Schrire, Robert. *Adapt or Die: The End of White Politics in South Africa.* New York: Ford Foundation, 1991.

Shinn, James, ed. *Weaving the Net: Conditional Engagement with China.* New York: Council on Foreign Relations Press, 1996.

Silber, Laura, and Allan Little. *Yugoslavia: Death of a Nation.* New York: TV Books, 1996.

Spector, Leonard S. *The Undeclared Bomb.* Cambridge, Mass.: Ballinger Publishing Co., 1988.

Spector, Leonard S., with Jacqueline R. Smith. *Nuclear Ambitions.* Boulder, Colo.: Westview Press, 1990.

Spector, Leonard S., Mark McConough, and Evan Medeiros. *Tracking Nuclear Proliferation: A Guide in Maps and Charts.* Washington, D.C.: Carnegie Endowment for International Peace, 1995.

Spence, Jack, George Vickers, and David Dye. *The Salvadoran Peace Accords and Democratization, A Three Year Progress Report and Recommendations.* Cambridge, Mass.: Hemisphere Initiatives, 1995.

Spiegel, Steven S., and David J. Pervin, eds. *Practical Peacemaking in the Middle East: Volume I, Arms Control and Regional Security.* New York: Garland Publishing, Inc., 1995.

————. *Practical Peacemaking in the Middle East: Volume II, The Environment, Water, Refugees, and Economic Cooperation and Development.* New York: Garland Publishing, Inc., 1995.

Stanley, William. *Protectors or Perpetrators? The Institutional Crisis of the Salvadoran Civilian Police.* Washington, D.C.: Washington Office on Latin America and Hemisphere Initiatives, 1996.

Study Commission on U.S. Policy toward Southern Africa. *South Africa: Time Running Out.* Berkeley, Calif.: University of California Press, 1981.

Summers, Lawrence H.,and Shekhar Shah, eds. *Proceedings of the World Bank Annual Conference on Development Economics, 1991.* Washington, D.C.: The World Bank, 1992.

Thatcher, Margaret. *The Downing Street Years.* New York: Harper Collins, 1993.

Thomas, Raju, ed. *Perspectives on Kashmir: The Roots of Conflict in South Asia.* Boulder, Colo.: Westview Press, 1992.

Tsao, J. *China's Development Strategies and Foreign Trade.* Lexington, Mass.: Lexington Books, 1987.

van Bergeijk, Peter A. *Economic Diplomacy, Trade, and Commercial Policy: Positive and Negative Sanctions in a New World Order.* Aldershot, England: Edward Elgar, 1994.

Vance, C. *Hard Choices: Critical Years in American Foreign Policy.* New York: Simon and Schuster, 1983.

Walker, W., and M. Lonnroth. *Nuclear Power Struggles.* London: Allen & Unwin, 1983.

Wolfers, Arnold. "Power and Influence: The Means of Foreign Policy." In *Discord and Collaboration: Essays on International Politics.* Baltimore, Md.: Johns Hopkins Press, 1962.

Woodward, Susan. *Balkan Tragedy: Chaos and Dissolution after the Cold War.* Washington, D.C.: Brookings Institution, 1995.

The World Bank. *Bosnia and Herzegovina, Toward Economic Recovery.* Washington, D.C.: The World Bank, 1996.

World Bank. *World Debt Tables, 1992–93.* Vol. 2, *Country Tables.* Washington, D.C., 1993.

Zartman, I. William. *Ripe for Resolution: Conflict and Intervention in Africa.* New York: Oxford University Press, 1985.

———, ed. *Elusive Peace: Negotiating an End to Civil Wars.* Washington: The Brookings Institution, 1995.

Articles

Agrell, W. "The Bomb that Never Was: The Rise and Fall of the Swedish Nuclear Weapons Programme." In *Arms Races: Technological and Political Dynamics,* edited by N. P. Gleditsch and O. Njølstud. Oslo, Norway: International Peace Research Institute, 1990.

Alam, Shahid. "Some Implications of the Aborted Sale of Russian Cryogenic Rocket Engines to India." *Comparative Strategy* 13, no. 3 (July–September 1994).

American-Israel Political Action Committee. "The Year in Review." *Near East Report,* special supplement, 18 December 1995.

Ashwin, Mulan, and Jordana Friedman. "Development Versus Defense: Aid as a Tool for Peace." *Research Report,* Council on Economic Priorities (March/April 1995).

Aviation Week and Space Technology. "Space Pacts Boost India." 13 February 1995.

Bajpai, Kanti, and Amitabh Mattoo. "First Strike!" *Pioneer,* New Delhi, 23 April 1995.

Baldwin, David A. "Foreign Aid, Intervention, and Influence." *World Politics* 21, no. 3 (April 1969).

———. "Inter-nation Influence Revisited." *Journal of Conflict Resolution* 15 (March 1971).

———. "Thinking About Threats." *Journal of Conflict Resolution* 15 (March 1971).

———. "The Power of Positive Sanctions." *World Politics* 24, no. 1 (October 1971).

———. "Power and Social Exchange." *American Political Science Review* 72 (1978).

Ball, Nicole. "Development Aid for Military Reform: A Pathway to Peace." *Policy Focus,* Overseas Development Council, no. 6 (1993).

———. "International Economic Actors." In *Coping with Conflict After the Cold War,* edited by Edward A. Kolodziej and Roger E. Kanet. Baltimore: The Johns Hopkins University Press, 1996.

Barber, Lionel, Harriet Martin, and Laura Silber, "Transatlantic Row Looming over Bosnia," *Financial Times,* 15 March 1996, 3.

Berthelemy, Jean-Claude, Remy Herrera, and Somnath Sen. "Military Expenditure Reductions in India and Pakistan: Analytic Perspectives." *Peace Economics, Peace Science, and Public Policy* 2, no. 3 (1995).

Blair, Edmund. "The Rewards of Peace." *MEED Middle East Business Weekly,* 15 April 1994.

———. "Seeking a Mandate for Palestine." *MEED Middle East Business Weekly,* 3 June 1994.

Blustein, Paul. "A Loan Amid the Ruins: World Bank Shifts Aid to Rebuilding War-torn Countries," *Washington Post,* 13 February 1996.

Bollag, Burton. "Educators Begin the Difficult Task of Rebuilding Bosnian Higher Education." *Chronicle of Higher Education,* 3 May 1996.

Bookmiller, Robert J. and Kirsten Nakjavani Bookmiller. "Behind the Headlines: The Multilateral Middle East Talks." *Current History* 95, no. 597 (January 1996).

Borden, Anthony. "Moving Dayton to Bosnia." *The Nation,* 25 March 1996.

Brown, Kenneth. "Mostar, Without Bridges, Without Light." *Mediterraneans* no. 7 (1995).

Brynen, Rex, and Jill Tansley. "The Refugee Working Group of the Middle East Multilateral Peace Negotiations." *Palestine-Israel Journal* 2, no. 4 (Autumn 1995).

Chanda, N. "Superpower Triangle." *Far Eastern Economic Review* 128, no. 13 (1985).

———. "No Boat to China." *Far Eastern Economic Review* 128, no. 21 (1985).

———. "Ships That Pass. . . ." *Far Eastern Economic Review* 132, no. 21 (1986).

Child, Jack. "The Arias Plan: 1987–1988 Summits." In *The Central American Peace Process, 1983–1991.* Boulder, Colo.: Lynne Rienner Publishers, 1992.

Chul Koh, Byung. "Confrontation and Cooperation on the Korean Peninsula: The Politics of Nuclear Proliferation." *Korean Journal of Defense Analysis* 6, no. 2 (Winter 1994).

Clad, James. "The Aid Lever." *Far Eastern Economic Review* 150, no. 40 (4 October 1990).

Cortright, David. "The Coming of Incrementalism." *The Bulletin of the Atomic Scientists* 52, no. 2 (March/April 1996).

Crocker, Chester A. "South Africa: A Strategy for Change." *Foreign Affairs* 59 (Winter 1980).

Crossette, Barbara. "Civilian Effort for Peace in Bosnia Seen Lagging," *New York Times,* 3 January 1996, A5.

Crumm, Eileen M. "The Value of Economic Incentives in International Politics." *Journal of Peace Research* 32, no. 3 (1995).

Cummings, B. "The Political Economy of China's Turn Outward." In *China and the World.* 2d ed., edited by Samuel S. Kim. Boulder, Colo.: Westview Press, 1989.

Cupitt, R. "Export Controls: The Perspective of the Czech and Slovak Federal Republic." In *International Cooperation on Nonproliferation Export Controls,* edited by G. Bertsch, R. Cupitt, and S. Elliott-Gower. Ann Arbor, Mich.: University of Michigan Press, 1994.

"Current Events Malawi: Doing Life." *Africa Events,* February 1993.

de Soto, Alvaro. "Implementation of Comprehensive Peace Agreements: Staying the Course in El Salvador." *Global Governance* 1, no. 2 (1995).

de Soto, Alvaro, and Graciana del Castillo. "Obstacles to Peacebuilding." *Foreign Policy* no. 94 (1994).

Der Spiegel. "Mostar: Jagt den Deutschen davon." 12 February 1996.

Deutsch, Karl. "On the Concepts of Politics and Power." *Journal of International Affairs* 21, no. 2 (1967).

Dobbs, Michael. "The Misery of Mostar." *Washington Post National Weekly Edition,* 25 September–1 October 1995.

Dobbs, Michael, and Dana Priest. "Now the Real Work Begins: In Bosnia, The Civilian Tasks May be More Difficult Than the Military Ones." *Washington Post National Weekly Edition,* 18–24 December 1995.

"Documents: Resolutions Adapted at the NPT Extension Conference." *Arms Control Today* 25, no. 5 (June 1995).

Doxey, Margaret. "International Sanctions: A Framework for Analysis with Special Reference to the U.N. and South Africa." *International Organization* 26 (1972).

Dryden, S. "Banking and Credit." In *The Post-Containment Handbook,* edited by R. Cullen. Boulder, Colo.: Westview Press, 1990.

Duffield, Mark. "The Political Economy of Internal War: Asset Transfer, Complex Emergencies and International Aid." In *War and Hunger: Rethinking International Responses to Complex Emergencies,* edited by Joanna Macrae & Anthony Zwi. London: Zed Books, 1994.

Dumas, Lloyd J. "Economics and Alternative Security: Toward a Peace-keeping International Economy." In *Alternative Security: Living Without Nuclear Deterrence,* edited by Burns Weston. Boulder, Colo.: Westview Press, 1990.

Eberstadt, Nicholas. "North Korea: Reform, Muddling Through, or Collapse?" *The National Bureau of Asian Research Analysis* 4, no. 3 (September 1993).

The Economist. "India and America: Almost Friends." 16 February 1991.

The Economist. "Nuclear Weapons: Going, Going." 12 October 1991.

The Economist. "Sweden's Baltic Bulwark." 9 July 1994.

The Economist. "Primer on the European Union Stability Pact." 18 March 1995.

The Economist. "Bosnia: Tender Shoots." 18 May 1996.

Evans, P. M. "Caging the Dragon: Post-War Economic Sanctions Against the People's Republic of China." In *The Utility of International Economic Sanctions,* edited by D. Leyton-Brown. New York: St. Martin's Press, 1987.

Fehrm, M. "Sweden." In *Nuclear Non-Proliferation: The Why and the Wherefore,* edited by J. Goldblat. London: Taylor and Francis, 1985.

Ferrari, Paul. "U.S. Security Aid in a New World Order." *Policy Focus,* Overseas Development Council, no. 2 (1991).

Fieldstein, J. S., and J. R. Freemen. "Theories of Cooperation." In *Three-Way Street: Strategic Reciprocity in World Politics.* Chicago, Ill.: University of Chicago Press, 1991.

Finegan, William. "Letter from Tuzla: Salt City." *The New Yorker,* 12 February 1996.

Fisher, Sharon. "Treaty Fails to End Squabbles over Hungarian Relations." *Transition,* 9 June 1995.

Frankel, Francine R. "India's Promise." *Foreign Policy* 38 (Spring 1980).

Gang, Ira N., and Haider Ali Khan. "Some Determinants of Foreign Aid in India, 1960–85." *World Development* 18, no. 3 (March 1990).

Ganguly, Sumit, and Kanti Bajpai. "India and the Crisis in Kashmir." *Asian Survey* 34, no. 5 (May 1994).

George, Alexander L. "Case Studies and Theory Development: The Method of Structured, Focused Comparison." In *Diplomacy: New Approaches in History, Theory, and Policy,* edited by Paul Gordon Lauren. New York: Free Press, 1979.

George, Alexander L., and T. J. McKeown. "Case Studies and Theories in Organizational Decision-Making." In *Advances in Information Processing in Organizations,* edited by R. Coulum and R. Smith. Greenwich, Conn.: JAI Press, 1985.

German Information Center. "German Politicians Express Support for

Embattled EU Administrator in Mostar." *The Week in Germany,* New York, 16 February 1996.

Gimstedt, O. "Three Decades of Nuclear Power Development in Sweden." In *Nuclear Power Experience: Proceedings of an International Conference on Nuclear Power Experience.* Vienna: International Atomic Energy Agency, 1983.

Graff, J. L. "Confronting a Tankless Task." *Time,* 17 June 1991.

Green, J. "Strategies for Evading Economic Sanctions." In *Dilemmas of Economic Coercion: Sanctions in World Politics,* edited by M. Mincic and P. Wallenstein. New York: Praeger, 1983.

Greffenius, Steven, and Jungil Gill. "Pure Coercion vs. Carrot-and-Stick Offers in Crisis Bargaining." *Journal of Peace Research* 29, no. 1 (1992).

Hamrin, C. L. "China Reassesses the Superpowers." *Pacific Affairs* 56, no. 2 (1983).

Hersh, Seymour. "On the Nuclear Edge." *The New Yorker,* 29 March 1993.

Hunter, Jane. "Laying the Ground for Arms Control Pacts." *MEI* no. 505, 21 July 1995.

Hurlburt, Heather. "Russia, the OSCE, and European Security Architecture." *Helsinki Monitor* 6, no. 2 (1995).

Hurwitz, Bruce."The Multilateral Peace Process." *Midstream* 40, no. 6 (August/September 1994).

Ignatieff, Michael. "The Missed Chances in Bosnia." *New York Review of Books,* 29 February 1996.

Inose, Hijiri. "Japan Promises Bosnia Aid—To a Limit." *Nikkei Weekly,* 26 February 1996.

International Trade Reporter. "U.S., Other Nations Reach Agreement on Restricting Nuclear Weapons Exports." 9 (1992).

Ip, Grep, "Trying to Make Peace Pay," *The Globe and Mail,* 1 July 1996.

Islam, Shada. "Bhutto's Bonus: IMF, Aid Donors Encourage Pakistan to Push Reform." *Far Eastern Economic Review* 157, no. 10 (10 March 1994).

Israeli Foreign Ministry. "Palestinians Propose Beginning Permanent Status Negotiations." *Israel Line,* 19 May 1995.

———. "Egypt Agrees to Drop Nuclear Issue from Agenda." *Israel Line,* 8 December 1995.

———. "Israel, Jordan, Palestinians Sign First Regional Agreement on Water." *Israel Line,* 14 February 1996.

Jensen, Lloyd. "Negotiating Strategic Arms Control, 1969–1979." *Journal of Conflict Resolution* 28 (1984).

Jervis, Robert. "Realism, Game Theory, and Cooperation." *World Politics* 40, no. 3 (April 1988).

Johansson, T. B. "Sweden's Abortive Nuclear Weapons Project." *The Bulletin of the Atomic Scientists* 42, no. 3 (1986).

Jordan Information Bureau. "Multilateral Working Groups Achieve Steady Progress in Water, Environment and Other Sectors." *Jordan: Issues and Perspectives*, no. 21 (September/October 1995).

Kant, Immanuel. "Essay on Eternal Peace." Reprinted in Appendix to Carl Joachim Friedrich, *Inevitable Peace*. Cambridge, Mass.: Harvard University Press, 1948.

Kapur, Ashok. "Western Biases." *The Bulletin of the Atomic Scientists* 51, no. 1 (January/February 1995).

Karl, Terry Lynn. "El Salvador's Negotiated Revolution." *Foreign Affairs* 71, no. 2 (Spring 1992).

Keesing's Record of World Events: New Digest for February 1996. "Bosnia-Hercegovina: Rome 'Mini Summit.' " London, 1996.

Kihl, Young Hwan. "Confrontation or Compromise on the Korean Peninsula: The North Korean Nuclear Issue." *Korean Journal of Defense Analysis* 6, no. 2 (Winter 1994).

Kirkpatrick, Jeane. "Dictatorships and Double Standards." *Commentary* 68 (November 1979).

Larson, Deborah Welch. "Crisis Prevention and the Austrian State Treaty." *International Organization* 41, no. 1 (Winter 1987).

Larsson, C. "History of the Swedish Atomic Bomb, 1945–1972." *Ny Teknik*, April 1985.

Leng, Russell. "Influence Techniques among Nations." In *Behavior, Society, and International Conflict, Volume 3,* edited by Philip E. Tetlock et al. Oxford: Oxford University Press, 1993.

Leng, Russell J., and Hugh G. Wheeler. "Influence Strategies, Success, and War." *Journal of Conflict Resolution* 23 (December 1979).

Levin, Andrew S. "Civil Society and Democratization in Haiti." *Emory International Law Review* 9, no. 2 (1995).

Levy, J. S. "Prospect Theory and International Relations: Theoretical Applications and Analytical Problems." *Political Psychology* 13 (1992).

Lijphart, A. "Comparative Politics and the Comparative Method." *American Political Science Review* 65 (1971).

Long, William J. "Trade and Technology Incentives and Bilateral Cooperation." *International Studies Quarterly* 40, no. 1 (March 1996).

Lynn-Jones, Sean M. "International Security Studies." *International Studies Notes* (Fall 1991/Winter 1992).

Malnes, Raino. " 'Leader' and 'Entrepreneur' in International Negotiations: A Conceptual Analysis." *European Journal of International Relations* 1, no. 1 (1995).

Mansfield, Edward D. "International Institutions and Economic Sanctions." *World Politics* 47, no. 4 (1995).

Maull, Hanns W. "Germany in the Yugoslav Crisis." *Survival* 37, no. 4 (1996).

Mazarr, Michael J. "Kim Il Sung, Up Close and Personal." *The New Yorker* 70, no. 4 (14 March 1994).

McNamara, Robert S. "The Post–Cold War World: Implications for Military Expenditures in the Developing Countries." In *Proceedings of the World Bank Annual Conference on Development Economics, 1991,* edited by Lawrence H. Summers and Shekhar Shah. Washington, D.C.: The World Bank, March 1992.

Mearsheimer, John J., and Stephen Van Evera. "When Peace Means War." *The New Republic,* 18 December 1995.

Miko, F. T. "Parliamentary Development in the Czech and Slovak Federal Republic." *CRS Review* (July 1991).

Millman, Joel. "El Salvador's Army: A Force Unto Itself." *New York Times Magazine,* 10 December 1989.

Milner, H. "International Theories of Cooperation Among Nations." *World Politics* 44 (1992).

Moffett, George. "Peace in Bosnia Hinges on Postwar Rebuilding." *Christian Science Monitor,* 20 December 1995, 1 and 18.

Montgomery, Tommie Sue. "Getting to Peace in El Salvador: The Roles of the United Nations Secretariat and ONUSAL." *Journal of Interamerican Studies and World Affairs* 37, no. 4 (Winter 1995).

Moravscik, Andrew. "Preferences and Power in the European Community: A Liberal Intergovernmentalist Approach." *Journal of Common Market Studies* 31 (1993).

———. "Explaining International Human Rights Regimes." *European Journal of International Affairs,* June 1995.

Morgenthau, Hans. "A Political Theory of Foreign Aid." *American Political Science Review* 56 (June 1962).

Nelson, Mark M. "Overseas Investors Find Serbian Leaders Corralling Economy," *Wall Street Journal,* 2 February 1996, A1, A10.

Nelson, Mark M., and Carla Anne Robbins. "Companies Jockey for Share of Effort to Rebuild Bosnia." *Wall Street Journal,* 24 November 1995.

Oksenberg, M. "A Decade of Sino-American Relations." *Foreign Affairs* 61, no. 1 (1982).

Ollapally, Deepa, and Raja Ramanna. "U.S.-India Tensions: Misperceptions on Nuclear Proliferation." *Foreign Affairs* 74, no. 1 (January/February 1995).

OMRI. *Pursuing Balkan Peace* 1, no. 23 (11 June 1996).

Ourdan, Rémy. "La rapprochement entre Serbs et Musulmans à Mostar pourrait préfigurer la réconciliation de tous les Bosniaques." *Le Monde,* 29 March 1996.

Park, Andrus. "Ethnicity and Independence: The Case of Estonia in Comparative Perspective." *Europe-Asia Studies* 46, no. 1 (1994).

Pedersen, Jorgen Dige. "The Complexities of Conditionality: The Case of India." *The European Journal of Development Research* 5 (1993).

Perlez, Jane. "Serbian Chief Moves on Opposition: Milosevic Also Tries to Reassert State Control of Economy," *New York Times*, 4 March 1996, A6.

————. "Balkan Economies Stagnate in Grip of Political Leaders." *New York Times*, 20 August 1996, A1, A4.

Peterson, Scott, "Bosnia Serbs Feel West's Cold Shoulder," *The Christian Science Monitor*, 15 May 1996, 6.

Potter, William. "Managing Proliferation: Problems and Prospects for U.S.-Soviet Cooperation." In *Strategies for Managing Nuclear Non-Proliferation*, edited by Dagobert Brito, Michael Intrilligator, and Adele Wick. Lexington, Mass.: Lexington Books, 1983.

Qiwei, C. "Why is China Opening to the Outside?" *Beijing Review*, April 1985.

Raser, J. R. "Learning and Affect in International Politics." *Journal of Peace Research* 2 (1965).

Reinicke, Wolfgang H. "Can International Financial Institutions Prevent Internal Violence? The Sources of Ethno-National Conflict in Transitional Societies." In *Preventing Conflict in the Post-Communist World: Mobilizing International and Regional Organizations*, edited by Abraham Chayes and Antonia Handler Chayes. Washington, D.C.: Brookings Institution, 1996.

Reiss, Mitchell. "Nuclear Rollback Decisions: Future Lessons." *Arms Control Today* 25, no. 6 (July/August 1995).

Richardson, Neil R. "International Trade as a Force for Peace." In *Controversies in International Relations Theory: Realism and the Neoliberal Challenge*, edited by Charles W. Kegley. New York: St. Martin's Press, 1995.

Robinson, Randall. Preface to *South Africa and the United States: The Declassified History*, edited by Kenneth Mokoena. New York: The New Press, 1993.

Robinson, Anthony. "The Uphill Track to Recovery," *Financial Times*, 13 June 1996, 11.

Rotblat, Joseph. "Past Attempts to Abolish Nuclear Weapons." In *A Nuclear-Weapon-Free-World: Desirable, Feasible?* edited by Joseph Rotblat, Jack Steinberger, and Bhalochandra Udgaonkar. Boulder, Colo.: Westview Press, 1993.

Roy, Denny. "The Myth of North Korean 'Irrationality.' " *The Korean Journal of International Studies* 25, no. 2 (Summer 1994).

Sahni, Varun. "Going Nuclear: Establishing an Overt Nuclear Weapons Capability." In *India and the Bomb: Public Opinion and Nuclear Options,* edited by David Cortright and Amitabh Mattoo. Notre Dame, Ind.: University of Notre Dame Press, 1996.

Schreiber, A. P. "Economic Coercion as an Instrument of Policy: U.S. Measures Against Cuba and the Dominican Republic." *World Politics* 25 (1973).

Schroeder, Paul W. "The New World Order: A Historical Perspective." *The Washington Quarterly* 17, no. 2 (Spring 1994).

Schweitzer, Glenn E. "A Multilateral Approach to Curbing Proliferation of Weapons Know-How." *Global Governance* 2, no. 1 (1996).

Seabolt, S. G. "United States Technology Exports to the People's Republic of China: Current Developments in Law and Policy." *Texas International Law Journal* 19 (1984).

Solingen, Etel. "The New Multilateralism and Nonproliferation: Bringing in Domestic Politics." *Global Governance* 1, no. 2 (May–August 1995).

Spurrier, Andrew. "Going for Growth." *MEED Middle East Business Weekly,* 7 January 1995.

Stedman, Stephen John. "The End of the Zimbabwean Civil War." In *Stopping the Killing: How Civil Wars End,* edited by Roy Licklider. New York: New York University Press, 1993.

Stein, A. "When Misperception Matters." *World Politics* 34 (1982).

Stein, Melanie H. "Conflict Prevention in Transition Economies: A Role for the European Bank for Reconstruction and Development?" In *Preventing Conflict in the Post-Communist World: Mobilizing International and Regional Organizations,* edited by Abraham Chayes and Antonia Handler Chayes. Washington, D.C.: The Brookings Institution, 1996.

Stevenson, Richard. "World Bank Gets Bosnia Aid Role." *New York Times,* 18 April 1996, A6.

Stremlau, John. "Clinton's Dollar Diplomacy." *Foreign Policy* 97 (Winter 1994/95).

Sullivan, Joseph G. "How Peace Came to El Salvador." *Orbis* (Winter 1994).

Sullivan, R. "The Nature and Implications of United States-China Trade Toward the Year 2000." In *China's Global Presence,* edited by D. Lampton and K. Keyse. Washington, D.C.: American Enterprise Institute, 1988.

Sutter, R. "Realities of International Power and China's 'Interdependence' in Foreign Affairs." *Journal of Northeast Asian Studies* 3, no. 4 (1984).

Svek, M. "Czechoslovakia's Velvet Divorce." *Current History* 91 (1992).

Tsebelis, George. "Are Sanctions Effective? A Game-Theoretic Analysis." *Journal of Conflict Resolution* 34, no. 1 (March 1990).

U.S. News and World Report. "An Assault on Nuclear Arms." 7 October 1991.

Ullman, Richard. "Redefining National Security." *International Security* 8, no. 1 (1983).

Van Hollen, Christopher. "Leaning on Pakistan." *Foreign Policy* 38 (Spring 1980).

Vickers, George R. "The Political Reality After Eleven Years of War." In *Is There a Transition to Democracy in El Salvador?* edited by Joseph S. Tulchin with Gary Bland. Boulder, Colo.: Lynne Rienner Publishers, 1992.

Wagner, R. H. "Economic Interdependence, Bargaining Power, and Political Influence." *International Organization* 42 (1988).

Wallenstein, P. "Characteristics of Economic Sanctions." *Journal of Peace Research* 5 (1968).

Wallin, L. "Sweden." In *Security with Nuclear Weapons: Different Perspectives on National Security,* edited by R. Cowen Karp. Stockholm: Stockholm International Peace Research Institute and Oxford University Press, 1991.

Wendt, Alexander. "The Agent-Structure Problem in International Relations Theory." *International Organization* 41 (1987).

———. "The Anarchy Is What States Make of It: The Social Construction of Power Politics." *International Organization* 46, no. 2 (Spring 1992).

———. "Collective Identity Formation and the International State." *American Political Science Review* 88 (1994).

Whitney, Craig R. "In Bosnia, Securing a Peace Depends on Roads, Refugees and Elections," *New York Times,* 26 March 1996, A6.

Zack-Williams, A. B. "The Deepening Crisis and Survival Strategies." In *Beyond Structural Adjustment in Africa: The Political Economy of Sustainable and Democratic Development,* edited by Julius E. Nyang'oro and Timothy N. Shaw. New York: Praeger, 1992.

Reports, Documents, Papers

Americas Watch. "El Salvador, Impunity Prevails in Human Rights Cases." New York, September 1990.

Arab Press Service. "Oman—Normalisation With Israel." Information Access Company Newsletter Database 31, no. 3, 4 March 1996.

Bajpai, Kanti. Remarks at the School of International Studies seminar, Jawaharlal Nehru University, New Delhi, India, 14 December 1995.

Ball, Nicole. *Pressing for Peace: Can Aid Induce Reform?* Policy Essay no. 6, Overseas Development Council, Washington, D.C., distributed by Johns Hopkins University Press, 1992.

Ball, Nicole, and Tammy Halevy. *Making Peace Work: The Role of the Inter-*

national Development Community. Policy essay no. 18, Overseas Development Council, Washington, D.C., 1996.

Blumenthal, Dan, and John Wilner, eds. "Building on Peace: Toward Regional Security and Economic Development in the Middle East." Conference proceedings, Washington Institute for Near East Policy, Washington, D.C., 9–11 September 1995.

Byrne, Hugh. "The Problem of Revolution: A Study of Strategies of Insurgency and Counter-Insurgency in El Salvador's Civil War, 1981–1991." Ph.D. diss., University of California, Los Angeles, 1995.

Chellaney, Brahma. "The Missile Technology Control Regime: Its Challenges and Rigors for India." Paper presented to the "Joint Indo-American Seminar on Nonproliferation and Technology," University of Pennsylvania, Philadelphia, Penn., 1994.

Christopher, Warren S. "Building Peace and Prosperity in the Middle East and North Africa: The Role of a Regional Development Bank." Remarks at an "Experts Meeting on the Middle East Development Bank," Washington, D.C., 10 January 1995.

Cole, P. A. "Neutralité du Jour." Ph.D. diss., Johns Hopkins University, 1990.

Colletta, Nat J., Markus Kostner, and Ingo Wiederhofer, with assistance of Emilio Mondo, Taimi Sitari, and Tadesse A. Woldu. *Case Studies in War-to-Peace Transition: The Demobilization and Reintegration of Ex-Combatants in Ethiopia, Namibia, and Uganda.* World Bank Discussion Paper no. 331, Africa Technical Department Series. Washington, D.C.: The World Bank, 1996.

Commission of the European Union. *Humanitarian Aid to the Former Yugoslavia: Prospects and Guidelines.* Brussels, 17 November 1995 [COM(95) 564].

———. *Humanitarian Assistance in Favour of the Victims of the Conflict in the Former Yugoslavia.* Brussels, 12 December 1995, Memo/95/137.

Commission on Security and Cooperation in Europe. *CSCE Helsinki Document 1992: The Challenges of Change.* Helsinki Summit Declaration, Helsinki, Finland, July 1992.

———. *Report on the Moscow Meeting of the Conference on the Human Dimension of the CSCE.* Washington, D.C., 1992.

———. Committees of Senior Officials. *Journals of the 24th, 25th, and 27th CSCE Committees of Senior Officials,* Washington, D.C., 1993 and 1994.

Cortright, David, and Amitabh Mattoo. "India's Nuclear Choices," Special Report of the Fourth Freedom Forum and the Joan B. Kroc Institute for International Peace Studies, University of Notre Dame, Notre Dame, Ind., November/December 1994.

Council of Europe. Parliamentary Assembly. *Report on the application of the*

Republic of Estonia for membership of the Council of Europe. Opinion no. 170, 13 May 1993.

————. Parliamentary Assembly. *Report on the application by Latvia for membership of the Council of Europe.* Comments of the Council of Europe(Rapporteur: Mr. Espersen), Doc. 7169, 6 October 1994.

The European Union. Foreign Affairs Council of Ministers. *Policy Paper on Former Yugoslavia.* Brussels, 6 November 1995, BIO/95/403/1.

Forsberg, Tuomas. "The Efficacy of Rewarding Conflict Strategies: Positive Sanctions as Face Savers, Payments and Signals." Paper prepared for the 37th Annual Convention of the International Studies Association, San Diego, Calif., 16–20 April 1996.

Gabriel, Jürg Martin. "Wirtschaftsanktionen: Begriffe, Faktoren, Theorien." no. 184. Institut für Politikwissenschaften, Hochscule St. Gallen, Beiträge und Berichte, 1992.

Gallucci, Robert. Remarks at "The U.S.-North Korea Nuclear Agreement: Current Status and Prospects for the Future," meeting at The Heritage Foundation, Washington, D.C., 15 June 1995.

Garris, J. H. "Sweden and the Spread of Nuclear Weapons: A Study in Restraint." Ph.D. diss., University of California, Los Angeles, 1972.

George, A. L. "Case Studies and Theory Development." Paper presented to the Second Annual Symposium on "Information Processing in Organizations," Carnegie Mellon University, Pittsburgh, Penn., 1982.

Girnius, Saulius. "Progress in Withdrawal of Troops from Lithuania?" *RFE/RL Research Report* no. 34 (28 August 1992).

————. "Relations between the Baltic States and Russia." *RFE/RL Research Report* no.33 (26 August 1994).

Goodby, James. "Averting Nuclear Chaos: A Challenge of Preventive Diplomacy," Statement at the Conference on "Bombs, Carrots, and Sticks: Economic Sanctions and Incentives and Nuclear Nonproliferation." University of Notre Dame, Notre Dame, Ind., April 1994.

Goodby, James. "Averting Nuclear Chaos: The Tasks before Us." U.S. Department of State Dispatch 4, no. 41 (11 October 1993).

Grenier, Yvon. "Foreign Assistance and the Market Place of Peacemaking: Lessons from El Salvador." Working paper series, Centre for Foreign Policy Studies, Dalhousie University, Halifax, Nova Scotia, 1995.

Gupta, Shekhar. "India Redefines Its Role." Adelphi Paper 293, International Institute for Strategic Studies, 1995. Printed by Oxford University Press, London.

Helsinki Commission. *Report on the Geneva Meeting of Experts on National Minorities.* Washington, D.C., 1991.

Hinton, Henry L., Jr. *Foreign Assistance—PLO Ability to Help Support Palestinian Authority Is Not Clear: Report to the Chairman, Committee on*

International Relations, U.S. House of Representatives. Federal Document Clearing House, Inc., GAO Reports. Washington, D.C., 1995.

International Crisis Group. *The European Union Administration of Mostar.* London, 13 June 1996.

Israeli Government. Ministry of Foreign Affairs. *The Middle East Peace Process: The Multilateral Negotiations.* November 1995.

Kaushal, Neeraj. "Peace(s) of Carrot(s): Urging Nuclear Restraint in South Asia." Paper presented at the conference on "Bombs, Carrots, and Sticks: Economic Sanctions and Nuclear Nonproliferation," University of Notre Dame, Notre Dame, Ind., April 1994.

Latin America Working Group. "El Salvador Delegation Report, June 1996." Washington, D.C., June 1996.

Lawrence, Stewart. "Postwar El Salvador: An Examination of Military Issues Relating to Reconstruction." Unitarian Universalist Service Committee, Cambridge, Mass., October 1991.

Leach, Jim, George Miller, and Mark Hatfield. *U.S. Aid to El Salvador: An Evaluation of the Past, A Proposal for the Future.* Report to the Arms Control and Foreign Policy Caucus, 99th Cong., 1st sess., Washington, D.C., 1 February 1985.

Linton, Steve. Presentation at Columbia University Center for Korean Research, New York, N.Y., November 1993.

Mattoo, Amitabh. "Prospects for Carrots and Sticks in South Asia." Paper presented at the Conference on Bombs, Carrots, and Sticks: Economic Sanctions and Nuclear Nonproliferation, University of Notre Dame, Notre Dame, Ind., April 1994.

McCain, John. Remarks at "The U.S.-North Korea Nuclear Agreement: Current Status and Prospects for the Future," meeting at The Heritage Foundation, Washington, D.C., 15 June 1995.

Milhollin, Gary. "Can Sanctions Stop the Bomb?" Keynote address delivered at the Conference on Economic Sanctions and International Relations, University of Notre Dame, Notre Dame, Ind., April 1993.

Nelson, Joan M., and Stephanie J. Eglinton. *Global Goals, Contentious Means: Issues of Multiple Aid Conditionality.* Policy Essay no. 10, Overseas Development Council, Washington, D.C., distributed by Johns Hopkins University Press, 1993.

Nye, Joseph. "Problems of Security Studies." Paper presented at the XIV World Congress of the International Political Science Association, Washington, D.C., August 1988.

Open Media Research Institute. *Pursuing Balkan Peace.* Special report, 21 May 1996.

Organization for Economic Cooperation and Development. Development Assistance Committee. *DAC Orientations on Participatory Development and Good Governance.* OCDE/GD (93) 191. Paris, 1993.

————. *Development Cooperation, 1995 Report*. Paris, 1996.

Organization for Security and Cooperation in Europe. Secretariat. *Report of the CSCE Office for Democratic Institutions and Human Rights Mission on the Study of Estonian Legislation Invited by the Republic of Estonia.* Prague, the Czech Republic, 1993.

————. Secretariat. *Mission Mandate Establishing OSCE Permanent Presence in Estonia.* CSCE/19 CSO/Journal No. 2, Prague, The Czech Republic, 1993.

Pelletreau, Robert. Federal News Service transcript of speech at the Woman's National Democratic Club in Washington, D.C., 25 January 1996.

Peres, Shimon. Federal News Service transcript of speech to Washington Institute for Near East Policy Breakfast Forum in Washington, D.C., 29 April 1996.

Population Reference Bureau, *World Population Data Sheet.* Washington, D.C: 1995.

Potter, William C. "The Politics of Nuclear Renunciation: The Cases of Belarus, Kazakhstan, and Ukraine." Occasional paper no. 22, The Henry L. Stimson Center, Washington, D.C., April 1995.

Rizvi, Haider. "The Prospects for Carrots and Sticks in South Asia." Paper presented at the Conference on Bombs, Carrots, and Sticks: Economic Sanctions and Nuclear Nonproliferation, University of Notre Dame, Notre Dame, Ind., April 1994.

Rosengrant, Susan. "Carrots, Sticks, and Question Marks: Negotiating the North Korean Nuclear Crisis." Case Studies in Public Policy, Kennedy School of Government, Harvard University, 1995.

Rowe, D. M. "The Domestic Political Economy of International Economic Sanctions." Paper prepared for the Annual Meeting of the American Political Science Association, Washington, 2–5 September 1993.

Schwarz, Benjamin C. *American Counter-Insurgency Doctrine and El Salvador: The Frustrations of Reform and the Illusion of Nation-Building.* National Defense Research Institute, RAND Corporation, Santa Monica, Calif., 1991.

Shanghai Joint Communiqué. In *Weekly Compiled Presidential Documents.* Vol. 8 Washington, D.C.: Office of the Federal Register, 1972.

Sheehy, Ann. Russian commentary reported in "The Estonian Law on Aliens." *RFE/RL Research Report* no. 38 (24 September 1993).

Snyder, Scott. "Possible Areas of Cooperation with the Democratic People's Republic of Korea." Asia Society research project for Rockefeller Foundation, 24 November 1993.

————. "The North Korean Nuclear Challenge: The Post–Kim Il Sung Phase Begins." Paper prepared for the United States Institute of Peace, Washington, D.C., December 1994.

————. "Dealing with North Korea's Nuclear Program: The Role of Incentives in Preventing Deadly Conflict." Paper prepared for the Carnegie Commission on Preventing Deadly Conflict, Washington, D.C., 1995.

Solis, Peter. "Reluctant Reforms: The Cristiani Government and the International Community in the Process of Salvadoran Post-War Reconstruction." Washington Office on Latin America, Washington, D.C., June 1993.

Stanley, William, and David Holiday. "Under the Best of Circumstances: ONUSAL and Dilemmas of Verification and Institution Building in El Salvador." Paper presented at Peacekeeping Conference, sponsored by North-South Center, Miami, Florida, 12 April 1996.

Stedman, Stephen John. Proposal at a symposium on "World Order, Global Justice, and the Perils of Anarchy." Michigan State University, 29–31 March 1996.

Stein, Janet Gross. Remarks on "Panel on Preventing Deadly Conflict." Annual Meeting of the American Political Science Association, San Francisco, California, 31 August 1996.

Sutter, R. *Sino-Soviet Relations: Recent Improvements and Implications for the United States.* Issue Brief 86138, Library of Congress, 1986.

"Trilateral Statement by the Presidents of the United States, Russia, and Ukraine." Reprinted in "Select Documents From the U.S.-Russian Summit." *Arms Control Today* 24, no. 1 (January/February 1994).

U.S. Citizens Election Observer Mission. "Free and Fair? The Conduct of El Salvador's 1994 Elections." Washington, D.C., June 1994.

U.S. Congress. House. Committee on Foreign Affairs. *United States-China Relations: A Strategy for the Future.* 91st Cong., 2d sess. 6 October 1970. Committee Print.

———. Subcommittee on International Economic Policy and Trade, and on Africa. *Testimony of Chester Crocker: The Anti-Apartheid Act of 1985.* 99th Cong., 1st sess., 17 April 1985.

———. *Legislative Options and United States Policy toward South Africa.* 99th Cong., 2d sess., 9 April 1986.

———. *The President's Report on Progress toward Ending Apartheid in South Africa and the Question of Future Sanctions.* 100th Cong., 1st sess., 5 November 1987.

———. *Approval of Extension of Most-Favored-Nation Treatment to Czechoslovakia.* 101st Cong., 2d sess., 15 November 1990.

———. Committee on International Relations. *Testimony of James Baker to the House Committee on International Relations.* 104th Cong., 1st sess., 12 January 1995.

U.S. Congress. Joint Committee on Atomic Energy. *International Cooperation in the Peaceful Uses of Atomic Energy Through the Instrument of the Bilateral Agreement for Cooperation.* Vol. 2 of *Review of the International*

Atomic Policies and Programs of the United States, 86th Cong., 2d sess., 1960.

U. S. Congress. Senate. Committee on Governmental Affairs. *Factsheet: U.S. Aid Policies and Pakistan's Bomb: What Were We Trying to Accomplish?* Washington, D.C., n.d.

———. Committee on Foreign Relations. *U.S. Policy toward South Africa.* 99th Cong., 1st sess., 24 April 1985.

———. Committee on Foreign Relations. Subcommittee on Near Eastern and South Asian Affairs. Statement by Robert H. Pelletreau, 11 May 1995, in "FY 1996 Economic Programs for Promoting Peace in the Middle East." *U.S. Department of State Dispatch* 6, no. 21 (22 May 1995).

U.S. Department of State. "Atomic Energy (Cooperation for Civil Uses)," 1966. TIAS no. 3477. *U.S. Treaties and Other International Agreements,* vol. 7, pt. 1, 1966.

———. "Atomic Energy (Cooperation for Civil Uses)," 1966. TIAS no. 6076. *U.S. Treaties and Other International Agreements,* vol. 17, pt. 1.

———. "Organizational Meeting for Multilateral Negotiations on the Middle East." *U.S. Department of State Dispatch,* 3, supplement no. 2 (February 1992).

———. "President Clinton Meets with Baltic Presidents." *U.S. Department of State Dispatch* 4, no. 40 (October 4, 1993).

———. DPRK Joint Statement, 11 June 1993.

———. *U.S.-DPRK Press Statement,* 19 July 1993.

———. *Country Reports on Human Rights Practices 1993.* April 1994.

———. "Remarks of President Clinton in Riga, Latvia, on 6 July 1994." *U.S. Department of State Dispatch* 5, no. 31 (1 August 1994).

———. "Casablanca Declaration." *U.S. Department of State Dispatch* 5, no. 45 (7 November 1994).

———. Remarks of Robert H. Pelletreau, U.S. Assistant Secretary of State for Near Eastern Affairs, 31 October 1994, in "Overview of the Multilaterals." *U.S. Department of State Dispatch* supplement 5, no. 10 (November 1994).

———. "U.S.-Oman Support for Middle East Desalination Research Center." Text of joint U.S.-Oman communiqué released in Washington, D.C., 2 June 1995. *U.S. Department of State Dispatch* 6, no. 24 (12 June 1995).

———. *Country Reports on Human Rights Practices 1995.* April 1996.

———. Office of Spokesman. *Address by Secretary of State Warren Christopher before the Legislative Assembly of El Salvador.* Legislative Assembly, San Salvador, 26 February 1996.

U.S. National Security Council. *Statement of Policy on Peaceful Uses of*

Atomic Energy, General Considerations. Doc. 5507/2. Washington, D.C.: Government Printing Office, 12 March 1955.

U.S. Office of Technology Assessment. *Technology Transfer to China.* Washington, D.C.: Government Printing Office, 1987.

United Nations. Development Program. *Human Development Report, 1992.* New York, N.Y., 1992.

———. *Adjustment toward Peace: Economic Policy and Post-war Reconstruction in El Salvador.* Report prepared by James Boyce, et al. San Salvador, May 1995.

United Nations. Security Council. *Statement initiating bilateral dialogue with North Korea.* 8 April 1993. S/25562.

———. Truth Commission for El Salvador. *De la locura a la esperanza: La guerra de doce anos en El Salvador.* New York, 1993.

van der Stoel, Max. Letter to Estonian Foreign Minister Velliste, May 1993. Secretariat, Organization for Security and Cooperation in Europe, Communication No. 192.

———. Letter to Latvian foreign minister Georgs Andrejevs, 10 December 1993. Secretariat, Organization for Security and Cooperation in Europe, Reference No. 1463/93/L.

van de Sand, Klemens. "Enhancing Security through Development: Security-related Concepts, Criteria, and Incentives in German Development Policy." Paper delivered at the Conference on Bombs, Carrots, and Sticks: Economic Sanctions and Nuclear Nonproliferation, University of Notre Dame, Notre Dame, Ind., April 1994.

Väyrynen, Raimo. "Toward a Theory of Ethnic Conflicts and Their Resolution." Occasional Paper 6:OP:3. Joan B. Kroc Institute for International Peace Studies, University of Notre Dame, Notre Dame, Ind., 1994.

Waslekar, Sundeep. "Track Two Diplomacy in South Asia." Occasional paper, Program in Arms Control, Disarmament, and International Security, University of Illinois, Urbana-Champaign, Ill. 2d ed., October 1995.

White House. Press Office. *Factsheet: Conventional Arms Transfer Policy.* Washington, D.C., 17 February 1995.

Wilcox, Wayne. *The Emergence of Bangladesh.* Foreign Affairs Study Number Seven, American Enterprise Institute, Washington, D.C., 1973.

Wood, Elizabeth. "Economic Structure, Agrarian Elites, and Democracy: The Anomalous Case of El Salvador." Paper prepared for the Latin American Studies Association conference, Washington, D.C., 26–30 September 1995.

The World Bank. *Projects in Support of the Priority Reconstruction Program in Bosnia and Herzegovina.* Washington, D.C., 10 May 1996.

The World Bank Central Europe Department, and the European Bank for Reconstruction and Development. *Bosnia and Herzegovina: Priorities for Recovery and Growth*. Discussion papers nos. 1, 2, and 3 prepared for the first donor's meeting, Brussels, 21–22 December 1995.

Index

absolutist policy, negotiating with, 66
Ackerman, Gary, 67
actor(s): international economic, 176n12; local vs. external powers, Bosnia-Herzegovina, 160–61; single, 52n8
Ad-Hoc Liaison Committee (AHLC), 255
Advani, Lal Kishan, 150n24
Afghan War: Pakistani arms and, 134; U.S. aid to Pakistan and, 45, 285
African Development Bank, 261n1
African National Congress (ANC), 210, 220
Agency for International Development (AID), 188, 194
Agreed Conclusions of February 1994 (N. Korea), 68
Agreed Framework of October 1994 (N. Korea), 4, 41, 42–43, 53n14, 55; elements in, 69–70; incentives use in, 74–75, 81n50; merits debated, 70–73; North-South dialogue and, 71–72, 76
AID (Agency for International Development), 188, 194
Alliance for Democracy, 253
ally: internal, 89, 98; need for stable, 46, 75
Americas Watch, 201n4

Angola: Cuban troops in, 212, 215, 217; demilitarization support, 243
Anti-Apartheid Act, Comprehensive, 205–6
apartheid, 209–10, 218–20
appeasement, 16n1, 116n15, 277–79
Arab-Israeli peace process, 254
Arafat, Yassir, 256, 257
ARENA party, 195–96
Argentina, 248, 270
Arias, Oscar, 201n1
arming-and-partitioning, refugees and, 162–63
arms exports, 243
Aronson, Bernard, 190, 192
ASEA (Swedish civilian nuclear power company), 89, 98
Asia Society study group, 127, 130, 141, 142
Asian Development Bank, 261n1
Asia-Pacific Economic Cooperation (APEC) meeting, 67
Assad, Hafez al, 213
association-exclusion, 269. See also membership incentives
Atomic Energy Act, U.S., 51n2, 94, 95
Atomic Energy Commission, U.S. (AEC), 95, 98, 99
Atoms for Peace program, U.S., 22, 25, 88, 94, 274
Atwood, Brian, 196

About the Contributors

Nicole Ball is a fellow at the Overseas Development Council in Washington, D.C. She has written widely on the relationship between military security and development in non-OECD countries and on the role of development assistance agencies in supporting war-to-peace transitions. Her publications include *Security and Economy in the Third World* (Princeton University Press, 1988) and *Making Peace Work: The Role of the International Development Community* (Overseas Development Council, 1996).

David Cortright is president of the Fourth Freedom Forum in Goshen, Indiana, and fellow at the Joan B. Kroc Institute for International Peace Studies at the University of Notre Dame. He is the recipient of a research and writing award for peace and international cooperation in 1990 from the John D. and Catherine T. MacArthur Foundation. Cortright has authored and edited several books, including (with George Lopez) *Economic Sanctions: Panacea or Peacebuilding in a Post–Cold War World?* (Westview Press, 1995).

Virginia I. Foran is research director of the Security Assurances Program of the Carnegie Endowment for International Peace. She has been director of the Nuclear Non-Proliferation Project of the National Security Archives and a foreign affairs specialist in the Office of the Assistant Secretary of Defense for International Security Policy. She is the author of *The Making of U.S. Foreign Policy: U.S. Nuclear Non-Proliferation Policy, 1945–1990* (London: Chadwyck-Healey, 1992).

Jordana D. Friedman is director of the International Security Program at the Council on Economic Priorities, where she pursues research and advocacy on global military spending, regional security, and arms control issues. Ms. Friedman holds a B.A. in Social Studies from Harvard University and an M.A. in International Relations and International Economics with a specialization in Security Studies from the Paul H. Nitze School of Advanced International Studies of the Johns Hopkins University.

Jeffrey Herbst is associate professor of politics and international affairs at the Woodrow Wilson School of Princeton University. He is the author of *U.S. Economic Policy Towards Africa: Promoting Reform in the 1990s* (Council on Foreign Relations, 1992) and is the coeditor (with Walter Clarke) of *Learning from Somalia: The Lessons of Armed Humanitarian Intervention* (Westview Press, 1997).

Heather F. Hurlburt is a speechwriter for Secretary of State Madeleine Albright. She served on the U.S. Delegation to the OSCE from 1990 to 1994, assisting in developing the organization's institutions and its response to post–cold war conflicts in Europe. She has also been a program director at the Carnegie Endowment for International Peace and a staff member of the U.S. Commission on Security and Cooperation in Europe.

William J. Long is professor and graduate programs director at the Sam Nunn School of International Affairs at the Georgia Institute of Technology. His research focuses on international trade and technology transfers and their relationship to national security, economic competitiveness, and international cooperation. He is the author of two books, *U.S. Export Control Policy* (New York: Columbia University Press, 1989); and *Economic Incentives and Bilateral Cooperation* (Ann Arbor: University of Michigan Press, 1996).

Amitabh Mattoo is an associate professor at the School of International Studies, Jawaharlal Nehru University. He is a former visiting fellow at the Joan B. Kroc Institute for International Peace Studies at the University of Notre Dame, and is the coeditor (with David Cortright) of *India and the Bomb: Public Opinion and Nuclear Options* (University of Notre Dame Press, 1996).

Caleb S. Rossiter founded and directs Demilitarization for Democracy, a research and advocacy organization in Washington, D.C., dedicated to making demilitarization in the developing world a central concern of U.S. foreign policy. He is the former deputy director of the Congressional Arms Control and Foreign Policy Caucus and was a fellow of the Center for International Policy.

Scott Snyder is a program officer in the Research and Studies Program of the U.S. Institute of Peace. He is the author of several articles and book chapters on Korea, is a frequent media commentator on Korean issues, and has visited North Korea three times in conjunction with academic study groups, most recently in July 1995. Previously, Mr. Snyder was acting director of the Contemporary Affairs Department at the Asia Society.

Leonard S. Spector is a senior associate at the Carnegie Endowment for International Peace and director of the Endowment's Nuclear Non-Proliferation Project, with staff and activities in Washington, D.C., and Moscow. Mr. Spector has been active in the nuclear nonproliferation field for nearly twenty years and, before joining the Endowment in 1984, served as chief counsel to the Senate Energy and Nuclear Proliferation Subcommittee. He is the author of six books on the spread of nuclear arms and comments frequently on nuclear issues in the media.

Geoff Thale is the associate for El Salvador at the Washington Office on Latin America. He was executive director of the El Salvador Policy Project from 1993 to 1995 and of the National Agenda for Peace in El Salvador from 1988 to 1993. He also served as East Coast director of the NEST foundation raising funds for rural communities and refugees in El Salvador.

Raimo Väyrynen is professor of government at the University of Notre Dame and the John M. Regan, Jr., director of the Joan B. Kroc Institute for International Peace Studies. He is former dean of the faculty of social sciences at the University of Helsinki and past secretary general of the International Peace Research Association. He is the author and coeditor of a dozen books and has published more than 140 journal articles.